The Pension Challenge

The Pension Challenge

Risk Transfers and Retirement Income Security

EDITED BY

Olivia S. Mitchell and Kent Smetters

OXFORD
UNIVERSITY PRESS

OXFORD
UNIVERSITY PRESS
Great Clarendon Street, Oxford OX2 6DP
Oxford University Press is a department of the University of Oxford.
It furthers the University's objective of excellence in research, scholarship,
and education by publishing worldwide in
Oxford New York
Auckland Bangkok Buenos Aires Cape Town Chennai
Dar es Salaam Delhi Hong Kong Istanbul Karachi Kolkata
Kuala Lumpur Madrid Melbourne Mexico City Mumbai Nairobi
São Paulo Shanghai Taipei Tokyo Toronto
Oxford is a registered trade mark of Oxford University Press
in the UK and in certain other countries
Published in the United States
by Oxford University Press Inc., New York

First published 2003

British Library Cataloguing in Publication Data
Data available
Library of Congress Cataloging in Publication Data
(Data available)
ISBN 0-19-9266913
Typeset by Newgen Imaging Systems (P) Ltd., Chennai, India
Printed in Great Britain
on acid-free paper by
Biddles Ltd., Guildford & King's Lynn

Preface

This book is the newest in the Pension Research Council series on challenges and opportunities in retirement security. In it, we explore several types of risk that confront employees, retirees, companies, and governments in the retirement context.

Our focus in this volume is on how pension systems can help protect against such risks, particularly in light of the current uncertain economic and financial global environment. Of particular interest is the question of whether and how financial products and systems can be better designed to meet and manage retirement risks. Examples considered in this book include guarantees and hedges for pension investments, catastrophe bonds, and alternative regulatory structures and investment restrictions intended to protect unwary or unwitting pension plan participants. Chapters draw important lessons from a wide range of countries, focusing on both developed and developing countries. Contributors include finance and insurance sector experts, development economists, regulators, and academics.

Primary sponsorship for the volume was generously provided by the Financial Services Forum under the leadership of George Votja, through a grant to the Pension Research Council at the Wharton School. Additional funding for our activities was provided by the Financial Institutions Center at Wharton, the Michigan Retirement Research Center in conjunction with the Social Security Administration, and the Pension and Welfare Benefits Administration of the U.S. Department of Labor. We are also grateful for assistance from the Boettner Center for Pensions and Retirement Research and the Penn Aging Research Center, both at the University of Pennsylvania. The Pension Research Council is proud to continue its affiliation with the Wharton School and to recognize the invaluable efforts of our Senior Partners and Institutional Members noted at the end of this volume. We are also grateful for the excellent work of Pension Research Council staffers Victoria H. Jo, Joseph V. Hirniak, and Christina Choi. On behalf of the Pension Research Council at the Wharton School, we thank our collaborators and the contributors who brought this work to fruition.

The Pension Research Council

The Pension Research Council of the Wharton School at the University of Pennsylvania is an organization committed to generating debate on key policy issues affecting pensions and other employee benefits. The Council sponsors interdisciplinary research on the entire range of private and social retirement security and related benefit plans in the United States and around the world. It seeks to broaden understanding of these complex arrangements through basic research into their economic, social, legal, actuarial, and financial foundations. Members of the Advisory Board of the Council, appointed by the Dean of the Wharton School, are leaders in the employee benefits field, and they recognize the essential role of social security and other public sector income maintenance programs while sharing a desire to strengthen private sector approaches to economic security.

More information about the Pension Research Council is available at the web site: <http://prc.wharton.upenn.edu/prc/prc.html>

Contents

Figures

Tables

Notes on Contributors

Zvi Bodie is Professor of Finance at Boston University School of Management; he also serves on the Pension Research Council Advisory Board and is a member of the Financial Accounting Standards Board Task Force on Interest Methods. Previously he visited Harvard's School of Business Administration and served on the finance faculty at MIT's Sloan School of Management. His research interests include investment, portfolio choice, and finance. Dr Bodie received the Ph.D. in economics from the Massachusetts Institute of Technology.

David Cummins is Harry J. Loman Professor of Insurance and Risk Management at the Wharton School of the University of Pennsylvania. He is the Executive Director of the S.S. Huebner Foundation. He received his Ph.D. from the University of Pennsylvania.

Suzanne Doyle is a Ph.D. student at the School of Economics, University of New South Wales in Sydney, Australia.

Arthur Fliegelman is Vice-President and Senior Credit Officer in the Financial Institutions Group of Moody's Investors Service where he serves as lead analyst for a portfolio of life insurance companies and evaluates insurance company creditworthiness. Previous positions include principal at A. Fliegelman & Associates, an investment research and consulting firm specializing in the insurance industry; analyst at Salomon Brothers specializing in insurance company investment issues; senior analyst in CIGNA Corporation's investment affiliate responsible for coordinating the company's insurance and investment process; and investment consultant with Hay Associates. Mr Fliegelman received his MBA in finance and insurance from the Wharton School. He is also a Chartered Financial Analyst and an active member of the New York Society of Security Analysts; he is also Vice-Chair of the NYSSA's Committee for Improved Corporate Reporting.

Peter Forsyth is a Professor of Computer Science at the University of Waterloo. His research interests concern numerical solution of partial differential equations, solution techniques for large sparse matrices, and computational finance. Previous positions include Director of the Institute for Computer Research at Waterloo, President of Dynamic Reservoir Systems, and a Senior Simulation Scientist with the Computer Modelling Group.

Jeremy Gold is Proprietor of Jeremy Gold Pensions in New York. He received his Ph.D. in Insurance and Risk Management from the Wharton School of the University of Pennsylvania.

Marie-Eve Lachance is a Ph.D. student at the Insurance and Risk Management Department of the Wharton School.

Christopher M. Lewis is Managing Director of the Enterprise Risk Advisory and Technology firm NetRisk and an Instructor-in-Residence in the Finance Department at the University of Connecticut. His areas of expertise include the management and measurement of natural disaster risk, operational risk, and the contingent pension liability of the Pension Benefit Guaranty Corporation. Previously Mr Lewis assisted agencies of the Federal Government (e.g. OMB and OFHEO) and private sector clients in the development and implementation of sound risk management programs.

Raimond Maurer is Professor of Investment, Portfolio Management, and Pension Systems Goethe University Frankfurt/M. His research focuses on the insurance and mutual fund industry, investment analysis, real estate finance, and pension systems. He is a Member of the German Society of Insurance Mathematics, the German A.F.I.R. Group (Actuarial Approach for Financial Risk), and Research Fellow of the Center for Financial Studies. He received his Doctorate and Habilitation in Business Administration from Mannheim University.

Moshe Arye Milevsky is Associate of Professor of Finance at the Schulich School of Business, York University, and the Executive Director of the Individual Finance and Insurance Decisions Center at the Fields Institute, Toronto, Canada. His areas of interest span finance and insurance, with recent research examining mortality-contingent claims. He received his Ph.D. in Finance from York University.

Olivia S. Mitchell is the International Foundation of Employee Benefit Plans Professor of Insurance and Risk Management, and Executive Director of the Pension Research Council, both at the Wharton School of the University of Pennsylvania, and also a Research Associate at the National Bureau of Economic Research. Her research focuses on private and public insurance, risk management, public finance and labor markets, and compensation and pensions, with a US and an international focus. Previously she taught at Cornell University, visited Harvard University and the University of New South Wales, served on the US Department of Labor's ERISA Advisory Council, and served on the Board of Alexander and Alexander Services, Inc. She recently served on President Bush's Commission to Strengthen Social Security. She received her Ph.D. in Economics from the University of Wisconsin-Madison.

Robert Palacios is Senior Pension Economist in the Social Protection Unit of the World Bank. He was a member of the team that produced the Bank's major policy paper on global pension system reform, and since then he has worked in Africa, Asia, Eastern Europe, and Latin America. He is also responsible for managing the World Bank's "Pension Reform Primer" an applied research working paper series. His current interests include estimating unfunded pension liabilities, managing public pension reserves, and converting defined contribution balances into annuities.

John Piggott is Professor of Economics at the University of New South Wales in Sydney, Australia. His research interests include pension investments and the determinants of lifetime accumulation and decumulation. He received the Ph.D. in Economics from the University of London.

David Rajnes is a Research Associate with the Employee Benefit Research Institute (EBRI) in Washington, DC. His work focuses on issues related to retirement and labor markets including the Retirement Confidence Survey. Previously he served as a statistician at the US Bureau of the Census, and he has also served as a consultant on pension reform and related issues for the US Agency for International Development, the World Bank, the International Labour Office, and the International Monetary Fund. He has graduate degrees in economics from both the American University and Johns Hopkins University.

Krishna Ramaswamy is Edward Hopkinson, Jr Professor of Investment Banking and Professor of Finance at the Wharton School of the University of Pennsylvania. Dr Ramaswamy received the Ph.D. from Stanford University.

Scott A. Robinson is an Analyst in the Life Insurance Group at Moody's Investors Service where he tracks national insurers including property-and-casualty, and life and health insurers. Previously he was an AVP for the Trust Company of the West and worked with AXA Financial. He received the Masters Degree in Actuarial Science from Georgia State University, and he is a Fellow of the Society of Actuaries and a member of the American Academy of Actuaries.

Christian Schlag is Professor of Derivatives and Financial Engineering at the Goethe University Frankfurt/M. His primary research focuses on valuation of derivative securities and empirical capital market research.

Kent Smetters is an assistant professor in the Insurance and Risk Management Department at The Wharton School at The University of Pennsylvania. Previously he worked at the Congressional Budget Office, visited the Stanford Economics Department, and served as Deputy Assistant Secretary for Economic Policy of the US Treasury. His research interests include intergenerational risk sharing and risk sharing within households. He received the Ph.D. in Economics from Harvard University.

John Turner is a Senior Policy Advisor in the Public Policy Institute at AARP. Previously he taught at George Washington University; he was a Fulbright Scholar in France; he worked for the International Labor Office; and he also worked at the US Social Security Administration and the US Labor Department. His research interests include global pension reform. He received the Ph.D. in Economics from the University of Chicago.

Stephen P. Utkus is a Principal at The Vanguard Group where he leads the R&D group within Vanguard's participant education department. He is responsible for developing education, guidance and advisory programs for participants in employer-sponsored retirement plans. Previously he worked in new product development and investment advisory services at Vanguard; he was also an investment strategist and analyst in a Philadelphia financial planning firm. He earned the MBA in finance from the Wharton School.

Kenneth Vetzal is an Associate Professor with the Centre for Advanced Studies in Finance at the University of Waterloo. His research interests focus mainly on numerical valuation of complex derivative instruments. He holds a Ph.D. in Finance from the University of Toronto.

Jan Walliser is an economist in the African Department of the International Monetary Fund. His research interests include intergenerational redistribution through fiscal policy, tax reform, macroeconomic aspects of pension reform, and annuitization of retirement income. He received the Ph.D. in Economics from Boston University.

Heath Windcliff holds a M. Math degree from the University of Waterloo and he is currently completing his Ph.D. He studies in the Department of Computer Science there. His research interests include the development of mathematical approaches for valuing and hedging exotic derivative securities, and object-oriented techniques in scientific computing.

Abbreviations

ABS	Asset-Backed Securities
ACPM	Association of Canadian Pension Management
AIR	Assumed Investment Return
AIME	Average Indexed Monthly Earnings
ALPS	Aircraft Lease Portfolio Securitizations
ARC	Annualized Return on Capital
AS-Funds	Altersvorsorge-Sondervermögen
AWI	Averaging Wage Index
Bakred	German Federal Banking Supervisory Authority
BIC	Banking Investment Contract
bps	Basis Points
CAPM	Capital Asset Pricing Model
CBO	Congressional Budget Office
CBOT	Chicago Board of Trade
CDD	Cooling Degree Days
CDO	Collateralized Debt Obligation
CIM	Commercial Investment Mandate
CLO	Collateralized Loan Obligation
CMBS	Commercial Mortgage-Backed Securities
CME	Chicago Mercantile Exchange
CML	Capital Market Line
CMO	Collateralized Mortgage Obligations
CPP	Canada Pension Plan
CPPIB	Canada Pension Plan Investment Board
CRRA	Constant Relative Risk Aversion
CSSS	Commission to Strengthen Social Security
CTE	Conditional Tail Expectation
DAX	German Stock Index
DB	Defined Benefit
DC	Defined Contribution
DSC	Deferred Sales Charge
EBRI	Employee Benefit Research Institute
EETC	Enhanced Equipment Trust Certificates
EGTRRA	Economic Growth and Tax Relief Reconciliation Act of 2001
EMTR	Emerging Market Trade Receivables
EP	Employee Pension
EPS	Earnings-Per-Share

ERISA	Employee Retirement Income Security Act of 1974
ESOP	Employee Stock Ownership Plans
ETC	Equipment Trust Certificates
ETI	Economically Trageted Investments
EV	Equivalent Variations
FDIC	Federal Deposit Insurance Corporation
FILP	Fiscal Investment and Loan Program
FRN	Floating Rate Note
GAO	General Accounting Office
GDP	Gross Domestic Product
GIC	Guaranteed Investment Contract
GIPF	Government Pension Investment Fund
GMIB	Guaranteed Minimum Income Benefits
HDD	Heating Degree Days
HELOC	Home Equity Lines of Credit
IA	Individual Account
IA	Immediate Annuities
ICI	Investment Company Institute
IFSSR	Investment Fund of Social Security Reserves
IPA	Individual Pension Account
IPB	Irish Pensions Board
IRR	Internal Rate of Return
IRS	Internal Revenue Service
KAGG	German Investment Company Law
LIBOR	London-Interbank-Offer Rate
MAR	Market Value Adjustment
MEL	Mean Excess Loss
MER	Management Expense Ratio
MOHLW	Minister of Health, Labor, and Welfare
NCEO	National Center for Employee Ownership
NEPA	National Energy Policy Act
NP	National Pension
NTMA	National Treasury Management Agency
NZSE	New Zealand Superannuation Fund
OASDI	Old Age Survivor and Disability Insurance
OECD	Organization for Economic Cooperation and Development
OLS	Online Library Service
OSFI	Office of the Superintendent of Financial Institutions
P&L	Profit and Loss
P-AL-B	Professional, Arms-Length Board
PBGC	Public Benefit Guaranty Corporation
PCS	Property Claims Services
POB	Pension Obligation Bond
PWSPC	Pension Welfare Service Public Corporation

REXP	German Bond Index
RMBS	Residential Mortgage-Backed Securities
S&P	Standard & Poor's
SE	Shortfall Expectation
SERPS	State Earnings Related Pension Scheme
SPDA	Single Premium Deferred Annuities
SPIA	Single Premium Immediate Annuity
SPR	Special Purpose Reinsurer
SPV	Special Purpose Vehicle
STRS	State Teachers Retirement System
TCE	Tail Conditional Expectation
TIAA-CREF	Teachers Insurance and Annuity Association College Retirement Equities Fund
TSP	Thrift Savings Plan
USDOL	US Department of Labor
VaR	Value at Risk
VIA	Variable Immediate Annuities
YMCA	Young Men's Christian Association

Chapter 1

Overview: Developments in Risk Management for Retirement Security

Olivia S. Mitchell and Kent Smetters

This volume evaluates advances in retirement risk management by exploring developments that hold out new promise for enhancing old-age income security. Recent volatility in capital markets, along with longer-term trends in pension system design, has prompted questions about how well the evolving retirement system is performing. These issues are taking on additional force as massive global demographic change is producing the largest group of retirees in human history. Such economic and demographic challenges prompt policymakers, academics, financial practitioners, and pension participants young and old, to search for innovative and creative responses to what promises to be a more risky global retirement environment than in the past.

Over the years, employers and governments around the world have tried to protect against retirement insecurity by setting up defined benefit (DB) pension schemes. Under such plans, retirement benefits depend on service and salary, and benefits are usually paid as a lifelong annuity to long-term employees who worked until retirement age. Yet as we show below, the traditional DB model has increasingly been supplanted with defined contribution (DC) plans in many countries. In the case of a DC plan, retirement saving tends to be more subject to employee control throughout the life cycle. For example, DC participants can often decide whether and how much to contribute to the plan, as well as where to invest the plan assets during the accumulation phase. Additionally, at retirement, DC plan assets can frequently be taken in a lump-sum form, rather than automatically converted to lifelong annuities.

Converting from DB to DC plans, offers participants several advantages. On the accumulation side, workers gain more control over their retirement saving decisions, which may spur more attention to individual decision-making and responsibility. Members may also be better protected from the political risks that plague public pay-as-you-go retirement schemes.[1] Nevertheless, workers and retirees also take on new types of risk in DC plans. For instance, some people might save too little, or make poor investment choices, or have their portfolios eroded through administrative fees.

In addition, participants bear uncertainty associated with investment returns and over how long they will live in retirement.

There is surely no uniquely perfect retirement system design that will apply to all countries for all economic circumstances, but there are just as surely lessons to be learned about how to make pensions more resilient. This volume provides a range of new perspectives on how to better manage the wide range of retirement risks as capital and labor markets continue to evolve. In particular, with the market downturn and several highly-publicized corporate collapses, policymakers and plan members have begun to find appealing the idea of adding additional structure to both DC and DB plans—structure that would help protect plan participants against a range of risks. Below, we offer a brief analysis of why the traditional defined benefit pension plan appears to be abandoned in favor of defined contribution plans. We also discuss some key risks that both defined contribution and defined benefit plans convey upon plan members, and we highlight some of the ways recommended by contributors to this volume, for managing these retirement risks.

Trends from Defined Benefit to Defined Contribution Plans

Conventional DB retirement plans pay retirement benefits based on a prespecified formula set by the plan sponsor, which can be a government, an employer, or some other entity. For example, in the United States, a private sector DB plan might pay a retirement benefit equal to 2 percent of the worker's average wage during the last 5 years of work multiplied by his years of employment. A 30-year worker with earnings averaging $50,000 per year over the last 5 years before retirement could anticipate a yearly retirement annuity of $30,000 ($= 0.02 \times \$50,000 \times 30$). This worker would therefore receive a "replacement rate," which is the pension benefit relative to his final pay, of 60 percent. In most DB plans the retiree continues receiving this benefit until he dies; some plans might pay some benefit to a surviving spouse, as well. The DB approach is also prevalent in global public pension systems: almost 170 nations have national social security retirement programs, many of which are based on the DB framework. In some cases, benefit payments are structured as a simple percent of final pay, while in others, more elaborate formulas are used that include redistributive features as well as survivors' benefits.

An important historical appeal of the DB model was that it allowed workers to plan for retirement without requiring much knowledge about saving rates, portfolio choice, capital market risk, or mortality trends. In particular, as long as the plan sponsor can pay the benefits, the retirement payout is unrelated to the sponsoring firm's stock value or to the investment performance of pension reserves. Furthermore, pension legislation in many countries requires plan sponsors to make good on these promises even if the underlying value of the pension reserve suddenly decreases. In the United States, for instance, by law pension benefits must be paid even if the value of the pension pools falls; consequently, corporate stockholders are seen to bear pension investment risk, rather than DB plan participants. Moreover, since DB plans typically have paid out life annuities, the plan sponsor bears mortality risk as well.[2]

The past two decades have seen a rather pronounced movement away from the DB and toward a DC model. Under the DC approach, a worker contributes directly to his own retirement account that is then invested into a financial portfolio. The retirement benefit is then directly related to his own contributions (plus the sponsor's, if any), as well as investment income earned over time. Figure 1-1 shows that the number of DB plans declined over time in the United States, while DC plans have grown dramatically, particularly the very popular 401(k) plans. In 1975, assets held in DC plans comprised 29 percent of all pension assets (including Individual Retirement Account funds), and the DC share has grown to 72 percent by 2001 (Poterba et al., 2001). During that same period, more than two dozen countries, spanning five continents, reformed their national retirement systems to include DC individual accounts (see Table 1-1). In most of these cases, participants exert some control over how their money is invested (subject to some constraints), and they receive the risk and reward for those investments. In yet

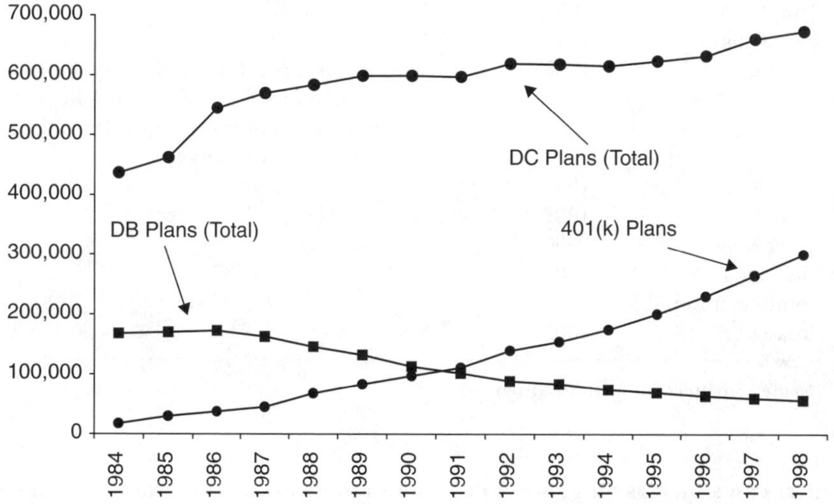

Figure 1-1. Trends in US Private Sector Pension Plans (number of plans by type). *Source*: Authors' computations from data provided by the US Department of Labor, Pension and Welfare Benefits Administration. <www.dol.gov>.

TABLE 1-1 Global Developments in Personal Account Retirement Systems

Country	*Year Personal Accounts Introduced*	*Voluntary Participation Choice?*
Chile	1981	New workers must join new system; current workers may choose between systems
Switzerland	1985	No
UK	1986	Yes
Denmark	1990	No
Australia	1992	No
Colombia	1993	Yes, workers are allowed to switch back and forth every 3 years
Peru	1993	Yes
Argentina	1994	Yes
China	1995	No
Uruguay	1996	Employees >40 years can choose; those <40 years and new workers must join new system
Bolivia	1997	No
Mexico	1997	No
El Salvador	1998	All new and young workers must join new system. Older workers must remain with old system. Workers age 36–55 (men)/50 (women) may choose
Hungary	1998	No
Kazakhstan	1998	No
Sweden	1998	Workers born before 1938 stay in old system; those born after 1953 in new system; gradual transition from old to new system for others
Costa Rica	1999	
Poland	1999	Yes
Hong Kong	2000	No
Nicaragua	2000	
Dominican Republic	2001	
Croatia	2002	Yes

Source: Smetters and Park (in progress).

other cases such as Singapore, Provident Funds have been established into which workers contribute; here participants are allocated a fixed return, akin to so-called "cash balance" plans.

While the movement toward DC plans seems to be a global phenomenon, we believe that somewhat different factors explain the DB to DC shift in the private versus the public sector. Specifically, we shall argue that the private sector change mainly reflects labor market dynamics, whereas the changes experienced in national retirement systems tend to be more reflective of demographic and political risks.

Challenges to Private Sector Pensions

Traditionally private sector DB pensions have had an important role in attracting and retaining workers (Lumsdaine and Mitchell, 1999). One way they do this is by offering additional lifetime compensation for those workers who remain with their employers for life (Clark and McDermed, 1990). In exchange for this positive aspect of DB plans, however, many also build in a "job-lock effect," discouraging workers from leaving their jobs early in their careers.[3]

The way job-lock works may be illustrated with a simple example. Suppose that a new employee, call her Jane, works for the same firm for 3 years, and she earns \$30,000 in the first year, \$40,000 in the second year, and \$50,000 in the third year. We further suppose that the company's DB formula specifies a yearly retirement benefit equal to one-quarter of the wage earned in Jane's last year of employment times the number of years she worked with the firm. At retirement, the employee would then be entitled to a benefit equal to \$37,500 ($= \frac{1}{4} \times \$50,000 \times 3$). Now alternatively, suppose that Jane earned the same annual salary each year, but instead she changed firms annually, working at three different companies, each having the same retirement formula. In this second case, when Jane retires, she will be entitled to a benefit from the first company equal to \$7,500 ($= \frac{1}{4} \times \$30,000 \times 1$), plus \$10,000 from the second firm ($= \frac{1}{4} \times \$40,000 \times 1$), plus a benefit of \$12,500 from the third company ($= \frac{1}{4} \times \$50,000 \times 1$). The total benefit in the second case would be \$30,000, or \$7,500 less than if she had remained with the first firm the entire time. Consequently the retirement formula provides a clear incentive to stay with the same employer, even if the worker's skills become more valuable with another company.

This hypothetical worker's benefit entitlement would have been even lower had she failed to "vest" before changing jobs. Vesting refers to the point at which a worker gains a legal right to an eventual retirement benefit. In the United States, vesting rarely occurred before 10 years of service until recently, but legal changes now require vesting in private pensions within 3 years of coverage (Sass, 1997). In any event, groups with higher job turnover rates, such as women, are much more prone than men to fail to vest under DB plans. This potential inefficiency has become particularly key as more women entered the labor force over the past two decades. Hence one motivation for the movement from DB to DC plans is to reduce this labor market distortion.[4]

To be sure, some "job-lock" might be efficient, especially in industries that require a fair amount of on-the-job training: employers can use job-lock to recapture some of their training investment. But fewer industries today are characterized by extensive on-the-job training; moreover, other mechanisms (such as deferred stock options) have been devised to provide incentive-based deferred compensation. As a result, DC plans are seen as more compatible with a mobile workforce in that they offer more portability: employees typically can roll over their accounts on changing employers, which undoes the job-lock problem quite readily.[5]

Another rationale for the shift on pension offerings notes that employers in many developed countries have begun to face tight labor markets in particular skill areas along with global product–market competition (Lofgren et al., 2001; Mitchell et al., 2003). The combination suggests that compensation packages must be more flexibly designed so as to accommodate the diverse needs of a more heterogeneous and less rapidly growing workforce. For example, a DC plan typically offers employees more control over how much to contribute, how their money is invested, and how to withdraw it, as compared to traditional DB plans.[6] In addition, DC plans are more flexible in terms of retirement age, unlike DB plans that generally subsidize early retirement but penalize continued work at older ages.[7] Both factors suggest that DC plans are more likely to grow more popular in the private sector, in the future.

Challenges to Public Sector Pensions

Pension plans in the public sector have also undergone substantial change in the last two decades. Traditionally, national social security systems were of the DB variety, mostly operated on a pay-as-you-go basis. Operating them on an unfunded basis means that participants are exposed to fluctuations in annual tax revenues, inasmuch as current revenues are needed to pay benefits each year. Consequently, workers find themselves exposed to the risk that shortfalls will require raising taxes, and retirees in traditional DB systems worry about unexpected costs and possible benefit cuts due to demographic changes and political uncertainty.

Appreciation of these risks over the last two decades prompted many countries to follow in Chile's footsteps, after that nation adopted a DC structure in 1981 for its national retirement system (Schwarz and Demirguc-Kunt, 1999). Many developing countries appear to have followed suit in response to situations of crisis and breakdown in their national programs; very few set aside adequate public pension reserves for their national old-age systems.[8] In developed countries, DC partial or full conversions appear to have been motivated by forecasts of future demographic change and long-run cost concerns (Smetters and Park, in progress).

Plan Design and Investment Risk

Adopting a DC plan affords workers and retirees additional, and sometimes welcome, control over their retirement saving and income. On the other hand, this added flexibility also brings new risks, some of which workers and retirees appear relatively ill-equipped to handle. In this section we discuss ways in which plan sponsors transfer retirement system risks to participants, and how this risk transfer can be better handled by good plan design.

The main source of risk we focus on here is investment risk, which is key since the value of DC accounts at retirement depends on the worker's and sponsor's contributions, as well as the investment returns earned over the working lifetime.[9] In the case of private sector conversion from DB to a DC plan, the risk is transferred directly from shareholders to workers. In the case of national social security DB to DC conversions, the nature of the risk transfer likely depends on what happened to promises made under the traditional system and how those promises were spread between pensioners and taxpayers. New risks faced by workers under national DC plans might actually be *less* than risks borne under the unfunded old system, though DC investment risks may seem more transparent to workers.

It is essential to note that investment risk is unavoidable when attempting to advance-fund future retirement consumption, irrespective of whether a pension system is based on the defined-benefit model or the defined-contribution model. While those who oppose augmenting social security systems with personal saving accounts often point to investment risk as a reason to oppose them, they miss an important point: *true* advance funding of future pension liabilities *always* requires an increase in capital holdings, and the risk associated with capital assets must be borne by someone. In a DB model, this risk tends to be passed on to future social security taxpayers in the form of risky tax rates, or to beneficiaries in the form of risky benefits. In a pure DC model, this risk is borne by beneficiaries and so it must be managed.

Although investors sometimes think that investment risk becomes less important over the long run, most experts know that this position is not accurate (e.g. Bodie, 1995; Chapter 2, this volume). Indeed, there have been 15 years in the twentieth century alone in which the real value of the US stock market fell over 40 percent in the succeeding decade.[10] The stock market declined by about 50 percent in real terms, between 1973 and 1975, and it did not return to its pre-1973 level for almost a decade. More recently, the US stock market has given up almost 5 years of growth including the earnings during the fast-growth late 1990s. Even at prevailing values, price-earnings ratios exceed their historic average, and a high price-earnings ratio may foretell yet another decline, following a "mean reversion" process outlined by various financial economists.[11] Also, though US capital markets have performed well over the last century, the same has not been true for major foreign markets, which returned an average real return of 1.5 percent over the century (Goetzmann and Jorion, 1996).

One important lesson from the literature is that DC plan participants must have access to high-quality, trustworthy investment advice, as well as financial education so they can accurately assess the risk/return mix in their pension plans. A survey conducted of the TIAA-CREF participant pool suggests that most people in that sector appear to follow the standard rules for investing (Bodie and Crane, 1997).[12] On the other hand the group surveyed was better educated and more highly paid than on average, so questions remain about whether employees more generally would follow this tactic. A different approach is to ask whether employees tend to receive good advice from financial service firms and investment advisory services. Bodie (Chapter 2, this volume) reviews a number of advice provider websites, and he concludes that a great deal of the information provided is logically flawed and sometimes even counterproductive. For example, he illustrates that the standard advice proffered is tilted toward risky investments, and it also offers little advice about protection against market declines. He concludes that more easy-to-understand advice and safer investment products are needed to simplify the complex task of investing for retirement.

Concern that DC participants might hold unbalanced investment portfolios in retirement plans is the focus of two studies that examine the role of employer stock. This issue has become especially important following the demise of Enron and other large employers. Mitchell and Utkus (Chapter 3, this volume) explore why many DC plans became heavily concentrated in company stock, the result of a policy conflict between wanting workers to own the company and hence align their interests with the firm's, versus the more traditional need to hold a diversified retirement portfolio. One striking finding is that 401(k) plan participants tend to believe that their *own* firm's company stock is safer than *other* individual company stock, and also safer than a stock market index. The authors assemble a wide range of data on this topic and outline policy options for future plan design. In a related chapter, Ramaswamy (Chapter 4, this volume) tackles the difficult issue of measuring the level of plan diversification when a worker holds a great deal of his DC pension assets in his employer's stock. The diversification measure he develops computes how "close" the participant's portfolio is to the point on an efficient capital market frontier that would produce the same expected return. Ramaswamy's measure can be computed without knowing the expected returns to all the pension assets, and he shows that many common DC plan portfolios are so badly diversified that they would require very costly insurance to hedge these underlying risks.

The risk of nondiversification must be distinguished from general investment risk that arises from fluctuations in market returns. A person who elects an undiversified portfolio might forego larger returns even when the market returns as a whole does well. Research shows that peoples' DC portfolio choices follow the "path of least resistance," by passively opting for the enrollment and investment options suggested by their employers (Choi et al., 2003). Consequently, good plan design regarding automatic enrollment, investment choice, and financial education can have a powerful impact on influencing, saving, and portfolio choices. A similar point applies to national social security retirement systems. In the Swedish DC pension system, one-third of participants chose the "standard" fund in 2000, which was the fund assigned to those who did not elect any fund (Weaver, 2001). For this reason, the Commission to Strengthen Social Security (CSSS, 2001) recommended that a standardized portfolio be offered for those who failed to elect a particular investment mix.

Another reason that investment risk in the DC system is of concern is that public and private pension systems may interact with each other, sometimes in complex ways. For example, Australia has for many years had both a national mandatory DC system and also a means-tested old-age benefit for the poor. The concern is that retirees have substantial flexibility in their pension investments and pension payouts, an interaction that opens the possibility of strategic participant behavior. The potential for moral hazard in this circumstance is explored by Doyle and Piggott (Chapter 5, this volume), who evaluate how participants perceive the cost versus the benefit of having a minimum pension benefit assured, versus a flat-rate benefit paid regardless of the value of assets in their personal account. They find that inflation-protected products have lots of value.

A different reason investment risk can arise results from confusion about how capital market risk should be assessed by pension policymakers. For example, when President Clinton proposed to invest the US Social Security surplus in the stock market, government scorekeepers "scored" this plan using risky expected stock returns. The problem with this approach is that it does not explicitly discount for market risk, and as Smetters (2002) shows, this scoring method imposes a large actuarial unfunded liability on future generations. A similar problem arises with state-level pension systems and, to a lesser extent, private pension plans, as illustrated by Gold (Chapter 6, this volume). The author also goes an important step further by pinpointing how actuarial standards can result in this costly bias. Concern over interference in valuing and investing pension assets has been highlighted by Iglesias and Palacios (2000), who emphasize how political factors may play an important role in reducing DB plan investment returns. To protect against this, several developed nations have restructured pension governance and investment options to limit the usage of pension monies for social projects that often earn low (or negative) real rates of return. Palacios (Chapter 7, this volume) examines a range of "best practices," and he contends that additional transparency, better reporting, and competitive market benchmarks can yield higher pension plan investment returns.

Global Developments in Retirement Risk Transfer

One approach to managing the investment risks that workers face in a defined-contribution plan is to offer them some form of guarantee. A simple approach would promise a participant contributing to a DC plan that he would receive a minimum rate of return on his investments, or guarantee that the DC account would be of a minimum size when the worker attains retirement age. Lachance and Mitchell (Chapter 8, this volume) estimate the actuarial cost of providing different types of DC plan guarantees, which they estimate using arbitrage pricing techniques. Though pension guarantees have been previously analyzed, this chapter considers a wider range of guarantee structures and builds on methodology pioneered by Cox, Ingersoll, and Ross (1985). This chapter confirms that many pension guarantees can be quite expensive. In addition, the authors also show that some potentially attractive guarantees might be more affordable. In particular, a "real principal" guarantee would return to a participant the real value of his contributions, a structure akin to that adopted in the new "Japanese 401(k)" plans (Clark and Mitchell, 2002). Since the guarantee is price indexed but the larger economy grows in real terms, this financial promise could be offered at fairly reasonable costs. On the other hand costs may be especially large if the plan guarantees a rate of return promised under a former DB social security system (Smetters, 2002).

DC plan guarantees are also offered in Germany, and are the subject of an examination by Maurer and Schlag (Chapter 9, this volume). Under the German Retirement Saving Act, supplemental DC pensions were created to offset reductions in traditional DB state benefit promises. To qualify for a special tax status, providers of these supplemental DC products must ensure the nominal value of workers' investments at retirement. The authors examine different ways in which providers can hedge such risks, as well as their associated costs. Alternative guarantees in Canadian "segregated funds" are examined by Vetzal, Forsyth, and Windcliff (Chapter 10, this volume). Here a guarantee is provided after a specified time, on the initial principal invested. These contracts include a reset provision that allows investors to lock in gains, as the value of the mutual fund increases; other features may also be included such as a death benefit paid off immediately on the investor's death. The authors describe hedging strategies that can be used by firms offering these contracts. Using numerical models they conclude that segregated contracts are quite expensive to offer, but that some of the risks can be reduced quite significantly using fairly simple active (or dynamic) hedging strategies.

Guarantees are quite prevalent in many pension plan systems around the world. For example, Chile was the first country to convert its complex DB system to one based on personal accounts. The Chilean system then guaranteed that each plan would yield a rate of return not too far from the average return and it also "tops up" personal accounts on retirement, so as to ensure that individual accounts are large enough to finance a benefit equal to approximately 75 percent of the minimum wage (Walliser, Chapter 11, this volume). This guarantee produces a retirement benefit equal to about 25 percent of the average wage in the economy (Diamond and Vadés-Prieto, 1994). Walliser also surveys other mandatory retirement systems and groups them into two general types, and he further discusses economic rationales for and incentives created by these guarantees. Pension guarantees have also been offered in a wide range of voluntary DC plans, as discussed by Turner and Rajnes (Chapter 12, this volume). These authors demonstrate that guarantees typically differ from those offered in a mandatory system: that is, voluntary DC plans tend to offer a fixed nominal rate of return, while relative rate of return guarantee tend to be offered by mandatory plans. They argue that the more generous voluntary system guarantees are more likely to encourage plan participation.

While many may find attractive the provision of guarantees in pension plans, there remains the key issue of how to finance the costs of providing different guarantees. These calculations are important because guarantees sometimes seem to be "free"; this is the case, for example, on government budget balance sheets that only report contemporaneous flows of revenues and costs, but ignore potential insurance liabilities down the road. Yet such guarantees can represent considerable risk to future taxpayers or, in the case of private sector, substantial risks for the party holding the short position of these contracts.

One of the most important diversification strategies for pension systems is to find investment vehicles whose returns are not highly correlated with the performance of the rest of the economy. For example, a worker who loses his or her job faces a second tragedy if the value of his pension plan also sharply decreases in value. Cummins and Lewis (Chapter 13, this volume) investigate a new class of derivative securities whose returns are tied to events such as catastrophes and weather. They argue that these securities might be quite useful to institutional investors, such as a mutual fund, because of the low correlation of their returns with other financial investments. Moreover, these securities pay a rate of return that is often much higher than other low-correlation securities, such as government bonds. But Cummins and Lewis argue that some caution is in order: these markets are quite thin, and so this premium might reflect liquidity problems.

Additional issues pertinent to pension payouts are taken up in the study by Fliegelman, Milevsky, and Robinson (Chapter 14, this volume). Their focus is whether and how insurers will be able to "make good" on promises to pay lifelong annuities. To this end, they propose that insurers can do several things, including offsetting mortality exposure via life insurance products and sensible product design. For example, they indicate that restricting investment options of plan participants can reduce volatility of returns and hence the value of the option granted to the contract holder. In addition, they recommend distributor and participant education as product complexity increases. Finally they explore alternative financing mechanisms including reinsurance that might permit insurers to access product design and mortality expertise of reinsurers, though they also note that reinsurers have traditionally been less than willing to accept longevity risk unless it is priced very conservatively.

Conclusions

Ultimately, retirement income products that offer new promise for old-age income security must better handle the increased volatility resulting from capital market investment, along with longer-term trends in pension system design, that have prompted concerns regarding how effectively retirement systems can perform. Policymakers, academics, financial practitioners, and pension participants are engaged in an active search for innovative responses to the emerging global retirement environment.

This research shows that the pension market is far from exhausted. Indeed, more workers than ever before seek sensible pension designs to help them save during the accumulation phase, and also to help them manage pension payouts in retirement. Maintaining insurer financial integrity and profitability is essential, including protecting for the long-tailed nature of payout annuity contracts. In addition, more work remains to be done on how to better protect retiree minimum pension guarantees, ultimately the core concern of retirement plan designers.

Notes

[1] For a discussion of political risk in the case of the US Social Security system see Schieber and Shoven (1999) and Cogan and Mitchell (2002). Other countries are discussed in World Bank (1994).

[2] For a more extended discussion of US pension law and solvency issues the reader is referred to McGill et al. (1996); for more on annuities see Brown et al. (2001).

[3] Many analysts have examined labor market impacts of DB plans; for reviews see Mitchell (1982) and Gustman et al. (1994).

[4] DC plans did not technically replace existing DB plans in most cases; rather, existing workers are often allowed to contribute to new DC plans, and new companies now typically elect the DC form; for a review see Mitchell (2000).

[5] Some DC firms do match a portion of employee contributions and then impose a vesting period similar to that in DB plans, before the matched contributions become the employee's personal property. In this case, some job-lock still exists though it is less important relative to traditional DB plans.

[6] The job-lock problem can also be addressed with a cash-balance DB plan that promises a fixed rate of return on contributions. Nevertheless these plans are costly to administer and typically do not give employees portfolio choice. Any employee seeking a relatively predictable rate of return could, of course, obtain it in a DC plan by investing in low-risk bonds.

[7] Cash balance plans can also encourage continued work; see Clark and Schieber (2002).

[8] While a few have done so, as in the case of Asian Provident Funds, these assets are often invested in fairly poor-performing assets. For a discussion of pension plans for governmental employees see Mitchell and Hustead (2000).

[9] For other risks we do not address here see Brown et al. (2000) and Bodie, Hammond, and Mitchell (2002).

[10] These include 1908–12, 1937, 1939, 1965–66 and 1968–73 (see Campbell and Shiller, 1998).

[11] Campbell and Shiller (1998*a*) argue that the price–dividend ratio is a powerful predictor of future prices, contrary to the efficient market hypothesis. On these grounds, they forecast a 38 percent loss in the real value of stocks over the next decade.

[12] One important exception was that participants often failed to "tax minimize," which means they did not figure out a contribution and asset mix that would reduce lifetime taxes paid on retirement saving and dissaving.

References

Bodie, Zvi. 1995. "On the Risk of Stocks in the Long Run." *Financial Analysts Journal* May/June: 18–22.

— 2001. "Financial Engineering and Social Security Reform." In *Risk Aspects of Social Security Reform*, eds. John Campbell and M. Feldstein. Chicago: University of Chicago Press, pp. 291–320.

— and Robert Merton. 1993. "Pension Benefit Guarantees in the United States: A Functional Analysis." In *The Future of Pensions in the United States*, ed. R. Schmitt. Pension Research Council, Philadelphia: University of Pennsylvania Press, pp. 194–234.

— and Dwight B. Crane. 1997. "Personal Investing: Advice, Theory, and Evidence." *Financial Analysts Journal* 53: 13–23.

—, Brett Hammond, and Olivia S. Mitchell (eds.) 2002. *Innovations in Financing Retirement*. Pension Research Council, Philadelphia: University of Pennsylvania Press.

Brown, Jeffrey, Olivia S. Mitchell, James Poterba, and Mark Warshawsky. 2001. *The Role of Annuity Markets in Financing Retirement*. Cambridge: MIT Press.

Campbell, John and Robert Shiller. 1998*a*. "Stock Prices, Earnings and Expected Dividends." No. 858 in Cowles Foundation Discussion Papers from Cowles Foundation, Yale University.

——— 1998*b*. "Valuation Ratios and the Long-Run Stock Market Outlook." *Journal of Portfolio Management* 24(2): 11–26.

Choi, James, David Laibson, Brigitte Madrian, and Andrew Metrick. 2002. "Defined Contribution Pensions: Plan Rules, Participant Decisions and the Path of Least Resistance." *NBER Tax Policy and the Economy*. The MIT Press: 67–113.

Clark, Robert L. and Ann A. McDermed. 1990. *The Choice of Pension Plans in a Changing Regulatory Environment.* Washington: AEI Press.

— and Olivia S. Mitchell. 2002. "Strengthening Employment-Based Pensions in Japan." *Benefits Quarterly,* Second Quarter: 22–43.

— and Sylvester J. Schieber. 2002. "Taking the Subsidy Out of Early Retirement: Converting to Hybrid Pensions." In *Innovations in Retirement Financing,* eds. Zvi Bodie, Brett Hammond, and Olivia S. Mitchell. Pension Research Council, Philadelphia: University of Pennsylvania Press, 149–174.

Cogan, John, and Olivia S. Mitchell. 2002. "The Role of Economic Policy in Social Security Reform: Perspectives from the President's Commission." Pension Research Council Working Paper 2002–13. <prc.wharton.upenn.edu/prc.prc.html>.

Commission to Strengthen Social Security (CSSS). 2001. *Strengthening Social Security and Creating Personal Wealth for All Americans: Final Report.* <www.csss.gov>.

Congressional Budget Office. 1999. *Social Security Privatization: Experiences Abroad.* Washington: US Government Printing Office.

Cox, John C., Jonathan E. Ingersoll Jr., Stephen A. Ross. 1985. "An Intertemporal General Equilibrium Model of Asset Prices." *Econometrica* 53(2): 363–384.

Diamond, Peter A. and Salvador Valdes-Prieto. 1994. "Social Security Reforms." In *The Chilean Economy: Policy Lessons and Challenges,* eds. Barry P. Bosworth, Rudiger Dornbusch, and Raúl Labán. Washington: The Brookings Institution, 257–357.

Goetzmann, William N. and Philippe Jorion. 1996. "Global Stock Markets in the Twentieth Century." *Journal of Finance* 54(3): 953–980.

Gustman, Alan S, Olivia S. Mitchell, and Thomas L. Steinmeier. 1994. "The Role of Pensions in the Labor Market." *Industrial and Labor Relations Review* 47(3): 417–438.

Iglesias, Augusto and Robert J. Palacios. 2000. "Managing Public Pension Reserves: Evidence from the International Experience." Washington: Pension Reform Primer, World Bank.

Lofgren, Eric, Steven A. Nyce, and Sylvester J. Schieber. 2001. "Designing Total Reward Programs for Tight Labor Markets." Pension Research Council Working Paper 2001–17. <prc.wharton.upenn.edu/prc.prc.html>.

Lumsdaine, Robin and Olivia S. Mitchell. 1999. "New Developments in the Economics of Retirement." In *Handbook of Labor Economics,* eds. Orley Ashenfelter and David Card. Amsterdam: North Holland, pp. 3261–3308.

Marcus, Alan J. 1985. "Spinoff-Terminations and the Value of Pension Insurance." *Journal of Finance* 40(3): 911–924.

— 1987. "Corporate Pension Policy and the Value of PBGC Insurance." In *Issues in Pension Economics,* eds. Zvi Bodie, John Shoven, and David Wise. Chicago: University of Chicago Press, pp. 49–76.

McGill, Dan, Kyle Brown, John Haley, and Sylvester Scheiber. 1996. *Fundamentals of Private Pension Plans,* 7th edn. Pension Research Council. Philadelphia: University of Pennsylvania Press.

Mitchell, Olivia S. 1982. "Fringe Benefits and Labor Mobility." *Journal of Human Resources* 17(Spring): 286–298.

— 2000. "Developments in Pensions." *Handbook of Insurance,* ed. Georges Dionne. Boston: Kluwer Academic Publishers, 873–899.

—— and Edwin Hustead (eds.) 2000. *Pensions for the Public Sector.* Pension Research Council, Philadelphia: University of Pennsylvania Press.

——, James M. Poterba, Mark J. Warshawsky, and Jeffrey R. Brown. 1999. "New Evidence on the Money's Worth of Individual Annuities." *American Economic Review,* September: 1299–1318.

——, David Blitzstein, Michael Gordon, and Judy Mazo (eds.) 2003. *Benefits for the Workplace of the Future.* Philadelphia: University of Pennsylvania Press.

Pennacchi, George G. 1999. "The Value of Guarantees on Pension Fund Returns." *Journal of Risk and Insurance* 66(2): 219–237.

Pesando, James. 1982. "Investment Risk, Bankruptcy Risk, and Pension Reform in Canada." *Journal of Finance* 37(3): 741–749.

Poterba, James M., Steven F. Venti, and David A. Wise. 2001. "The Transition to Personal Accounts and Increasing Retirement Wealth: Macro and Micro Evidence." NBER Working Paper 8610, November.

Sass, Steven. 1997. *The Promise of Private Pensions: The First Hundred Years.* Cambridge: Harvard University Press.

Schieber, Sylvester J. and John B. Shoven. 1999. *The Real Deal: The History and Future of Social Security.* New Haven: Yale University Press.

Schwarz, Anita and Asli Demirguc-Kunt. 1999. "Taking Stock of Pensions around The World." World Bank. <http://www.worldbank.org/wbi/pensions/ pdfpublications/schwarz.pdf>.

Smetters, Kent. 2002. "Controlling the Costs of Minimum Benefit Guarantees in Public Pension Conversions." *The Journal of Pension Economics and Finance* 1(1): 9–34.

—— and Cindy Park. In progress. *A Matter of Trust: Understanding Worldwide Social Security Reforms.* The Wharton School, University of Pennsylvania.

Weaver, Kent. 2001. "Reforming Social Security: Lessons from Abroad." Working Paper. Washington: The Brookings Institution.

World Bank. 1994. *Averting the Old-Age Crisis.* Washington: The World Bank.

Part I

Plan Sponsors and Retirement Income Risk

Chapter 2

An Analysis of Investment Advice to Retirement Plan Participants

Zvi Bodie

Around the world, the primary responsibility for providing an adequate retirement income has been shifting from governments, employers, and trade unions, to individuals. Pension plans are shifting from the defined benefit form to defined contribution, in which plan participants must make investment decisions. Evidence abounds that people consistently make certain mistakes because of lack of knowledge, faulty logic, cognitive dissonance, and biased statistics. This chapter examines the quality of the online investment education materials and advice offered at websites designed specifically for people planning for retirement. The first section of the chapter titled "Time Horizon and Risk Tolerance: The Trouble with Online Advice" analyzes the content of these websites, and it concludes that much of the advice offered there is misleading and potentially quite harmful. The second section titled "Defined Benefit, Defined Contribution, and Individual Choice" considers what might be done to improve the advice and to develop better investment products.

While there are significant differences in the level of technical sophistication among the websites and optimization tools, their qualitative advice is strikingly uniform.[1] The educational materials at these websites generally agree on the following set of principles for investing money earmarked for retirement:[2]

- Investors should diversify their total portfolio across asset classes, and the equity portion should be well-diversified across industries and companies.
- The longer your time horizon, the more you should invest in equities.

Table 2-1 summarizes some of the key findings from an examination of the major websites.[3]

Time Horizon and Risk Tolerance: The Trouble with Online Advice

Economic theory provides no necessary connection between a person's time horizon and his risk tolerance. Thus, one can have a horizon of 30 years

TABLE 2-1 Retirement Investment Advice in Websites

Issue	*Quicken*	*Smart Money*	*mPower (Money Central)*	*Financial Engines*
Does the fraction in stocks automatically increase with time horizon?	Yes	Yes	No	No
Is there a risk-free (e.g. TIPS or I-bonds) option?	No	No	No	No
Is there any mention of different stock market forecasts of experts?	No	No	No	No

Source: Author's survey.

and be extremely averse to risk, or a horizon of 1 year and be very tolerant of risk. Indeed, for utility functions that exhibit constant relative risk aversion (CRRA), Merton (1969) and Samuelson (1969) have shown that the proportion of total wealth optimally held in risky assets is the same regardless of age. Their models show that very risk-averse people should choose to invest in such a way as to minimize the volatility of their lifetime consumption flow. If a risk-free lifetime annuity is available, then they should purchase it.

Stocks for the Long Run

Yet the standard advice offered by the financial services industry is that a longer time horizon implies greater risk tolerance.[4] For example, *Smart-Money University* puts it this way:

> Where to invest your retirement savings shouldn't be that complicated. It depends largely on a single factor: time. The more time you have before you plan to retire, the more aggressively you should be invested in equities. If, as for many people, the stock market makes you nervous, check out *Time vs. Risk* for an interactive demonstration of why this simple axiom holds true in good times and bad. History shows quite clearly that equities are your best long-term investment option.[5]

A popular rule of thumb says that the fraction of one's portfolio to invest in stocks should be 100 minus one's age. Using this rule, 70 percent of one's investments should be in stocks if one is 30 years old; 30 percent should be in stocks if one is 70. The reasoning behind this advice goes as follows:

> stocks' year-to-year volatility make them poor choices to finance short-term goals: For example, stocks' spectacular 1995 return of 37.6 percent (as measured by the S&P 500) compares with the low 1994 return of 1.3 percent. But, over longer periods of

time, fluctuations like these have tended to settle down—as you can see in the chart. Stock returns for twenty-year periods ranged from a low of about three percent to a high of around 17 percent. Over thirty-year periods, stock returns narrowed, ranging from 8.5 to 13.5 percent. That's why, although investing in stocks is hardly risk-free and past results certainly don't guarantee future performance, their historical pattern suggests that stocks may be an appropriate alternative for you to consider if your goal is a longer-term one.[6]

Unfortunately, this reasoning is invalid, and it may also be dangerously misleading. The apparent reduction in risk is a statistical illusion arising from the fact that the measure of return used is an average compound rate. As students of introductory statistics are taught, the dispersion of an n-year average declines, as n grows.[7] But the dispersion of the average compound rate of return is not a relevant parameter for the purpose at hand. For a person investing a lump sum now to have, say, $1 million in 30 years time, the relevant parameter is not the dispersion of the annual rate of return, but the dispersion of the value of the portfolio in 30 years. The dispersion of long-term holdings does not fall with time.

This same mistake is often made in educational materials depicting the trade off between risk and reward (the "efficient portfolio frontier") for different time horizons. Using mean and standard deviation of average compound rates of return, the slope of the curve gets steeper as the time horizon lengthens, implying that equities are a better choice, the longer one's horizon. But this is because the expected annualized risk premium remains fixed, while the annualized standard deviation declines: again, a statistical illusion.[8]

The financial advice in the websites that report probability of success or failure as their summary measure are also misleading, but in a more subtle way. To see why, compare the *probability* of a shortfall with the *cost of insuring* against a shortfall.[9] A shortfall occurs if the value of a stock portfolio at the horizon date is less than the value an investor would have received by investing in safe bonds (e.g. Treasury bonds) maturing on that same date. If, as history suggests, the *expected* average compound return on stocks exceeds the risk-free rate of interest, it is indeed true that the probability of a shortfall declines with the length of the investment time horizon (Figure 2-1). But this fact does not have the favorable implications many investment advisers think it has.

The Truth about the Risk of Stocks in the Long Run

The simple economic fact is that there is no "free lunch" for the long-term investor in the risk-reward department. The probability of a shortfall is a flawed measure of risk because it completely ignores the *severity* of the financial loss should a shortfall occur.[10] A measure that does take proper

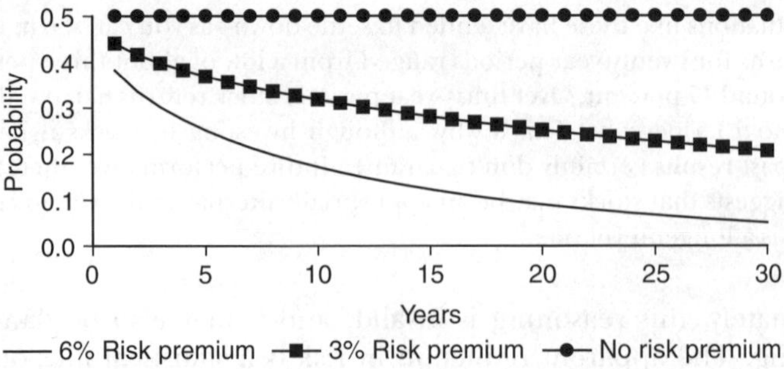

Figure 2-1. Probability of a shortfall. (*Source*: Author's computations.)

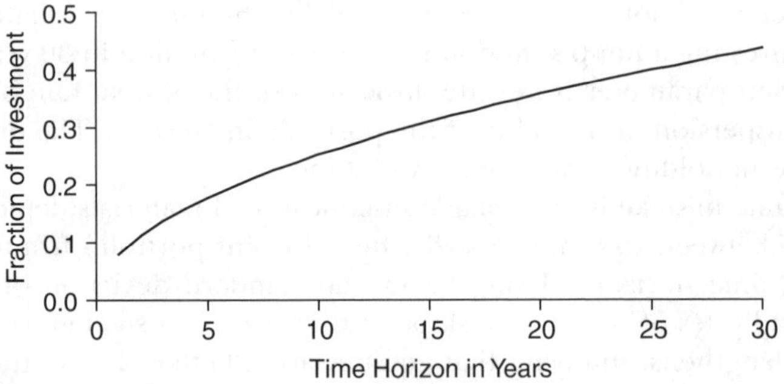

Figure 2-2. Cost of shortfall insurance. (*Source*: Author's computations.)

account of both the likelihood *and* the severity of a potential shortfall is the price an investor would have to pay to insure against it.

If stocks were truly less risky in the long run, then the cost of insuring against earning less than the risk-free rate of interest should decline as the length of the investment horizon increases. But reality is quite the opposite. The structure of insurance against shortfall risk is effectively a put option with maturity equal to the investment horizon and with a strike price set at the forward price of the underlying stock portfolio.[11] According to theory and in actual practice, the put price representing the cost of insuring against a shortfall *increases* as the investment horizon lengthens. (See Figure 2-2.)

This pattern is easily confirmed for maturities up to 3 years by inspection of prices for exchange-traded puts on individual stocks and on broad stock-index portfolios. The same result holds uniformly for proprietary pricing models used by investment and commercial banks to assess their own cost for longer-maturity puts that they sell over the counter. For very long maturity puts, this cost ranges from one-third to a half of the value of the equity portfolio to be insured and so there is typically little commercial interest.

In short, the insurance cost, and hence the risk, of shortfall over long time horizons is anything but small (see Bodie, 1995; Lachance and Mitchell, Chapter 8, this volume).

The Importance of One's Earnings Profile

Clearly the conventional reasoning linking age and equity investing is fundamentally flawed, but there are good reasons for linking age and portfolio mix. A critical, but often overlooked, determinant of optimal asset allocation is the risk profile of the individual's future labor income. Typically the ratio of future labor income to other assets (such as retirement savings) is large when investors are young, and eventually it decreases as they approach retirement.

If one's future labor income is relatively secure, it might be optimal to start out in the early years with a high proportion of one's investment portfolio in stocks, and decrease it over time as suggested by the conventional wisdom. However, this conventional wisdom may *not* apply to those who face substantial risk in their labor income: entrepreneurs or stock brokers, for example, whose income is highly sensitive to stock market risk. For such investors, their human capital already provides a large stock market exposure and the *opposite* policy may be optimal, that is, to start out with a relatively low fraction of the portfolio in stocks and increase it over time.[12]

The Conservative Investor

To assess the strength of the pro-equity bias at websites for retirement plan participants, I performed a simple test by adopting the stance of an ultraconservative investor to see if there was any mention of risk-free investments such as inflation-protected bonds. When asked questions designed to elicit my risk tolerance, I answered them in such a way as to indicate as little tolerance as possible for risk of any kind. In theory, the financial advice should result in a portfolio designed to minimize the volatility of my lifetime consumption. If all post-retirement consumption is to be financed from accumulated savings, then the portfolio should consist entirely of fixed-income securities denominated in units of the consumption good.

Unfortunately, in *none* of the many models I tested did this ever turn out to be the case. Instead, I was always advised to invest a substantial fraction of my portfolio in stocks (at least 30 percent). This was true even when I notified the advice program that I was starting my retirement. As shown in the next section, retirees who are drawing down their retirement savings to finance their spending face special risks when they invest in equities.

The Situation of Retirees

Most websites emphasize the fact that people may live a long time after they retire. The average male retiring at 65 can expect to live 19 more years,

TABLE 2-2 Drawdown of Retirement Fund Assuming 10% Per Year Rate of Return

Year	Rate of Return (%)	Amount in Fund ($)	Interest Earned ($)	Amount Withdrawn
1	10	1,000,000	100,000	117,460
2	10	982,540	98,254	117,460
3	10	963,335	96,333	117,460
4	10	942,209	94,221	117,460
5	10	918,970	91,897	117,460
6	10	893,407	89,341	117,460
7	10	865,288	86,529	117,460
8	10	834,358	83,436	117,460
9	10	800,334	80,033	117,460
10	10	762,907	76,291	117,460
11	10	721,739	72,174	117,460
12	10	676,453	67,645	117,460
13	10	626,638	62,664	117,460
14	10	571,843	57,184	117,460
15	10	511,567	51,157	117,460
16	10	445,264	44,526	117,460
17	10	372,331	37,233	117,460
18	10	292,105	29,210	117,460
19	10	203,856	20,386	117,460
20	10	106,781	10,678	117,460
21		0	0	

Source: Author's computations.

to age 84. The average woman retiring at age 65 can expect to live 23 more years, to age 88. Therefore, the reasoning goes, one should remain substantially committed to stocks even after one retires.

This advice is especially problematic, however, because during retirement one is drawing down one's assets. The resultant standard of living will depend not only on the *average* rate of return one earns during retirement, but also on the *time path* of returns. Even if the average rate of return is high, one can run out of money long before one expires. For example, suppose one planned to save a total of $1 million, expecting to live for 20 years after retirement, and assume an average rate of return of 10 percent per year.[13] The annual retirement income to be withdrawn is calculated to be $117,460 per year. Table 2-2 shows that by withdrawing this amount at the end of each year, the original fund will be exhausted in precisely 20 years, *provided that one earns 10 percent in each and every year.*

But suppose that the rate of return varied over the 20 years. Even if the average is 10 percent per year, it makes a big difference whether

TABLE 2-3 Drawdown of Retirement Fund When Rate of Return during First 10 Years Is Zero

Year	*Rate of Return*	*Amount in Fund ($)*	*Interest Earned ($)*	*Amount withdrawn at end of year ($)*
1	0	1,000,000	0	117,460
2	0	882,540	0	117,460
3	0	765,081	0	117,460
4	0	647,621	0	117,460
5	0	530,162	0	117,460
6	0	412,702	0	117,460
7	0	295,242	0	117,460
8	0	177,783	0	117,460
9	0	60,323	0	117,460
10	0	−57,137	0	117,460

Source: Author's computations.

the higher-than-average returns occur early or late in the 20-year span. Suppose that during the first 10 years your rate of return is below average and during the last 10 years it is above average. One might not make it past the 10th year. For example, suppose the rate of return is zero in the first 10 years, and 20 percent per year in the last 10 years. Since the fund would earn no interest at all during the first half of the period, one would completely run out of money by the 9th year, as shown in Table 2-3 and in Figure 2-3.

This is not merely a far-fetched hypothetical situation. Suppose that in January 1973 a retiree had a fund of $1 million. The average rate of return on a value-weighted portfolio of all stocks on the NYSE during the 20 years starting in 1973 was a healthy 12.78 percent per year. Suppose the retiree was conservative and assumed only a 10 percent rate of return, thus taking out $117,460 each year. The pattern of actual annual returns and remaining funds is shown in Table 2-4 and depicted in Figures 2-4 and 2-5.

Let's take a detailed look at what could have happened. The stock market declined 14.75 percent in 1973, so at the end of the year only $852,500 was left. After taking out $117,460, only $735,040 was left. In 1974 the market dropped another 26.5 percent, reducing the account balance to $540,990. At the end of 1974, he again took out $117,460, leaving a new account balance of $423,530. In other words, by the end of 1974, he had less than half of the original $1,000,000 left, even though he only took out a total of $234,920. In 1975 the market gained 37.2 percent, lifting his balance to $581,337. After withdrawing $117,460, the balance was $463,878. In 1976

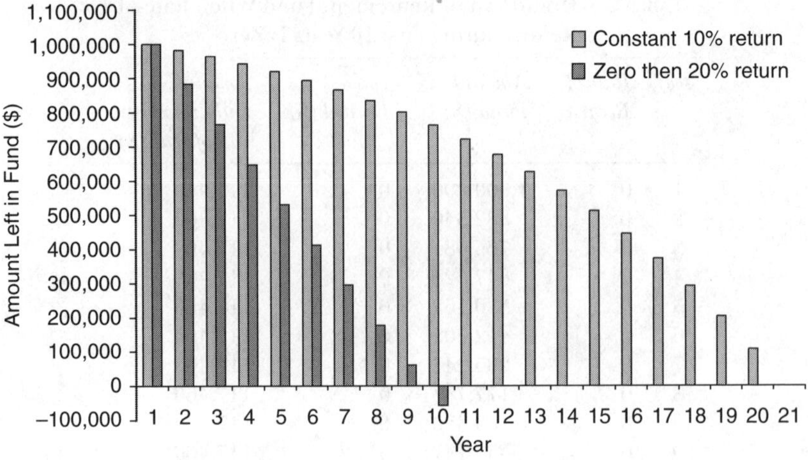

Figure 2-3. How long will $1 million last? (*Source*: Author's computations.)

TABLE 2-4 Actual Values for Retiree Starting in 1973

Year	*Rate of Return (%)*	*Amount in Fund ($)*	*Interest Earned ($)*	*Amount Before Withdrawal ($)*	*Amount Withdrawn ($)*
1973	−14.75	1,000,000	−147,500	852,500	117,460
1974	−26.40	735,040	−194,051	540,990	117,460
1975	37.26	423,530	157,807	581,337	117,460
1976	23.98	463,878	111,238	575,116	117,460
1977	−7.26	457,656	−33,226	424,430	117,460
1978	6.50	306,971	19,953	326,924	117,460
1979	18.77	209,464	39,316	248,780	117,460
1980	32.48	131,321	42,653	173,974	117,460
1981	−4.98	56,514	−2,814	53,700	117,460
1982	22.09	−63,760	−14,085	−77,844	117,460

Source: Author's computations.

the market climbed 23.8 percent, raising the balance to $575,116, from which he again took $117,460, leaving a balance of $457,656. The next year, 1977, was a bad year with a market return of −7.2 percent. The account balance declined to $424,430, from which he withdrew $117,460, and so on. By the time he reached 1981, he had only $56,514 left in the fund. That year his return was −4.98 percent and he could no longer take out $117,460 to live on. Thus we see that even though *on average* from 1973 through 1992

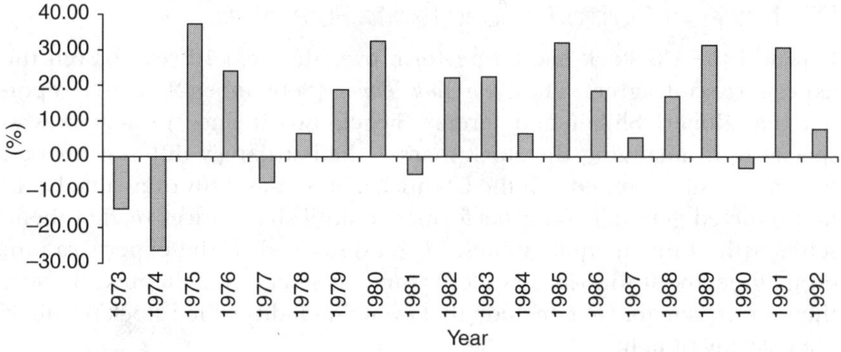

Figure 2-4. Rate of return on New York Stock Exchange. (*Source*: Wharton research data services <http://wrds.wharton.upenn.edu>.)

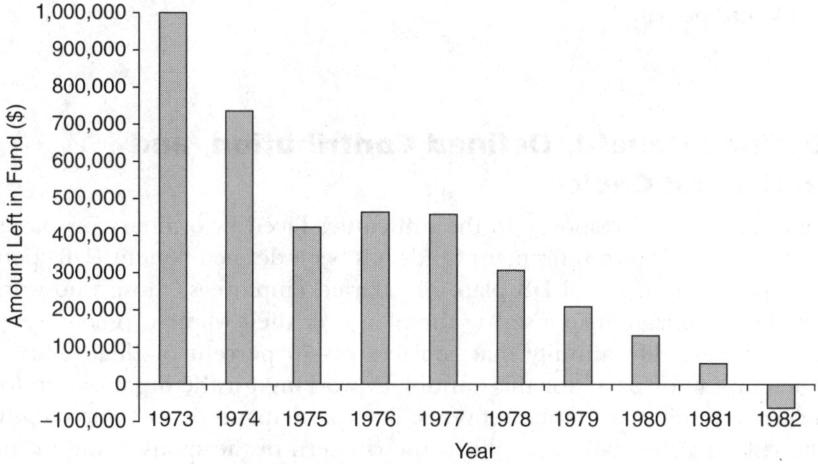

Figure 2-5. Funds remaining for retiree who started withdrawing in 1973. (*Source*: Author's computations.)

the market returned a rate of return of 11.3 percent per year, and he had been counting on only 10 percent per year, he ran out of money before the 10th year.

Matters would have been even worse for a retiree in Japan. The Japanese market reached its peak in 1989, just over 40,000 on the Nikkei 225, its major stock index. It then plunged to about 12,000, and despite temporary recoveries, it has remained depressed ever since.

Differences of Opinion among Expert Forecasters

How will the US stock market perform over the next 10 years? Even the experts cannot agree. The *New York Times* (September 2, 2001) reported that Robert Shiller and Jeremy Siegel, two finance professors who specialize in analyzing the stock market, had strikingly different market forecasts. Shiller argued that the US stock market was vastly overvalued, and he predicted generally poor performance until share prices realign themselves with "fundamental" values. Siegel disagreed. If the experts cannot even agree about the *mean* rate of return on stocks over the next decade, then it is reasonable to conclude that even a well-diversified stock portfolio is a risky investment.

Another piece of conventional wisdom holds that one should invest in stocks because they are a good hedge against inflation. In fact, the evidence is that stocks are not a good hedge against inflation. The decade of the 1970s was the only prolonged period in the past century when the United States experienced significant inflation, and that is precisely the period when stocks did poorly.[14]

Defined Benefit, Defined Contribution, and Individual Choice

One institutional response to the difficulties faced by ordinary people in managing their own retirement funds has been defined benefit (DB) pension plans. In a typical DB plan for salaried employees, those who work for the organization sponsoring the plan over their whole careers receive a guaranteed life annuity that replaces 60–70 percent of final salary.[15] The employee "pays" for this annuity by working for the organization for a certain minimum number of years. Plan participants do not worry about the risk of a shortfall, since this is the concern of the sponsor and in the United States, the Pension Benefit Guaranty Corporation (PBGC).[16]

But traditional DB pension plans have been on the decline in the United States, eclipsed by cash-balance plans and defined contribution (DC) plans, which transfers the risk to those who may be least qualified to manage it.[17] For the average participant in an employer-sponsored plan, the switch to self-directed pension plans might therefore cause a decline in welfare, even when offset by other benefits of greater monetary value.

The tendency in the last several years has been to offer participants in self-directed retirement plans more and more investment options. Economists generally believe that people are made better off when offered more choices, as long as they can always choose what they had before.[18] But if people do not have the knowledge to make choices that are in their own best interests, increasing the number of choices may not necessarily make them better off.

In fact, it could make them more vulnerable to exploitation by opportunistic salespeople or by well-intentioned, but unqualified, professionals.

An analogy with medical care may clarify this point. Most of us look to physicians and other medical professionals to guide our choices about health maintenance practices and treatments for illnesses. We would probably not be better off if the number of alternatives increased without our understanding enough about them to make rational choices. Like surgery, asset allocation is a complex procedure, requiring much knowledge and years of training. No one would imagine that patients could perform surgery to remove their own appendices after reading an explanation in a brochure published by a surgical equipment company. Yet prevailing practice seems to expect employees to choose an appropriate mix of stocks, bonds, and cash after reading a brochure published by an investment company. Some of them are likely to make serious mistakes, and the educational materials distributed to retirement plan participants by financial service firms confirm these fears. Participants are led to believe that stocks are not risky in the long run. Online asset allocation tools are heavily biased toward equity investment. Rarely is mention made of truly safe long-term investments, such as government inflation-protected bonds and real annuities.

Protection Against a Market Decline

Starting with the emergence of exchange-traded options and the discovery of the option pricing model in 1973, a variety of financial service firms have been selling investment products that offer protection against a stock market decline.[19] In Germany it seems likely that insured equity-linked retirement saving products will become the norm, as a result of the pension reform legislation passed in 2001. A key feature of Germany's pension reform is that to qualify for state subsidies, all savings vehicles must carry a guarantee of principal.[20]

Escalating Life Annuities

The modern theory of contingent claims analysis provides the framework for the production and pricing of new and improved retirement income products with protection against both market declines and the risk of outliving one's resources.[21] Let me illustrate using the example of a class of contracts that I call "escalating annuities."[22]

Traditional annuities in the United States, including those provided by DB plans have a glaring defect: they are not protected against inflation. Today it is possible for financial intermediaries to efficiently produce annuities that are protected fully or partially against inflation by hedging the liability with inflation-protected government bonds.[23] Moreover, they can also be combined with upside participation in the performance of various stock market indexes. As an example, consider an escalating life annuity with a minimum benefit linked to the cost of living. Payments increase with inflation and with the performance of a market index, and increases are locked in for life.

Escalating annuities are designed to provide a guaranteed minimum standard of living defined in terms of a flow of lifetime consumption (rather than a stock of wealth). They allow retirees to gradually increase their consumption if the stock market performs well without jeopardizing the standard of living to which they have become accustomed. Note that this is very different from a variable annuity benefit, which can either go up or down over time depending on market performance.

To make the example more concrete, let us assume that a typical customer reaches age 65 with $1 million in his self-directed retirement account. He seeks to retire and live off his income from Social Security (say $15,000 per year) and the income generated by his $1 million retirement account. How would a hypothetical escalating life annuity work? One simple design would be to allow the annuitant to choose the fraction of his $1 million that would go into the guaranteed real annuity. Assume he chooses 90 percent, and that this establishes a guaranteed real floor of $55,000 per year.[24] Together with his Social Security income, this gives him a real income floor of $70,000 per year. The other $100,000 in his retirement account would be invested in equities or equity derivatives to produce growth in real income. Each year part of this risky fund would be used to purchase additional guaranteed real annuity income.[25]

The upside leverage of the escalating annuity could be increased by investing the $100,000 at risk in a series of equity call options maturing in each of the next 10 years. If on the annual expiration date, the call is in the money, then the proceeds are used to increase the guaranteed income floor. If it is out of the money, the floor remains unchanged for another year.

Currently, exchange-traded options have maturities as long as 3 years. Firms that sell structured equity participation securities have issued notes with maturities of 10 years. It is not hard to imagine that innovative firms might issue even longer-dated index call options over the counter.

Conclusions

Increasingly, the complex problem of investing so as to provide a secure retirement income is being transferred from governmental institutions and private sector employers to people who lack the knowledge and the training to handle the risk. As we have seen, the educational materials and investment advice provided to those people by financial service firms is often dangerously misleading. One practical solution to the dangers posed for individuals and for society at large is to design and produce a new generation of investment products that insure people against severe market declines. Advances in the science of finance and market innovations over the past several decades have made this a feasible task.

Notes

1 A major distinction is between websites that give advice in terms of from three to five generic asset categories and those that give more specific recommendations based upon the user's actual holdings. Some use a Markowitz efficient portfolio frontier analysis. The more sophisticated websites, such as *Financial Engines* or *mPower*, simulate probability distributions of retirement wealth or retirement income.

2 See Bodie and Crane (1997) for a more complete statement of generally accepted investment principles. Ameriks and Zeldes (2001) report a similar finding.

3 My survey was done during the month of December 2001.

4 *Financial Engines* was the only exception.

5 See <http://university.smartmoney.com/Departments/Investing101/RiskvsReward/index.cfm?story=timevsrisk>.

6 Taken from TIAA-CREF "Principles of Sound Investing."

7 The variance of the annualized rate of return declines with the length of the holding period as long as there is no perfect positive serial correlation in stock returns. Empirically stock returns exhibit either no serial correlation or negative serial correlation. See in Bodie, Kane, and Marcus (2002), pp. 254–256.

8 See Merton (1992) for a demonstration that characterizing rates of return solely in terms of mean and variance is valid only when the time interval is extremely short and there are no big "jumps."

9 See Bodie (1995).

10 The term *severity* as used here is meant to capture not just the *magnitude* of a shortfall but also its *weight* in terms of its Arrow-Debreu state-claim price. For a detailed discussion of this point see Bodie (2002).

11 Bodie (1995).

12 See Bodie, Merton, and Samuelson (1992).

13 This example is taken from Bodie and Clowes (2003).

14 See Bodie (1976).

15 The employer-provided benefit is typically integrated with Social Security benefits, and the combination of the two replaces roughly 70 percent of earnings only for those at the bottom of the income scale.

16 This guarantee is capped by the PBGC. Above the cap, the employee is at risk of default by the plan sponsor. For plans terminated in 2001, the cap was $40,704.60 per year. It is adjusted annually.

17 The AFL-CIO writes: "Defined benefit plans remain the best and soundest vehicles for building and safeguarding retirement income and security." <www.aflcio.org/publ/estatements/feb2002/governance.htm>.

18 But even economists acknowledge that there are exceptions, for example, when people have problems with self-control. Offering a shot of whiskey to a recovering alcoholic does not increase his welfare.

[19] For a discussion of such products, see Bodie and Crane (1999) and Maurer and Schlag (Chapter 9 this volume).

[20] Deutsche Bank has already structured principal-guaranteed transactions of funds and mixed equity, and fixed-income portfolios. <www.risk.net/investor/archive/oct01/pension.htm>.

[21] For a discussion of the many other risks of old age that can be addressed with innovative financial products, see Bodie, Hammond, and Mitchell (2001).

[22] Dybvig (1995) uses the term "ratcheting" to describe this time-pattern of consumption.

[23] See Bodie (1990, 1997).

[24] This is an approximation based on quoted rates on Lincoln National Life's Inflation-Proofer annuity.

[25] I am assuming that the worker has no bequest motive.

References

Ameriks, John and Stephen Zeldes. 2001. "How Do Household Portfolio Shares Vary With Age?" TIAA-CREF Institute Working Paper. <www.tiaa-crefinstitute.org>.

Bodie, Zvi. 1976. "Common Stocks as a Hedge against Inflation." *Journal of Finance* May: 459–470.

— 1990. "Inflation Insurance." *The Journal of Risk and Insurance* 57(4) 634–645.

— 1995. "On the Risk of Stocks in the Long Run." *Financial Analysts Journal* May–June: 18–22.

— 1997. "Inflation-Protected Retirement Plans." In *Managing Public Debt: Index-Linked Bonds in Theory and Practice*, eds. Marcello De Cecco, Gustavo Piga, and Lorenzo Pecchi. Cheltenham, UK: Edward Elgar Publisher, pp. 33–49.

— 2002. "Life-Cycle Finance in Theory and in Practice." Boston University School of Management Working Paper.

— and Michael Clowes. 2003. *Worry-Free Investing: A No-Risk Approach to Achieving Your Lifetime Financial Goals*. New York, NY: Financial Times/Prentice Hall.

— and Dwight B. Crane. 1997. "Personal Investing: Advice, Theory, and Evidence." *Financial Analysts Journal* 53 (November–December): 13–23.

—— 1999. "The Design and Production of New Retirement Savings Products." *Journal of Portfolio Management* 25(January–February): 77–82.

—, P. Brett Hammond, and Olivia S. Mitchell. 2001. "New Approaches to Analyzing and Managing Retirement Risks." *Benefits Quarterly* 17(4): 72–83.

—, Alex Kane, and Alan Marcus. 2002. *Investments*, 5th edn. Boston: McGraw-Hill Irwin.

—, R. C. Merton, and W. Samuelson. 1992. "Labor Supply Flexibility and Portfolio Choice in a Life-Cycle Model." *Journal of Economic Dynamics and Control* 16: 427–449.

Dybvig, Philip H. 1995. "Dusenberry's Ratcheting of Consumption and Investment Given Intolerance for any Decline in Standard of Living." *Review of Economic Studies* 62: 287–313.

Merton, Robert C. 1969. "Lifetime Portfolio Selection Under Uncertainty: The Continuous-Time Case." *Review of Economics and Statistics* 51(August): 247–257.

— 1992. *Continuous-Time Finance*, revised edn. Oxford: Basil Blackwell.

Samuelson, Paul A. 1969. "Lifetime Portfolio Selection by Dynamic Stochastic Programming." *Review of Economics and Statistics* 51(August): 239–246.

Chapter 3

The Role of Company Stock in Defined Contribution Plans

Olivia S. Mitchell and Stephen P. Utkus

In the United States, defined contribution (DC) pensions have often relied on employer common stock as an essential component of their investment portfolios, particularly in the case of plans sponsored by large employers. Company stock in retirement plans has also been used to encourage stock ownership among rank-and-file employees, with the intent of enhancing employee productivity and boosting shareholder value. It is against this backdrop that existing stock market shocks have highlighted the dangers to DC plans of heavy reliance on a single company's stock. Prominent firms including Lucent, Enron, and Worldcom, have seen their stock prices drop precipitously or collapse entirely, prompting lawsuits from plan participants who lost billions of dollars of retirement saving. These and other company stock losses have kindled Congressional debate regarding the proper role of company stock in DC plans over the extent to which these plans should emphasize investment diversification in pursuit of retirement security, on the one hand, versus potential productivity gains that might be attributed to employee stock ownership, on the other.

This chapter explores several aspects of this debate. First, we offer essential background regarding the role of company stock in US pension plans. After surveying the legal and fiduciary status of company stock, we briefly review the role of Employee Stock Ownership Plans (ESOPs) and combined 401(k)/ESOP (or KSOP) plans. Second, we analyze holding patterns of company stock in DC retirement plans. Next, we evaluate explanations offered for why employers and employees tolerate (or even prefer) high levels of company stock holdings, and then we provide an assessment of the impact of concentrated holdings of company stock on retirement incomes. A final section sketches policy alternatives and concludes.

Company Stock in US Defined Contribution Pensions

Employers in the United States may elect to offer retirement programs in addition to paying into the national mandatory Social Security system, and they are encouraged to do so by a variety of federal income tax incentives. About half the civilian private-sector labor force is covered by a company-sponsored retirement plan. Many plan types and plan designs are permissible under current law: some employees receive a promise of future retirement benefits in defined benefit (DB) plans, while others receive a promise of a fully funded current contributions to DC plans. Total private pension assets stand at about $4 trillion, roughly divided between DB and DC plans.

Two decades of growth have firmly established the central importance of DC plans in the US retirement marketplace. There are now over 700,000 corporate DC pension plans covering nearly 56 million workers and managing over $2 trillion in assets; all evidence points to increasing growth in this sector for the foreseeable future.[1] By comparison, there are only 56,000 DB retirement plans covering about 23 million active participants (see Table 3-1), and DB plans continue to decline over time in terms of number and coverage.

TABLE 3-1 Aspects of US Private Sector Pension Plans: 1985–2001

Year	*Total*	*DB Plans*	*DC Plans*	*401(k) Only*
A. Number of Pension Plans				
1985	632,135	170,172	461,963	29,869
1990	712,308	113,062	599,245	97,614
1995	693,404	69,492	623,912	200,813
1998	730,031	56,405	673,626	300,593
2001[a]	758,000	51,000	707,000	361,000
B. Number of Active Pension Plan Participants (000)				
1985	62,268	29,024	33,244	10,339
1990	61,831	26,344	35,488	19,548
1995	66,193	23,531	42,662	28,061
1998	73,328	22,994	50,335	37,114
2001[a]	78,000	22,500	55,500	43,800*
C. Pension Plan Assets ($ millions)				
1985	1,252,739	826,117	426,622	143,939
1990	1,674,139	961,904	712,236	384,854
1995	2,723,735	1,402,079	1,321,657	863,918
1998	4,021,849	1,936,600	2,085,250	1,540,975
2001[a]	4,000,000	1,900,000	2,100,000	1,700,000

Source: Data from 1985 to 1998: Form 5500 Reports provided by PWBA-USDOL: Tables E1, E23, E8, E11.

[a] Authors' estimates based on US DOL and Federal Reserve Board data.

Note: A portion of participants may be covered by one or more DB or DC plans. *43.8 million estimate for 401(k) plans in 2001 is for active participants. Eligible 401(k) participants are estimated at 58.4 million based on 75% participation rate.

The Pension Legal and Fiduciary Framework

The key legislation governing US private sector retirement plans is the Employee Retirement Income Security Act of 1974 (ERISA). This law requires plan fiduciaries, who usually include the plan sponsor as well as plan administrators and advisers, to manage a retirement plan in the participants' best interest. ERISA further requires that fiduciaries must comply with an "*exclusive purpose*" rule, indicating that the fiduciary must be exclusively loyal to participants and beneficiaries; a "*prudent man*" rule, specifying that the plan fiduciary must act with the "care, skill, prudence, and diligence" that a prudent person acting in a similar capacity would use; and a "*diversification rule,*" requiring that the fiduciary diversify the plan's investments with regard to type of investment, geographic area, dates of maturity, and industrial sector to reduce the chances of large losses (GAO, 1997; Joint Committee, 2002).

At the time of ERISA's adoption, the dominant US retirement plan was the DB plan, and one of the principal goals of the new law was to ensure adequate private funding of private sector DB benefits. Motivated by the failure of several high-profile companies and their pensions, including Studebaker Corporation in 1963, ERISA mandated investment diversification requirements for private DB plans. Moreover, it established the Pension Benefit Guaranty Corporation, a federal agency that guarantees a portion of private defined benefit pensions in the event of corporate bankruptcy. In order to mitigate the moral hazard problem of sponsors investing their pension assets heavily in their own company stock, and leaving the liabilities to the Pension Benefit Guaranty Corporation (PBGC) in the event of bankruptcy, Congress instituted a 10 percent limit on DB plan holdings of employer stock.

It is an interesting historical footnote that at the time of ERISA's passage, Congress chose not to extend that same percent limit to DC retirement plans.[2] This was mainly because, at that time, DC plans consisted mainly of profit-sharing plans to which employers made variable plan contributions based on company earnings, and ESOPs, which by design encouraged employers to make employer stock contributions in an effort to foster employee ownership. DC plans were thus not widely used as a retirement income vehicle and at many large firms, they were supplemental to DB programs. Many prominent employers viewed DC plans as vehicles for promoting employee stock ownership and so they objected to limitations on company stock holdings.[3]

Some also argue that Congress exempted DC plans from the diversification standard and cap so as not to constrain ESOPs, which were explicitly intended to encourage employee investment in employer stock (Hunter, 1994). Consequently DC plans had to comply with the exclusive purpose and prudence standards of ERISA, but not the diversification fiduciary standard nor the explicit 10 percent limit on company stock holdings.[4,5]

Five years after ERISA passed, Congress authorized the creation of 401(k) plans. Previously, the Internal Revenue Service as tax authority had crafted regulations allowing employees to make tax-deferred contributions into profit-sharing plans. The Revenue Act of 1978 codified these rules into section 401(k) of the Internal Revenue Code, which in effect permitted a type of DC profit-sharing financed by pre-tax employee contributions. As such, 401(k) plans were also exempted from the 10 percent cap on company stock holdings. The subsequent explosive growth of 401(k) plans produced an environment in which this plan type is now the dominant form of private sector retirement plan, accounting for over 80 percent of all DC assets and 40 percent of all private sector retirement assets (authors' estimate, year-end 2001). In tandem, the use of company stock has now become widespread among many private sector retirement arrangements, even though Congress originally authorized it for ancillary retirement plans like profit-sharing plans and ESOPs.

Even before the equity bear market, there were inklings of the exposure arising from concentrated DC stock holdings. In 1997 the retail chain Color Tile filed for bankruptcy, at which point 80 percent of its retirement plan proved to be invested in company assets, and the firm's failure produced substantial losses for plan participants.[6] Concern over the Color Tile case prompted Congress to reconsider imposing a mandatory 10 percent cap on DC company stock holdings, but many large employers opposed a cap. Congress consequently adopted a narrower restriction, prohibiting employers from compelling workers from investing 10 percent more of *their own 401(k) contributions* in company stock unless employees could reallocate those investments at will. This new rule did not prohibit employees from voluntarily holding company stock over the 10-percent cap nor did it apply to ESOPs or profit-sharing plans (England, 1997).

The equity bear market of 2001–2002 once again made participants and policymakers aware of the risks associated with undiversified DC plan investments. Several prominent firms with company stock in their 401(k) plans experienced severe drops in stock prices (see Table 3-2),[7] leading to related litigation directed at plan sponsors and providers.[8] Since company stock is statutorily exempt from ERISA's diversification requirement in DC plans, this litigation mainly focused on plan sponsors' alleged failure to comply with ERISA's prudence standard.

Worries over exposure to company stock in DC plans have spurred several employers to change the structure of their DC plans. Federal Mogul, a manufacturer reeling from asbestos litigation, saw its share price collapse from \$70 to \$1 per share, at which point the company ended employer-matches of stock contributions to its retirement plan and eliminated company stock as an investment option altogether (Jacobius, 2001*a*,*b*). Polaroid Corporation and US Airways, two firms that became bankrupt, appointed independent trustees to oversee company stock holdings in retirement plans. Other

TABLE 3-2 Recent Performance of Company Stock in Corporate 401(k) Pension Plans

Company	*% of DC plan in Company Stock*	*% Stock Price Change 3/00-12/01*
Polaroid	19	−99.6
Enron	41	−99.6
Global Crossing	16	−97.5
Weirton	16	−96.4
Crown Cork & Seal	11	−92.5
Providian Financial	19	−91.8
KS City Southern	80	−91.8
Lucent Technologies	16	−89.2
Owens Corning	25	−88.5
Montana Power	25	−88.0
Northern Telcom	30	−86.6
Corning	32	−86.0
W.R. Grace	11	−84.3
Chiquita Brands	11	−82.8
ADC Telcom	46	−80.4

Source: Authors' derivations from Farrell (2002).

sponsors have begun to liberalize restrictions imposed on diversification of company stock holdings (Chen, 2002*a*,*b*). These and other losses due to company stock in DC plans have also fed into the broader national debate about corporate governance, the role of the accounting profession, and the ways in which stock and stock options are used in executive compensation packages.[9]

Employee Ownership and Employee Stock

Controversy over company stock has focused mainly on the role of 401(k) plans, though it must be acknowledged that the issue is far more complex since employers are permitted flexibility in retirement plan design under US pension law. In particular, many of the largest so-called 401(k) plans that hold high levels of company stock are actually not garden-variety 401(k) plans. Instead, they are what is known as "combination" plans, mixing 401(k) features with a profit-sharing plan, or 401(k) features with an ESOP in a design known as a KSOP. Hence understanding the role of company stock in DC plans also requires a perspective on ESOPs and KSOPs in the US retirement market.

An ESOP is a defined contribution retirement plan in which the employer makes discretionary contributions of company stock to workers' accounts.[10] Philosophical support for ESOPs derives from an era when policy interest in workers' ownership of their firm's stock trumped the need to diversify portfolio investments. Louis Kelso, a California businessman, promoted the virtues of employee stock ownership during the 1950s; later, Peter Drucker espoused them as a vehicle for "worker capitalism" (Drucker, 1979). The exact number of ESOPs today is in some dispute: the National Center for Employee Ownership (NCEO) reports that there are 11,500 ESOPS covering almost 9 million employees and holding about $500 billion in assets (NCEO, 2002), while Perun (2000) finds fewer ESOPS, in the order of 8,100 such plans, or just over 1 percent of all retirement plans.

Tax law specifically authorizes such plans to invest principally, if not exclusively, in the stock of the employer.[11] ESOPs are thus intended to encourage employee ownership of a firm's stock, and they are also used to accumulate wealth for retirement. As per the structure that exists, most ESOPs typically restrict participants from diversifying company stock though sponsors may adopt more liberal rules. The existing law stipulates that ESOPs may require participants to hold company stock until (the later of) age 55 or 10 years of service; apart from that point, participants may *begin* diversifying gradually but need not fully diversify until the participant attains at least age 60. Since the US median retirement age is now 62, ESOPs give workers approaching retirement little chance to recover financially in the event of a collapse in their employer's stock price.

Unlike other DC plans, ESOPs offer a unique privilege making them a tax-preferred vehicle to the plan sponsor, via the ability to *leverage* plan assets.[12] In an employee-owned firm, this feature allows an owner to use an ESOP to acquire bank financing for capital investment, and then company earnings are used to pay off the debt over time. In publicly held firms, leveraged ESOPs are used by managers to undertake leveraged buyouts or to stave off hostile takeovers.[13] An important rationale is that employees' voting control may be exercised over the entire block of leveraged shares held by the plan.[14] Thus employees sympathetic to management can, through a leveraged ESOP, exert voting authority over a block of shares larger than that which they own directly. Leveraged ESOPs also bring other benefits.[15] While interest payments on an ESOP loan are deductible to the company, like other corporate interest payments, employers may also use dividends paid on the unallocated ESOP shares to defray those interest payments. This in essence allows dividend income to be transferred to participant-shareholders free of corporate income tax.[16,17]

Media reports about the concentration of company stock in retirement programs have sometimes confused the difference between ESOPs and 401(k) plans. For instance, some 401(k) plans named as having high concentrations of employer stock are actually ESOP-centered programs.

The confusion is understandable: although the purpose of an ESOP is to provide for *employee ownership* of the company's shares, ESOPs sometimes appear to be *retirement* plans, especially when they are combined with other types of DC retirement plan features. As one example, the Procter and Gamble (P&G) retirement program has some 95 percent of its assets invested in company stock. It is not a garden-variety 401(k) plan; rather, it is an ESOP, a profit-sharing, and a 401(k) plan, wrapped into one. Within the P&G plan, both ESOP and profit-sharing components are invested in P&G stock. The company does not offer a DB plan; instead, it views the stock-oriented profit-sharing component as a substitute for a DB plan. A 401(k) feature of the plan allows participants to invest their own monies in a range of diversified investment choices for retirement or in P&G stock (Jacobius, 2001*a*; Peale, 2002). With ESOP and profit-sharing components invested heavily in stock, and with employees making voluntary 401(k) contributions to P&G stock, the plan is, not surprisingly, highly concentrated.

A partial list of well-known US companies holding high levels of company stock in their corporate plans includes P&G, Abbott Laboratories, Anheuser-Busch, Ford Motor Company and Pfizer (see Table 3-3). Each of these firms uses a combination of a 401(k) plan and ESOP feature, known as a KSOP.[18] Some also use leverage to gain the tax and ownership benefits noted above. Employers' decisions to create hybrid ownership/retirement programs have blurred the distinction between plans designed to enhance employee ownership and plans designed to maximize retirement security.[19] Recent legislation further confounds the distinction between traditional retirement plans and stock ownership plans, as in the 2001 Economic

TABLE 3-3 Company Stock and Tax Savings From Large Hybrid 401(k) and ESOP Plans (KSOPs)

Company	*% of DC plan in Company Stock*	*Estimated ESOP Deduction from EGTRRA ($ millions)*
Abbott Laboratories	82	28
Anheuser-Busch	83	15
Bank of America	43	8
Ford Motor	50	90
Marsh & McLennan	61	10
McDonalds	74	4
Pfizer	82	23
Procter & Gamble	92	127
SBC	38	56
Verizon	51	31

Source: Authors' derivations from Schultz and Francis (2002*b*).

Growth and Taxpayer Relief Reconciliation Act (EGTRRA) that embodied an attractive new tax incentive for plan sponsors to create ESOPs by making stock dividends reinvested in the ESOP tax-deductible.[20] Though Congress thought this to be a narrowly written tax benefit for ESOPs, it has proved to be advantageous to many sponsors of traditional 401(k) plans since with a simple plan amendment, the traditional 401(k) plans can be converted to a KSOP, often with a substantial corporate tax deduction (Anand, 2001; Schulz and Francis, 2002*a*,*b*). Estimated tax deductions for certain large employers converting to the KSOP structure are reported in Table 3-3.

In all, it is clear that ESOPs and KSOPS are playing a dual role in the company stock debate. For large, publicly traded firms, leveraged ESOPs may be used for tax and financial reporting benefits, and to enhance employee voting control in corporate control and takeover transactions. In smaller firms, leveraged ESOPs have played an important role in financing employee–owner acquisitions. And for privately held firms, succession and other tax benefits flow to the company's original stockholders, as a result of ESOPs.

Patterns of Concentrated Company Stock Holdings

Next we describe how and where concentrated stock positions arise in DC retirement plans.[21] There is no central source of data on company stock exposure, so we review both government statistics and firm surveys to gauge patterns of exposure. Data from the US Department of Labor (USDOL; data provided to authors on special request) suggests that about 16 percent of DC assets were invested in employer stock in 1998 (see in Table 3-4).[22] Rolling the estimates forward, we estimate that DC assets stood at $2.1 trillion in 2001, so company stock holding amounted to $340 billion at year-end.[23] The fraction of plan assets in employer stock also varies across plan type, with stock bonus plans/ESOPs being the most concentrated, and profit-sharing/thrift saving plans (which include 401(k) plans) somewhat less so. By the end of the 1990s, each plan type appeared less concentrated than in 1993; this trend likely resulted from the growth of small 401(k) plans, which are less likely to offer company stock.

The conclusion that only 16 percent of DC assets overall are concentrated in company stock gives a misleading view since it represents an average over all DC plans in the United States, and it includes plans that do not offer company stock as an investment option. To measure exposure to company stock *among plans offering company stock*, we rely on data from the Participant-Directed Retirement Plan Data Collection Project sponsored by the Employee Benefits Research Institute (EBRI) and Investment Company Institute (ICI).[24] According to this survey, company stock represented 19 percent of 401(k) assets, a figure comparable to the USDOL's 16 percent

TABLE 3-4 Company Stock Holdings within DC Plans Over Time

	Employer Securities as % of Plan Assets		
	1993	*1996*	*1998*
Total DC plans	17.4	15.5	16.2
Profit-sharing and thrift saving	17.6	12.8	14.4
Stock bonus/ESOP	51.3	48.9	41.6
Target benefit	0.5	0.4	0.4
Money purchase	1.2	1.7	2.4

Source: Authors' derivations from published and unpublished data from USDOL Form 5500 Series for various plan years.

TABLE 3-5 Prevalence of Company Stock in 401(k) Plans

	Plans Offering Company Stock (%)	*Plans not Offering Company Stock (%)*
Plans	3	97
Participants	42	58
Assets	59	41

Source: Authors' estimates based on VanDerhei (2002).

estimate for all DC plans.[25] Nevertheless, exposure levels in 2001 are far higher among the plans offering company stock: here, company stock accounted for 29 percent of plan assets.

Another key fact is that company stock is available in only a small fraction of all DC plans: only 3 percent of 401(k) plans actually offer company stock as an investment option (see Table 3-5). Yet because these plans are mainly sponsored by large firms, they account for a substantial subset of the DC plan participant and asset universe. Consequently, those firms offering company stock include 42 percent of all DC plan participants and 59 percent of all DC plan assets.[26] To put it differently, only 3 percent of 401(k) plans offer company stock, but some 23 million DC plan participants have access to company stock within their employer plans, and those DC plans command assets of $1.2 trillion, in total.

Other surveys confirm the conclusion that company stock held in DC plans is a large-firm phenomenon: the Profit-Sharing/401(k) Council of

TABLE 3-6 Participants With Concentrated Holdings in Company Stock

Asset Allocation to Company Stock (%)	*Millions of Participants*
0	8.0
1–20	4.4
21–40	3.0
41–60	2.3
61–80	1.4
Over 80	3.9
Total	23.0

Source: Authors' estimates based on Holden and VanDerhei (2001*b*) and VanDerhei (2002).

Notes: Total over 20%: 10.6 million participants; Total over 60%: 5.3 million participants.

America reports that 72 percent of plans with 5,000+ participants offer company stock as an investment option, while only 6 percent of firms with fewer than 100 employees do (PSCA, 2001). A different survey by Fidelity Investments (2001) shows that 62 percent of plans with 2,500+ participants offer company stock, while only 2 percent of firms with less than 500 employees do. Asset allocation levels to company stock are also a function of plan size. Company stock represents 43 percent of average assets among plans with 5,000+ employees, but less than 10 percent of assets in small plans (PSCA, 2001).

Because company stock is more common among plans sponsored by large firms, concentrated positions in company stock also affect a substantial number of plan participants. We estimate the number of DC participants with concentrated positions in company stock within plans offering company stock in Table 3-6, drawing on EBRI/ICI concentration data for 401(k) plans. Out of approximately 23 million DC participants offered company stock, it appears that just over 12 million participants are less concentrated, holding 20 percent or less of their DC plan balance in company stock. Meanwhile, we estimate that nearly 11 million plan participants have a concentrated stock position exceeding 20 percent. Of these, some 3 million participants hold company stock worth 21–40 percent of their account balances; 2.3 million participants hold 41–60 percent; and 5.3 million participants exceed 60 percent of account balances in company stock.

TABLE 3-7 401(k) Plan Asset Allocation Patterns by Degree of Direction (%)

Type (% of total plans)	*Equity Funds*	*Company Stock*	*Balanced Funds*	*Bond Funds*	*Money mkt/GIC Funds*	*Other*
All 401(k) plans	51	19	8	5	14	3
All plans w/company stock (%)	44	29	6	4	15	2
All plans w/company stock and full participant direction (%)	46	22	10	3	17	2
All plans w/company stock where employer directs match (%)	26	53*	5	1	13	2

Source: Holden and VanDerhei (2001*b*) and VanDerhei (2002).

Note: *Includes 33% of employee monies and 20% of employer monies.

Two elements of employer plan design seem to be closely associated with high levels of company stock holdings. One is some employers' requirement to direct employer's own contributions into company stock. Industry surveys show that the requirement to direct employer contributions into company stock is common though not necessarily dominant for plans offering company stock. The Vanguard Group found that 45 percent of plans direct employer contributions to stock, while 55 percent did not.[27] Moreover, the decision to direct contributions to stock appears to be a function of firm size, with large firms more likely to direct contributions in company stock than small firms. Mercer (2001) finds that 19 percent of all plans surveyed, forced a contribution into stock, while 39 percent of larger plans did. When employers direct contributions on a plan's holdings of company stock, the impact appears to be profound (see Table 3-7). In the EBRI/ICI subsample of 401(k) plans where participants could freely chose to invest employer contributions, 22 percent of total assets were held in company stock; by contrast when the employer directed his own contributions into company stock, the average stock exposure was exceptionally high, at 53 percent of average plan assets. Of this total, 20 percent was employer-matching contributions, and 33 percent represented employee voluntary contributions. Since larger firms tend to restrict contribution investment choice, the result is that company stock concentration levels are highest among large firms offering DC plans (Purcell, 2002).

Another plan design factor contributing to stock concentration is employer-imposed restrictions on participants' ability to diversify employer investments in company stock. To understand these restrictions we turn

TABLE 3-8 Survey Results on Qualified Plan Restrictions

A. Overall Stock Direction

Plans that direct contributions into stock:	45%
Plans that do not direct contributions	55%

B. Directed Plans: Restrictions Imposed by DC Plans with Contributions Directed to Company Stock

Restriction	*% of plans imposing*		
	Hewitt, 2001	*Mercer, 2001*	*Vanguard, 2001*
Age	34	40	37
Age/service, including ESOP	22	15	
Restricted until termination	19	12	21
Holding period	3	6	9
Vesting/Other	3	—	1
Subtotal	81	73	68
No restrictions	15	19	13
Caps/maximums	—	—	5
Other	4	8	14
Subtotal	19	27	32
Total	100	100	100

C. Discretionary Plans: Restrictions Imposed by DC Plans with Employer Contributions Not Made in Company Stock

Restriction	*% of plans imposing*
No restriction	48
Caps/maximums	20
Subtotal	68
Age/age service/ESOP	5
Restricted until termination	4
Holding period	2
Vesting/Other	21
Subtotal	32
Total	100

Source: Hewitt (2001); Mercer (2001); Vanguard (2001).

to surveys of qualified plan restrictions conducted by Hewitt Associates, William M. Mercer, and The Vanguard Group. In analyzing these survey results, we have classified plan restrictions into one of two categories: *directed plans*, where the company directs all or part of employer contributions to company stock, and *discretionary plans*, where all contributions are invested at the discretion of the employee. Table 3-8 reveals that employers who direct their plan contributions be invested in company stock are also those who restrict participant diversification; in effect, these employers mandate employee share ownership. By contrast, employers who leave all investment decisions to employees are also those who permit diversification, or even discourage concentrated company stock holdings through caps or other limits. In effect, this second group appears to take a more voluntary approach to employee share ownership.

It is not generally appreciated that restrictions vary widely across directed plans. In some cases, employers specify limits as a function of age, service, or vesting (including statutory ESOP limits); in others, workers must hold stock until termination; and a few set mandatory holding periods. But again reflecting employer heterogeneity, a few directed plans permit immediate diversification, and yet others cap employee stockholding to discourage concentrated positions.[28] Some plans impose trading limits, either to discourage short-term day trading or to restrict participants' ability to buy or sell during blackout periods. Among discretionary plans, the tendency is for employers to encourage flexibility and diversification: most allow full flexibility, or impose caps, and other limits to discourage concentrated holdings. Overall, concentration patterns in company stock have three key characteristics. First, a small fraction of DC plans actually offers company stock, though because these are the largest firms, they include an estimated 23 million of participants and nearly 60 percent of all DC plan assets. Second, just under half of plans offering company stock direct employer contributions into stock, again more common among larger firms. Third, restrictions on diversification go hand in hand with the decision to direct contributions into stock. Larger employers that direct contributions to stock also typically restrict participants' ability to diversify, in effect, taking a mandatory approach to employee stock ownership. Meanwhile, smaller employers tend to take a more employee-voluntary approach, leaving investment decisions to participants; they are less likely to impose restrictions, or if they do, they set caps on stock holding.

Rationales for Concentrated Stock Holdings

Concentration in a single company's stock, as described here, flies in the face of modern portfolio theory and its central tenet of diversification. As a rule, investors should not expect to be rewarded for assuming single-stock risk, since investing in a single stock must be a zero-sum game across investors, with participants in the aggregate earning the market return. Retirement plan participants would therefore, according to this view, hold in their portfolios no more than a market-weighted share of their firm's company stock. Further, workers would theoretically be expected to value company stock holdings according to their certainty-equivalent: namely, due to an individual stock's volatility, a 401(k) plan with a match in stock would be valued at less than a 401(k) plan with the same dollar match in cash. Deviations from the diversified "norm" would lead well-informed employers and workers to discount benefit packages that encouraged or mandated the holding of company shares. On the other hand, as the data indicate, it appears as though some employers and participants may either tolerate or actually prefer single-stock exposure. This section considers potential explanations for why employers and plan participants might depart from the theoretically implied norms.

Employer Motivations

Several explanations might be considered for why some firms encourage and/or mandate employee holdings of company stock, the most widespread of which is that doing so is believed to align stakeholder interests. Employee ownership of company shares, whether within a DC retirement plan or via other stock ownership programs, is argued to boost efficiency, worker productivity, employee morale, and, ultimately, the sponsoring firm's value. Employee–owners are thus thought to be more aligned with the business goals of the firm and as a result should be expected to perform at a higher level.

This motivational view is pervasive, is undoubtedly influential among executives who offer company stock within DC plans, and, as we have shown, given the opportunity, workers do buy employer stock. Yet the open question is whether employee stock holdings have a positive effect on important company outcomes. Evidence on this topic is inconclusive.[29] Firms that promote stock ownership tend to have employees with more positive attitudes about their firms, but the link to firm performance is not automatic. Companies with ESOPS report 6 percent higher productivity holding other factors constant (Blasi, Conte, and Kruse 1996). On the other hand, compulsory stock ownership in DC plans is also more characteristic of large firms, yet the evidence is weakest in favor of employee ownership among such firms.[30] Productivity gains are smaller in larger firms, perhaps as a result of the fact that workers are less likely to feel they can influence bottom-line results (the "free-rider" problem). In fact, large companies' restrictions on diversifying out of company stock may be an attempt by managers to overcome the inherent productivity problems of large-scale operations. It is also worth noting that studies on employee ownership are drawn from a period of exceptional equity market returns; whether more normal equity market results motivate workers is far from clear.

Another issue is whether employee–ownership incentives are influential for workers below the executive ranks. Traditionally stock compensation was restricted to managerial employees, but it has been extended through the rank and file. About half of all stock plans offered to US nonmanagerial workers as of 1998 had been either expanded or added after 1996, and there seems to be a trend toward increased stock coverage (Lebow et al., 1999). The growth of DC plans has also produced more concentration in stock among mid- and lower-level employee ranks. Having said that, stock option programs, a major source of equity compensation, are still skewed toward upper-income earners. The Bureau of Labor Statistics (BLS, 2000) reports that 13 percent of employees earning $75,000 or more had options grants, while only 1.5 percent of employees earning $35,000 to $49,999 had such grants.

A different reason that employers might foster employee purchase of company stock is that it could potentially place company stock into friendly hands to maximize managerial interests, say in a takeover defense or to effect leverage buyouts. For sixty-five of the largest corporate DC plans in the United States, we have calculated employee holdings as a percent of outstanding market capitalization. In that sample, DC plan participants controlled some 5.9 percent of the outstanding market capitalization of the average firm. These data represent only DC company stock holdings and exclude other types of stock ownership plans such as employee stock purchase plan and stock options; they also exclude unallocated shares in leveraged ESOPs that the employees may indirectly control. In a tight takeover battle, a 6-percent position held by employees might be very influential (presumably only if employees act in concert). Combined with other employee holdings and stock held by senior management, the total figure of employee-owned stock could be very significant. Nonetheless, overall, the data indicate that DC participants own a small minority holding in the largest firms.

A different, and prominent, argument for employee ownership is that workers may be more productive and amenable to management proposals if they are shareholders.[31] If true, equity-linked compensation would be expected to be widespread in DC plans, and more broadly as well. Nevertheless, equity-linked compensation is rare among rank-and-file employees, remaining limited to highly compensated managers.[32] One reason may be employee risk aversion: to the extent that workers feel that stock exposes them to greater uncertainty than cash compensation, they would demand a risk premium in compensation. Within a retirement plan, well-informed employees would demand more stock to offset the uncertainty and compensate for restrictions imposed on the stock sale. Low or moderate-income workers are also likely to be risk averse, since they have only undiversified human capital, and their largest financial asset is likely the company-sponsored retirement plan.[33]

Some who favor the use of company stock in DC plans argue that contributing stock to their retirement plans costs employers less than when they contribute in other forms, or that equity compensation in effect is "cheaper" than cash compensation (Ward, 2001; Hedges and Neikirk, 2002). By this argument, if employers were prohibited from making contributions in the form of employer stock, the effective cost of employer contributions to retirement plans would be higher. If required to find a substitute for stock, employers would replace existing stock contributions with less generous cash contributions. The simplest version of this argument is that stock contributions to a DC plan are cheaper when the employer issues new shares. By issuing new shares and contributing them directly to the plan, the firm avoids spending cash on a matching contribution. Issuing new shares preserves cash flow, so this approach might be expected to be popular among cash-strapped firms. The dilemma, of course, is that issuing new shares to the retirement plan dilutes existing shareholders' interest; economically, the firm's net present value has been reduced, whether the contribution is in cash or in stock. There is little evidence on the prevalence of issuing new shares for retirement plan contributions. Only half of all firms buy stock in the open market to finance their DC plan contributions, and half issue new stock (Benartzi, 2001); this finding, however, is based on a sample of firms that do or do not make 11K filings with the SEC (needed when new shares are issued), so it may simply reflect different interpretations of when an 11K filing is needed. Anecdotally, several plan sponsors have suggested to the authors that common practice at large employers is to always expense plan contributions, whether made in cash or stock.[34] Still others have indicated that the impression that "stock is cheap" may come from older leveraged ESOPs, where plan contributions are reported on financial statements at historic cost, not market value.

It is unclear how common the practice is of issuing new shares. To the extent that some make this argument, it is possible that they are engaged in a kind of "mental bracketing," a narrow framing of the cost issue, which overemphasizes the impact of a cash contribution on reported earnings, and downplays the economic cost of shareholder dilution. A cash contribution reduces reported earnings-per-share (EPS) immediately and is highly visible to shareholders. Diluting existing shareholders by issuing new shares has a much smaller, and less visible, effect; and any reduction in the firm's share price from the dilution is likely to be swamped by daily stock price volatility.[35]

A different cost argument relates to ESOPs. Here the benefits are more concrete, relating to the unique issuance, tax, and leverage features of ESOPs. Through KSOP programs, public firms may garner higher tax benefits for their 401(k) plans and enjoy other benefits if the ESOP component is leveraged. In terms of issuance, smaller privately held or family firms may find issuing shares to an ESOP a lower-cost and more flexible method for raising investment capital, without the need to resort to public capital markets. Tax benefits accrue when certain private firms are sold to employee-owned ESOPs, and when dividends are used for interest on a leveraged ESOP loan. In 2001, EGTRRA also boosted tax savings on reinvested ESOP dividends.

Finally, in assessing the cost argument, the issue of cost-effective stock contributions is sometimes confused with two other questions: the question of employer generosity with stock, and the certainty-equivalent value of stock contributions. Under the existing DC system, employers contributing stock seek two objectives: encouraging (or mandating) employee stock ownership, and providing a competitive retirement savings benefit. If policy were to restrict employers' ability to offer (or mandate) stock ownership, the argument is that companies might reduce retirement contributions and/or redirect them to other forms of stock ownership. This argument is not necessarily about the inherent cost advantages of company stock; rather, it reflects the employer's desire to encourage stock ownership.

A critical issue in assessing the value of employer stock contributions is how to account for the underlying volatility of the stock. The certainty-equivalent of company stock may be worth much less than the dollars contributed by the employer, depending on the participant's risk aversion and the fraction of other wealth in company stock (Lambert, Larcker, and Verrecchia, 1991). In other words, a smaller cash contribution with no volatility might be deemed as valuable to plan participants as a higher stock contribution with stock-specific volatility. As one example, Meulbroek (2002) estimates that $100,000 in company stock is only worth $42,000 to an employee with nondiversified holdings. In other words, if restrictions on company stock in employer plans are implemented, and employers decide to replace stock contributions with less generous cash contributions, the change may actually not be welfare-reducing for employees. Employees could be better or equally well off depending on the size of the reduction, the volatility of the stock, participants' risk aversion, and participants' total holdings in company stock.

Two other factors may help explain why employers use company stock in DC plans, particularly larger firms that mandate DC plan stockholding. One is the existence of some other retirement plan such as a defined benefit pension, and the other relates to the volatility of common stock. On the first point, the evidence indicates that large companies are more likely to offer *both* DB and DC plans; the former are usually traditional DB plans, though some firms have substituted cash balance plans instead. Rosen (2002) reports that three-quarters of all ESOP participants heavily concentrated in company stock also have some other form of retirement plan, although as we note above, many ESOPs are associated not with large firms offering company stock, but instead with small employee-owned firms. Out of the ninety-six largest corporate DC plans described in a trade publication survey, we find that all but one also offer a DB plan.[36] A Vanguard in-house survey of employers offering company stock in their DC plans showed that 77 percent of plans with 2,500+ active participants also had a DB plan. Having multiple plans may explain why some employers tolerate high concentrations of company stock: in the event of a stock value collapse, workers would still have a retirement benefit from another better-diversified plan. It may also explain why participants might allocate their own contributions to company stock within a DC plan: long-term employees with a guaranteed DB income stream (or with other diversified DC assets) might reasonably seek greater single-stock risk in the DC plan with company stock.

Though this argument makes sense, the data show that having a DB plan cannot explain the pattern of company stock in DC plans. One reason is that traditional DB plans tend to be back-loaded, and hence are not very valuable to workers in the event of layoff or company bankruptcy; rather, it is the long-tenured employees near retirement that may enjoy a significant DB pension. Large firms offering cash balance plans, by contrast, are in the opposite position since they provide a benefit that grows more evenly across the employee's work career. In terms of legal exposure of the employer, offering a DB or other DC plan may be perceived as a possible way of mitigating legal risks arising from lawsuits, though no court precedent exists on the issue.

A different factor that could explain company stock holdings is the risk and return characteristics of company stock itself. Many people would contend that "blue chip" stocks are less risky than stocks of smaller firms: as evidence, we note that the top twenty (and the top 100) stocks in the S&P 500 are between two and two-and-a-half times as volatile as a broad market index such as the S&P 500, while small stocks are four times as risky or more. It may be that managers of larger firms with "blue chip" stocks are more willing to assume the fiduciary risks of concentrated holdings, given the generally lower volatility of their shares as a group, whereas managers of smaller firms with riskier stocks are not.

Employee Motivations

Next we turn to the question of why employees might hold company stock in their retirement plans. One rationale relies on the fact that earning profiles for many young employees are relatively independent of stock market returns, so some equity investment may be recommended. Research analyses uses individual-level income information to explore how employee compensation covaries with aggregate equity returns, long-term bond returns, and returns on other assets (Davis and Willen, 2000; Baxter, 2001). The findings indicate that aggregate equity returns are uncorrelated with occupational income changes, implying that younger savers would do well to hold diversified equities in their portfolios. The research also indicates that in several occupations, income shocks are correlated with portfolios concentrated in large companies and specific industries. These patterns indicate that holding a diversified equity portfolio can make good financial sense, and that younger workers should diversify out of a large firm stock.

In practice, this theoretically appealing advice may be confounded with several factors. One is that workers might be persuaded by the appeal of employee ownership: that is, they might want to own part of their own firms. A second argument is that the tax code makes holding company stock through DC plans appealing, since the purchase of company stock is with pre-tax funds, and participants do not pay retail brokerage commissions. While these same tax and price incentives exist for all diversified investment options within the plan, the one exception is the special long-term capital gain treatment of company stock upon distribution.[37] A third rationale for participants' holdings is the information argument. Employees may feel they have a superior understanding of the firm and its business prospects. This "insider" perspective might induce participants to overweight company stock holdings in the hopes of realizing excess returns on the stock when the firm's results are reported to public shareholders. If this hope is realized, this informational advantage could lead to a conflict of interest between employee and public shareholders; also, as noted below, few informational advantages might actually exist.

As employees near retirement, many should perceive that company stock investment is unduly risky, since it substantially boosts the variance of eventual retirement incomes. This would apply even for employees of larger companies whose stock price volatility can be at least twice that of a market portfolio. Older workers near retirement may also focus less on future price appreciation and more on downside risk (i.e. the chance of losing money). Offsetting this expectation is the role of other income and wealth holdings. Some 60 percent of DC participants say they are saving outside their employer's plan according to a recent poll (Vanguard, 2001), and many also have housing equity. Further, participants often have spouses or partners with 401(k) and other retirement benefits, and they may feel comfortable taking a concentrated bet on their company's stock if they have these other assets. Finally, if returns to human capital and company stock are believed to be uncorrelated, people may feel more comfortable investing in stock.

Behavioral explanations can be added to conventional reasons for why employees hold company stock. One is employee myopia regarding the risks of company stock: a survey of national DC plan participants showed that participants systematically err in assessing the risks of their company stock (Figure 3-1), rating employer stock as less risky than a diversified equity mutual fund.[38] Moreover, that survey showed that participants properly rated "individual stocks" as more risky than an equity mutual fund, but they considered their employer's stock as less risky (in effect they perceived their own company stock as less risky than other individual stocks). Despite the fact that average volatility of an individual stock is at least twice the volatility of a diversified market portfolio, participants rated individual stocks as only slightly more risky.

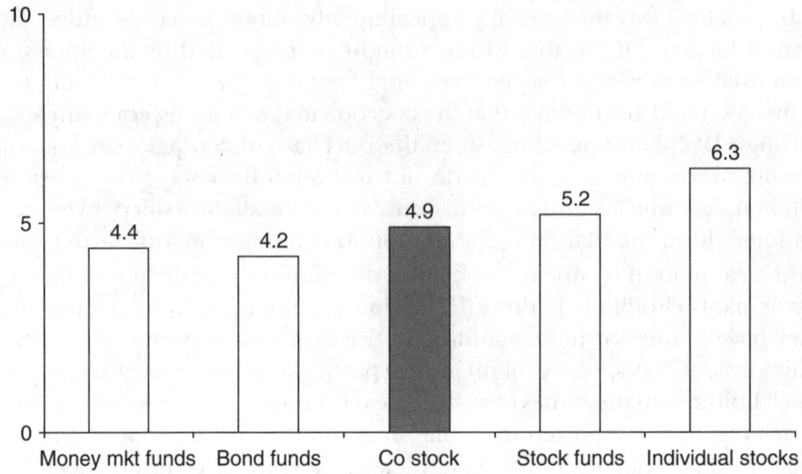

Figure 3-1. Participant knowledge about risk/return of company stock. (*Source:* Vanguard 2001*a*.)

Another factor influencing participant allocations to company stock is past investment performance. Participants' decisions to invest their own monies in company stock appear to be related to the stock's long-term total return performance, particularly over 10-year periods (Benartzi, 2001).[39] When a stock ranks in the top performance quintile, participants devote about 40 percent of their own assets to company stock; if the stock ranks in the bottom performance quintile, participant holdings of stock fall to 10 percent of portfolios. Participants' decisions to over-or under-weight company stock do not seem to depend on "inside information" regarding their firm's prospects: they tend to overweight stocks that later deteriorate and underweight stocks that improve.

Company stock investment decisions by DC plan participants are unusual in another important respect: participants' portfolio mixes are influenced not only by their own preferences and behavior, but also by their employer's plan design decisions. Thus Benartzi and Thaler (2001) find that participants held more equity when the investment menu includes more equity funds; and conversely, participants held less equity when the menu included more fixed income funds. Employers play an important role in the case of company stock, because they select the menu of available investment options, including whether or not to offer company stock in the first place. In addition, as we have seen, some employers direct their contributions to stock and furthermore restrict its diversification; in so doing, they tend to be seen as implicitly endorsing company stock as an investment and encouraging employees to invest their own funds as well. This has been termed the "endorsement effect" in the literature (Benartzi, 2001).

Table 3-7 offers some evidence of an endorsement effect. If participants make all retirement plan investment decisions, holdings of company stock amount to 22 percent of plan assets; by contrast when an employer directs employer contributions to company stock, total holdings of company stock soar to 53 percent of assets. Of that 53 percent, 33 percent is the participant's money and 20 percent is the employer's. Arguably there are differences in directed versus discretionary plans that account for some of the difference. Employers who direct contributions to stock are more likely to be large, well-known companies; their "blue chip" stock may be somewhat less volatile; and they may be somewhat more likely to offer a DB or other DC plan. Still, the difference in asset allocation patterns between these two groups is striking and suggestive of an endorsement effect. Further, a persuasive case can be made that participants follow the "path of least resistance" in making contribution and investment choices within retirement plans. One such path may be to accept an employer's decision to invest the employer contribution in company stock, and to mimic to some extent that decision in one's own portfolio (Choi et al., 2001).

Company Stock and Retirement Income Security

Two distinct goals drive current policy toward tax-qualified retirement saving in the United States, namely, employee ownership and retirement saving. The policy goal of employee ownership has been encouraged in several different ways. For instance, ERISA exempts company stock from its diversification standard; employers may contribute in company stock and restrict its diversification; no cap is required for company stock in DC plans comparable to that on DB plans; and participants are afforded special tax treatment for company stock on distribution. ESOPs, whether standalone or integrated with a 401(k) feature, also have an array of tax, leverage, and other advantages; the passage of EGTRRA as noted earlier enhances the tax benefits further. Currently, tax subsidies amounting to $55 billion (in 2002)[40] and exceptions in fiduciary law permit employers to encourage or mandate employee holdings of company stock in DC plans.

Some firms have therefore emphasized employee ownership aspects of their tax-qualified retirement programs, a finding enunciated in a 1983 opinion of the US Court of Appeals for the Fifth Circuit. Although it referred narrowly to ESOPs, it did summarize the broader arguments regarding company stock in retirement savings plans:

> Congressional policies [...] seem destined to collide.... On the one hand, Congress has repeatedly expressed its intent to encourage the formation of ESOPs... Competing with Congress' expressed policy to foster the formation of

ESOPs is the policy expressed in equally forceful terms in ERISA: that of safeguarding the interests of participants in employee benefit plans by vigorously enforcing standards of fiduciary liability.[41]

By contrast, ERISA's prudence and diversification standards derive from a view of the world consistent with modern portfolio theory, which holds that workers should not own stock in a single factory. Instead, they should be encouraged to own a representative fraction of all factories by investing through a fully diversified market portfolio. Departure from a market weighting of any one company's stock will result in labor and capital earnings becoming positively correlated, so firm bankruptcy puts wages and financial assets at risk.

In order to assess the impact of holding company stock on retirement security, we model retirement incomes for participants holding company stock, taking a system-wide view. The analysis considers three hypothetical portfolios: one invested 100 percent in company stock, a second invested 100 percent in a market portfolio, and a third invested in a 50/50 mix of the two. The hypothetical participant in this exercise receives $50,000 in labor earnings and has a total of 10 percent of earnings contributed to his DC plan; his pension contributions are assumed to grow non-stochastically at 3 percent (to account for inflation). Returns on company stock and the market portfolio are assumed to be normally distributed with identical expected mean returns of 10 percent. Consistent with the individual stock risk presented earlier, the volatility of company stock is set at 40 percent, twice that of the market volatility of 20 percent. Terminal wealth is log-normally distributed.

The range of results for retiree wealth 30 years hence is generated by a Monte Carlo simulation; results are given in Figure 3-2. One finding is that median expected wealth declines due to the compounding of more volatile returns, as the percentage of company stock increases in the participant's portfolio. Median wealth with the market portfolio amounts to $830,000, but is about half that, $411,000, with the company stock portfolio. Extremes of wealth are greater in the best-case company stock scenario, where there is a 5 percent chance of making $4.1 million, versus only $2.7 million with a market portfolio. Yet in the worst-case scenario, the ordering of outcomes is reversed: the market portfolio provides a low of $281,000 while the company stock investor ends up with only $66,000 in retirement.

In the aggregate then, more volatile company stock is expected to produce greater wealth extremes in DC plans: there are a few retirement outcomes where DC participants are either exceptional winners or losers. The problem is that policymakers tend to be concerned with downside risk where people forfeit substantial DC assets to firm bankruptcy (e.g. "Enron losers"), rather than the upside risk (e.g. the "Microsoft winners"). Also, median wealth for

(A) Assumptions

Initial worker income:	$50,000	Expected return, company stock:	10%
Contribution rate:	10%	Volatility, company stock:	40%
Contribution growth rate:	3%	Correlation, market and company stock	0.9
Expected return, market:	10%		
Volatility, market:	20%		

(B) Wealth outcomes in 30 years

	Expected Wealth in 30 years		
Portfolio mix	5th Percentile ($)	Median ($)	95th Percentile ($)
100% market portfolio	281,000	830,000	2,733,000
50% company stock, 50% market portfolio	139,000	615,000	3,384,000
100% company stock	66,000	411,000	4,070,000

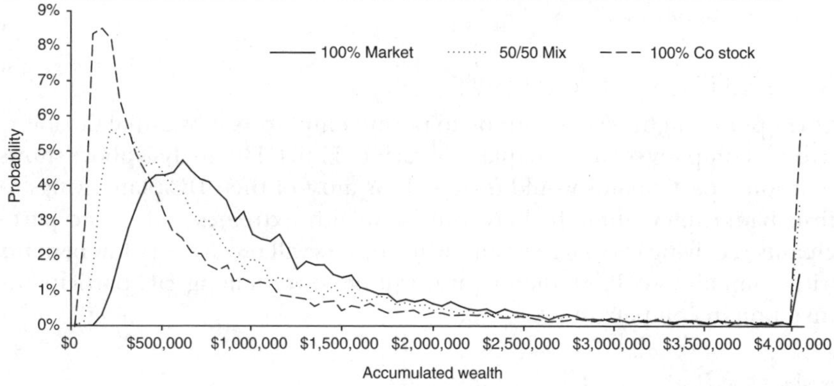

Figure 3-2. Wealth outcomes and company stock. (*Source*: Authors' computations using Monte Carlo simulations and assumptions above.)

DC participants with company stock may be lower,[42] a perhaps counterintuitive finding that results directly from greater volatility of company stock compounding at a lower rate. In other words, greater diversification would boost employees' median wealth but simultaneously reduce extreme outcomes at both ends of the spectrum. Therefore, curtailing bankruptcy risk for company stock losers also limits the chance of outsized gains for company stock winners.[43] As a consequence, policymakers face the quandary of whether to permit DC pensions to produce such widely disparate outcomes. Downside, as well as upside, risk from company stock is particularly concentrated for long-tenure employees working for a single firm whose DC assets are bound up tightly with the company. When the stock value drops precipitously, such long-tenure workers will experience a substantial loss of lifetime savings. Diversification would logically limit such extreme worst-case as well as best-case outcomes, while less obviously, it will also increase median wealth among all DC plan participants holding company stock.

The dilemma for policyholders is that making DC plans more diversified will not produce readily observable benefits for employers and participants. Thus in the long term, median retirement wealth will likely grow, but it will be difficult to compare results with a company-stock-heavy system. Some participants would suffer bankruptcy losses though these will be relatively few; meanwhile, diversification restrictions will be highly visible, particularly at very successful firms.

Policy Choices and Outcomes

Several policy options have been suggested to encourage DC plan diversification. This section evaluates their potential impact on employer and employee behavior.

Maintain the Status Quo

One option might be to continue to permit employers substantial flexibility to offer company stock in DC plans of various kinds. The analysis above shows that some participants would forfeit all or most of their DC plan savings to firm bankruptcy, though there will be wealth extremes with some participants receiving very large wealth while others will receive very low benefits with company stock. Median wealth will be lower among DC participants investing in company stock.

Enhance Participant Risk Disclosure

DC plan participants seem to systematically underestimate the risks inherent in company stock, based on evidence provided above. Plan designers seeking to encourage diversification might require periodic disclosure statements encouraging participants to limit their own company stock holdings to some stated limit such as 10 or 20 percent of assets. In view of participants' poor understanding of the risks, repeated risk disclosure might be useful. A difficulty with disclosure, whether passive or active, is that plan sponsors may perceive a conflict regarding their dual roles as company executives seeking to promote employee ownership, and plan fiduciaries seeking to ensure diversification. Perhaps "safe-harbor" disclosure statements could be provided by regulators.

Promote Participant Investment Advice

To encourage further diversification, disclosure might be combined with expanded use of third-party advice providers. Today advice is rarely offered with DC retirement plans, and various proposals have been made to simplify the fiduciary rules surrounding the provision of advice, the subject of a separate policy debate. Yet providing plan participants with investment advice will encourage diversification only if those with highly concentrated positions are actively encouraged to sell those holdings, even when such sales might be against the employer's wishes. It is worth noting that the leading providers of advice rely on participants to determine how much company stock they want; they do not explicitly instruct participants to sell company stock as many independent financial planners might (Halsey, 2002).

Strengthen Fiduciary Oversight

Implicit in the national policy debate as well as employers offering DC plans is the inherent conflict of interest that arises between promoting stock ownership and encouraging diversification. One approach to addressing this conflict would be to propose tougher conflict-of-interest standards, to focus fiduciaries on the risks associated with DC plan investments (Olsen, 2002). A different tack would require that an independent fiduciary be responsible for monitoring company stock performance and recommending steps that employers could take to minimize concentrated stockholdings.

Restrict DC Participants from Holding "Too Much" Company Stock

To discourage participants from holding "too much" company stock, some have recommended minimizing employer restrictions on participants' ability to diversify employer contributions. A different approach would set a statutory cap on company stock holdings in DC plans such as the 10-percent maximum for DB plans. A third proposal, recommended by Olsen (2002), would provide employers with a choice of company stock regimes. If the employer elected to direct contributions into stock to encourage employee ownership, these employees could be prohibited from investing their own contributions in stock. This would prevent the "doubling down" of investments in company stock, when employees concentrate their purchases of stock on top of company contributions. Alternatively, an employer could offer stock as simply another investment option in the plan, but would not direct contributions to stock. Rather, it would be up to the participant to decide whether or not to allocate employer and/or employee monies to the option. A different set of choices pertains not to participant or plan design behavior, but instead focuses on tax subsidies. One option would phase out EGTRRA dividend reinvestment incentives for ESOPs and long-term capital gain treatment for distributions of stocks to participants. To raise the relative costs of making contributions in stock, the tax deduction for stock contributions to retirement plans could be reduced.

In assessing these and other options to restrict company stock holdings, we note that there are two competing views regarding the degree of regulation that public policy should impose. Those policymakers that focus on the flexibility of the retirement system, employer support for employee ownership aspects of DC plans, and the central role of individual investment decisions, are likely to emphasize voluntary diversification by participants. By contrast, policymakers concerned about the company executives acting as independent fiduciaries for their stock, participant myopia about risks and performance, and participant inertia generally, are likely to consider statutory rules that mandate diversification. Additionally, any policy change would have to take into account the varied role of ESOPs as standalone plans or hybrid KSOPs, as leveraged or unleveraged plans, and as plans sponsored by public versus private, family, or employee-owned firms.

Develop New Pension Investment Protections

To protect against excessive company stock in DC plans, employers could also offer plan participants insurance against severe loss of company stock value. As with Enron, Worldcom, Kmart, and Polaroid, the dilemma is that if the firm self-insures, there will likely be no assets available in the worst-case scenario of bankruptcy, and if the firm obtains third-party insurance, that coverage could be contested. There is also the moral-hazard problem, of firms with insurance "betting the farm" on company stock. Another alternative might be to require DC plans to offer one or two guaranteed investment options such as those discussed in this volume (Lachance and Mitchell, Chapter 8, this volume). Indeed more than one legislator has already proposed that DC plans offer insured investment products, perhaps on a federal level (Joint Committee, 2002). More research on the feasibility, structure, and cost of guarantees is clearly required.[44]

Proposals that would alter the role of company stock in private DC plans might also change employer and employee behavior. The key question is how employers and employees might respond to plans to require diversification. To the extent that actual company stock holdings reflect inertia and risk myopia by both employers and employees, relatively little might change. On the other hand, sponsors or participants with most of their assets in company stock might assign a higher utility to equity-linked compensation than those with, say, 15 percent in company stock. Some of this is employer-based, though as noted earlier, 55 percent of plans offering stock do not direct contributions to stock and are liberal in allowing participant diversification. Even among the 45 percent of company stock plans that direct employer contributions to stock, some have no restrictions on diversification nor do they impose caps.

Some worry that new plan formation could decline, or sponsors might terminate retirement plans, in response to changes in company stock rules.

In our view, this seems unlikely. Plan formation is principally a concern among smaller firms where company stock is generally not offered; workers' preferences for wages and firm profitability are reported to be the main obstacles to offering retirement benefits (EBRI, 2001). In terms of plan termination, virtually all large US corporate employers offer DC plans, and though most offer company stock, there is still heterogeneity in the level of stock concentration and the types of restrictions imposed. The universality of DC benefits among large firms would suggest that employers would continue to maintain some DC retirement program in order to remain competitive in the labor market.

Alternatively, some employers may reduce retirement plan contributions when faced with caps or limits on stock. Stock contributions could be replaced with smaller cash contributions or simply smaller stock contributions than before, as the DC plan environment becomes less favorable toward holding company stock. In times of labor scarcity, employers cutting stock contributions would be reducing pay so employers would be expected to have to boost other forms of compensation over time to remain competitive. The substitution may be less than one-for-one on an after-tax basis in the hands of employees, since the employer is no longer directing compensation to a tax-qualified plan.[45]

Yet a different employer response might be to redirect existing retirement plan contributions into other forms of stock compensation. Several choices come to mind as alternative vehicles: for instance sponsors might use stock options, though this might increase accounting scrutiny about options' dilutive effect and the substitution of visible compensation expense for less-transparent option grants. A different possibility would be employee stock purchase plans, which are typically voluntary and lack the compulsory nature of directed employer contributions in DC plans. A third avenue would provide employees with direct grants of stock from the company. These might come in the form of a special restricted class of shares, if feasible. However, compared with options, grants are expensed on income statements under current financial reporting standards; as a result, they are less advantageous in management's eyes compared with options. Since none of these options has the tax benefits, market appeal, and transparency (in terms of public and media scrutiny) as do DC plan contributions, it is unlikely that there would be a direct and complete substitution effect, with employers reducing current retirement plan contributions by $1 and redirecting the same $1 to one of these other forms of compensation. Ultimately, substitution will hinge on employees' value associated with mandatory stock contributions in DC plans as well as employer valuation of these contributions.

Assuming that employers who preferred large holdings of company stock by employees will direct some of their contributions to other forms of equity compensation, what might be the impact on retirement plans? One possibility is that employee DC plan participation rates might fall. Evidence indicates that plan participation rates rise with employer matching contributions, though there is some question as to whether it is the size, or the mere existence, of the match that counts most. Large firms, which more often offer company stock, already have lower participation rates, perhaps because they are also more likely to offer another retirement plan. Also as noted above, movement toward diversification and less company stock could raise median wealth, while reducing the chances of exceptional wealth and loss of all assets due to company bankruptcy. On the other hand, depending on workers' preferences and other wealth, risk-averse workers may accept a decrease in total compensation as a result.

The dynamics of employer contributions are further complicated by nondiscrimination testing in DC plans. Nondiscrimination rules require that non-highly compensated employees contribute at some minimum rate; the goal is to ensure that the tax benefits associated with a DC plan are not simply provided to highly compensated employees. If non-highly paid employees fail to contribute, highly paid employees will also be limited in their ability to contribute. Employers who decide to reduce plan contributions made in stock (and thereby decrease participation or savings rates among non-highly compensated workers) could inadvertently lead to savings restrictions on highly compensated employees, decreasing the value of the retirement plan benefit for this segment of the employee population.

Finally, what impact might a policy change have on employees? Today an estimated 11 million participants have concentrated stock positions exceeding 20 percent of account assets. If forced to diversify, some of these people will believe themselves worse off since they were required to modify their desired stockholdings. On the other hand, since some participants underestimate the risks of owning company stock, and employer plan design and past performance have a strong influence on their decision to invest, this group might experience lower current satisfaction but greater later benefit in retirement. Yet others will perceive no reduction in welfare, possibly because they are concentrated in stock on an involuntary basis, through a misunderstanding of the risks, or inertia. Given the tendency of participants to overweight stock holdings based on past performance, employees perceiving the greatest welfare reduction will be those employed by firms with a history of strong stock performance.

Conclusions

This chapter has focused on the role of company stock in employer-sponsored retirement plans, with special attention to how US employers have used company stock within DC plans in an effort to promote employee share ownership, particularly among rank-and-file workers. The stated aim of such ownership is to improve morale, worker productivity, and shareholder value. The data show that only 3 percent of DC plans actually offer company stock as an investment in the United States, but since these plans are sponsored by large firms, around half of all private sector DC plan participants, 23 million workers, have access to company stock in their DC plans. Of these, some 11 million participants hold concentrated stock positions exceeding 20 percent of account balances; and 5 million hold positions exceeding 60 percent of account balances. It is surprising that concentrated DC company stock holdings appear to be driven by employer belief that restricting diversification will enhance productivity, in view of the lack of strong evidence on this point. A different explanation is systemic participant decision-making error, where participants erroneously view employer stock as less risky than a diversified equity fund or other individual stocks. There also appears to be evidence favoring the "endorsement effect," in which participants take employer decisions to direct and restrict company stock investments as an implicit recommendation.

Retirement systems with concentrated stock positions will always have some participants forfeit DC plan savings to firm bankruptcy. Company stock in retirement portfolios also leads to greater extremes in accumulated wealth because of its higher volatility, and a lower median wealth, as compared to a system of diversified investments. Policy options for encouraging additional diversification include additional risk disclosure, liberalization of restrictions, maximum caps or limits on company stock, and other strategies. We find that rule changes will have little immediate impact on plan formation or termination, but they may influence employers to redirect some portion of retirement plan contributions to other forms of equity-linked compensation, such as options, stock purchase plans, or stock grants. Whether reductions in stock contributions are welfare-reducing depends on the certainty-equivalent value of such stock contributions, not simply on a change in the dollar value of the contribution.

In the end, policymakers face a dilemma. Most proposed reforms, restrictions, and advice, discourage the purchase of top-performing stocks. These will also be highly visible, especially after the fact, while long-term improvements in retirement wealth due to diversification will be difficult to measure and potentially diffuse. Reductions in bankruptcy risk will affect only a relatively small group of participants, and the utility gain to risk-averse participants whose plans become diversified may be even harder for politicians to identify.

Notes

[1] Aggregate 2001 statistics based on the authors' estimates from US Department of Labor and Federal Reserve Board data appear on Table 3-1. The existing official data on pension assets and participants are from 1998 taken from Form 5500 data filed with the US Department of Labor.

[2] Interestingly, the early legislative proposals for ERISA developed early in the Kennedy administration included a 10-percent cap on company stock for *both* DB and DC plans devised by the Commission on Money and Credit. Cap plans then resurfaced several times, in a cabinet working group on pensions during the Kennedy commission, in pension reform proposals developed during the Johnson Administration, and in the pension debate leading up to ERISA's drafting.

[3] One key opponent of a 10-percent cap on employer stock in DC plans was Sears Roebuck from Chicago, which offered a profit-sharing plan invested exclusively in Sears' stock. Because of the stock's strong performance through much of the 1950s and 1960s, it proved difficult to persuade employees to diversify: that profit-sharing plan yielded very generous payouts to its participants, paying retirees sometimes five times their pre-retirement salaries. Unwillingness to limit profit-sharing programs such as Sears' led to the elimination of the 10 percent cap on DC plans proposed in the 1970s; see Gordon (1984).

[4] Technically, "individual account" DC plans, in which accounts are maintained for individual workers, are exempted from ERISA's diversification requirement (Buckley, 2001). These plans include the 401(k) plan (a type of profit-sharing plan), and also traditional profit-sharing and ESOP plans. Another type of DC plan is the money purchase pension plan, in which employer contributions are based on a fixed percentage of pay. These latter plans are considered a form of "pension plan"; they are not guaranteed by the PBGC, but they are subject to the same 10-percent cap on stock holdings as are DB plans. Money purchase plans are also required to offer employees an annuity option upon distribution of plan assets. Finally, some pre-ERISA DB and DC plans are exempt from the 10-percent rule.

[5] Regulations issued in 1992 under ERISA section 404(c) provide a modest incentive for employers to end directed contributions into company stock. Under these regulations, sponsors are provided limited fiduciary liability relief for employee investment decision-making, as long as certain conditions are met. The most important requirement is that participants must exercise independent control over plan assets and must have an opportunity to diversify plan assets among a range of investments. Thus, plans where the employer directs contributions into company stock are ineligible for 404(c) protection, whereas discretionary plans where the participant makes all investment choices are (assuming they meet other technical requirements).

[6] This was not precisely a garden-variety company stock purchase plan. England (1997) reported that the Color Tile 401(k) plan had purchased several stores from the parent firm and then leased them back to the company at below-market rates. Subsequently "(s)ome of these stores stopped making their lease payments, cutting cash flow into the plan. Plan administrators froze payouts, telling participants in a May 10 letter that they had no idea when they might resume or what value could be recovered from these investments."

[7] The debate over company stock has focused on precipitous drops in stock values, but single-stock risk can also be felt more gradually, over longer periods. One such instance is the bankruptcy of Kmart Corporation in January 2002. Kmart reported that 14 percent of its DC plan was invested in company stock at the time of its bankruptcy (Schneyer, 2002), though stock accounted for some 28 percent of plan assets in 1995 (Paton, 2002). Indeed, over the decade ending in 2001, Kmart was one of

the poorest performing stocks in the Standard & Poor's 500 Index, losing 75 percent of its value as compared to a gain of 238 percent for the S&P 500. In a similar vein, the bankruptcy of Polaroid Corporation in 2001 reflected a long-term deterioration in its core business (Krasner, 2002; Deutsch, 2001).

[8] Targets of litigation included telecommunications firms Lucent Technologies, Nortel Networks, Global Crossing, Qwest, SBC, and Worldcom; energy companies Enron Corporation, CMS Energy, Duke Energy, Halliburton and Williams Companies; and firms such as Providian Financial Corporation and Rite Aid Corporation (Plan Sponsor, 2002). Litigation against IKON Office Solutions was settled in May 2002 with the firm agreeing to end restrictions on participants' ability to diversify employer stock contributions after 2 years of service.

[9] Senior executives at several firms allegedly reaped substantial gains from the sale of personal stock holdings prior to losses incurred by nonexecutive workers. Executives were said to have distorted financial results in order to maximize reported company earnings and stock option gains. Worldcom reported billions of dollars in accounting errors that masked true earnings; at Enron and elsewhere, sham transactions were ostensibly used to boost short-term earnings and stock prices. The accounting firm Arthur Andersen was convicted of obstruction of justice in the Enron case.

[10] For more on ESOPS see Hallman and Rosenbloom (2000) and Smiley and Brown (2000).

[11] The tax law definition that ESOPs must invest "principally" in employer securities would seem to imply that some diversification would be common in ESOPs. The US Department of Labor has suggested as much (in an *amicus* court brief filed by the DOL Secretary in *Moench v. Robertson*, a 1995 court case involving an ESOP). Yet most ESOPs are heavily invested in stock of the sponsoring employer.

[12] In a leveraged ESOP, the plan, using either bank debt or a loan from the employer, buys a large block of employer shares, which are held as "unallocated" (not yet designated to individual participants). Each year, as the employer makes tax-qualified contributions to the ESOP, a portion of the bank debt, both principal and interest, is paid off, and a corresponding value of the unallocated shares is transferred to individual employee accounts. Under prior law, the bank making the ESOP loan also received special tax incentives.

[13] For example, in 1988, Polaroid Corporation utilized an ESOP to buy back shares and maintain independence in the face of a hostile bid from Shamrock Holdings (Deutsch, 2001). This contemporary case is illustrative of the risks involved in an undiversified ESOP. Polaroid filed for bankruptcy in 2001, and employees lost substantial savings accumulated in the Polaroid ESOP (Krasner, 2002).

[14] When tallying shareholder votes, unallocated shares are generally voted in the same proportion as the allocated shares held by and voted by employees. However, plan fiduciaries are still required to exercise prudent judgment and may vote contrary to employee decisions.

[15] Leveraged ESOPs also offered certain financial reporting benefits in the past. Under old accounting rules (grandfathered for certain firms), ESOP debt could remain off of the employer's balance sheet. Contributions to the ESOP could be reported at historic cost, not market value, understating the cost of pensions, at least during the term of the ESOP loan. Some existing ESOPs still take advantage of these benefits. As a result, firms report higher earnings on their shareholder financial statements than they otherwise might.

[16] Principal payments on the loan are seen as deductible too, as they are in the form of tax-qualified employer contributions to the plan. Freiman (1990) argues that employers have overstated these tax benefits, as both interest and dividend payments on ESOP loans constitute a form of compensation, which would otherwise be deductible if paid under a different form. Chaplinsky and Niehaus (1991) reaffirm that it is the tax sheltering of dividend payments that offers a meaningful tax benefit. To maximize this benefit, some employers utilize high-yielding preferred stock, rather than low-yielding common shares, in a leveraged ESOP.

[17] Other ESOP benefits accrue to family- or privately-held firms. ESOPs are a tool of succession planning, providing liquidity to a founding family or owners through a private sale to employees. Owners of privately-held firms receive tax benefits when they sell their holdings to an ESOP (Perun, 2000). Privately-held firms also used ESOPs as a source of investment capital; in effect, selling shares to employees through an ESOP offers a private equity capital market for the owners' shares, as well as the opportunity to borrow against that equity. Overall, only 10 percent of ESOPs are sponsored by publicly traded firms, while 90 percent are sponsored by private firms (NCEO, 2002). However, a much higher percentage of ESOP participants and assets are in publicly traded ESOPs because of the public firms' larger size. ESOPs in private firms are supported by a larger percent of employee salary than in publicly traded firms (8–10 percent of pay versus 4–6 percent; NCEO, 2002).

[18] In an ESOP, employers make discretionary contributions of employer stock to workers' accounts. In a KSOP, participants make voluntary 401(k) contributions to the 401(k) portion of the program. The employer provides a ESOP stock contribution and may also make a matching 401(k) contribution to the 401(k) portion, which may or may not be directed into company stock. The plan may or may not include a profit-sharing contribution, made in cash or stock. The ESOP component may or may not be leveraged.

[19] A number of prominent firms have taken a similar tack, replacing DB benefits backed by diversified portfolios with programs based on company stock. In a so-called "floor offset" plan design, the employer gradually reduces or eliminates benefits under a traditional DB pension plan as it increases company stock contributions to an ESOP. Such programs have further reduced corporate pension expense, but they also have the effect of increasing company stock concentration among workers (Schultz and Francis, 2002*a*). Since 1987, floor-offset arrangements have been generally prohibited if company stock in the DB and ESOP plans exceeds 10 percent of assets. At the same time, the floor-offset programs of a number of prominent employers (including Enron Corporation) were grandfathered under the 1987 law (Kandarian, 2002).

[20] Under EGTRRA, employers can more readily qualify for a corporate tax deduction for dividends reinvested in an ESOP by participants. Earlier tax law allowed a similar deduction, but typically required payment of the dividend to the employee. In order to qualify for the ESOP deduction, sponsors must recast their 401(k) plan as an ESOP, at least insofar as the employer contribution is concerned. Sponsors must give participants the right to receive dividends in lieu of being reinvested in the plan. There are also technical requirements that must be met, including requirements for separate nondiscrimination testing and participant pass-through voting.

[21] Company stock holdings by employees may result from other programs including stock option offerings, employee stock purchase plans, and a wide range of executive

compensation arrangements (Lambert et al., 1991; Hall and Murphy, 2001). We do not consider these here, focusing instead on what workers tend to see as retirement systems.

[22] These data are drawn from plans that must file Form 5500 with the USDOL; they exclude life insurance reserves used to fund corporate retirement plans.

[23] This estimate is derived by projecting the 1998 USDOL data from 5500 plans to 2001 (see Table 3-1). Our figure agrees with other estimates in the literature; see Benartzi (2001). Higher estimates suggest that company stock represents $500 billion of DC assets, but this figure uses an erroneous calculation (it applies the 29 percent of company stock in 401(k) plans that offer company stock to all DC assets including plans lacking stock).

[24] The EBRI/ICI dataset includes more than 35,000 plans with a 401(k) feature, 12 million active 401(k) plan participants, and nearly $580 billion in 401(k) assets; see Holden and VanDerhei (2001*a,b*) and VanDerhei (2002).

[25] Kruse (2002) indicates that DOL data do not separately account for company stock holdings held within collective trusts. According to his calculations, if these holdings are properly reflected in the overall totals, the percent of DC plan assets in company stock rises from 16 to 20 percent, a figure consistent with data from EBRI/ICI.

[26] The EBRI/ICI data also indicate that, within the 3 percent of plans offering company stock, 29 percent of plan assets are invested in company stock. Applying this measure to our estimates for 401(k) and DC plan assets for 2001, it suggests a range for company stock holdings of $290 billion to $359 billion, confirming the results from the USDOL data of $340 billion.

[27] Survey results provided to the authors encompassed 173 sponsoring firms and 264 qualified plans as of June 2001. The sample represented $65 billion in DC plan assets covering an estimated 5 percent of the market value of company stock in 2001. Fidelity (2000) and Hewitt (2001) find near-identical results.

[28] There is no evidence that when restrictions are lifted, rank-and-file participants diversify out of company stock, while executives offered stock options do appear to exercise some portion at the point of vesting (Hall and Murphy, 2001).

[29] Even and Macpherson (forthcoming) as well as Ippolito (1998) summarize the positive arguments, noting that employee ownership provides workers with an opportunity to own a stake in the firm that can enhance shareholder value. A number of other studies is reviewed in Kruse and Blasi (1997) and Kruse (2002); a recent extension is found in Oyer and Schaefer (2002).

[30] Related research has also evaluated stock-based executive compensation, since in the US context, a substantial portion of deferred compensation is in the form of company stock or stock options. The evidence shows that chief executives in key industrial companies receive about one-third of their compensation in the form of stock options (Leonard, 1990; Murphy, 2000; Abowd and Kaplan, 1999). Research indicates that company performance is positively associated with executive holding of stocks or stock options, but by much less than one-for-one. In other words, firms compensating key employees using conditional and long-term incentive plans did experience higher equity returns than those lacking such plans, but net shareholder benefits were not necessarily positive.

[31] Under current tax law, company equity offerings are more tax effective from the employee side if provided in the retirement plan instead of in other stock-based (e.g. stock option) plans.

[32] Oyer and Schaefer (2002) estimate that the top five executives of firms, accounting for 2 percent of employment, receive 31 percent of the Black-Scholes value of stock options grants; non-executive employees earning more than $75,000, accounting for another 4 percent of employment, receive 61 percent of the Black-Scholes value. Meanwhile, employees earning under $35,000, accounting for two-thirds of employment, receive just under 2 percent of options value. The National Center for Employee Ownership, cited in Leonhardt (2002), indicates that in 2000, 75 percent of options outstanding were held by the top five executives in options-granting companies.

[33] Social security benefits represent the largest social entitlement program; see Moore and Mitchell (2000).

[34] For this reason, we avoid the nomenclature of employers "making their 401(k) matching contribution in stock"; instead it appears to be common to make a cash contribution and direct that it be invested in stock.

[35] For example, consider a firm with $1 billion in earnings, 200 million shares outstanding, and a share price of $80. EPS is $5.00 per share and the firm's market capitalization is $16 billion. A $50 million cash contribution to a DC plan will reduce reported EPS by 5 percent to $4.75. Yet issuing an additional $50 million in shares (625,000 shares at the market price) would require an offsetting decline in the stock price from $80 to $79.75, or about 0.31%, to maintain the firm's existing market value. The percentage decline in share price is small in relation to the normal stock market volatility, whereas the reported reduction in earnings is widely publicized to investors.

[36] This compilation of the largest ninety-six corporate DC plans is extracted from a survey of the 200 largest DC plans in the trade publication *Pensions & Investments* (2002); we exclude from the initial list public plans and plans sponsored by mutually owned or privately-held firms. Though few in number, these ninety-six private pension plans account for $520 billion in aggregate DC plan assets; the average firm has $5.4 billion in DC assets.

[37] Given the obscurity of this tax provision, it is debatable how large a factor it plays in participants' initial investment decisions.

[38] John Hancock Financial Services (2001) reports similar results.

[39] Purcell (2002) also reports that stock performance contributes to plan-level concentration in company stock.

[40] OMB (2002) notes that this refers to both the tax expenditure due to the exclusion of employer contributions and earnings in 401(k) and ESOP plans.

[41] *Donovan v. Cunningham*, 716 F.2d 1455, 1466 (5th Cir. 1983).

[42] If inducing employees to hold stock actually increased productivity, overall returns might rise. However, as we noted earlier, there is hardly a proof of this point.

[43] A few caveats are in order. Employees often change jobs during their careers, so job changes will keep some participants from accumulating too much in a single stock. Our analysis reflects the worst-case results for a long-tenure employee. If participants accumulate several single-stock positions during a career, the retirement outcome will depend on the correlation of returns among the old and the new stocks. Finally, this analysis models outcomes only from the DC component of retirement incomes. Sponsors who also provide a corresponding DB (or other non-company stock DC) plan will mitigate the risk to total retirement income for covered employees, assuming there is a meaningful vested and accrued DB payout (and taxable savings).

[44] See <http://prc.wharton.upenn.edu/prc/2002confb.html> for a range of studies on this topic.

[45] How much less the cash-equivalent value of company stock in pensions plans might be worth is unclear. The fact that it can be substantially less than dollar for dollar is demonstrated by Hall and Murphy (2000), Lambert, Larcker, and Verrecchia (1991), and Meulbroek (2000*a*,*b*), among others, in the case of executives, but similar metrics have not been derived for rank-and-file employees.

References

Abowd, John M. and David S. Kaplan. 1999. "Executive Compensation: Six Questions that Need Answering." *Journal of Economic Perspectives* 13: 145–168.

Anand, Vineeta. 2001. "Employers Get a Gift: Treasury Department OKs Break for ESOPs." *Pensions & Investments*, 24 (December): 3.

Baxter, Marianne. 2001. "Social Security as a Financial Asset: Gender-Specific Risks and Returns." NBER WP 8329.

Benartzi, Shlomo. 2001. "Excessive Extrapolation and the Allocation of 401(k) Accounts to Company Stock." *Journal of Finance* LVI (5): 1747–1764.

— and Richard Thaler. 2001. "Naïve Diversification Strategies in Retirement Savings Plans." *American Economic Review* 91(1): 79–98.

Blasi, Joseph, Michael Conte, and Douglas Kruse. 1996. "Employee Stock Ownership and Corporate Performance among Public Companies." *Industrial and Labor Relations Review* 50(1): 60–79.

Buckley, Allen. 2001. "Eligible Individual Account Plans and ERISA's Fiduciary Duties." *Journal of Pension Benefits* 9(1).

Bureau of Labor Statistics (BLS). 2000. "Pilot Survey on the Incidence of Stock Options in Private Industry in 1999." <www.bls.gov>.

Chaplinsky, Susan and Greg Niehaus. 1991. "Tax Advantages of ESOP Financing." *Benefits Quarterly* Third Quarter: 26–30.

Chen, Kathy. 2002*a*. "Enron Official Failed to Warn Participants of 401(k) Plan." *The Wall Street Journal* February 6: C1.

— 2002*b*. "Pension Plans Are Adjusted After Enron." *The Wall Street Journal* January 29: A2.

Davis, Steven J. and Paul Willen. 2000. "Occupation Level Income Shocks and Asset Returns: Their Covariance and Implications for Portfolio Choice." NBER WP 7905.

Deutsch, Claudia H. 2001. "Market Place: For Polaroid, the Bad News Seems to be the Only News." *New York Times* October 4: 2001. <www.nytimes.com>.

Drucker, Peter. 1976. *The Unseen Revolution: How Pension Fund Socialism Came to America.* New York: Harper & Row.

Employee Benefits Research Institute (EBRI). 2001. "The EBRI 2001 Small Employer Summary of Findings." <www.ebri.org.sers>.

England, Robert Stowe. 1997. "Protecting the Participant: Washington Lawmakers Ponder Tighter Regulations for 401(k) Plans." *Plan Sponsor* February. www.assetpub.com/archive/ps/97–02psfeb/feb97PS44.html.

Even, William E. and David A. Macpherson. 2003. "Benefits and Productivity." In *Benefits for the New Workplace*, eds. Olivia Mitchell, David Blitzstein, Michael Gordon, and Judy Mazo. Philadelphia: University of Pennsylvania Press.

Farrell, Chris. 2002. “The Problem with Pension Plans.” *Business Week Online.* Sound Money 1/11/02. New York: McGraw Hill. <www.businessweek.com/bwdaily/dnflash/jan2002/nf20020111_3044.htm>.

Fidelity Investments. 2001. *Building Futures: A Report on Corporate Defined Contribution Plans.* Boston: Fidelity Investments.

Freiman, Howard A. 1990. “Understanding the Economics of Leveraged ESOPs.” *Financial Analysts Journal* March–April: 51–55.

General Accounting Office (GAO). 1997. *401(k) Pension Plans: Extent of Plans” Investments in Employer Securities and Real Property.* Washington, DC: November.

Gordon, Michael S. 1984. “The Employee Retirement Income Security Act of 1974: The First Decade: An Information Paper: Why Was ERISA Enacted?” Special Committee on Aging, US Senate. Washington: US GPO, August.

Hall, Brian and Kevin Murphy. 2000. “Optimal Exercise Prices for Executive Stock Options.” NBER WP 7548 (February).

——— 2001. “Stock Options for Undiversified Executives.” Working Paper, Harvard Business School.

Hallman, G. Victor III and Jerry S. Rosenbloom. 2000. “Employee Stock Compensation Plans.” In *Handbook of Employee Benefits,* ed. J. Rosenbloom. New York: McGraw Hill.

Halsey, Nicole. 2002. “Advice Providers Differ on Company Stock Treatment.” *Plansponsor.com.* February 11. <www.plansponsor.com/content/News/Finance/enronadviceprov>.

Hedges and Neikirk. 2002. “Enron Failure May Not Be Enough to Bring Around Lasting Financial Reforms.” Chicago: *Chicago Tribune.* February 11.

Hewitt. 2001. *Survey Findings: Trends and Experience in 401(k) Plans 2001.* Chicago: Hewitt Associates.

Holden, Sarah and Jack VanDerhei. 2001*a*. “Contribution Behavior of 401(k) Plan Participants.” *ICI Perspective* 7(4), Washington.

——— 2001*b*. “401(k) Plan Asset Allocation, Account Balances, and Loan Activity in 2000.” *ICI Perspective* 7(5), Washington.

Hunter, Barry D. 1994. “ERISA’s Authorization of Unlimited Fiduciary Self-Dealing: Employer Stock Acquisition by Defined Contribution Plan Trustees.” *Journal of Pension Planning and Compliance* Fall. 20(3): 27–45.

Ippolito, Richard A. 1998. *Pension Plans and Employee Performance: Evidence, Analysis, and Policy.* Chicago: University of Chicago Press.

Jacobius, Arleen. 2001*a*. “P&G Debuts New, Improved DC Plan.” *Pensions & Investments* 9 July: 1.

—— 2001*b*. “Company Stops Contributing its Stock to 401(k).” *Pensions & Investments.* 3 September: 1.

John Hancock Financial Services (2001). *Insight into Participant Investment Knowledge and Behavior,* Seventh Defined Contribution Plan Survey.

Joint Committee. 2002. Joint Committee on Taxation, *Background Information Relating to the Investment of Retirement Plan Assets in Employer Stock,* (JCX-1-02), February 11.

Kandarian, Steven. 2002. “Statement” on the Pension Benefit Guaranty Corporation, before the Committee on Finance, United States Senate, February 27. <www.pbgc.gov/news/speechs/test_02_27_2002.htm>.

Krasner, Jeffrey. 2002. "Polaroid workers dealt new setback on stocks." *The Boston Globe* January 20. <www.boston.com/dailyglobe2/020/nation/Polaroid_workers_dealt_new_setback_on_stocks.html>.

Kruse, Douglas. 2002. "Research Evidence on Prevalence and Effects of Employee Ownership." Testimony for the Subcommittee on Employer-Employee Relations, Committee on Education and the Workforce, US House of Representatives, February 13.

— and Joseph Blasi. 1997. "Employee Ownership, Employee Attitudes, and Firm Performance: A Review of the Evidence." In *Human Resources Management Handbook.* Part 1, eds. D. Lewin, D.J.B. Mitchell, and M. Zaidi. Greenwich, CT: JAI Press.

Lambert, Richard, David Larcker, and Roe Verrecchia. 1991. "Portfolio Considerations in Valuing Executive Compensation." *Journal of Accounting Research* 29(1): 129–149.

Lebow, David, Louise Sheiner, Larry Slifman, and Martha Starr-McCluer. 1999. "Recent Trends in Compensation Practices." Washington DC: Board of Governors of the Federal Reserve System, Working paper, July.

Leonard, Jonathan S. 1990. "Executive Pay and Firm Performance." *Industrial and Labor Relations Review* 43(3): 13–29.

Leonhardt, David. 2002. "Stock Options Said Not To Be As Widespread as Backers Say." *New York Times,* July 18: C1. Citing data on stock options from National Center for Employee Ownership, <www.nceo.org.22>.

Mercer. 2001. William M. Mercer, *Survey on Employee Savings Plans: 2000–2001.* New York: Mercer.

Meulbroek, Lisa. 2000*a*. "The Efficiency of Equity-Linked Compensation: Understanding the Full Cost of Awarding Executive Stock Options." Harvard Business School Working Paper.

— 2002*b*. "Company Stock in Pension Plans: How Costly Is It?" Harvard Business School, Working Paper 02-0258.

Moore, James and Olivia S. Mitchell. 2000. "Projected Retirement Wealth and Saving Adequacy." In *Forecasting Retirement Needs and Retirement Wealth,* eds. O.S. Mitchell, B. Hammond, and A. Rappaport. Pension Research Council. Philadelphia, PA: University of Pennsylvania Press, pp. 68–94.

Murphy, Kevin J. 2000. "Executive Compensation." In *Handbook of Labor Economics* 3, eds. Orley Ashenfelter and David Card. Amsterdam, New York, and Oxford: Elsevier Science, North-Holland, pp. 2485–2563.

NCEO. 2002. "A Comprehensive Overview of Employee Ownership." downloaded 1/22/02. http://www.nceo.org.

Olsen, Erik. 2002. "Testimony Before the Senate Committee on Governmental Affairs on Retirement Security: 401K Crisis at Enron." February 5. <www.senate.gov/~gov_affairs/020502olsen.htm>.

Office of Management and Budget (OMB). 2002. Budget of the US Government. Chapter 6, Tax Expenditures. <www.whitehouse.gov/omb/budget/fy2003/index.html>.

Oyer, P. and S. Schaefer. 2002. "Why Do Some Firms Give Stock Options to All Employees?" GSB Stanford University working paper. January.

Paton, James. 2002. "Kmart Dive Shows Employee Risk." *Reuters,* January 27. <news.lycos.com/news/story.asp?section=Business&storyID=324020>.

Peale, Cliff. 2002. "Enron Debacle Spurs P&G to Examine ESOP: Company Considers more Diversification." *The Cincinnati Enquirer* 18 (January). <enquirer.com/editions/2002/01/18/fin_enron_debacle_spurs.html>.

Pensions & Investments. 2002. "The Top 200 Pension Funds/Sponsors", January 21: 12.

Perun, Pamela. 2000. "Employee Stock Ownership Plans: A Status Report." *The Retirement Project Brief Urban,* Urban Institute, Washington.

Plan Sponsor. 2002. "Insights on Company Stock." Web page on Enron and related company stock controversies. <www.plansponsor.com/eprise/main/PlanSponsor/News/Finance/costockindex>.

Purcell, Patrick J. 2002. "Employer Stock in Retirement Plans: Investment Risk and Retirement Security." Congressional Research Service, Washington.

Rosen, Corey. 2002. "New Data Show that ESOPS and 401k Plans Heavily Invested in Company Stock Are More Likely to Have Other Retirement Plans As Well." February 17, <www.nceo.org/columns/cr107.html>.

Schneyer, Fred. 2002. "Kmart: Our 401K Plan is Still Safe." *Plansponsor.com.* January 24. <www.plansponsor.com/content/news/finance/kmartbankrupt>.

Schulz, Ellen E. and Theo Francis. 2002*a*. "Enron Pensions Had More Room at the Top." *Wall Street Journal* January 232002, p. A4.

——— 2002*b*. "Companies" Hot Tax Break: 401(k)s." *Wall Street Journal,* January 31, 2002, p. C1.

Smiley, Robert W. and Gregory K. Brown. 2001. "Employee Stock Ownership Plans." In *Handbook of Employee Benefits,* ed. J. Rosenbloom. New York: McGraw Hill.

VanDerhei, Jack. 2002. "The Role of Company Stock in 401(k) Plans—Written Statement for the House Education and Workforce Committee." Employee Benefits Research Institute, Washington, DC. February 13.

Vanguard Group. 2001. "Expecting Lower Returns in the Short Run." *Vanguard Participant Monitor.* Vanguard Center for Retirement Research, November.

Ward, Judy. 2001. "The Match Game." *Plan Sponsor* November: 104, 106.

Chapter 4

Company Stock and Pension Plan Diversification

Krishna Ramaswamy

Defined contribution (DC) plans are an important and growing form of private retirement system in the United States,[1] and they are growing increasingly popular in the rest of the world as well (see Walliser, Chapter 11, this volume and Turner and Rajnes, Chapter 12, this volume). In many of these plans, the employee's contribution to the plan is matched by the employer, so there is a strong incentive to participate. A notable feature of such plans is that the employee takes charge of his own investment decisions, thereby bearing the risk of fluctuating returns to the chosen investments. By contrast, the defined benefit (DB) plan specifies a promised benefit formula for the employee, and the employer funds the plan and selects its investment portfolio. In this latter case, the risk of DB plan asset returns is borne by company shareholders, together with the Pension Benefit Guaranty Corporation in the US context.

A key feature of a DC plan, often perceived as a plus, is that it empowers the beneficiary to take charge of his retirement planning in accordance with his income and preferences. Nevertheless market volatility and corporate bankruptcies have underscored the lack of adequate diversification in the portfolios of many DC plan participants. DC participants with lopsided portfolios, holding a great deal of company stock, have suffered losses when their employers experience financial distress. Sometimes employees hold undiversified positions because the firm's matching contribution is made in company stock, and this investment may not be altered until they attain a certain age (typically 50 or 55). Even when an employee is permitted to direct his employer's matching contribution, the data indicate that employees tend to invest substantial amounts in company stock, and hence they are inadequately diversified.[2] Note, however, that there is no insurance provided to DC plan participants to protect them against the avoidable decline in their portfolios due to overweighted company stock. By contrast, DB plan sponsors have access to insurance against decline in plan assets, and furthermore

I am grateful to Olivia Mitchell and Steve Utkus for their comments, to Ron Stambaugh and Craig MacKinlay for helpful discussions, and to Choong-Tze Chua and Alexander Grantcharov for research assistance.

they are restricted from owning more than 10 percent of company stock in the plan portfolio (see Mitchell and Utkus, Chapter 3, this volume).

What causes employees to sometimes ignore the sensible advice that they should diversify, given that they are surely provided such advice from many sources? The fact that this question is hard to answer points out that academics may have failed to educate practitioners and professionals who dispense investment advice to the typical DC plan participant.[3] Finance textbooks, of course, show that dividing a portfolio's wealth equally among an increasing number of (randomly chosen) equities lowers portfolio variance. Furthermore, Modern Portfolio Theory shows that knowledge of the means, variances, and covariances can help find a portfolio that minimizes risk at every level of expected return. Surprisingly, these ideas have apparently not been harnessed to assess the diversification level of a typical 401(k) plan participant's portfolio.[4]

This chapter makes two contributions. First, it develops a measure of the diversification level in a DC plan participant's portfolio. This measure computes how much additional risk reduction can be had by reallocating investments among the choices permitted *within* the DC plan, without changing the expected return of the currently chosen portfolio. (Of course, the participant may be constrained from reallocating that part of his portfolio held in company stock.) I call this an "efficiency" measure, related to the closeness to the frontier discussed in Kandel and Stambaugh (1995). It computes the reduction in risk available by moving to the mean–variance efficient frontier, at the participant's chosen level of expected return. It should be emphasized that in the current context, we confine ourselves to examining the diversification of the individual's 401(k) plan assets; thus we ignore the possibility that he might have sizable assets and achieve diversification outside the plan.

Second, the chapter shows that the plan participant can privately avail himself of insurance against the decline in his wealth attributable to his undiversified position within the DC plan. This insurance takes the form of an option contract that gives the recipient the higher of the return to company stock or a diversified (suggestively, index) portfolio over a given future term: the resulting return would be applied to the dollar amount invested in company stock. This insurance gives the participant a rate of return at least as great as on the diversified index, when applied to the amount invested in company stock. Indeed, if the employer so chooses, this insurance can be attached to the matching contribution made in company stock. The cost of the insurance can be borne by (or shared between) the plan participant and the employer, providing thereby the proper incentive to both to realize the benefits of a diversified portfolio. Even if the DC plan participant elects to self-insure and avoid the purchase of this option, the cost of the insurance can serve as a "monetized" version of the diversification measure.

In an early and closely related study directed at separating the components of *ex post* portfolio performance, Fama (1972: 559) calculates a measure he calls *diversification*, defined as the "extra portfolio return the manager's winners have to produce in order to make concentration of resources in them worthwhile." This quantity is precisely the difference in return (using an *ex ante* interpretation) that is required to compensate for having to take an undiversified position. Brennan and Torous (1999) have looked at the cost (in terms of loss of certainty equivalence, using specific preference assumptions) to investors in choosing an inadequately diversified position. Meulbroek (2002) evaluates the cost to an employee of the grant of company stock within a DC plan; her assessment of this cost relates to the value that is lost due to the lowered level of diversification, an assessment closely related to Fama's computation of the foregone return. This lost value serves as a measure of a dollar discount to the share price at which the employee would have the same Sharpe-ratio (expected excess return to total portfolio risk, or standard deviation of return) as the market portfolio. The efficiency measure described in the present chapter at the plan participant's chosen level of expected return computes the fraction of total risk that the employee takes, that is rewarded, from the menu of assets within the DC Plan. In contrast to Fama's and Meulbroek's analysis, which is embedded in a capital market equilibrium, I have embedded the problem within the more narrow context of a set of DC plan menu assets.

In what follows, I first show how the measure of diversification efficiency is computed. Next, I show how one can use Margrabe's formula to find the cost of private insurance for a DC plan portfolio that has a fraction allocated to company stock, where I specialize that insurance to apply to the company stock holdings, although it can be regarded in a more general context. A final section concludes.

DC Plans and Portfolio Diversification

A typical participant in a DC plan is permitted to allocate his contribution, as well as his company's matching contribution (if and when that is permitted under plan rules), between at least four to five professionally managed investment alternatives (Mitchell and Schieber, 1998). One of these alternatives may be a money market fund; one may be a bond fund; one of the funds might be a balanced fund, combining equities and bonds in an active mix; and the remaining alternatives tend to be equity funds, of which one might be a low-cost passive vehicle. Employees are typically offered a company stock fund as an investment choice, and especially for larger firms, the company's matching contribution is made in company stock. In some plans, the employer's matching contribution in company stock is not subject to the employee's self-directed asset allocation decision until the worker attains a certain age. It is possible then for the portfolio allocation of the employee's assets within the DC plan to become lopsided and inadequately diversified, and especially so if the employee allocates part of his own contribution toward company stock.

The benefits of diversification are by now very well known. In an early paper, Samuelson (1967) showed that the outcome of diversification—equal division of investment among N alternatives, sometimes called naive diversification—follows, whenever the joint distribution of returns to securities shows symmetry in the interdependence among them. Finance textbooks usually depict the variance (risk) reduction available from dividing a portfolio's wealth equally among an increasing number of securities, the conclusion being drawn either from a simulation or from portfolios with successively increasing numbers of randomly chosen equities. Benefits from international diversification are also shown to depend on the strength of correlation between domestic and foreign market indices. Indeed, more sophisticated models for risk decomposition permit examination of the exposure of a chosen portfolio to particular risk factors, to industry sectors, and to investment styles.

Bernheim (1998) notes that the average employee may have other financial assets and private savings elsewhere, outside 401(k) plan assets, but those savings typically will not guarantee an adequate level of post-retirement income. One could argue that even though the employee's 401(k) investments are not diversified, his overall savings may well be, although there is little evidence supporting such a conclusion. In addition, as is often observed, the employee's human capital is at least partly dependent on the company's fortunes, which might make a further tilt toward company stock within the DC plan questionable.

Is it possible to design a measure that assesses the level of diversification of an individual's portfolio in the DC plan context? Conventional measures of portfolio diversification rely on the number of securities within the portfolio and the strength of the average correlation between these securities (Goetzman and Kumar, 2001). Using these might lead an observer to conclude that there is a sufficient number within the participant's portfolio, even though the weighting of one particular security (company stock) might be several multiples of the weight in any other security.

Another measure relates to the familiar mean–variance efficient frontier, which is the locus of all minimum risk (variance of return) positions at different levels of reward (expected return). Given an individual's particular portfolio chosen from his set of opportunities; one may seek a feasible portfolio chosen from the same set with less risk, at the same level of expected return as the chosen portfolio. It would tell investors how "close" their actual portfolios are to an efficient choice. The measure itself is not new, having been proposed by Kandel and Stambaugh (1995) as a measure of closeness to the mean–variance efficient frontier.[5]

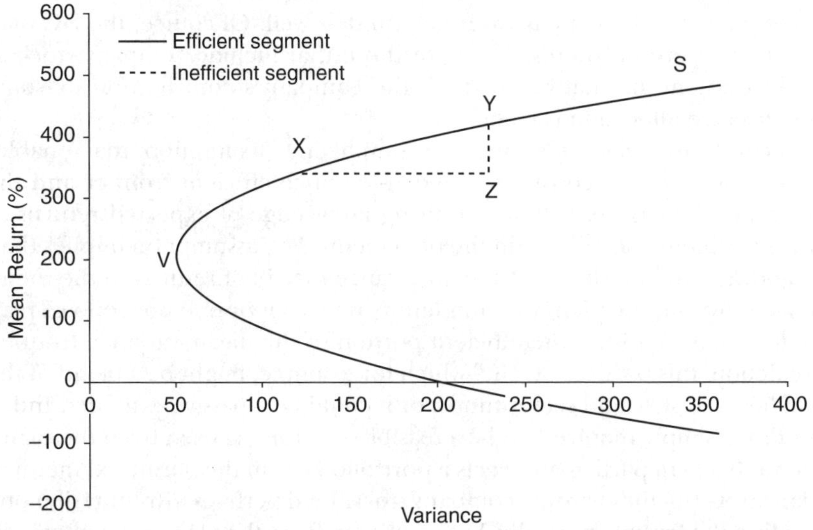

Figure 4-1. Portfolio efficient frontier. (*Source*: Author's computations.)

In the familiar mean–variance framework, this involves moving from the point (Z) representing the individual's portfolio due west to the point (X) on the efficient frontier, as shown in Figure 4-1. Then the ratio of the variance of X to that of Z

$$\eta_z = \frac{\sigma_X^2}{\sigma_Z^2} \tag{1}$$

represents a measure of how diversified Z is relative to X. At one extreme, the measure η_z approaches 0: this happens when $\sigma_X^2 \gg \sigma_Z^2$, or when the individual's chosen portfolio Z is "far" from the frontier and extremely undiversified given the investment alternatives available to him. At the other extreme, η_z is equal to 1.0, when Z is on the frontier and coincides with X. Here the individual has chosen an efficient portfolio, and no further reduction in risk is possible at the chosen level of expected return.

In the current context, when investment allocations among risky assets within a DC plan are of interest, we can adapt the computation of the frontier in useful ways. First, we make the set of investment choices into which a plan participant allocates his 401(k) wealth as the primitive assets with which the mean variance frontier is generated. One may properly call such a frontier one that embodies "constrained" mean–variance efficiency with respect to the assets in the DC plan menu, which is itself a subset of the very large universe of equity securities and portfolios on offer in the capital markets. As described above, the typical DC plan menu includes at least three to four mutual funds, including a stable value fund and a balanced fund, and some menus include a passive Index fund as well. Of course, the DC plan menus that are of interest to us are those that include company stock as an investment alternative in which the company's contribution or some self-directed allocation is made.

Second, we make a strong but simplifying assumption that enables computation of the constrained mean–variance efficient frontier and the "closeness" measure, *without* requiring knowledge of expected returns to the investment choices within the plan menu. The assumption implies that, in addition to knowledge of the covariance matrix of returns to the menu of assets within the plan, we can identify one asset or one portfolio of plan menu assets that is on the efficient portion of the mean–variance frontier. We denote this portfolio as "S," which for example, might be a blend of the S&P500 and style and sector funds; or it could be a passive extended Index fund. We simply require S to be a feasible portfolio chosen from the plan's menu. If a plan participant elects a portfolio Z from the permitted menu of plan assets (including some company stock, held perhaps involuntarily) one can find the feasible portfolio X, also chosen from the plan menu, that is on the mean–variance efficient frontier and that has the same expected return as her chosen portfolio Z. The efficiency measure of how well portfolio Z is diversified can then be computed. This measure varies between zero and one, where a value of one indicates the ideal—an efficiently chosen investment at its level of expected return. This may not be achievable if the plan participant cannot reallocate the company's matching contribution made in company stock.

In order to compute this measure η_z, we must know the location of Z and X. Essentially, one must know the locus of the mean–variance frontier, given the set of investment opportunities. This requires knowledge of the vector of expected returns and the variance–covariance matrix of the returns and the investment alternatives, and access to a standard optimization program that will trace the frontier. As long as there is a sufficient history of the returns to these investment alternatives, the covariance matrix can be estimated: indeed there are several commercially available risk measurement services that can be used in this context.

Estimation of the vector of expected returns given to the list of available plan assets is more difficult. Assessing the *ex ante* return for company stock requires forecasting future earnings, which is difficult. Worse still, this forecast might be the subject of disagreement when analyzing the influence of company stock contributed into the plan participant's portfolio. Forecasting the expected returns to other investment alternatives within the plan menu is equally difficult, whether we use a top-down or bottom-up approach. A model-based approach requires forecasts of market risk premiums in the context of an equilibrium pricing model.

It is also well known that the average returns computed from historical data (as estimates of expected returns) have low precision, and that their use in constructing mean–variance efficient portfolios can lead to extreme weights. Indeed, in practice, restrictions must be placed to constrain these weights to acceptable levels, or some form of shrinkage must be employed in adjusting the mean vector of returns.

The objective is to compute the η_z measure for any individual's portfolio chosen from a menu of the DC plan, restricting the information available to only the covariance matrix of returns and without recourse to a forecast of the expected returns to each of the assets offered in the DC plan menu. This appears clearly impossible in practice, for with that restricted information set, one can only identify the global minimum variance portfolio V in Figure 4-1. It turns out, however, that with one additional assumption, one can compute the η_z measure for any portfolio Z chosen from that DC plan menu. This assumption requires that: (A) *One known portfolio combination of the DC plan assets is on the efficient segment of the minimum variance frontier constructed from the DC plan menu.*

Figure 4-1 indicates the portfolio referred to in Assumption (A) as S; we require it to be on the positively sloped portion (the efficient segment) of the frontier.[6] This ensures that we know another point on the mean–variance frontier, or equivalently one of the portfolios other than V, chosen from the DC plan menu, that is on the mean–variance efficient frontier. Notice that one need not forecast the expected returns to portfolio S or even portfolio Z.

If the plan menu offers a low cost passive index fund, then many may find the assumption that that passive vehicle was chosen as portfolio S to be reasonable. If, in addition, the plan menu offers other style or sector funds that provide exposure to value or growth stocks, or international assets, for example, then a predefined and suitable mixture of these assets can be assumed to be point S on the frontier.

Assumption (A) is strong: it supplants the need to forecast expected returns to all the assets in the DC plan menu. Because the DC plan sponsor usually chooses from available investment funds to put into the menu of plan choices, it is typically the case that each of these choices is reasonably diversified in terms of its own holdings, on a stand-alone basis. In some instances, where the plan participant has not elected to self-direct an allocation across the plan menu, the employer employs a default allocation with an acceptable diversification level and an acceptable trade-off of risk and return to some risk-averse investor (Choi et al., 2002).[7] Nevertheless, it need not follow that this choice, or a particular combination of available choices, is on the minimum–variance frontier. Indeed, individuals with heterogeneous beliefs might disagree as to the values of the expected returns, so that they may not agree that a particular portfolio S is on the efficient frontier.[8]

Computation of the Efficiency Measure

We next demonstrate how assumption (A) permits us to compute our efficiency measure η_z for a given portfolio Z. We define $\tilde{r}_j$ as the return to any asset (or portfolio) j, and Ω as the ($N \times N$ positive definite) covariance matrix of the returns to the $i = 1, 2, \ldots, N$ risky investment alternatives within the DC plan's menu of offerings. Let the N-th investment alternative be company stock. The individual's total wealth in the 401(k) or DC plan is comprised of investments made with his own contributions, as well as matching company contributions. If individual Z elects to direct part or all of those amounts, the vector $w_Z = \{w_{Z_i} i = 1, 2, \ldots, N\}$ represents the resulting investment proportions in each of the N investment alternatives, with

$$\sum_{i=1}^{N} w_{Z_i} = 1 \tag{2}$$

These investment proportions are computed using the aggregate wealth (including all company match contributions) in the plan.

The variance of the return on his portfolio is given by:

$$\sigma_Z^2 = w_Z' \Omega w_Z \tag{3}$$

The *global* minimum variance portfolio V has an associated vector of investment proportions w_Z, which is the solution to

$$\underset{\{w_{V_i}, i=1,2,\ldots N\}}{\text{Min}} \quad w_V' \Omega w_V \quad \text{subject to} \sum_{i=1}^{N} w_{V_i} = 1 \tag{4}$$

Notice that short sales are permitted, so the resulting global minimum variance portfolio may have some negative weights. Of course, the global minimum variance portfolio would not be optimal for any one unless he is "infinitely" risk-averse. These weights can be computed with the knowledge of the covariance matrix alone, so given this information we can compute the variance of V as:

$$\sigma_V^2 = w_V' \Omega w_V \tag{5}$$

To compute the η_Z measure, we need to find the portfolio X that is on the frontier with the same mean as the individual's chosen portfolio Z. The following three well-known properties of the mean–variance frontier (see Huang and Litzenberger, 1988), in addition to Assumption A, are sufficient to locate the investment weights in portfolio X:

Property 1. The investment proportions in any portfolio on the minimum variance frontier are a weighted sum (with weights that sum to unity) of the investment proportions of any two distinct portfolios that are also on the minimum variance frontier.

Property 2. The covariance of the return on any portfolio with the global minimum variance portfolio V is equal to the variance of the global minimum portfolio's return, σ_V^2.

Property 3. The covariance of any portfolio Z with the portfolio X that is on the minimum variance frontier and that has the same expected return as Z is equal to the variance of the return to the frontier portfolio X. The first property is well-known: it says that the mean–variance frontier is spanned by any two portfolios that are on the frontier.[9] It enables us to identify X as a weighted average of the investment proportions in two portfolios that are known to be on the frontier. In terms of our notation, if portfolios S, X, and V are known to be on the frontier, then there is a number λ such that:

$$\lambda w_{S_i} + (1 - \lambda) w_{V_i} = w_{X_i} \quad \text{for } i = 1, 2, \ldots, N \tag{6}$$

The second and the third properties follow from the fact that the frontier portfolios V and X have minimum variance, so that the separate portfolio combinations of either Z and V or of Z and X, respectively, attain their minimum variances when the weight on Z is set to zero. In other words Properties 2 and 3 state that:

$$\sigma_{ZV} \equiv \text{Cov}(\tilde{r}_Z, \tilde{r}_V) = \sigma_V^2 \quad \text{and} \quad \sigma_{ZX} \equiv \text{Cov}(\tilde{r}_Z, \tilde{r}_X) = \sigma_X^2. \tag{7}$$

To find the value of λ we use these properties to compute

$$\text{Cov}(\tilde{r}_Z, \tilde{r}_X) = \text{Cov}(\tilde{r}_Z, \lambda \tilde{r}_S + (1 - \lambda)\tilde{r}_V) \tag{8}$$

Using Property 3, the above relation is set equal to

$$\text{Var}(\tilde{r}_X) = \text{Var}(\lambda \tilde{r}_S + (1 - \lambda)\tilde{r}_V) \tag{9}$$

The solution for λ from the above two relations is

$$\hat{\lambda} = \frac{\sigma_{SZ} - \sigma_V^2}{\sigma_S^2 - \sigma_V^2}. \tag{10}$$

Given this value for $\hat{\lambda}$ we can show that the efficiency measure η_z for portfolio Z is

$$\eta_z = \frac{\sigma_x^2}{\sigma_z^2} = \hat{\lambda}^2 \frac{\sigma_S^2}{\sigma_z^2} + \{1 - \hat{\lambda}^2\} \frac{\sigma_v^2}{\sigma_z^2} \tag{11}$$

It is easy to verify that if the investor chooses S as her optimal portfolio so that $Z = S$, then $\hat{\lambda} = \eta_z = 1$; and if he chose a portfolio on the mean variance efficient frontier, such as $Z = X$, then by construction $\eta_z = 1$.[10]

It is natural to ask, in this context, whether it is possible to find a portfolio Y, which has the same variance as Z but a higher expected return. That frontier portfolio would be due north of Z in the mean–variance diagram, as shown in Figure 4-1. Then the portfolios in the segment XY would be preferred (by the preferences of investors using mean variance analysis) to portfolio Z, as they would all offer either a higher mean return or a lower variance, or both, relative to Z. In order to compute the investment proportions in portfolio Y, we would use Property 1 to find a number γ such that Y is a combination of V and S, satisfying the variance condition

$$\sigma_Z^2 = \mathrm{Var}(\tilde{r}_y) = \mathrm{Var}(\gamma \tilde{r}_s + (1-\gamma)\tilde{r}_v). \tag{12}$$

Solving the above relation for $\hat{\gamma}$,

$$\hat{\gamma} = \sqrt{\frac{\sigma_z^2 - \sigma_v^2}{\sigma_s^2 - \sigma_v^2}}, \tag{13}$$

so that the weights in portfolio Y can be recovered from

$$w_{Yi} = \hat{\gamma} w_{Si} + (1-\hat{\gamma}) w_{Vi}, \quad i = 1, 2, \ldots, N. \tag{14}$$

Note that if $\sigma_Z^2 = \sigma_S^2$ then $\hat{\gamma}$=1 and Y= S.

Portfolios along the segment XY on the efficient frontier in Figure 4-1 will be strictly preferred to portfolio Z by all risk-averse plan participants with preferences that are described by the mean and variance of their portfolio returns. It should be emphasized that it is not possible to fix a measure of "closeness" of the chosen portfolio Z to portfolio Y without having information on the vector of mean returns to the available assets.

A more general analysis that examines the diversification level of a portfolio that is chosen from the larger universe of all capital assets—not just the DC plan menu—would find that the frontier would offer opportunities for even further risk reduction at every level of expected return; the efficient frontier would be to the left of the frontier constrained to DC plan choice as shown in Figure 4-1. If we then specify a different portfolio, S', on that frontier, then we could find the westward frontier portfolio, X', and recompute the efficiency measure η_z in the same way as shown above. Those computed measures would generally be smaller (reflecting the possibly additional risk reduction obtainable from the larger universe of assets) than computed from the constrained frontier. If, in addition, we were to estimate expected returns and risks to the larger universe of assets, and we assumed the existence of a riskless asset, then the frontier would collapse[11] to the familiar Capital Market Line (CML). In this case, we could compute both the reduction in risk to the CML at the same level of expected return as Z, and the foregone expected return at the same level of risk as Z (Meulbroek, 2002).

The efficiency measure η_z is equal to the square of the correlation coefficient between portfolios Z and X; it is therefore the same as the diversification measure corresponding to the R^2 of a market model regression of the returns to portfolio Z regressed on a chosen benchmark X. Such a measure is discussed in Sharpe (1970). Many performance measurement services (for example, Morningstar) report the R^2 measure in the context of a regression of fund returns on the returns to a chosen market index. Here we have found portfolio X from the knowledge of the DC plan menu's choices and designed it to have the same mean as the participant's chosen portfolio Z.

Sample Calculations

Suppose now that the 401(k) portfolio Z chosen by a plan participant has a fraction w_{zn} of the portfolio wealth invested in company stock, the N-th asset, either by virtue of the company contribution made in locked-up company stock or due to a self-directed contribution. The remaining fraction $(1 - w_{zn})$ is distributed among the other choices within the plan menu. Then the η_z measure for his portfolio would indicate the extent to which his portfolio was undiversified.

We can easily compute η_z for different values of the fraction invested in company stock. For simplicity, assume that the remaining fraction is invested in the mean–variance efficient portfolio S; the efficiency numbers therefore correspond to a "best" case, and in practice, participant portfolios are likely to be less efficient at each level of company stock holding. The following parameters are used: $\sigma_v = 0.1, \sigma_s = 0.18$, and we use cases with low, average, and high risk companies whose "market" betas β_n computed with respect to S are 0.8, 1.0, and 1.2 respectively.

Table 4-1 shows values for the efficiency measure η_z for holdings of company stock from 10 percent to 90 percent. Mitchell and Utkus (Chapter 3, this volume) report that the fraction of self-directed wealth in 401(k) plans averages nearly 30 percent; when the company match contribution is included, it averages approximately 53 percent. The table shows that for these values of the holdings of company stock the efficiency measures are, in the best case, 0.64 and 0.39, respectively. In some larger firms (Purcell, 2002), participants have holdings of company stock as high as 90 percent, and for these portfolios, the η_z measure is the least in each case.

It is noteworthy that DB plans are restricted to holding no more than 10 percent in company stock; at that level of holding, and assuming that the balance is in an efficient portfolio, the efficiency measure is in the 90-percent range for the three cases shown in Table 4-1.

Insurance Against a Decline in Portfolio Wealth due to Company Stock Investment

The diversification measure discussed in the previous section has the potential to be a useful tool, especially to those familiar with Modern Portfolio

TABLE 4-1 Values of the Diversification Measure η_z

Company Weighting w_{zn}	*Low Risk* ($\sigma_n = 0.35, \beta = 0.8$)		*Average Risk* ($\sigma_n = 0.48, \beta = 1.0$)		*High Risk* ($\sigma_n = 0.60, \beta = 1.2$)	
	σ_z	η_z	σ_z	η_z	σ_z	η_z
0.1	0.1793	0.97	0.1855	0.94	0.1920	0.91
0.2	0.1843	0.88	0.2012	0.80	0.2182	0.74
0.3	0.1945	0.76	0.2250	0.64	0.2544	0.56
0.4	0.2093	0.63	0.2546	0.50	0.2968	0.43
0.5	0.2277	0.51	0.2881	0.39	0.3432	0.33
0.6	0.2489	0.41	0.3245	0.31	0.3922	0.27
0.7	0.2723	0.33	0.3628	0.25	0.4429	0.22
0.8	0.2973	0.26	0.4025	0.20	0.4948	0.18
0.9	0.3236	0.21	0.4432	0.16	0.5475	0.15

In constructing the table, we assume the standard deviation of the return to the global minimum variance portfolio, $\sigma_v = 0.1$; and the standard deviation of the return to portfolio S, $\sigma_s = 0.18$.

Source: Author's computations.

Note: These computations assume that the DC plan participant has a fraction w_{zn} of his portfolio Z, including the company matching contribution, in company stock, the N-th asset; and the balance of the portfolio investment proportion $(1 - w_{zn})$ in a feasible portfolio S, which is on the efficient portion of the minimum variance efficient frontier, constructed with the assets within the DC plan menu. The measure η_z is the ratio of the variance of his portfolio Z to the variance of a portfolio X that is on the efficient frontier and that has the same expected return as Z.

Theory. To others, it may appear to take on the aspect of an amulet, with no easily comprehensible benefit to increasing the diversification level within their portfolios. Nevertheless, it is possible to provide the DC plan participant with a more immediate and tangible measure of his undiversified stance by monetizing this measure into a price.

Suppose the DC plan participant were offered insurance, for a fee, that would give him the return on the better performing of two assets: company stock, or a well-diversified efficient portfolio S, both feasible choices within his DC plan menu. This return guarantee would be applied to the dollar value of his chosen investment in company stock, at the expiration of the term of the insurance. This insurance contract is equivalent to providing him with an exchange option, first analyzed by Margrabe (1977). The exchange option here permits the DC plan participant to exchange his ownership of shares in company stock for a fixed number of units of the efficiently diversified portfolio S at the option's expiry date. The right to "swap" his ownership of the company stock into a fixed number of units of the diversified portfolio S would be exercised if the value of the latter were greater than the value of the shares invested in company stock, on the final maturity date of the option.

It is possible for competitive market makers to provide this insurance in a more general setting. For example, it is theoretically possible to provide the plan participant insurance against the "bad" outcome that his investment in a portfolio (Z) chosen from the plan menu, including company stock, might decline *relative* to the performance of the more efficient portfolio X, just as in the previous section. This form of insurance has the property that it must be tailor-made to every participant's chosen portfolio. Rather than discuss the private provision of diverse insurance to a heterogeneous pool of investors with different needs, we confine the discussion here to insurance and the related exchange options that apply to company stock and an efficient portfolio as the benchmark. This focuses attention on the main reason a typical plan participant's portfolio becomes prone to substantial and precipitous declines: overweighting in company stock. By making available the option to swap that investment for a diversified alternative, we would provide him with an insured position at the termination of the option—in the event that company stock declined—providing, thereby, education on the benefits of diversification. Furthermore, a firm that provides a matching contribution in company stock would then recognize the cost incurred in protecting the employee's retirement savings from declines due to the presence of the company stock granted to the employee, at least for the period during which the company stock remained locked in the participant's portfolio.[12]

It is well-known that the Margrabe exchange option's value can be found without resorting to investors' aversion to risk or knowledge of expected returns, by using the assumptions and ideas that underlie the Black-Scholes analysis. The exchange option's price depends upon the volatilities of company stock and the efficient portfolio S, and on the correlation between them. In particular, we assume that the employer's matching contribution is \$1,000 in company stock; that the volatilities of the continuously compounded rate of return on company stock and diversified benchmark portfolio S are given by σ and σ_s, respectively; that the correlation coefficient between the returns on these assets is given by ρ, and that these assets pay a continuous dividend at rate q and q_s, respectively. Then the current (date t) value of the exchange option that permits the participant to exchange the company stock for the future (date T) value of \$1,000 initially invested in the diversified benchmark S is given by:

$$1{,}000 \exp\{-q_s(T-t)\}N(d_1) - 1{,}000 \exp\{-q(T-t)\}N\left(d_1 - \hat{\sigma}\sqrt{T-t}\right), \tag{15}$$

where:

$$\hat{\sigma} = \sqrt{\sigma^2 + \sigma_s^2 - 2\rho\sigma\sigma_s}, \qquad d_1 = \frac{(q_s - q + 0.5\hat{\sigma}^2)(T - t)}{\hat{\sigma}(T - t)}, \tag{16}$$

and the function $N(x)$ represents the standard cumulative normal probability evaluated at x. The volatility $\hat{\sigma}$ is the standard deviation of a position that is effectively long \$1 in the benchmark asset S and short \$1 in company stock.

By virtue of a self-directed allocation or due to the company's matching contribution, an investor who owns \$1,000 worth of company stock and acquires the exchange option will have a dollar amount at the option's expiry date T that guarantees a return that is the greater of the return on company stock or the benchmark asset S.

Sample Valuations

Next we compute the cost of such an insurance policy and show that it becomes very expensive for longer terms. We assume typical parameters for the company stock ($\beta = 1, \sigma = 48$ percent), and we further assume that the volatility of the benchmark asset S is $\sigma_S = 18$ percent. For simplicity, we posit that neither the stock nor the benchmark asset S pays dividends. The cost of insurance to obtain the better performing return between company stock and portfolio S on every \$1,000 invested in company stock turns out to be \$178, or 17.8 percent for a one-year term, a cost that will appear prohibitive to most investors.[13] Administration proposals suggest a 3-year term over which a company's matching contribution may not be reallocated. If an employee wished to purchase such insurance for 3 years, the cost would rise to \$303, or 30.3 percent.[14] If we were to use stocks with varying volatilities, then Figures 4-2 and 4-3 show the cost of the option for 1- and 3-year terms, respectively; in these graphs we have retained the β of the company stock at one.

Clearly, an undiversified position can involve a substantial implicit insurance cost. For cases where the employer's matching contribution is made in company stock, the price of the exchange option is equivalent to a cost imposed on the employee (who might otherwise hold an efficient, well-diversified alternative) for the term that the granted stock remains untradeable.

Implementation

A provider of this form of portfolio insurance will typically seek to hedge by buying a number of units in portfolio S and shorting a certain number of shares in company stock, both these numbers corresponding to the hedge ratios dictated by Margrabe's formula. In actual implementation, however, it is possible (for example) for the grant of company stock to be coupled with exchange options, in which case no explicit short position must be held.

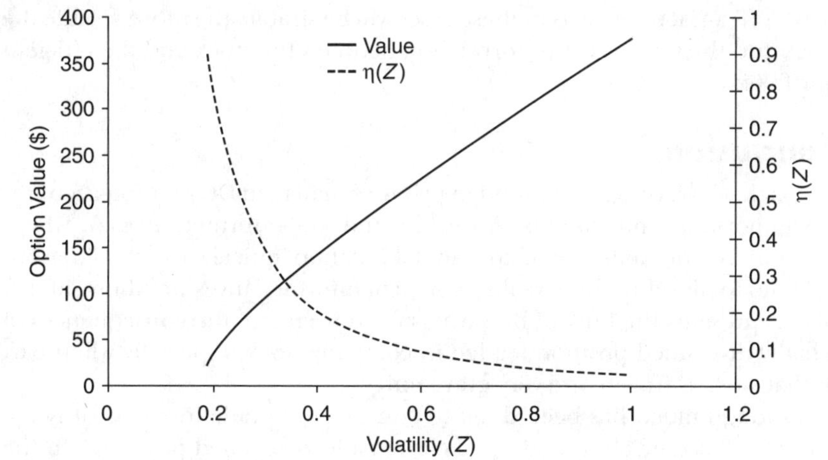

Figure 4-2. Exchange option value (1 year). (*Source*: Author's computations.)

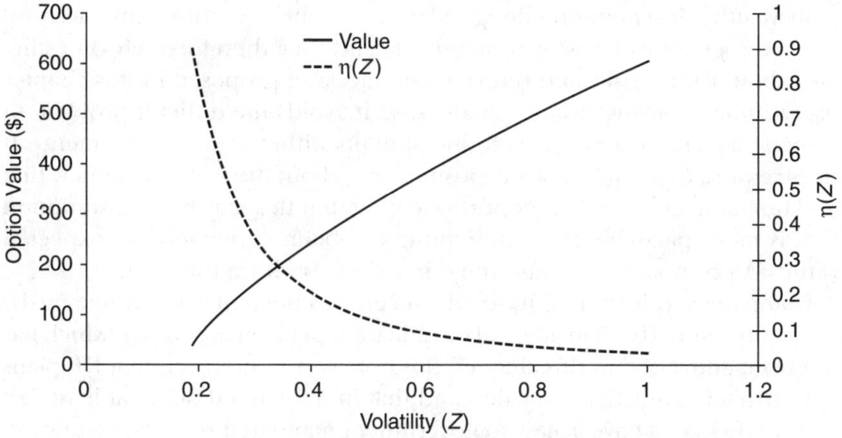

Figure 4-3. Exchange option value (3 year). (*Source*: Author's computations.)

Here the insurance is effected by shifting funds between company stock and the feasible efficient portfolio S, such that at the terminal date, the funds are totally in the better performing of the two assets. Of course, such shifting of funds implicitly assumes that the company stock is tradeable.

One way in which the insurance can be effected would be to grant the matching contribution in company stock and in the efficient portfolio S, in equal dollar amounts. Then instructions would be given to trade out of the underperforming asset and into the better-performing asset in incremental amounts each period. If such a procedure were implemented with the incremental trades corresponding to the changing hedge ratios in Margrabe's formula, then the portfolio will implicitly replicate the insurance option. Transactions costs in these cases will be sizable, the more volatile the stock and the weaker is the correlation between the stock and the efficient portfolio.

Conclusion

The lack of diversification found in privately managed DC pension accounts has important ramifications. A wealthy and well-informed investor whose position is not well-diversified can take action quickly to avoid serious declines to his retirement wealth. For an ill-informed investor, whose 401(k) plan represents the bulk of his savings for retirement, the consequences of a badly diversified position loaded in company stock, especially when part of that stock is frozen, are very grave indeed.

Although much has been done to educate and guide investors, it is still the case that they often end up eliciting badly diversified positions. In the case of 401(k) portfolios, much of this might be avoidable. A first step in this direction is to design a measure that reveals to an investor how efficiently chosen his 401(k) portfolio is, on a stand-alone basis, ignoring his non-DC plan wealth. Most measures designed to answer such questions must account for heterogeneous investor preferences, and they therefore rely on estimates about future risks and returns. The measure proposed in this chapter uses standard mean–variance analysis, so it avoids the difficult problem of forecasting the mean returns to investments within the DC plan menu. It does require us to make a strong assumption about the frontier, namely that we know at least one efficient portfolio on it, but this may be an assumption that is more palatable than attempting to obtain agreement on expected returns to company stock and the other choices within the plan.

Companies typically emphasize the incentive effects of stock ownership by their employees (both inside and outside their pension accounts), which has not been addressed in this chapter. It is noteworthy, however, that DB plans have stricter diversification rules, and that in the United States at least, DB plan participants have access to government-mandated pension insurance. Our research shows that a privately obtainable insurance policy would be very costly, if it were to assure that 401(k) investments in company stock will do at least as well as a diversified position, even in the short term.

Notes

[1] For a comprehensive discussion of these issues, see Mitchell and Schieber (1998).

[2] This finding is not new, for the allocations by retail investors in equity portfolios have been distributed across a handful of (typically three to four) stocks. Early evidence on this point is provided by Blume and Friend (1975) and more recent analysis by Goetzman and Kumar (2001).

[3] Several studies have documented the allocation and participation behavior of DC plan participants and suggested explanations; see Benartzi (2001) Benartzi and Thaler (2001) and Choi et al. (2001).

[4] Many online services provide a simulation platform where investors may evaluate the impact of various allocation alternatives on retirement wealth (see Bodie, Chapter 2, this volume). These platforms typically employ forecasts of expected returns to the investment choices (including company stock), which may be the source of substantial difference of opinion when advocating a shift in allocation. This procedure for assessing how efficiently a plan participant has diversified his 401(k) portfolio requires more information than the measure described below.

[5] The connection between mean variance efficiency of a portfolio and the diversification level characterized by the smallness of weights in the portfolio is studied by Green and Hollifield (1992). They show that the existence of a well-diversified portfolio on the frontier depends on a bound that relates expected returns on the portfolio to its covariance with other assets.

[6] The figure is an example drawn with a level of $\sigma_S > \sigma_Z$. The arguments in the body of the text are general and apply even when $\sigma_S \leq \sigma_Z$.

[7] One could argue that default allocation sometimes invests in money funds or bonds and that it *ought* to have a larger allocation to equities, but that is not the thrust of the present chapter.

[8] Indeed, it is well known that a test of whether portfolio S is on the efficient frontier is equivalent to a test of whether expected returns to assets are linearly related to their betas with respect to S (see Fama, 1976; Roll, 1977). Kandel and Stambaugh (1995) show that the closeness of a portfolio to the frontier need not imply a nearly linear relationship between expected returns and betas.

[9] Property 1 in conjunction with Assumption A (and knowledge of the covariance matrix of plan asset returns) says in effect that the investment proportions of all portfolios that are frontier portfolios are known. This means that agreement as to S being on the frontier is equivalent to agreement as to the investment proportions of all frontier portfolios, but what we cannot specify is their location as to scale along the Y-axis in the traditional mean–variance diagram.

[10] If the employee chooses the global minimum variance portfolio so that $Z = V$ then $\hat{\lambda} = 0$ and $\eta_Z = 1$; but this would be a suboptimal choice. It is possible that the value of $\hat{\lambda}$ is negative: this occurs only if the investor's chosen portfolio has a lower expected return than the minimum variance portfolio V.

[11] Here the plot referred to is that of mean returns versus standard deviation of returns.

[12] We can always interpret our computations and Figure 4-1 to portfolio Z in the general case; it is possible to consider the cost of the insurance as applying to either portfolio Z or to company stock.

[13] Plan participants and company managers might disagree as to the volatility levels and correlation assumed in computing the cost of the insurance. I have chosen parameter values that are representative; the correlation between company stock and the index portfolio S is given by $\rho = \beta \times (\sigma_S/\sigma) = (0.18/0.48) = 0.375$. The higher the correlation coefficient, the lower the cost of the insurance, *ceteris paribus*. It should be noted, however, that even favorable estimates for volatilities and correlations will give prohibitive expensive premiums, as shown in the figures that follow.

[14] Not surprisingly, a 25-year old employee who wanted to buy an insurance policy on company stock that he cannot reallocate until he is 50 years old, would have to pay $739 per $1,000 of stock, retaining the assumption that this is an average beta company stock.

References

Benartzi, Shlomo. 2001. "Excessive Extrapolation and the Allocation of 401(k) Accounts to Company Stock." *Journal of Finance* 56(5): 1747–1764.

— and Richard Thaler. 2001. "Naïve Diversification Strategies in Defined Contribution Plans." *American Economic Review* 91(1): 79–98.

Bernheim, B. Douglas. 1998. "Financial Illiteracy, Education Retirement Savings." *Living with Defined Contribution Pensions*, eds. O. S. Mitchell and Sylvester J. Schieber. Pension Research Council. Philadelphia. PA: University of Pennsylvania Press: 38–68.

Blume, Marshall E. and Irwin Friend. 1975. "The Asset Structure of Individual Portfolios and Some Implications for Utility Functions." *Journal of Finance* 30: 585–603.

Brennan, Michael J. and Walter N. Torous. 1999. "Individual Decision Making and Investor Welfare." *Economic Notes* 28(2).

Choi, James, David Laibson, Brigitte Madrian, and Andrew Metrick. 2001. "DC plans: Plan Rules, Participant Decisions, and the Path of Least Resistance." Rodney White Center for Financial Research, Working Paper No. 001–02, Philadelphia, PA: The Wharton School.

Fama, Eugene F. 1972. "Components of Investment Performance." *Journal of Finance* 27(3): 551–567.

— 1976. *Foundations of Finance.* New York, NY: Basic Books.

Goetzman, William and Alok Kumar. 2001. "Equity Portfolio Diversification." NBER Working Paper 8686. Cambridge, MA.

Green, Richard C. and Burton Hollifield. 1992. "When will Mean–variance Efficient Portfolios be Well-diversified?" *Journal of Finance* 47(5): 1785–1809.

Huang, Chi-fu and Robert H. Litzenberger. 1988. *Foundations for Financial Economics.* New York, NY: North-Holland.

Kandel, Shmuel and Robert F. Stambaugh. 1995. "Portfolio Inefficiency and the Cross-Section of Expected Returns." *Journal of Finance* 50(1): 157–184.

Margrabe, William. 1978. "The Value of an Option to Exchange One Asset for Another." *Journal of Finance*, March: 177–186.

Meulbroek, Lisa. 2002. "Company Stock in Pension Plans: How Costly Is It?" Working Paper 02–058. Boston, MA: Harvard Business School.

Mitchell, Olivia S. and Sylvester J. Schieber (eds.) 1998. *Living with Defined Contribution Pensions.* Pension Research Council, Philadelphia, PA: University of Pennsylvania Press.

Purcell, Patrick J. 2002. "The Enron Bankruptcy and Employer Stock in Retirement Plans." Congressional Research Service. Washington: The Library of Congress.

Roll, Richard. 1977. "A Critique of The Asset Pricing Theory's Tests: Part I." *Journal of Financial Economics* 4: 129–176.

Samuelson, Paul A. 1967. "General Proof that Diversification Pays." *Journal of Financial and Quantitative Analysis.* Chapter 210 in *The Collected Papers* of Paul Samuelson, Vol 3, ed. R. C. Merton. Cambridge, MA: MIT Press.

Sharpe, William F. 1970. *Portfolio Theory and Capital Markets.* New York, NY: McGraw Hill.

Chapter 5

Integrating Payouts: Annuity Design and Public Pension Benefits in Mandatory Defined Contribution Plans

Suzanne Doyle and John Piggott

Defined contribution (DC) style retirement systems have proliferated as partial or complete substitutes for mandatory social security, spawning a growing literature on their possible economic impacts,[1] but associated payout structures have received surprisingly little attention. Nevertheless, DC type retirement provision support and individual retirement accounts pose special challenges for the payout phase. Adverse selection in the voluntary annuities market, prudential considerations, and the implications of interactions between annuity payouts and first pillar type social welfare, all suggest that DC retirement systems require some government regulation regarding the nature of associated retirement benefits.

Unlike traditional DB funds, regulations and employer obligations associated with the accumulation phase typically expire at retirement, even if pension options are offered by the accumulation fund. Any payout regulations must therefore be separately stipulated. In practice, a range of options is specified, ranging from lumpsum withdrawal to full annuitization, sometimes subject to the personal circumstances of the retiree.

This chapter focuses on the design of annuities and similar retirement income instruments. It is especially concerned with interactions between annuity preference and underlying publicly provided safety net support. Because DC-type plans expose individuals to investment and inflation risk, governments often provide guarantees on pension fund benefits, as well as non-means tested transfers to the retired. These influence not only the choice of accumulation portfolio, but also the choice of retirement product, through providing a retirement income floor. They further complicate the analysis of annuity and retirement income markets.

The authors are grateful to conference participants, especially Zvi Bodie, Olivia Mitchell, and Andrew Samwick for comments. Lance Fisher, Geoffrey Kingston, Sachi Purcal, and Mike Sherris provided comments and discussion on earlier drafts. They acknowledge financial support from the Economic and Social Research Institute, Cabinet Office, Government of Japan, and the Australian Research Council. All opinions remain the authors' own.

We focus on the interaction between private sources of retirement income and first pillar government transfers. Two forms of government support are modeled: a "pension guarantee," which is withdrawn dollar for dollar with the private payout, and a non-means-tested public pension offered to all retirees at a flat rate. Results emphasize the welfare impacts of alternatives under a range of income assumptions. A number of themes emerge. First, for most retirees, annuities that expose the retiree to investment risk are preferred to annuities guaranteeing certain payments, when the government shares the investment risk by guaranteeing a minimum pension. Second, on an expected basis, in the lower range of wealth accumulations, which characterize an immature mandatory retirement system, these products may generate a lower expected *government* payout than life annuities offering full investment risk coverage. Third, inflation-protected annuity products are highly valued, especially by the rich and risk-averse, though except for the poor, inflation indexed products yielded lower expected public liabilities. This is because over time, the real value of the level annuity can more quickly erode to the point where a pension guarantee is activated. Finally, some products which offer partial longevity insurance such as phased withdrawals may be preferred by consumers to full longevity insurance products, but the former are often associated with high levels of implied government liability.

We begin by detailing the retirement products we consider and present our modeling approach. We conclude by reporting estimates of consumer preference toward alternative products, along with their budgetary implications.

Characterizing Retirement Income Products

For modeling purposes, we focus on five different retirement income instruments, which cover alternative patterns of exposure to longevity, investment, and inflation risks:

1. *Level Life Annuities.* These provide insurance against longevity risk and guarantee a certain payment per period, thus insuring against investment risk. But payments are fixed in nominal terms, so annuitants are fully exposed to inflation risk.
2. *Variable Annuities.* These provide insurance against longevity risk, while at the same time delivering higher expected returns by transferring investment risk to the annuitant. The annuity is written on the basis of an assumed investment return (AIR). Payouts, however, are adjusted by the relationship between the performance of the underlying portfolio, which may be specified by the annuitant, and the AIR. Because investment risk is borne by the annuitant, the AIR may be significantly higher than the risk-free rate.

3. *Inflation-indexed Annuities.* Even a modest inflation rate of 3.5 percent will halve purchasing power in 20 years. Combined with 1-percent wage productivity growth, purchasing power relative to community standards will halve in 16 years. For a retiree with a life expectancy of 15 or more years, as a male retiring at sixty-five would have in most OECD countries, erosion of purchasing power through inflation is thus a significant risk. For longer-lived women, the risk is even greater. While escalated annuities partially address this problem, they do not offer insurance against unanticipated inflation, which may be a larger danger to annuitant welfare.
4. *Term Annuities.* It is possible to purchase an annuity, which provides a guaranteed income stream for a specified period. This kind of product is available for retirement provision in some countries, with a long term. In our calculations, we assume life expectancy as the term set. This product does offer insurance against investment risk, but it offers no longevity insurance.
5. *Phased withdrawals.* The phased withdrawal appears at first sight to be more like a pure investment instrument than a retirement income stream product. Its essence is that a sum of money is invested at retirement, in a portfolio over whose composition the retiree has considerable control. Both income and capital can be drawn down to meet the retiree's needs. The drawdowns, however, are limited to a range, with both upper and lower bounds. These are often set such that the upper bound carries with it an expectation of an even income flow until the life expectancy of the retiree at the point of retirement. The lower bound is set so that withdrawals can be made until the actuarial probability of survival from the date of purchase approximates zero. These "valuation factors" apply to the account accumulation each year.

Retirement Income Payout Streams and First Pillar Benefits

We use a stochastic numerical simulation approach to study consumer preference and government budgetary implications of a number of stylized annuity type payout instruments offered in countries with mandatory DC retirement systems. For convenience, Australian data are used to specify the accumulation, risk-return, and longevity parameters of the model, since this is one of the few developed countries with a fully fledged private DC-type mandatory retirement system. But we consider policy specifications, which are quite general, including some not in operation in Australia.

Calculations of the income flows associated with our menu of annuities are based on variants of standard actuarial formulae. We incorporate stochastic processes for both inflation and real rate of investment returns by assuming that these follow geometric Brownian motion. Assuming that there is no borrowing or lending, these income flows along with stochastic inflation allow us to calculate real consumption in each period in retirement.

The indices associated with both inflation and investment variables grow at trend rates, which are continuously disturbed by random shocks. This "proportional random walk" implies that the volatility of the time path is proportional to the level of the associated index. We further assume that the inflation and real investment return processes are independent.[2] Each of the reported experiments is based on 5,000 draws from a standard normal distribution.

The simulations reported here assume three retirement accumulations, of $100,000, $200,000, and $300,000, to represent low, medium, and high income levels. A full-time worker on average earnings might be expected to accumulate between $150,000 and $200,000 at retirement age 65.[3] These accumulations differentially impact on first-pillar support. For the payout phase, we have assumed a real safe rate of return of 3.5 percent, an expected inflation rate of 3.5 percent, a risky rate of return of 10 percent, and real wage growth of 1 percent. The current real return on a 20-year indexed government bond is 3.68 percent. While inflation over the last century has averaged 4 percent, existing long-term inflation forecasts are somewhat lower; changed Central Bank policy is sometimes appealed to in defense of these lower figures.

The above values imply an equity premium of 3 percent. This may be low by conventional standards, but in a very thorough study, Siegel (1992) argues that over the last two centuries, the equity premium may have been closer to 3–4 percent than to the 6–7 percent range frequently used. He suggests that the high equity premium observed over the sixty-five years to 1990 was due primarily to depressed rates of return on fixed income assets, and that it is unlikely to endure in the future. Because of the long time horizons involved, we have chosen a conservative equity premium estimate. In the stochastic simulations, the return on equities is assumed to have a standard deviation of 0.2. Inflation is assumed to have a standard deviation of 0.02.

Mortality is specified using Australian population survival probabilities, which are compiled by the Australian Government Actuary (1994) every 5 years. For this analysis we use the 1995–97 life tables, modified to reflect the projected cohort mortality improvements that a 65-year-old purchasing an annuity now might experience over time. Australian mortality is close to the OECD norms.

The first pillar payouts are specified to 25 percent of male average weekly earnings, of about $40,000 a year in Australia (2000). The first pillar is thus indexed to wage growth. The 25 percent calibration is consistent with the levels of pension guarantee offered in Switzerland and Chile, and it is also the approximate value of the full "Age Pension" in Australia. In our central case, the guarantee is withdrawn dollar-for-dollar with annuity payments.

These amounts are indexed to wage growth, assumed here to be 4.5 percent nominal.

Results

One way of assessing efficacy of annuity products involves comparing their payout structures at different points in time. Direct comparison of income streams generated by different annuity products offers only a limited guide to their value to consumers, however. Of greater importance are individual preferences toward alternative income (or consumption) profiles. In assessing the effectiveness of alternative policies, economists often base their recommendations on metrics associated with individual welfare, or utility. This approach is readily adapted to the present problem. We adjust the income flows, which different annuity types yield for assumed inflation. Income-tested public sector first pillar payments are then added in. The resulting real income in each period is assumed to finance consumption in that period alone—there is no borrowing or lending in retirement, and no other source of income. This gives an estimate of consumption for each period, and provides the basis for the utility score calculation.[4]

In what follows, we assume a 65-year-old Australian male retires in 2000, having accumulated a retirement benefit throughout his working life. For simplicity, we focus on three income levels, which we represent by the annuity purchase price, and we use male average cohort life expectancy, an assumption justified by mandatory annuity purchase.[5] Table 5-1 reports product-by-product equivalent variations (EVs) for the five retirement income products identified above, in the policy context of a pension guarantee equal to 25 percent of average earnings, offset dollar-for-dollar with private retirement income. The interpretation of the EVs is that they give an estimate of how much an individual would have to pay as a lump sum, at the point of retirement, to make him indifferent between a level life annuity and the alternative. In each case, we assume that only one alternative is available, and that purchase is mandatory, avoiding issues of potential adverse or differential selection across products.

It is convenient to begin by pointing out the salient characteristics of the income streams generated by the menu of products considered here. Longevity insurance offered by the level life annuity, the variable annuity, and the CPI indexed annuity, means that there is no sudden drop in income late in retirement. This is, however, present in the case of the term nominal annuity, and to some degree also with the phased withdrawal.[6] A rather different pattern of income variation is implied by instruments, which expose the purchaser to investment risk. The variable annuity offers longevity risk cover but investment risk exposure; the phased withdrawal exposes the purchaser to both risks.

TABLE 5-1 Consumer Welfare and Public Liability for Alternative Retirement Payout Products (Individual Male aged 65)

	First Year Annuity Income ($)	*First Year Total Income ($)*	*EV ($)* $\gamma = 0.5$	$\gamma = 5$	$\gamma = 10$	*PV ($) Pension Guarantee Payouts*
A: Purchase Price $100,000						
Level	10,976	10,976	n/a	n/a	n/a	33,934
Variable	15,613	15,626	59,089	39,384	30,312	30,242
CPI-indexed	8,394	10,273	−6,519	−7,007	−7,376	33,286
Term	10,719	10,721	−2,333	−2,357	−2,366	48,033
Phased withdrawal	10,723	11,174	26,285	15,599	10,483	44,887
B: Purchase Price $200,000						
Level	21,951	21,951	n/a	n/a	n/a	3,747
Variable	31,226	31,226	79,530	4,335	−20,988	11,745
CPI-indexed	16,788	16,788	−3,409	19,430	55,447	0
Term	21,438	21,438	−5,383	−6,904	−9,098	27,949
Phased withdrawal	21,401	21,401	13,118	−25,057	−41,472	20,241
C: Purchase Price $300,000						
Level	32,927	32,927	n/a	n/a	n/a	505
Variable	46,839	46,839	103,713	−48,703	−88,152	6,284
CPI-indexed	25,181	25,181	1,181	54,100	153,035	0
Term	32,157	32,157	−18,831	−61,086	−91,226	27,933
Phased withdrawal	32,168	32,168	1,149	−84,579	−112,207	12,867

Source: Authors' computations.

The first message from Table 5-1 is the high value placed on the variable annuity by low-income individuals, or by those with low risk aversion. The variable annuity offers a significantly higher expected rate of return, and this is a preferred product for those who are less risk averse, or for low-income individuals heavily reliant on government benefit. Equally important is the pattern of government liabilities reported in the right hand column of the table. Again, for low-income individuals, the expected present value of government payout for the variable annuity is less than for the level annuity, and also for all other retirement instruments we consider. This occurs because at low incomes, the higher expected payouts from the variable annuity reduce government liability relative to instruments, which offer insurance across more dimensions of retirement risk. These latter instruments offer a lower payout than the expected income from a variable annuity.

For the more risk-averse high income groups, however, the variable annuity comes last. For these individuals, there is little downside protection from government support, because their expected retirement incomes lie above the safety net range. At the same time, their preferences are specified so that they have an intense aversion to income volatility resulting from the exposure to investment risk associated with a variable annuity. The CPI-indexed annuity is the preferred retirement instrument for the rich and risk-averse. The strong preference in our calculations for this annuity type, compared with market experience, where demand is consistently reported to be weak, is surprising. One possible explanation is that CPI-indexed annuities are offered with far higher loadings in the commercial market than level annuities, which inhibits demand.[7]

In general, the term annuity fares worst in terms of its appeal to consumers. This is probably because there is no consistency of exposure to volatility over time. For the first 15 years, a safe, smooth return is offered; this appeals to the very risk averse, while those less averse to risk miss out on the higher expected returns generated by products associated with riskier portfolios. After that time, there is a considerable movement in consumption flows, which the risk averse dislike. No matter how preference toward risk is specified, this product has unattractive features. Furthermore, the public pension payout associated with term annuity purchase is much higher than for the level life annuity. This product may, of course, score better if a bequest argument were incorporated into the preference function.

Given our "medium" assumption over phased withdrawal drawdown, the first year payout from the allocated annuity is not particularly high. But the EVs are such that the allocated annuity ranks second overall to the variable annuity, given a purchase price of $200,000. However, as with the term annuity, the expected present value of public pension payments are high, given that the retiree relies on these payments as their only income source later in life.

It is difficult to capture the phased withdrawal's appeal in the preference framework used here. It generates a significant value of expected bequests, and also leaves considerable discretion over capital drawdown for the duration of life expectancy. Neither of these features is captured in our preference function, yet both are valued by individuals.

Table 5-1 reports results that are substantively different in the degree to which first pillar support might be relied upon. For the base $200,000 case, Figures 5-1 and 5-2 reveal this clearly. The non-indexed annuity streams remain flat over time, but when combined with first pillar payouts, total retirement income increases over time as the increasing pension guarantee comes into play for the latter stages of the annuity payout.

Sensitivity of our findings to changes in the assumed values of parameters is reported in Table 5-2. The safe real rate of return and the expected rate of inflation are varied for the base case of a $200,000 accumulation. Results

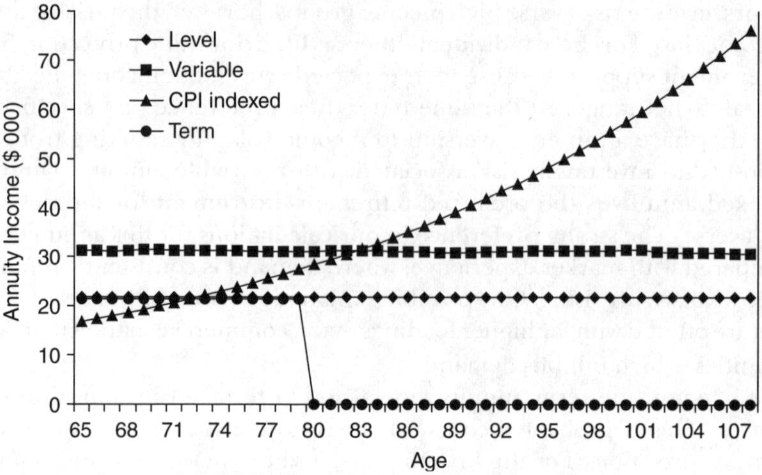

Figure 5-1. Expected annuity income paths. (*Source*: Author's computations.)

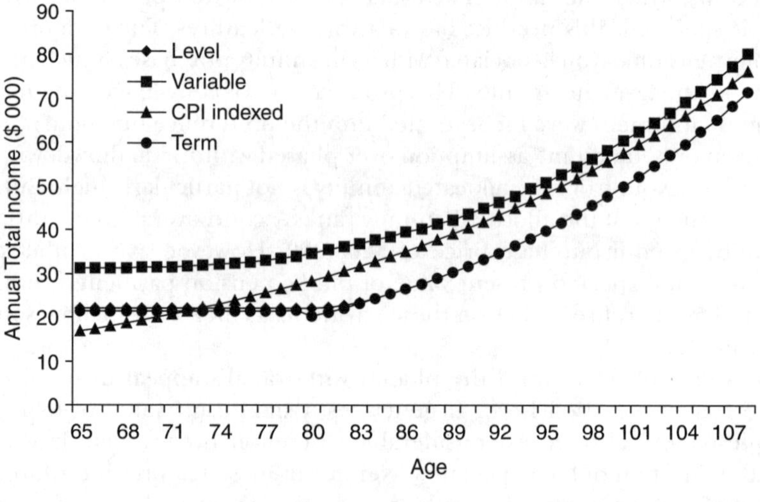

Figure 5-2. Expected total income paths with pension guarantee. (*Source*: Author's computations.)

suggest that first-year annuity payouts are quite robust across these ranges. When we turn to EV calculations, however, we find that some results are highly sensitive to the values of parameters assumed. Their interpretation requires a recognition that the payouts reflect both annuity income and first pillar government benefits. In most cases, rankings do not alter. Where

TABLE 5-2 Parameter Sensitivity Analysis: Inflation and Rate of Return

	2.5%			4.5%		
	First Year Income ($)	*EV ($)*		*First Year Income ($)*	*EV ($)*	
		$\gamma = 1.5$	$\gamma = 5$		$\gamma = 1.5$	$\gamma = 5$
A: Safe rate of return						
Level	20,382	n/a	n/a	23,542	n/a	n/a
Variable	31,226	74,358	20,070	31,226	37,526	−9,474
CPI-indexed	15,398	−5,017	9,779	18,284	6,388	28,665
Term	20,154	−2,618	−3,059	22,752	−8,560	−11,305
Phased withdrawal	21,401	16,331	−11,586	21,401	−12,710	−36,880
B: Inflation rate						
Level	20,382	n/a	n/a	23,542	n/a	n/a
Variable	29,320	53,328	1,244	33,159	55,412	6,798
CPI-indexed	16,643	2,046	13,438	16,954	−1,049	26,064
Term	20,154	−5,321	−8,548	22,752	−6,885	−7,162
Phased withdrawal	21,278	2	−26,959	21,525	601	−23,281

Source: Authors' computations.

Notes: Results reported for $200,000 premium, male 65-year old purchase.

reversals do occur, the explanation can in most cases be found in the relative impacts on first pillar support of relative changes in the payouts of the annuities.

EV values also appear highly sensitive to changes in the underlying real safe rate. The mechanism here relates to the level annuity benchmark. As the safe rate moves up or down, the relative importance of inflation and the equity premium change. For example, in the case of the variable annuity, an increase in the safe rate from 2.5 to 4.5 percent reduces the EV by half for individuals with γ set equal to 1.5, and reverses the ordering when γ is set equal to 5.

Because pension guarantee benefits are indexed to the real wage, the CPI insured instruments do best in limiting public liability, except for the low accumulation group. This public liability associated with non-indexed benefits increases with the expected inflation rate. For expected inflation of 1.5 percent, for example, the expected public liability associated with the variable annuity is $16,000, compared with $11,745 in the standard specification. As well, increases in the real safe rate reduce expected public outlays for instruments whose payouts are based upon safe returns. A level annuity is associated with an expected present value payout of $2,760 if

TABLE 5-3 Parameter Sensitivity Analysis: Equity Premium and Maximum Drawdown ($200,000 premium, male)

	Equity Premium 4%			*Max Drawdown Phased Withdrawal Annuity*		
	First Year Income ($)	*EV ($)*		*First Year Income ($)*	*EV ($)*	
		$\gamma = 1.5$	$\gamma = 5$		$\gamma = 1.5$	$\gamma = 5$
Level	21,951	n/a	n/a	21,951	n/a	n/a
Variable	33,104	66,716	10,688	31,226	54,742	4,335
CPI-indexed	16,823	1,385	20,266	16,823	1,385	20,266
Term	21,438	−5,632	−6,904	21,438	−5,632	−6,904

Source: Authors' computations.

Note: Results reported for $200,000 premium, male 65-year old purchase.

TABLE 5-4 Summary of outcomes for universal pension: Male $200,000

	First Year Annuity Payout ($)	*First Year Total Payout ($)*	*EV ($)*			*PV ($) Universal Pension*
Level	21,951	32,221	n/a	n/a	n/a	133,165
Variable	31,226	41,496	69,620	−27,025	−81,084	133,165
CPI-indexed	16,823	27,093	147	9,817	24,197	133,165
Term	21,438	31,708	−33,738	−114,196	−154,757	133,165
Phased withdrawal	21,401	31,671	−5,246	−68,489	−107,324	133,165

Source: Authors' computations.

Note: Results reported for $200,000 premium, male 65-year old purchase.

the real safe rate is 4.5 percent, compared with $3,747 in the central case specification. First year annuity payout variation, while small, can lead to major differences in first pillar liability.

Table 5-3 reports results from two further variations on our central case specification. Increasing the equity premium leads to higher payouts for instruments relying on risky portfolios. Altering the drawdown pattern of the phased withdrawal changes early year payouts, but also the later year reduction in private income.

Finally, we turn in Table 5-4 to consider the impact of a universal pension to sit beneath private retirement income, rather than a minimum pension guarantee, in which benefits are withdrawn dollar-for-dollar. The clearest

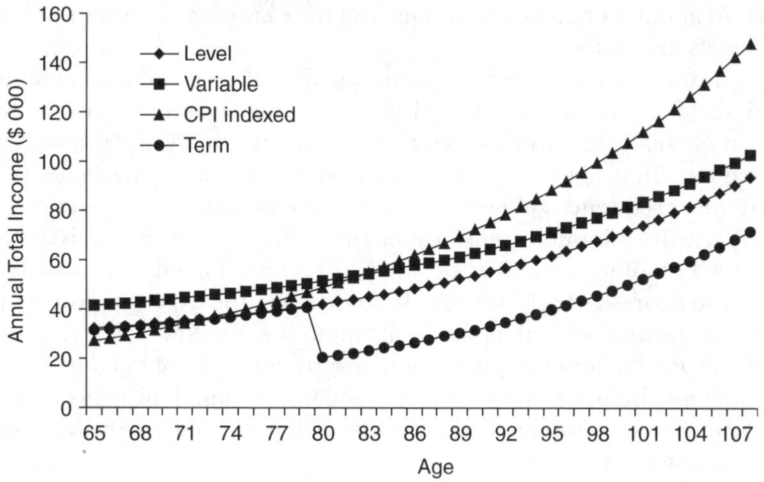

Figure 5-3. Expected total income paths with universal pension. (*Source*: Author's computations.)

impact is that government benefits and therefore retirement income flows, are higher across a wider range of wealth accumulations. These government benefits become more important later in life, as Figure 5-3 indicates.

Consumer preference across annuity types varies with this alternative first pillar design. The variable annuity retains its ranking as the most preferred product for the cases we consider, even though the risk-sharing inherent in the pension guarantee design considered earlier is no longer present. But the replacement of a guarantee with a fixed demogrant does reduce the desirability of the phased withdrawal, whose ranking across the five alternatives drops to fourth. Otherwise, however, the consumer preference ordering across products is the same as that generated in the pension guarantee case.

Conclusion

This chapter investigates the consumer preference and government budget implications of alternative annuity designs in a private mandatory retirement provision environment. We assume a retirement policy framework in which mandatory DC accumulations are paid out at retirement, and regulations over retirement income streams must be separately stipulated. A social welfare safety net is assumed, in which either a minimum pension is guaranteed by the government, or a universal social welfare payment is provided. The minimum pension is similar in broad structure to the US Supplemental Security Income Program (see for example Daly and Burkhauser, forthcoming), which offers a transfer to elderly US citizens or permanent residents equal to about 25 percent of average full time earnings, subject to income and assets means tests.

The insurance coverage and payout profiles of several different annuity products are considered. Numerical simulation of annuity payouts for a 65-year-old male, in the presence of longevity, investment, and inflation risk, is used to gain insight into the implications for social welfare benefits and consumer preference valuation of alternative products by the retiree. We find that with a minimum pension guarantee, the variable annuity is the most preferred of all the annuities we study, for a broad band of accumulation levels and degrees of risk aversion. In some cases, the expected government outlays associated with first pillar obligations are also lower. These findings hold only for the lower accumulation groups, but in a policy context, these are perhaps the most important. Annuity mandation, and concern about government responsibility for individual welfare in retirement, is unlikely to be focussed on the rich.

Another broad finding is that inflation insured annuity products are popular, especially with the rich and risk-averse. As well, except for the poor, inflation-indexed products yield lower expected public liabilities than most other products. Finally, non-life instruments, especially when tied to risky investments, are popular, but they tend to be quite expensive for government revenue.

This chapter considers only two first-pillar safety net designs, which could be seen as two extremes between a variety of alternative tapered benefit structures. Other research not detailed here suggests that tapered benefits extend to higher income ranges the pattern of consumer preference and public outlays we report for the guarantee case. Extensions to our research could embrace alternative portfolio specifications, including especially portfolio insurance and protective put strategies, which offer some protection against downside risk; multiple individuals; and the implications of a preference specification in which habit formation is incorporated.

Notes

[1] Australia and Switzerland are among the developed nations to adopt mandatory policies, while among developing economies, Chile has the most mature system. More than a dozen countries, mostly from Latin America and the transition economies of central Europe, have either mandated private retirement provision or have stated their intention to undertake such reform. Further, a number of developed countries have either reformed their pension systems in this direction (e.g., the United Kingdom) or have debated doing so (the United States).

[2] This assumption is supported by evidence on the United Kingdom, Canada, and West Germany (Ely and Robinson, 1989), which suggests that in the short term, the correlation between the real stock return and the inflation rate are not significantly different from zero. Similar results hold for the Australian economy (Crosby, 1998).

[3] A worker on average earnings, who had been in full time employment continuously for 35 years to retirement in 2000, contributing 9 percent of earnings (the Australian mandatory rate), would have accumulated about $160,000 at retirement. Bateman and Piggott (1999) provide an account of the Australian mandatory Defined Contribution system, the Superannuation Guarantee.

[4] We assume a standard iso-elastic utility function, which allows for the incorporation of varying degrees of risk aversion.

[5] The possibility of reversion of the annuity to a spouse is ignored. Further, we ignore taxation and government benefit provisions, which specifically favor one annuity type over another.

[6] Our baseline drawdown assumption for the phased withdrawal is set halfway between the two extremes. In Table 5-4, we report the case of a phased withdrawal with maximum drawdown. This generates the same "over-the-cliff" drop as for the term annuity.

[7] This may be because of accentuated self selection in the indexed annuity market (only those with very long life expectancies care about inflation indexation), or because of a lack of long-dated indexed securities to provide insurers with suitable immunization against inflation risk.

References

Australian Government Actuary. 1994. *Australian Life Tables: 1990–92.* Canberra: Australian Government Publishing Service.

Bateman, H. and Piggott, J. 1999. "Mandating Retirement Provision: The Australian Experience". *Geneva Papers of Risk and Insurance* 24(1): 95–113.

Crosby, M. 1998. *Stock returns and inflation*, Mimeo, Department of Economics, University of Melbourne.

Daly, M. and Burkhauser, R. (Forthcoming). "The Supplemental Security Income Program". In *Means Tested Transfer Programs in the United States*, ed. Robert Moffitt, Chicago, IL: University of Chicago Press for the NBER.

Ely, D. P. and Robinson, K. J. 1989. "The Stock Market and Inflation: A Synthesis of the Theory and Evidence". *Economic Review*, Federal Reserve Bank of Dallas, March: 17–29.

Siegel, J. 1992. "The Equity Premium: Stock and Bond Returns Since 1802". *Financial Analysts Journal*, January–February: 28–38.

Chapter 6

Risk Transfer in Public Pension Plans

Jeremy Gold

Public pension plans, as the term is used in the United States, are defined benefit (DB) plans established by governments and their agencies to provide retirement benefits to their former employees. In these systems, retirement promises are made to employees in lieu of current wages. It is an economic truth that the wages given up are exchanged for the liabilities (promises) of defined benefit plans, and not for the plan assets. This is very different from the defined contribution (DC) plan case where it is reasonable to equate wages to plan contributions and thus plan assets. This economic distinction, generally reinforced at law as well, has not been well communicated to employees and has been particularly poorly communicated to employees subject to wage and benefit negotiations.

In the private sector, the primary economic purpose of pension plan contributions and plan assets is to secure (collateralize) the promised benefits made to the plan participants and beneficiaries. In the governmental sector, this primacy of purpose may be surpassed by a budgeting goal designed to minimize intergenerational wealth transfers.[1] In neither situation, however, is it reasonable to believe that the assets of the plan represent deferred wages. Plan liabilities have been exchanged for wages, but plan assets have not. The financial validity of this assertion lies in the observation that the taxpayers bear the risk of asset underperformance.

Whether the primary purpose is collateral or budgeting, annual actuarial valuations of public defined benefit pension plans are performed in order to determine plan liabilities, costs, and cash contributions. The incidence of cash contributions establishes the taxpayers' budget plan and the accumulation of the contributions is intended to build asset levels sufficient to provide benefit collateral. The actuarial methods and assumptions used are designed so that each generation bears its fair share of multigenerational costs. The actuarial process is intended to allocate risks fairly across generations as well. There is no intention to transfer costs, wealth, and/or risks *systematically* between generations.

The author acknowledges helpful comments and suggestions from Lawrence N. Bader, Francis Bernardi, Zvi Bodie, Jonathan F. Gold, Nick Hudson, Robert C. North, John Ralfe, and the editors. Opinions remain those of the author.

This chapter demonstrates that, while actuarial processes may appear intergenerationally fair on an expected basis, they systematically transfer risk away from early generations and toward later generations. The result is that *equal expected costs* imply *unequal risk-adjusted costs*, whenever risky assets are included in DB plans. This inherent bias favors current taxpayers, plan participants, and politicians, at the expense of future taxpayers.

We begin with an abstract example of an investment opportunity that illustrates the essential actuarial valuation flaw. The example, drawn from Bader (2001), illustrates how a clever politician may attempt to take advantage of this flaw. The politician is later challenged by a well-educated member of a generation that will be injured by the combination of actuarial error and risky investment. Next we show that such risk transfers can lead to suboptimal decisions (all of which burden future taxpayers), including: poor trade-offs of pension benefits for current wages in labor negotiations, skim funds, and pension obligation bonds (POBs). Lastly, we note that the suboptimal decisions flow from the actuarial anticipation of risky returns and not from the risky investments *per se.* Financial economics shows us how to amend the actuarial process to avoid intergenerational risk transfer.

An Investment Opportunity

In this section we step through an abstract investment opportunity to illustrate how actuarial anticipation of expected returns systematically transfers future returns to the first generation and foists risk upon subsequent generations. We later use the intuition from the abstract example in a more formal, more practical, model.

Figures 6-1 (a-b) show the simulated results of an investment strategy over 10 and 30 years, respectively. Each payoff point represents one trial. The trials, which occurred randomly, are shown in rank order. The mean payoff after 10 years is 1.03; the median is 0.77. There are twenty-two negative outcomes (worst = −0.74) and seventy-eight positive (best = 5.43). The corresponding 30-year statistics are 13.34, 7.85, 9 (−2.25), and 91 (64.12).

Because the mean and median are positive and because the number of trials with negative values is few, these payoffs appear to be valuable. Suppose that we were to offer this strategy in exchange for a certain payment today: what price might we receive? If, for example, the risk-free 30-year zero-coupon bond is priced at $0.23 per dollar of maturity value, might we be able to sell the random payoffs for as much as $0.90—that is, at about half of the present riskless value of the median payoff, well below one-third of the riskless price for the mean payoff?[2] What price might such a contract have in the existing capital markets?

A Bader Swap

Each of the 100 outcomes in each figure represents the end of a path. Let us look at the paths that underlie the 30-year case (Figure 6-2). The 100 equity

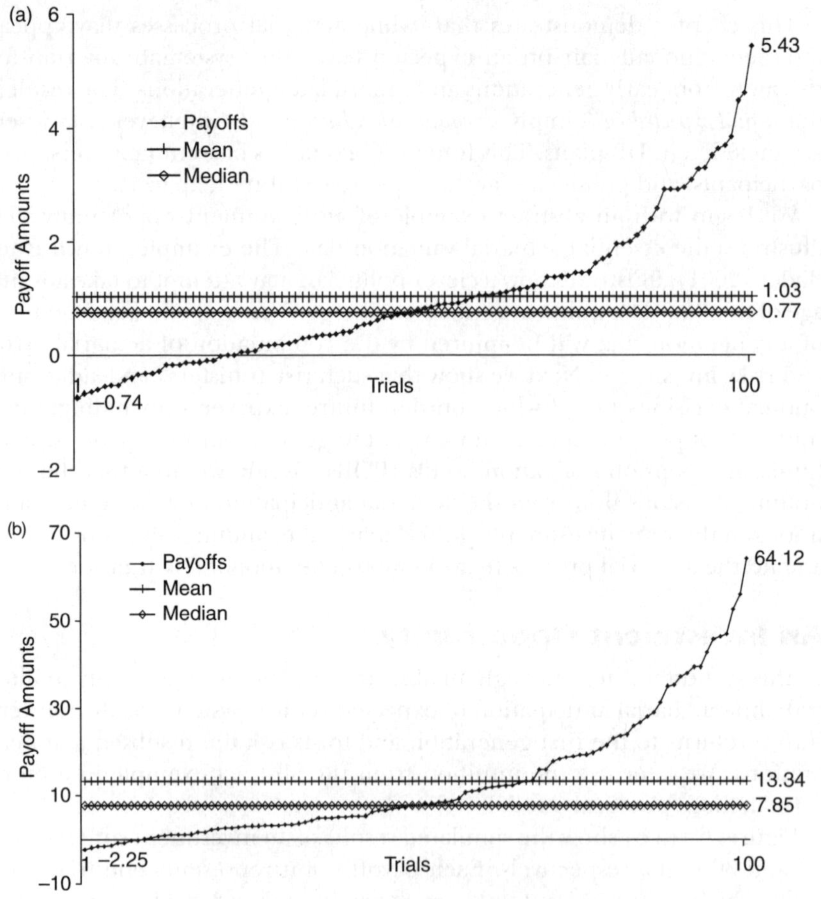

Figure 6-1. Investment payoffs over 100 random trials (ordered): (a) 10-year horizon, (b) 30-year horizon. (*Source*: Author's calculations.)

paths represent the random results from a $1 investment using a lognormal distribution with an expected annual return of 10 percent and an annual standard deviation of 16 percent. The mean and median paths are shown for the equity trials. The Treasuries earn 5 percent annually starting with a $1 investment.

How do these paths relate to the outcomes in Figure 6-1(b)? Each of those outcomes represents the result of an equity investment offset by a short position in Treasuries, a net cost of $0 today. From each of the equity endpoints in Figure 6-2, I have subtracted the endpoint of the Treasury path to get the corresponding payoff point for Figure 6-1(b). The Treasury path always ends with $4.32. The best equity path ends with $68.44 and thus the best payoff point shown in Figure 6-1(b) is $64.12. Notice that some of

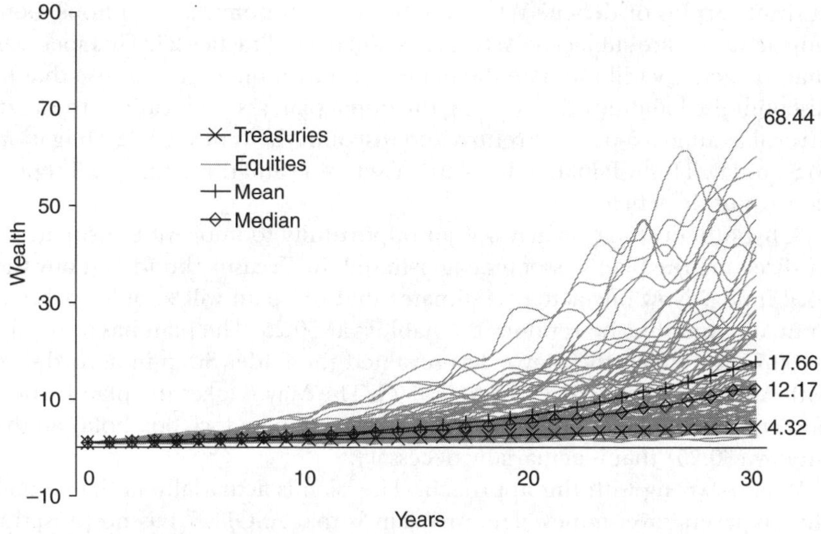

Figure 6-2. Investment payoff paths for equities versus treasuries: 30 year horizon. (*Source*: Author's calculations.)

the equity paths end up below the Treasury endpoint. These represent the nine negative payoffs. In particular, the worst case equity outcome is \$2.07 leading to a payoff of minus \$2.25. In other words the results in Figures 6-1(a-b) simulate a long S&P-like investment short a zero-coupon Treasury bond. What, then, should any market participant be willing to pay today for the outcome opportunities? Exactly nothing.

Can one really buy these outcome distributions for \$0? For a funded pension plan, the simple answer is: Yes. Bader (2001) illustrates how pension plans could develop such distributions without cost. Starting with a plan whose sole obligation might be \$4.32 due in 30 years and a Treasury asset of \$1 that will exactly meet that future obligation, Bader's plan sells the Treasury bond and buys a diversified equity portfolio, each with a \$1 current price.[3] Bader indicates that this is equivalent to a swap contract, so I have labeled Figures 6-1 (a-b) "Bader Swaps." Bader Swaps are worthless at inception but may have high expected future values. Algebraically:

$$P(t = 0) = 0$$

$$EP(t = 10) = 1.03$$

$$EP(t = 30) = 13.34$$

where P is value (price) and EP is expected future value.[4]

Consider a municipal pension plan with the same starting position as the Bader plan. How will an actuary value that plan's liabilities, assets, and current surplus or deficit? When establishing economic assumptions, pension actuaries are subject to Actuarial Standard of Practice 27. This specifies that the actuary will estimate the expected return on assets and use that to discount the liabilities. Thus, using the initial plan asset allocation, the actuary will assume a 5-percent return and discount the future $4.32 obligation to $1 today. This will match the plan's asset value and the actuary will report no surplus or deficit.

A hypothetical mayor may see an opportunity to improve the situation, by directing the plan's asset manager to sell the Treasury bond and buy the S&P index. Now our actuary estimates that the plan will earn 10 percent annually, and thus he revalues the liability at $0.25. The plan has a surplus of $0.75. In effect, the Mayor has revalued the Bader Swap in accordance with ASOP 27, such that $P(t = 0) = 0.75$. The Mayor takes the plan surplus and cuts today's taxes by $0.75, and the pension plan lock box holds all the money ($0.25) that is actuarially necessary.

What is wrong with this approach? The plan is actuarially sufficient and the taxpayers save money. The problem is that ASOP 27 has no prescription for accounting for risk. Pension actuaries consider themselves fiscally conservative, and individual actuaries might trim the expected return to a "conservative" 9 percent in this situation. An actuary who expected equities to return 10 percent and, nonetheless, assumed a 5 percent return for the all-equity plan, would be out of compliance with accepted actuarial standards. We shall see that the use of any assumption exceeding 5-percent in this instance results in an unintended risk-based transfer of wealth between generations. This is disturbing, because the use of a 5 percent assumption is intergenerationally fair, financially sound, and actuarially *unacceptable.*

When the 10 percent assumption is used, who wins? The Mayor, the taxpayers, and the actuary. Does anyone have to lose? The capital markets tell us that the Bader Swap is worthless; the Mayor and the actuary say it is worth $0.75. If it is really worth $0.75, then they should surely be able to get someone to pay $0.60 for it. Would any creditworthy market participant accept the pension plan obligation, the $1 in plan assets *and* pay the taxpayers $0.60 for the privilege? The answer is no, because the creditworthy market participant could short $1 in Treasuries and buy $1 of the S&P, and pay no one for the privilege. He would be taking a substantial risk by doing so. Financial economics explains that the expected future value on the Bader Swap is exactly the market compensation for taking that risk. If someone did take that risk, he would demand full compensation and have nothing to share with the taxpayers.

The Mayor Meets a Financially Astute Taxpayer

This intuition may be formalized with a model that illustrates how the risk may be measured and who bears it. Our model compares the fortunes of successive generations of taxpayers in order to detect systematic risk/wealth transfers among them. The generations are identified as Gen1, Gen2, ... Gen(n), ... GenN, and each has the same number of members, M. When the model begins, in Period 1, Gen1 is actively working and paying taxes. Gen2 is attending school. A number, G, of each generation's M members spend their work time as employees of the local government. In Period 2, Gen1 members are no longer working nor are they paying taxes, Gen2 members are working taxpayers and Gen3 members are in school. In Period 3, Gen1 is deceased, Gen2 is retired, Gen3 is working and Gen4 is in school.

As the system commences, Gen1 designs a public pension plan that will make a Period 2 payment of \$M/G to each of the G former governmental employees of Gen1. The plan continues period by period without amendment. The \$M/G payment to each of G recipients translates to \$1 from each of \$M taxpayers. But which taxpayer will pay how much and when? Some members of Gen1 suggest a PAYGO plan, saying "Let Gen2 members each pay \$1 next period." Under the PAYGO plan, each Gen($n > 1$) taxpayer will pay \$1 to the retirees of Gen($n-1$).

Gen2 members disagree, "The services provided by Gen1's public workers go to Gen1. Gen1 must set aside enough money to fund the plan fully." How much shall each Gen1 taxpayer contribute to the plan to prefund the pension benefit? The present value of \$1 due one period from now is:

$$\mathrm{PV} = \frac{1}{1+r}$$

where r is the rate of return. Following the principles of ASOP 27, actuaries assume that r is the expected rate of return on the money in the plan. For convenience, we modify the 5 percent Treasuries and 10 percent equities that were used above. Let the return on Treasuries be 5.2632 percent and let the expected return on equities be 9.8901 percent. If we invest in Treasuries, the actuary says we must set aside \$0.95; if we invest in equities, \$0.91 will suffice.

Because the town wants to remain in business, that retiree is going to receive \$M/G next year. Each future retiree has a riskless promise worth \$0.95M/G. But the Mayor and actuary propose that the city and its pension plan are long-term investors so they can afford to take risks that will average out in the long run. Each Gen1 taxpayer then contributes \$0.91 and the plan buys the S&P index; the \$0.91 is expected to grow to \$1 next year. If the assets are greater (or lesser) than \$1, the taxes of Gen2 will be lesser (or larger) by the difference.

Because, on average, the assets will be sufficient to pay the required \$1, members of Gen2 expect to pay the same tax that Gen1 must pay today. Our actuary says that that is right and that Gen2 members can expect to pay \$0.91 next year. The actuarial definition of parity is met when each

TABLE 6-1 Generational Balance Sheets

Sections	*Assets*	*Liabilities*
A: Gen1, Period1	Personal portfolio[a]	$9.1 Payable now
B: Gen2, Period1	Personal portfolio: $X S&P Y T-bills	(due Period 2) $0.91 expected Risk of Gen1's S&P investment
C: Gen2, Period 1, Analyzed	Personal portfolio: $X S&P Y T-bills	(due Period 2) $.91 for Gen2 employees 1.00 for Gen1 retirees −(0.91 S&P in plan as of Period 1)
D: Gen2, Period 1, Hedged	Personal portfolio: $(X−0.91) S&P (Y + 0.91) T bills	(due Period 2) $0.91 for Gen2 employees 1.00 for Gen1 retirees −(0.91 S&P in plan as of Period 1)
E: Gen2, Period 2, Projected	Personal portfolio	$0.91 for Gen2 employees $0.042105 for Gen1 retirees

[a] Invested as Gen1 sees fit. The personal portfolio for Gen2 (initially $X in the S&P Index, $Y in T-bills) is shown with greater detail in her balance sheets.
Source: Author's computations.

generation *expects* to pay the same amount. But one member of Gen2, a finance student, senses a problem. Whereas Gen1 is certain to pay $0.91, Gen2 may pay more or less than $0.91 depending on how the S&P performs.

To show this, she develops a balance sheet for Gen1 (Table 6-1) and a projected balance sheet for Gen2 (Table 6-1). The student reformulates the risk in terms of exposure to the pension plan.

Since the finance student has learned about hedging and arbitrage, she has planned for her own future with a portfolio that includes just the amount of risk and expected return that makes her comfortable (represented by an exposure to $X of equities). She decides to hedge to eliminate any extra risk thrust upon her by the pension plan. The hedge must be such that no matter how the $0.91 set aside by Gen1 performs, she bears the risk that she intended to take. Her S&P exposure is effectively $(X + 0.91) while her tolerance limits her to $X.[5] In order to establish her hedge, she realizes that she must sell $0.91 of S&P and invest the proceeds in T-bills (Table 6-1, Section D). Now her total S&P exposure is $X as she intended. She projects her balance sheet forward to Period 2 (Table 6-1, Section E) so that she may compare to Gen1 in Period 1, where the negative $0.91 in S&P exposure has cancelled out across the two sides of the balance sheet. The extra $0.91

she held in T-bills has grown by 5.2632 percent to $0.957895, which cancels out all but $0.042105 of the $1 that must be paid to Gen1 retirees.

Comparing to Gen1's balance sheet (Table 6-1, Section A) reveals that Gen2 is worse off by $0.042105. Each future generation will be in the same position as Gen2. How may we interpret this $0.042105 difference between Gen1 and later generations? Consider that the Gen1 public employees have riskless promises worth $0.95G/M equivalent to $0.95 per taxpayer. Gen1 taxpayers have been told that they need pay only $0.91 to provide $0.95 of riskless value, because the plan will take the equity risk. But our student has taught us that she is the actual risk bearer: if the plan had invested risklessly in T-bills to meet its riskless promise, Gen1 would have had to pay $0.95. Gen2 would have suffered no imposed pension risk and Gen2 would have had to pay $0.95 too.

Financial economics prescribes the use of a riskless discount rate for riskless liabilities, regardless of the actual investments. Had the actuary followed this prescription (in violation of ASOP 27), Gen1 and Gen2 would each face the same risk-hedged or risk-adjusted $0.95 cost. By paying only $0.91, Gen1 enjoys a risk-adjusted free lunch equal to $0.04 while subsequent generations have to pay $0.002105 more than the fair value of the benefits for their governmental workers. In effect, the $0.04 Gen 1 shortfall grows at riskless interest to $0.042105 (equals 0.04 times 1.052632). Gen2 pays the interest and passes on the $0.04 shortfall to Gen3. This continues until the final GenN is forced to pay $0.992105 representing the $0.95 needed to prefund GenN retirees, the $0.04 "borrowed" by Gen1 and one year's interest of $0.002105.

One last way to assess this risk/wealth transfer across generations is to recognize that Gen1 might have invested the full $0.95 value of its promise in T-bills. A decision by the plan to sell those T-bills and invest in the S&P would be recognized as a worthless Bader Swap and Gen1 would not have received the $0.04 windfall contrived by the Mayor and made possible by the ASOP 27 actuary.

In this example, the intergenerational transfers of risk have been converted to their certainty equivalents and reveal a $0.04 windfall for Gen1 that makes all subsequent taxpayer generations losers. This seems like a small "evil," so why should taxpayers worry? One reason is that initially it appeared that the work of $1 in Treasuries could be matched by only $0.25 in equities. In this latter example, we have $0.91 in equities doing the work of $0.95 in Treasuries.

Consider, further, that this example assumed that retiree benefits are due 1 year after the civil service employee provides service to the taxpayers. In a typical pension plan, however, the average worker may be 40+years old and the average retirement promise is kept some 30 + years later. This means that the discount process is more like the 30-year Bader Swap than it is like the one-period pension example. When we consider taxpayer and worker generations that are 30 years in length the intergenerational wealth transfer is very large. Supposing a $1 promise 30 years in advance, the riskless cost is $0.214639. Yet the actuary calculates a contribution requirement using equities equal to $0.059053. As in the Bader Swap example, the actuary's adherence to ASOP 27 enables an understatement of liabilities[6] by about 75 percent. This amplifies the impact, by assuming that the plan might be invested entirely in the S&P instead of in Treasuries. A more typical plan might invest about half of its assets in bonds and half in equities, so ASOP 27 would lead to an understatement of liability values by about 50 percent.

Implications of Liability Mismeasurement

The process defined by ASOP 27 is considered unbiased by actuaries because, on average, investment returns are neither under- nor overestimated. Yet financial economists deem the risky discount of riskless promises to be biased, because the resulting liabilities are systematically understated compared to the market value of similar promises. Understatement of the value of promises made to public employees leads to valuable risk transfers between generations and inferior decision-making by taxpayer representatives.

Three prominent examples of such poor decision-making are negotiated wage/pension trade-offs, skim funds, and POBs.

Negotiated Wage/Pension Trade-offs

Because actuaries undervalue promised future retirement benefits, governmental financial officers are prone to promise excessive retirement benefits in exchange for insufficient wage give-ups at the bargaining table. A $1 retirement benefit to be paid 30 years hence may have a riskless discounted value of $0.21, but it will be actuarially discounted to a value of $0.06. How much of today's wage should be given up by the employee in exchange for that future benefit? As we have shown any value less than $0.21 represents a real gain to the employee and any value greater than $0.06 creates an apparent gain to today's taxpayers. The $0.15 cost differential is always paid, by future taxpayers, with interest.

A simple test of this proposition may be made by asking insurance companies to offer deferred annuities to cover the promises made. Pension actuaries uniformly believe that insurance companies systematically and egregiously overprice such contracts. Shareholders of insurance companies will not, however, accept the risk of equity investment to fund fixed income annuities without full market compensation for the risk.[7] Since the full market compensation for the risk is priced in expectation by a Bader Swap, the insurance company shareholders must charge at least a riskless price for a riskless promise.

Observe that the use of a near riskless rate of discount, independent of the allocation of plan assets, would result in wage/benefit exchanges made at the value of the benefits promised with almost no regard to how those benefits are financed.

Skim Funds

When public pension plans invest in risky assets, actual investment returns may exceed the assumed returns. So-called "skim funds" exist in many arenas to share the pension plans' superior results with plan participants; no similar sharing is levied on participants when risky returns turn out to be inferior. Thus common skim funds designs look like financial call options. Defined benefit pension plans implement a portion of the employment contract under which employees accept reduced current cash contributions, in exchange for promises of conditional future retirement benefits. Employees "own" the pension plan liabilities; the assets stand to provide collateral for those liabilities. Risks taken with the assets are borne by the sponsor (or its constituent taxpayers) in the hopes of reducing the cash necessary to support the benefit promises. When the risks result in losses, the sponsor is responsible for increased future contributions. The justification for establishing skim funds frequently flows from a very different understanding of the nature of pension assets and liabilities. This view holds that plan assets represent employees' accumulated deferred wages, a view more consistent with the economic reality of defined contribution plans.

For many years, public DB pension plans trailed their corporate brethren in the proportion of their assets allocated to equities. Over the last two decades, however, public plans increased their equity exposure to the point where their equity exposure is, on average, not notably different from private sector plans. The public sector began to emulate the private sector with the intention of lowering the cost of benefit promises to the taxpayers who made the promises. The fundamental actuarial error represented by ASOP 27's treatment of the valueless Bader Swap allows this seeming cost reduction to be brought to taxpayers immediately.

If one were to view the taxpayers of all generations ensemble, it might be possible to conclude that the expected cost reduction would be a fair recompense for the added risks of equity investment. It would be incorrect, however, to conclude that taxpayers have received a windfall because they can execute a Bader Swap. Rather, taxpayers exchange wages for benefit promises, and then they elect to engage in a Bader Swap. Since the benefits promised remain unchanged, the risk inherent in the swap has not been shared with plan participants.

Nonetheless, as public sector pension plans began to reduce their holdings of bonds over time and increase their holdings of equities, negotiators for the plan participants demanded that the rewards from equity investments be shared between the participants and the taxpayers, taking advantage of the fable that ties wages to plan assets. Municipal politicians and managers, anxious to lower current costs by switching into equities, were willing to share the "gains" with participants, despite the risk that was borne entirely by taxpayers. The structure that emerged is the "skim fund," which redirects some of the "excess" returns earned by the taxpayers' acceptance of risk to provide previously unscheduled benefit increases. The very same actuarial error that encouraged equity investment, encouraged undervaluation of promises made in lieu of wages, and transferred risk from today's taxpayers to tomorrow's, is used to justify an asymmetric game in which today's taxpayers share rewards with tomorrow's participants, once again to the detriment of future taxpayers.

Observe that the use of a near riskless rate of discount, independent of the allocation of plan assets, would reduce the financial managers' incentive to invest in equities. Then, faced with demands for shares of equity rewards, the managers would be required to recognize the symmetric sharing of equity risks as well.

Pension Obligation Bonds

A third implication deriving from the fundamental actuarial misvaluation of the Bader Swap has prompted states to issue taxable POBs. To understand the taxable POBs, it is useful to begin with an earlier period in which municipal taxpayers benefited from a tax arbitrage to the detriment of federal taxpayers.

This began in the early 1980s, when some Wall Street public finance specialists found a loophole in the federal tax system that allowed states and municipalities to issue tax-exempt bonds, to cover past service contributions to underfunded DB public pension plans. Without taking on any net risk, the governmental entity could borrow at its below-Treasury tax-exempt rate, and then it could place the proceeds in the pension plan where it could be used to purchase comparable Treasury securities. This procedure provided a net gain to the local governments that clearly came at the expense of the federal purse. In a short period in the mid-1980s, billions of dollars of such transactions were undertaken.

In order to deliver the advantages of this arbitrage to taxpayers immediately, the pension plan actuary had to recognize that the pension plan assets purchased with the borrowing proceeds could be used to reduce the plan contributions by more than the debt service cost incurred by the borrowed. Since there were true arbitrage gains available, actuaries could establish methods and procedures to lower contribution costs for the life of the borrowing, while remaining certain that the pension plan would be at least as well funded as it otherwise would have been over the same period. In effect, the pure arbitrage met two useful constraints: (i) the municipality's total cash flow for debt service and pension contributions could be reduced, and (ii) the plan would always have assets at least as great as if the transaction had not been undertaken.

Within a few years, the Internal Revenue Service (IRS) declared that any future bond offerings used in such schemes would have to be taxable though it grandfathered the outstanding pension bond issues as tax-exempt. For several years following this ruling, Wall Street's public finance departments did not market or underwrite the issuance of pension bonds. But then managers of public pension plans decided that holding Treasury bonds was inconsistent with their long-term risk-return goals, and they undertook to redeploy the assets. Using Bader Swaps, as a result, the reduction in the level of contributions far exceeded the cost of debt service. The net reduction was so important, in fact, that the tax-exempt status of the bonds was only the smaller of the values added.[8]

Wall Street's public finance departments soon saw a new opportunity to market and underwrite pension bonds.

In the dozen or so years since the invention of this "actuarial arbitrage," the volume of POBs has swelled. Only recently has the wisdom of POBs been called into question, as recently in Philadelphia (Davies, 2001).

To review how taxable POBs work, the municipality first borrows at its taxable rate (which is greater than the comparable US Treasury borrowing rate) and contributes the proceeds to the pension plan. Next the fund managers invest the proceeds in diversified assets including equities. For the sake of illustration, we assume that all of the proceeds are invested in the S&P 500. The actuary then credits the fund with the expected return on the S&P and reduces the required plan contributions by that amount. Gold (2000) describes the taxable POB transaction by first assuming that the proceeds are invested in US Treasury securities that proportionally match the cash flows of the new municipal indebtedness. Since the municipality's borrowing rate is higher than that of the Treasury, the net cash flows would be unfavorable and the borrower would be a loser. In fact that is the economic truth of the matter. Without significant risk modification, the transaction is a loser for taxpayers. Nevertheless, the fund undertakes a Bader Swap, thus achieving the goal of the POBs. The actuarially generated gain on the Bader Swap generates more in *apparent* winnings than the first step *really* lost. Once again, the loss is reflected in the increased risk borne by future taxpayers and once again today's taxpayers and politicians are the winners. We observe that the use of a near-riskless rate of discount, independent of the allocation of plan assets, would eliminate the "actuarial arbitrage" gains from POBs, leaving nothing but the negative arbitrage that results from borrowing at above Treasury rates to earn near riskless rates.

Conclusion

I have argued that currently accepted pension actuarial methods embed a flawed understanding of the risk of equities and the improper valuation of market-to-market swaps. The existing approach was developed as

DB pension plans abandoned insurance companies and adopted trusteed arrangements after Second World War. The flaw has been extended by the accountants and by Congress when they incorporated actuarial principles into their prescriptions.

Few are aware of the problem because recognizing the error requires an integration of financial economics with actuarial science. Because the existing standards favor today's generation of managers, shareholders, taxpayers, politicians, and actuaries, even those who do perceive the problem are poorly motivated to correct it.

This problem has begun to be revealed, however. Consider the "legacy" pension obligations of the steel industry that received some attention in March 2002, when President George W. Bush chose to protect that industry with tariffs. A companion proposal, not adopted, would have had federal taxpayers bail out the underfunded pension plans of failed steel companies.

Consider too the recent actions of the Boots Company (2001), a UK firm elected to place its £2.3 billion plan in UK bonds matching the plan's projected outflows. It chose to forego the illusory gains from a Bader Swap but in doing so has had to explain its decision to shareholders, rating agencies, and other interested parties. The firm has said that its motivation was to reduce risks associated with mismatches between DB plan assets and plan liabilities. It is interesting that the Boots' transaction coincided with the adoption of Financial Reporting Standard 17 in the United Kingdom, a standard that provides a market-based liability valuation model and may serve to expose the risks of asset/liability mismatches. FRS 17 has been credited with increasing accounting transparency, motivating a slight shift in asset allocation to bonds from equity, and it has also been blamed for discouraging final average defined benefit plan formation and maintenance (Capleton and Cleary, 2002).

Unfortunately these are only small steps. The global accounting effort to implement a "fair value" accounting model for financial instruments by 2005 will require accounting to learn the lessons of arbitrage and proper risk-adjusted measurements. Nevertheless, the accounting project has thus far elected to exempt pension and welfare plans from its purview. The pension actuarial community has begun its own research and education effort designed to assess the implications of financial economics on the pension actuarial model. We should therefore begin to see the fair value paradigm influence securities analysts of pension plan finance.[9]

Notes

[1] Here we argue that the goal of intergenerational fairness may be served in expectation but it is often poorly served in value.

[2] Note that after paying such an amount, the final payoff will be negative 9 percent of the time, requiring a second payment at maturity. We assume that neither party will default.

[3] Bader had a $1 million obligation. Here we adjust to be consistent with our payoffs.
[4] These are sample means. Population means are 0.96 and 13.13.
[5] This equates to $X in his personal portfolio plus the effect of having a liability of minus $0.91 in S&P.
[6] Readers may note that the liabilities discussed here amount to benefits newly earned. The corresponding liability might be called the "Unit Credit Normal Cost" or the "Service Cost." These liability items may well approach the 30-year duration implied by the text. Aggregate pension liabilities more typically show durations that are about half as long.
[7] As shown by Bodie (1995), the price for equity risk is an increasing function of the period of time over which the risk is taken. Actuarial myth holds that the risk of equity ownership declines with time and that the equity risk premium is more truly a reward for patience than it is compensation for risk. See also Lachance and Mitchell (Chapter 8, this volume).
[8] The *true* value added, derived from below-Treasury borrowing to invest in Treasury securities, was often far outweighed by the *apparent* value added by the Bader Swap.
[9] See Bader (2002) and Capleton and Cleary (2002).

References

Actuarial Standards Board. 1996. Actuarial Standard of Practice No. 27. "Selection of Economic Assumptions for Measuring Pension Obligations."

Bader, Lawrence N. 2001. "Pension Forecasts, Part 2: The Model Has No Clothes". *Pension Section News, Society of Actuaries,* 14–15.

—— 2002. "Valuing Companies, Valuing Pension Plans". *Contingencies* 14(5).

Bodie, Zvi. 1995. "On the Risk of Stocks in the Long Run". *Financial Analysts Journal* 18–22.

Boots Company. 2001. "2001 Half Year Release". <www.halfords.com/content/files/BootsHalfyearResults0102.pdf>.

Capleton, Mark and Fred Cleary. 2002. "Is the UK Equity Market Moving into Retirement?" *UK Bond Tactics, Barclay's Capital.*

Davies, Dave. 2001. "City Pensions Lose Millions in Market". *Philadelphia Daily News.* October 29: 4.

Gold, Jeremy. 2001. "Actuarial Assumptions for Pension Plans Invite Arbitrage: The Case of Pension Obligation Bonds". *Risks and Rewards, Society of Actuaries* 6–7.

Chapter 7

Securing Public Pension Promises through Funding

Robert Palacios

There are several reasons to be interested in the way public pension reserves around the world are managed. To begin with, many countries have adopted a strategy of partial funding of public defined benefit (DB) schemes. For millions of current and future members of these schemes, in dozens of countries as diverse as Sweden and China, investment performance may affect the likelihood that their pensions will be paid as promised. Another motivation is related to the continuing debate over how to reform public pension systems increasingly perceived to be unsustainable. The focus is often not whether to increase the level of funding, but rather, the best way to do so. The trend toward funding is partly due to growing awareness of the implications of large unfunded pension liabilities. So, the "implicit pension debt" does pose an intertemporal fiscal constraint and financial markets will punish sovereigns that let it get out of control, despite the fact that this is nowhere reported on government balance sheets. The increased attention is also partly due to the fact that those who will bear the brunt of the intergenerational transfer that this liability represents are starting to protest.

Generating a higher funding ratio—defined as the size of pension reserves relative to pension liabilities—is one way to mitigate these negative effects. It can be achieved by reducing the liability (i.e. cutting benefits), increasing earmarked revenues (usually, raising payroll taxes), or improving the investment returns of an existing fund. In many cases, reform packages include two or even all three elements; increasing investment returns is clearly the least difficult, politically.

Nevertheless, the record of public pension fund managers suggests this is a strategy that often fails.[1] Around the world, reserves in partly-funded, public schemes have been used to subsidize housing, state enterprises, and various types of economically targeted investments (ETIs). They have also been used to prop up stock markets.[2] And frequently, they have probably led to larger public deficits than would have otherwise been the case, as money is simply channeled back to the central government, often at below-market rates of interest. The conflicting objectives of government or parastatal officials determining asset allocation have resulted in poor performance, measured by most reasonable standards. These decisions typically occur in a regulatory vacuum and there is often little public accountability or transparency.[3]

While proponents of centralized management may recognize the failings of the past, they argue that performance can be improved by changes to governance and investment policy, and they suggest that insulation from political interference is feasible. The attempt to do this in some countries involves adopting the standards and practices of well-developed private pension sectors, to the extent possible. Most reforms also envision an increased reliance on private asset managers. Nevertheless, decisions are ultimately made by trustees appointed by government and exempted from the regulatory oversight that would apply in the private sector.

Are there ways to shield public pension funds from the kind of political interference that has plagued them in the past? Is there a way to ensure appropriate incentives for trustees to make prudent investment decisions without the discipline of competition and independent supervision? This chapter reviews some of the key design issues and policy alternatives that would have to be addressed in order to answer these questions in the affirmative. It also reviews initiatives in five developed countries—Canada, Ireland, Japan, New Zealand, and Sweden—where new models of public pension fund management have been introduced. From these experiences, certain positive features of the schemes are summarized in a preliminary attempt to arrive at practical recommendations based on good practice in this area. The limitations of such an exercise must be kept in mind however, especially in light of the unrepresentative set of countries that has undertaken this type of reform. With this in mind, the last section addresses the role of country-specific conditions.

Policy Choices and Design Issues

Many of the issues raised in public pension fund management are similar or even identical to those that apply to private pension funds. In fact, several of the reforms described in the next section borrow directly or rely heavily on the rules developed for the private pension sector. But the analogy is far from perfect. None of the public funds examined here is governed by the statutes that apply to their private sector analogues, nor are they under the jurisdiction of the same supervisor.[4] This is due to the fact that there are considerations specific to public funds, ranging from their funding objectives to potential conflicts of interest. This section seeks to identify some of the key policy choices by highlighting limitations that apply in the case of public pension funds.

Pension Governance

In the broadest sense, pension governance refers to the: "processes and structures used to direct and manage the affairs of the pension plan, in accordance with the best interests of the plan participants. The processes and structures define the division of power and establish mechanisms for ensuring accountability."[5]

General governance parameters are usually set out in legislation, while detailed rules may be internal to the scheme in question. Public pension plans are usually subject to specific laws that are distinct from those that apply to the private sector. Responsibility is normally vested in a board of directors or trustees. Many public funds use representative rather than professional boards. Representative boards are often "tripartite," namely consisting of labor, employer, and government representatives. This usually means that there are few if any board members with expertise in finance or investment. Professional boards, by contrast, would normally include this expertise.

In addition to determining the composition of the board and its manner of selection (and dismissal), their specific duties might be clearly specified, especially as distinguished from management. In order to ensure that incentives to perform these duties are robust, it is normally recommended that those making decisions also bear a risk related to key outcomes. This is one of the more difficult policies to apply to public funds, partly because potential board members are unable to insure against the risk of political interference that might significantly affect their ability to perform their duties.[6] In fact, government representatives may themselves be a source of risk, due to inherent conflicts of interest.

There is significant scope for defining the role of management within a pension scheme. In some cases, internal managers are limited to selecting and overseeing external service providers. Outsourcing has become increasingly popular in private sector DB plans, but most public plans perform most or all functions internally. Whether internal or external, the responsibilities of managers should be clearly defined and the criteria for hiring and compensating them should result in the appropriate skill mix. A practical problem for many public funds is that human resource policies and salary scales used in the public sector may reduce the potential pool of qualified candidates for positions that are often highly remunerated in the private sector.

Perhaps the most important problem to resolve in designing public pension fund governance is the potential for conflicts of interest. Rules involving personal gain at the expense of members can be made explicit through codes of conduct. It is more difficult however, to avoid problems arising from inherent institutional conflicts that often arise when public officials are in a position to make decisions that may have collateral public policy impact. A typical example is that the Minister of Finance may be involved in decisions over asset allocation that can affect capital markets and government borrowing constraints.

Well-defined information flows between board, management, and members are essential to ensure that duties can be performed effectively and for the sake of accountability. The required frequency and type of information required should be clearly documented. In the case of information to members, it could be argued that standards should be higher for pension plans that receive mandatory contributions, including public pension plans.

Funding Objectives

Perhaps the most obvious difference between public and private plans is the extent to which they match assets and liabilities. Minimum funding requirements are applied to private DB schemes, recognizing the dangers of relying exclusively on the solvency of the sponsor. While definitions vary, countries with minimum funding standards typically aim to have sufficient funds on hand to meet accrued obligations at any given point in time.

By contrast, most public DB schemes do not follow these principles. Most were set up with significant unfunded liabilities, partly due to transfers made to early cohorts, as well as to the choice to begin with contribution rates much lower than what would have been required to accumulate reserves that matched accruing liabilities. When a government is a sponsor, the perception may be that tax revenues could always be increased as necessary to meet these obligations. Most public schemes did, nevertheless, build reserves during their initial phase, and many have made it explicit policy to partially fund future benefits in order to avoid a drastic increase in future payroll taxes.[7]

The level of funding needed in public plans must therefore be defined according to public policy objectives. These objectives will differ across countries (as seen below). The important point however, is that the target levels should be explicit and well-defined if they are to guide investment policy. In addition to fixing these long-term objectives, related tasks include determining actuarial and accounting assumptions, approving the appointment of the pension plan actuary, and evaluating investment performance.

Investment Policy

The board of a pension plan is responsible for setting the plan's overall investment policy. Best practice dictates that this should be explicit and in written form, reviewed periodically, and typically differentiates between the strategic, long-term plan and the annual plan. The board may also receive advice through external consultants or from a permanent advisory council.

A plan's investment policy is where targets are set for long run investment performance, risk tolerance, and the overall asset allocation strategy with a clear approach to portfolio diversification. Often, exposure to specific firms, markets, issuers or sectors will be explicitly limited. Exposure to specific firms may also be limited for other purposes, related to the corporate governance. In this regard, investment policy can also make explicit a board's position on shareholder activism, social investment, and economically targeted investments.

Some public pension plans accumulate a large asset base relative to domestic capital markets and public budgets. Consequently, the potential for a conflict between the long-term goals of the pension fund and other public policy objectives may recommend extra safeguards that would not be found in private sector regulations in addition to the need to diversify. For example, limitations on the amount of domestic government debt that can be held by the public plan might be considered a prudent way to avoid the temptation to relax fiscal constraints through coerced borrowing from the pension.

While these are best practice approaches, many public pension plans around the world lack this kind of investment policy. Most importantly, public plans rarely state as their fundamental objective (whether enshrined in the investment policy or not) that plan assets will be invested in the sole interests of plan participants. Indeed many public plans allow or even mandate that investments be made with other public policy objectives in mind.[8]

Investment Process

Within the broader investment framework, pension managers develop a plan to purchase and sell assets, implement this plan, and monitor the results. These results are then reported to the board and through them, to the members of the scheme. Other things constant, there are no obvious differences between public and private funds with regard to the implementation of a given investment policy. If anything, however, the standards of transparency for the process might well be expected to be highest in a public fund that receives mandatory contributions from members.

A plan's investment policy also lays out general approaches with regard to passive versus active investment, external versus internal asset management, hedging strategy, and other related topics. Implementing the strategy tends to be left to professional managers who in turn, may use external managers, custodians, and brokers. The method for selecting these external parties and evaluating their performance is an important part of defining the investment process and should be based on well-defined and objective criteria. These may include, for example, level of fees, experience, and expertise within certain sectors, or with certain types of financial instruments. It is imperative to keep systematic and accessible records as to the considerations and arguments for selection. Likewise, investment decisions within the scope of the overall asset allocation plan laid out in the investment policy are ideally based on objective criteria in line with the risk and return targets associated with individual asset classes.

Well-run pension plans benefit from an objective and quantifiable methodology for assessing performance over reasonable periods of time. Measuring performance is a two-step process that begins with an accurate measurement of results. This in turn requires the application of accepted accounting and valuation standards that allow for reasonable comparison with prescribed benchmarks. The second step is to compare these results to an objective predetermined benchmark(s). This assessment may focus, for example, on the net value added by internal or external managers, taking into account risk involved. Independent and external performance valuation can be very useful, especially where the resources available internally are scarce. The consequences of the assessment in terms of retention of managers and performance-related compensation can be explicitly described in the documentation of the investment process.

Reporting and Disclosure

A well-run pension plan must provide information to those who control and participate in the fund. For example, key elements of fund management, such as the investment policy, can easily be made available to the public. Performance, in terms of cost of administration, compliance with the law governing the fund, and investment returns, can be through annual and perhaps quarterly public reports. The veracity of the information can be ensured by regular independent audits. If anything, the standards for transparency for a public fund, where the liability of the board is usually circumscribed, can be expected to be higher than those that apply in the private sector.

Interdependence of Policy Choices

Effective policies in the five areas described above require coherent attention. The clearest example of the interdependence of these choices is the relationship between governance structure and investment policy. Legislation governing many public pension schemes often precludes the formulation of a sound investment policy, even by the most qualified and motivated trustees. Conversely, when a board is given more latitude, a weak governance structure can influence investment policy.[9] Studies find that the key determinant of public plan investment is overall asset allocation; an otherwise sound investment policy can still be undermined by weak investment processes (Brinson et al., 1991).

Reporting and disclosure provide an important source of discipline for private pension funds, but they are arguably of greater importance for public plans. This assertion is based on at least two limitations regarding accountability exclusive to public schemes. The first is personal liability of trustees.

Even in countries with a strong tradition in trust law, it has proven difficult to hold trustees of public pension plans to the same standards as their private sector counterparts. This violates one of the basic tenets of good governance, namely matching consequences with decisions. The second limitation is more fundamental. Almost without exception, public plans are not monitored by a supervisor with the objective of ensuring that the interests of members are served. Unlike members of private schemes, those forced to pay into public schemes do not receive protection from an agent with sufficient expertise and access to information. Public pension funds are therefore, to a large extent, self-policing monopolies.

This leaves only two avenues for accountability: representation of members on the board, and at the ballot box (if that option is available). It would seem difficult to devise an effective mechanism for selecting a well-versed representative for members of a national pension scheme (as opposed for example, to a scheme for civil servants or some other clearly differentiated group). Some options could result in populist policies that undermine the original funding objective; in practice, experience with representative pension boards in many countries has not been positive. The second avenue for accountability, the electoral process itself, raises much broader questions of governance given wide variance across countries.

In view of these limitations, the best and perhaps only source of discipline for public pension fund managers is a public that is well-informed on the subject, which can assess whether the funds are invested prudently. Achieving this level of public consciousness can be facilitated by civil society, academia, and the media, but only if accurate reporting and disclosure is in place.

Recent Initiatives in Developed Countries

Next, we review the efforts to improve public pension fund governance, that attempt to address each of the issues described above. Where possible, the evolution of the proposal and the rationale for the ultimate design of the schemes is discussed. Some key features are then compared across the five countries.

Five developed countries have substantially altered their strategy for funding public pension obligations since 1997.[10] Three of these countries, Canada (1998), Japan (2001), and Sweden (2001), reformed existing funding arrangements that had not performed well over the past several decades. Two other countries, New Zealand (2000) and Ireland (2000), launched initiatives for building pension reserves designed to offset the projected rising costs in their flat pension schemes due to population aging.

Table 7-1 provides some background on these five countries. Sweden and Japan have older populations, while Ireland has the youngest population of the set. Japan and Sweden also have more generous public pension

TABLE 7-1 Background Statistics for Five Countries with Public Pension Plan Initiatives

Country (Year Implemented)	*Population Over 60 (%)*[a]	*Public Pension Spending GDP (%)*[b]	*Public Pension Fund Assets GDP (%)*[c]	*Private Pension Fund Assets GDP (%)*[d]
Canada (1998)	16.5	5.4	10	48
Japan (2001)	23.1	6.9	34	19
Ireland (2000)	15.5	4.6	None	45
New Zealand (2001)	15.5	6.5	None	n.a.
Sweden (2001)	22.1	11.1	23	3

Notes:

[a] World Bank estimates for 2000.

[b] OECD Social Expenditure database figures for 1997.

[c] Figures for Canada for 1998, while figures for Japan and Sweden are for 2000.

[d] OECD Institutional Investors Yearbook, 2000. Figures are for 1998.

Sources: OECD (1996); OECD (2000); World Bank population database; author's computations.

promises than do the other three. These two factors explain observed differences in public pension spending relative to GDP, in the second column. Meanwhile, at the time of the reform initiatives, Japan and Sweden had already amassed large public pension reserves, Canada had accumulated a significant amount, and Ireland and New Zealand had none. Ireland and Canada had the most developed private pension fund industry and commensurately large assets.

Canada's CPP Investment Board

After an actuarial assessment revealed growing long-term imbalances in the Canada Pension Plan (CPP), a debate ensued over how to ensure the finances of the scheme set up three decades earlier. The idea of moving to fully-funded individual accounts was rejected, in favor of improving long-term finances of the existing public scheme. A package of reforms sought to smooth increases in contribution rates forecasted by government actuaries in two ways. First, the contribution rate was increased from 6 to 9.9 percent; and second, the CPP reserves were invested in the stock market beginning in 1999 to obtain higher expected rates of return. This required a shift away from the previous policy of automatically purchasing provincial government bonds. Yields on those bonds were below market rates, leading to relative low long-run returns for the CPP. There was also some evidence that the captive source of credit available to the provinces increased government consumption (von Furstenberg, 1979).

The Act proposed to phase out these purchases. According to the "Briefing Book" for the final CPP Legislation (CPP Investment Board (CPPIB), 2000): "The option of governments intervening in CPP investment policy to meet regional or economic goals was widely rejected during public consultations as being incompatible with the interests of plan members. Accordingly the Board and its responsibility to invest in the sole interests of plan members are foundations of the new investment policy." In keeping with this approach, the new investment regime explicitly excluded social or economically targeted investments. The focus was to increase equity holdings: initially, it was decided that investment in domestic equities would have to "substantially replicate" broad market indexes of publicly traded Canadian securities. This method was preferred because it reduced discretion of the fund managers and because passive indexation was considered less costly than the alternative. Foreign equity exposure was initially limited to 20 percent, to be raised later to 30 percent, in line with restrictions on Canadian private pension funds.

A key element insulating the funds from politicians hinged on the newly created and independent Investment Board. In consultation with provincial governments, the Finance Minister appoints the twelve members of the board. The briefing book describes the process as follows (Government of Canada, 1998: 37):

> A nominating committee will recommend qualified candidates for the board of directors to federal and provincial governments. Government employees are not eligible to be directors. The Board will be subjected to close public scrutiny. It will make investment policies public, release quarterly financial statements and an annual report and hold public meetings every two years in each participating province...This agency would be subject to "fiduciary duty to invest CPP funds in the sole interests of contributors and beneficiaries—that is, to maximize returns without undue risk of loss."[11]

The board's members would be appointed for staggered 3-year terms and would fulfill a set of criteria including:[12]

> sound judgment; analytical, problem-solving and decision-making skills; a genuine interest in, and dedication to, the CPP; the capacity to quickly become familiar with specific concepts relevant to pension fund management; adaptability, including the ability to work co-operatively with others (possibly witnessed in prior service on a board, association or committee); high motivation, with the time and dedication required to prepare for and attend Board meetings; ethical character and a commitment to serving the public, preferably with a sensitivity to the public environment in which the CPP operates; and strong communications skills.

Regarding the qualifications of the financial experts, these would include: "experience in a senior capacity in the financial industry; broad investment knowledge (e.g., securities and financial markets); experience as a chief financial officer or treasurer of a large corporation or government entity;

consulting experience in the pension area; and generally recognized accreditation as an investment professional (e.g., CFA, MBA, training in economics or finance)." Since the objective was to increase returns, the method of achieving this was to impose private sector portfolio criteria on the public fund, and to place the professional Board at arms' length from the government. Regarding investment rules, the government noted that most of these were taken from the Pension Benefits Standards Act. In other words, the existing regulatory framework for a well-developed private pension sector was the basis for the rules of the Investment Board.

Perhaps the most controversial of the private pension rules adopted for the CPP was the foreign investment limit which initially allowed up to 20 percent (rising to 30 percent by 2001) of the portfolio to be invested in foreign assets. Labor party politicians argued that the entire pool of CPP investments should remain in Canada to stimulate economic development. But reformers eventually succeeded in obtaining the same portfolio limits on foreign investment as applied to the private sector.

Investing in the market index was another way of avoiding political discussions over investment choices or potential conflicts of interest. If stock picking was disallowed, there would be little scope for political considerations to influence investment policy. At the same time, it was recognized that the size of the fund, combined with a lack of flexibility, might distort the market if other players were able to anticipate CPP investments. Also, it was pointed out that tracking the index could involve higher turnover than a buy and hold strategy, as the index weightings changed over short periods of time. Ultimately, the wording in the regulations allowed room for some active management.

These measures were intended to produce CPP investment policies that approximated what was found in the private sector. This comparison was possible because there was a significant private pension sector with a long track record to use as a benchmark. The existence of a large contractual savings sector, including close to 40 percent of gross domestic product (GDP) in pension assets alone, was an important consideration for the reform. At its peak, CPP reserves were still expected to be smaller than those held in private pension funds. Another consideration was the absorption capacity of capital markets, which were deemed well developed and able to absorb CPP investments. Analysts found that the projected flows of new CPP funds into equities would not overwhelm the supply of new issues, especially given that foreign investment option was available.

Another focus during the design phase was the issue of corporate governance. The CPPIB potentially would be in a position to exercise its shareholder voting power over Canada's leading corporations. One option was to agree to abstain from using this power. Instead, the government chose to retain voting privileges in order to be able to take advantage of its "voice" as an investor, in the same way as other institutional investors in

Canada. This was the background for the ultimate passage of the Canada Pension Plan Investment Board Act that came into force in 1998, which appointed a Board of Directors and launched a new Corporation. The Act clearly stated that the Board's objectives were:

(a) to manage any amounts that are transferred to it under section 111 of the Canada Pension Plan in the best interests of the contributors and beneficiaries under that Act; and (b) to invest its assets with a view to achieving a maximum rate of return, without undue risk of loss, having regard to the factors that may affect the funding of the Canada Pension Plan and the ability of the Canada Pension Plan to meet its financial obligations.

The process of nomination and appointment of this Board deserves special attention. Ministers of Finance from each of the nine participating provinces and the federal government select individuals (public and private sector) responsible for the nomination process. Next, this nominating committee recommends individuals that meet the criteria for Board members as laid out in the Act. The Minister of Finance of Canada then appoints the Board, consisting of twelve members, from those on this list. This unique arrangement has the advantage distancing the Minister of Finance and the Board. Terms are staggered with half of the directors serving 2-year terms and the remainder serving 3-year terms. Each can be reappointed for another 3-year term with a maximum of three terms or 9 years. The Chair can serve a fourth term. Members must agree to uphold a code of conduct and must disclose any potential conflicts of interest.

Reporting requirements include, (i) an annual independent audit,[13] (ii) annual report, (iii) quarterly financial statements, and (iv) public meetings in each province at least once every 2 years. In addition, the Finance Minister is required to initiate a special examination of management practices at least once every 6 years.

The CPPIB's investment policy flows from its stated objective to increase the funding ratio for the CPP from 8 to 20 percent by 2017. It also has made clear the target long-term rate of return is 4 percent in real terms. In order to achieve these targets, and in light of the CPP's historical investment in provincial bonds, the Board decided to invest new funds exclusively in equities. All asset management is done through external managers.[14] Initially, domestic equity holdings were concentrated in index funds replicating the Toronto Stock Exchange index; foreign equity holdings similarly focused on S&P 500 and MSCI EAFE index funds. By 2002 however, the Board had shifted its asset mix in favor of private equity funds. On a commitment basis, these represented about 17 percent of total assets of the fund, but only 3 percent on the basis of actual investment. The Investment Statement from April 2002 shown in Table 7-2, includes minimum and maximum investment shares.

TABLE 7-2 Permitted Investments by the CPPIB

Investment Activity	*Minimum (%)*	*Maximum (%)*
Public equities of which		
Canada	45	75
US	5	25
Other	5	25
Total	75	100
Private equities	0	10
Total equities	85	100
Real assets[a]	0	5
Nominal fixed income/cash	0	10
Foreign currency	10	35

Note: [a]Includes (i) real estate, (ii) natural resources, and (iii) real return bonds.
Source: Adapted from CPPIB Investment Statement, April, 2002.

Between year end 1998 and the first quarter of 2002, the fund had accumulated around 14 billion Canadian dollars, or about 1.3 percent of GDP. First-year returns were tremendous, driven by passive equity investments during a period of rapid international equity appreciation. Regulations allowed for some active equity investment in 2000. The Board decided to reduce its exposure to one particular firm, having what was perceived to be an excessively high weight in the overall Canadian equity portfolio. This policy allowed the CPPIB to outperform the index, as this particular stock had declined precipitously by March 2001.[15] After 40 percent returns in 2000, the decline in global equity markets in 2001 led to a negative return of about 9 percent for a cumulative annualized return of 14.8 percent. Administrative costs fell from 31 to 11 basis points between 2000 and 2001.

Ireland's National Pension Reserve

The Irish Pensions Board (IPB) issued a major pension policy report in May 1998, that recommended expanding voluntary private pension coverage through increased incentives, and an increase in the flat benefit which constituted Ireland's first pillar that had fallen over time relative to average income (IPB, 1998). To control future contribution rates as the country ages, and to reduce intergenerational transfers, the report recommended partial funding of the flat benefit. The projections suggested that the contribution rate with partial funding would have to increase from 4.84 to 6.24 percent, while the no-funding scenario would require an increase to 9.25 percent. The option of mandating private pension coverage towards the same objective was debated but ultimately rejected.

This new fund was to be set up with an independent managing body with statutory responsibility for investing solely for the purpose of maximizing returns; social investments were explicitly disallowed. In addition, the governing board was prohibited from investing in domestic government bonds, to avoid the temptation of increasing government consumption using a captive source of credit. In 1999, Minister of Finance Charlie McCreevy announced that the Government had extended the new funding strategy to public employees pensions as well. The combined package created a Social Welfare Pension Reserve Fund and a Public Service Pension Fund, into which budget surpluses totaling 1 percent of GDP were to be deposited annually through 2055. This contribution would not be discretionary and funding levels would be assessed periodically in actuarial reviews.

By 2001, the fund held approximately 7.5 billion Euros, or about 5.3 percent of Ireland's GDP.[16] The fund is controlled by a seven-member Commission independent from the national government, which works to maximize returns subject to a prudent level of risk. The initial investment policy adopted by the Commission was developed with the assistance of international consultants and is described in Table 7-3. The National Treasury Management Agency (NTMA) was designated as manager for the first 10 years, which in turn contracts out to private asset managers. Within this framework, the NTMA was seen as a manager of managers, on behalf of the Commission. The Commission did delegate the NTMA as the manager of the passive bond portfolio of the fund. So external managers manage about 85 percent of the total fund assets. The selection criteria for external managers were embedded in a tender process subject to certain European Union directives. In a two-step process, 600 applications were initially received from 200 investment managers, with 93 percent coming from outside of Ireland. Subsequently, three candidates were selected from a short list where criteria were scored quantitatively with regard to specific asset classes. The NTMA is responsible for monitoring the asset managers against a predefined set of benchmark indices. They report to the Commission regularly on the results,

TABLE 7-3 Irish National Pension Reserve Fund Asset Allocation Strategy 2001

Major Asset Classes	*Overall Allocation (%)*	*Share Passively Managed (%)*	*Share Actively Managed (%)*
Equities	80		
Eurozone	40	27.9	12.1
Global ex	40	14.2	25.8
Bonds	20	14.8	5.2
Total	100	56.9	43.1

Source: Maher (2001).

and the Commission in turn provides an annual report to the Irish Houses of Parliament, the Committee of Public Accounts, and the public.

Japan's National Pension Fund

Japan's flat national pension (NP) and its earnings-related employee pension (EP) insurance programs were originally intended to be fully funded from their inception in 1942. Benefits were subsequently raised and the funding ratio gradually declined, despite increased contribution rates. Even after a major reform in 1995 that reduced future benefit levels, Japan's rapid demographic aging and reliance on public pensions has produced one of the largest unfunded pension liabilities in the world. Japan also has one of the largest public pension reserves in the world. Therefore, the reform legislation that became effective in 2001 sought to reduce liabilities by reducing the accrual rate, raising the normal retirement age, and shifting from wage to price indexation (Sakamoto, 2001). Another feature of the reform was to change the way public pension reserves are managed. In the past, a substantial portion of public pension assets was borrowed by the central government in the form of non-marketable government bonds, and used to finance government projects. The rest of the money was invested in a combination of social projects (e.g. medical infrastructure, loans to members) and capital markets, some of which was managed by the "Pension Welfare Service Public Corporation" (PWSPC). A large portion of the funds (along with Post Office savings) could be categorized as economically targeted investments. There is also a mandatory transfer from the pension plans to the Fiscal Investment and Loan Program (FILP), which in turn makes loans to public agencies, municipal groups, and the central government. This allocation is determined during the formulation of the annual government budget.

The magnitudes involved are large. In March of 2000, assets of the NP and EP totaled about 34 percent of GDP. On the other hand, the liability to workers and pensioners was estimated to be 160 percent of GDP, yielding a funding ratio of about 22 percent (Sakamoto, 2001).

Figure 7-1 shows the evolution of FILP investments since 1955. The accumulated loan portfolio was more than 80 percent of GDP in 2000, of which around one-quarter came from the pension system. Over time, and as the funds grew relative to the economy, the proportion allocated to supporting industry and providing infrastructure was reduced, in favor of housing and social welfare spending including loans for education. Subsidies to small-and medium-sized enterprises also increased over the period, representing almost one-fifth of FILP investments by 2000. Clearly, public pension assets in Japan were used as a way to achieve a variety of public policy objectives.

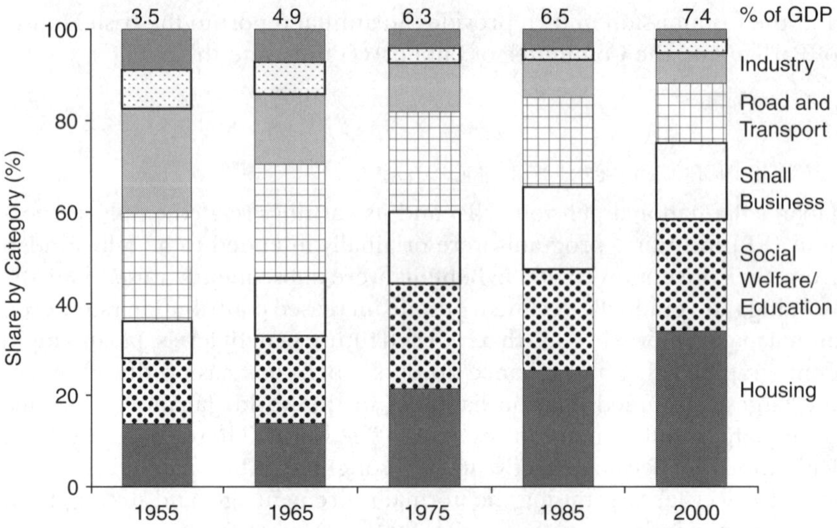

Figure 7-1. History of the fiscal investment and loan program. (*Source*: Japan—FILP 2000; Financial Bureau; Ministry of Finance.)

Pension reserves were invested differently after 1986. The first change allowed the PWSPC to use trust banks and insurance companies to manage assets, and by 1995, the proportion of total pension reserves invested in something other than government loans has risen from 1 to 20 percent. Figure 7-2 shows how this 20 percent was allocated in 1998: about half was loaned back to the government through the purchase of bonds, about 40 percent was held in equities, and almost a quarter was held in foreign securities. The corresponding figures expressed as a share of the total assets of the public pension scheme are about 8 percent in equities and 4 percent in foreign securities. In total, around 90 percent of Japanese pension assets are borrowed back by the government and used to finance public works projects and other programs.

Not surprisingly, historical rates of return on these government projects proved to be quite low. Between 1970 and 1995, the return was slightly higher than the yield on 1-year Treasury bills and almost 2 percentage points below the growth of income per capita (Iglesias and Palacios, 2000). Since pension liabilities tend to grow with wages, this differential alone accounts for significant erosion in the funding ratio. Demographic changes and increased benefits without corresponding increases in contribution rates explain most of the unfunded liability.

The purpose of investing in private securities was to raise returns. At first glance, the strategy appears to have been successful. As shown in Figure 7-3,

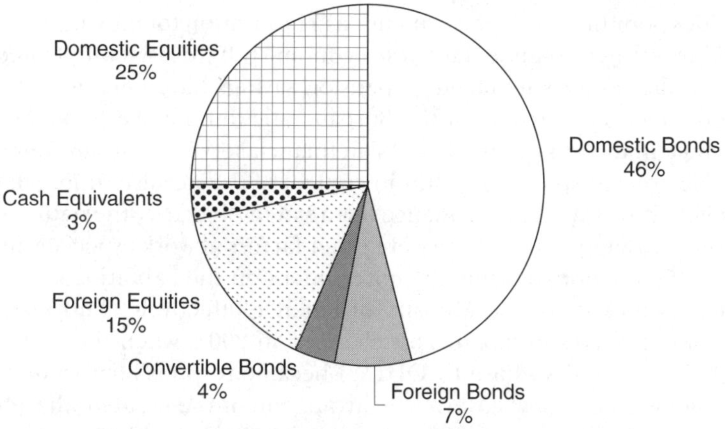

Figure 7-2. Portfolio of PWSPC, 1998. (*Source*: PWSPC (1999).)

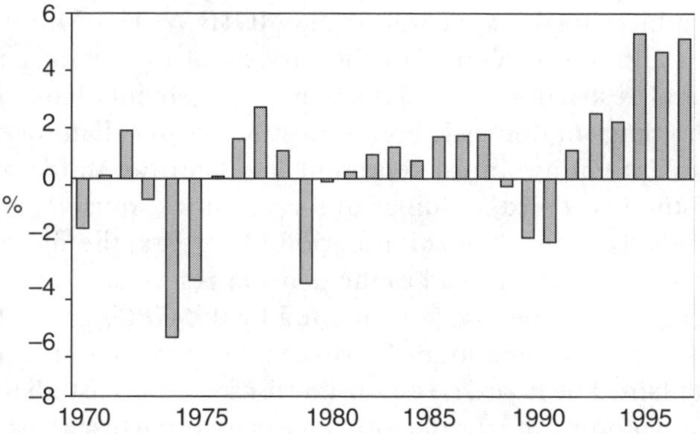

Figure 7-3. Gross pension fund returns minus T-bill rates, Japan, 1970–97. (*Source*: PWSPC (1999): IMF IFS statistics.)

returns relative to Treasury bill rates have risen since 1995. Nevertheless, returns on Japanese investments from 1986 to 1997 yielded the same compound return as the government loan portion of the portfolio, but with a much higher level of volatility. This was due to the stagnation in the domestic equity market during the 1990s, coupled with limited international diversification. The apparent improvement by the end of the period was due to the collapse in short term interest rates, a temporary effect due to a policy of holding bonds to redemption.[17]

Besides poor historical performance as a motivation for moving away from the old investment regime, Japanese economists have also complained that many public projects financed by pension savings have been wasteful and unproductive. The erosion of the bureaucratic dominance of the Ministry of Finance in the wake of the East Asian financial crisis in the late 1990s may have also created space for a shift in control of the massive fund. So, while improving investment performance was a stated objective, the nature of the final reforms suggest that there were other factors at work especially in light of the difficult choices facing the government on the liability side.

Since its inception, the Ministry of Finance effectively controlled public pension reserves in Japan. This changed in 2001, when the Minister of Health, Labor, and Welfare (MOHLW) became responsible for the funds. At the same time, a new governance arrangement was created whereby the MOHLW determined asset allocation in consultation with experts from a Subcommittee for Fund Management, themselves appointed by the same Minister. The management of the fund is now delegated to a three-person board known as the Government Pension Investment Fund (GIPF).[18] The Chairperson is appointed by the MOHLW who selects the two other Board members, subject to the approval of the MOHLW. The Minister sets the overall asset allocation. As part of the process of formulating investment policy, several restrictions and transition arrangements have been adopted. First, holdings of domestic bonds must be greater than foreign bonds. Second, foreign equities must represent less than two-thirds of domestic equity investments. Third, holdings in foreign stocks must be greater than foreign bonds. During a transition period of 7 years, the old loans made through the FILP will be repaid to the pension reserves.[19]

The investment process is implemented by the GPIF, whose Board may consult with a special committee of investment experts in setting its detailed investment plans. The Board is responsible for selecting custodians and asset managers and monitoring the performance of external firms based on stated and objective criteria. Contracts with external agents are reviewed every 5 years. All investments other than domestic bonds are managed externally. The GPIF also sets the explicit guidelines for internal management of the domestic bond portfolio. All shareholder voting rights are transferred to the external managers. The GPIF Board must present independently audited investment results to the MOHLW who in turn must disclose this to the Social Security Council, the Diet, and the general public, as part of its supervisory function. Independently audited financial statements and the auditor's report must be published annually.

New Zealand's Superannuation Fund

New Zealand is the only Organization for Economic Cooperation and Development (OECD) country that does not force workers to contribute to a publicly-mandated pension scheme. Instead, there is a general revenue-financed, universal flat benefit provided to every citizen with 10 years of residency since age 20, upon reaching age 65.[20] The Government has projected that spending on this program will rise from the current 4 percent of GDP to 9 percent in the next 50 years due to population aging.

In 2001, the government instituted a new funding effort by setting aside funds over a 40-year period. The Ministry of Finance stated the issue clearly (Government of New Zealand, 2000): "New Zealand's population is ageing. We need to start preparing now for the impending bulge in the cost of New Zealand Superannuation (NZS) that will accompany this trend. By setting aside some Crown resources toward retirement income now, while we can afford it, we will be able to smooth out the cost over time."[21]

Initially, the plan was resisted by the two main opposition parties, the Greens and the New Zealand First or National party. The Nationals favored tax cuts in the short run and insisted on keeping open the long-term option of moving to a system of individual funded accounts. The Government opposed individual accounts, arguing that lower-income workers and those with partial careers would not benefit equally, and that costs of administration could be high. The Green party held that the scheme was affordable on a pay-as-you-go basis because expenditures on children would be lower in light of population trends. It was also concerned about investment policy and argued that criteria include social or ethical investment. Some Parliamentarians argued that it made less sense to fund than to reduce the size of the national debt (Cullen, 2001).

After a heated debate, the Superannuation Act passed in 2001 with some compromises, including the inclusion of an investment criterion to deal with ethical investment and a provision allowing for future consideration of the conversion of the Superannuation fund into individual accounts. The New Zealand Superannuation Fund (NZSF) has several unique and innovative features. The first relates to the partial funding target, which is specified indirectly through a formula that determines the annual contribution from the budget. The formula is designed to generate a flow of annual contributions sufficient to meet the cost of the program over the subsequent 40 years, subject to revised annual estimates. Withdrawals from the Fund are expressly forbidden until 2020.[22] According to one study, the baseline scenario is for the Superannuation Fund to grow to around 6 percent of GDP by the year 2020 (McCulloch and Frances, 2001).

Governance of the NZSF is entrusted to a public corporation known as the "Guardians of New Zealand Superannuation Fund." It is run by a Board responsible for investing the Fund "on a prudent, commercial basis . . . ." Moreover, the Board is held to three standards:

(a) "best practice portfolio management
(b) maximizing return without undue risk to the Fund as a whole; and

(c) avoiding prejudice to New Zealand's reputation as a responsible member of the world community."

The five–seven members of the Board are first nominated by a committee. Established by the Minister of Finance, it must include at least four persons with "proven skills or relevant work experience that will enable them to identify candidates for appointment to the Board who are suitably qualified." The nominations are then considered by the Minister who must then consult with political parties in Parliament before he finally recommends to the Governor-General that the appointments be made.[23]

Once the appointments are made, the term of each Board member is limited to 5 years, unless he or she is reappointed. The Minister may remove any member from office for any reason that the Minister finds appropriate. Members must adhere to codes of conduct as laid down by the Minister and must generally behave in an honest and ethical manner, they must report any conflicts of interest as soon as possible. Liability of members as regards civil lawsuits and successfully defended criminal actions is indemnified and such costs fall on the Budget. For the purposes of the indemnification, members are never personally held liable provided the member acted in "good faith." The Minister is further empowered to "give directions" to the Guardians in writing, in a document that must be presented to the House of Representatives and published in the official gazette. The Guardians are obliged to take it into advisement and tell the Minister how they propose to respond, to be documented in the Annual Report.

The Board lays out an investment policy and reviews it annually. The Act does not set maxima or minima or impose any other limits or mandates. The Board may appoint one or more external agents to manage the investments, as well as a custodian. Performance reviews are required as soon as possible after July 2003 and then again at a maximum of 5-year intervals. These reviews are performed by an independent firm or person appointed by the Minister. Following the review, the Minister presents a report to the House of Representatives.

Sweden's National Pension Fund

A key aspect of the Swedish pension reform of 1999 was the introduction of "notional accounts," which are unfunded individual accounts where contributions equivalent to 16 percent of wage are credited to members and accumulated with interest until retirement (Disney, 1999). The notional interest rate is set equal to the average growth of incomes and the notional balance is finally converted into an indexed annuity, although during low or negative growth periods, real benefits may be reduced. The concept has since been adopted in several other countries including Latvia, Poland, and Italy. There is also a new funded component in the Swedish pension system. The contribution to this "second pillar" or Premium Savings Fund is 2.5 percent of payroll, with assets privately managed by asset managers selected by members from among dozens of mutual fund options. In order to control costs, recordkeeping and information flows are centralized, and transactions are executed in blocks rather than at the retail level. There are also complicated caps on fees charged by the mutual funds.

Sweden also instituted another pension change that has received less attention, namely, the reform of management of public pension reserves. This reform entailed the conversion of five existing funds into four new entities with different governance rules and investment policies.[24] After a transfer from the old reserves back to the central government, the remaining stock of reserves to be distributed between the four funds was equivalent to around 23 percent of GDP.

Prior to the reform, different statutory restrictions on investments applied to the separate funds. These limits prohibited investment in equities in the first three funds and limited foreign securities to less than 10 percent of assets in all five funds. Actual domestic and foreign equity holdings represented 23 and 9 percent of total assets, respectively. Fixed income instruments, including government bonds, mortgage, and other bonds represented 60 percent of the portfolio. The rest was in real estate, direct loans, and cash. The average annual compounded return between 1961 and 1995 was 2.1 percent, compared to 0.9 and 2.5 percent on short-term bank deposits and income growth respectively (Iglesias and Palacios, 2000). The reform created four funds of equal size. Each fund now has a board consisting of nine members, two of which are nominated by employers and two by employee organizations. Criteria for appointment exist but are vague and would appear to allow for much flexibility; members are chosen based on "competence to promote the management of the fund."

Investment restrictions on these new funds are significantly less onerous than those in the old regime. The objective was stated in terms of maximizing return subject to stated risk tolerances in the best interest of members. Two important constraints on investment policy are a 30 percent minimum required allocation to fixed income instruments with high ratings (low credit risk), and a 40 percent foreign currency exposure rule for investments outside Sweden. This limit does not apply to investments where currency risk is hedged. Finally, up to 5 percent of the fund can be invested in unlisted securities.

The law further states that "there shall be no industrial or economic policy goals in the management of the funds"; nevertheless, it also stipulates that investment policy should state how environmental and ethical considerations were taken into account albeit "without relinquishing the overall goal of high return on capital" (Government of Sweden, 2001). In order to prevent these funds from becoming too important in the Swedish stock market, a maximum of 2 percent of the market value of a Swedish firm can be held by any of the four funds. In addition, voting rights are limited to 10 percent in

TABLE 7-4 Reference Portfolios, Returns, and Costs for Swedish AP Funds 1–4 (2001)

	Percentage of Total Assets			
	AP1	*AP2*	*AP3*	*AP4*
Swedish shares	12	20	16.3	22.5
Foreign shares	45	40	32.6	40
Hedged	30	10		
Fixed income	40	40	44	32.5
Real estate	3	n.a.	7	0
Return 2001 (%)	−4.1	−3.7	−4.2	−5.0
Costs (bp)	8	20	8	13

Source: Author's computations from Fund Annual Reports.

listed companies and 30 percent in unlisted venture capital firms. Table 7-4 provides data on the "reference portfolios." While there is some variation, the tendency is to invest about 40 percent in fixed income instruments and 50–60 percent in equities. Of the latter, between 60 and 80 percent are foreign securities.

With regard to the investment process, the new Swedish systems set measurable targets with clear time limits for the purpose of monitoring performance. It also requires that a minimum of 10 percent of assets be managed externally. One fund, AP 2, contracted out management of 75 percent of the portfolio, but intends to reduce this significantly. Another, AP 3, contracted out about 25 percent of its asset management activities. The funds produce reports that are audited and available to the public. As public agencies, they are subject to Sweden's "open government policy act" which demands a high level of transparency. The Ministry of Finance sends an annual letter to the parliament reporting fund performance, drawing on international investment consultants.

Finally, it is interesting to note that explicit attention was given to the impact on the Swedish economy anticipated from these changes, and provisions were made to mitigate them. In particular, the Government recognized public finance concerns over the shift out of government bonds, as well as the potential impact on capital markets through the potential increase in demand for Swedish shares. Phasing in higher limits on foreign securities—starting at 5 percent and increasing steadily to 40 percent for unhedged investments—was justified by concerns about pressure on the exchange rate.

TABLE 7-5 Indicators of the Five New Public Pension Funds (2001)

	Canada	*Ireland*	*Japan*	*New Zealand*	*Sweden*
Assets in US$ (billions)	9.0	6.8	207.5	0.25	48.4
Assets/GDP (%)	1.3	5.3	5.4	0.5	22.9
Funding ratio (%)	8	n.a.	22	n.a.	n.a.
Costs/assets (%)	0.12	n.a.	0.16	n.a.	8–20

Source: Author's computations based on country Fund Reports.

Comparing the Initiatives[25]

Across the five country experiences documented here, three have long experiences with funding their public pension systems, so their reforms sought to improve on past performance. Two of the three—Japan and Sweden—had very high levels of unfunded pension liabilities relative to national income. Both also had very large reserves before the reform, while Canada had a moderate level. Ireland and New Zealand did not have public pension reserves before these initiatives.

Table 7-5 summarizes the key indicators and reveals large variation in the magnitudes involved, in both absolute and relative terms. Combined assets of the Swedish funds are by far the largest of the five countries relative to the size of the economy. The smallest fund by this measure is the incipient Superannuation fund in New Zealand. In absolute terms (in US$), the massive reserves in Japan subject to the new management system are by far the largest, at over $200 billion, projected to reach $1.2 trillion by 2008. The Swedish funds hold almost $50 billion, followed by Canada and Ireland at $9 and $7 billion, respectively. New Zealand's initial contribution to the fund in 2001 comes only to about $250 million. The costs of administering the funds range from about 12 to 20 basis points in the four countries where data are available.

Tables 7-6 and 7-7 summarize key features of the country experiences regarding governance and investment policy. Some important similarities and differences can be observed. With the exception of Japan, there was an attempt to create some distance between government bureaucrats or line ministries and the pension fund. In Canada, this was done by appointing a nominating committee that is not under the direct supervision of the Minister of Finance who ultimately appoints the board of directors. The situation is similar in New Zealand, where a nominating committee made up of private sector and professionals with relevant background submits candidates to the Governor-General. No such buffer exists in the case of Ireland, although board members must have the requisite professional background for the position. In Sweden, the Government must choose four of the nine board members from among the individuals nominated by employer and

TABLE 7-6 Comparison of Public Pension Plan Governance and Transparency

	Canada	*Ireland*	*Japan*	*New Zealand*	*Sweden*
Who acts as the fiduciary?	Professional board	Professional Board	Minister	Professional board	Hybrid board
How are these individuals appointed?	Finance Minister selects from a short list of nominees	Finance Minister appoints	Minister of Health and Labor designated by law	Governor-general selects based on list of nominees	Government appoints five and selects two each from employer/ee nominees
Are annual external audits required?	Yes	Yes	Yes	Yes	Yes
What share of portfolio is managed externally?	All	85%	Roughly one third	All	At least 10%
Are manager selection and monitoring criteria explicit and objective?	Yes	Yes	Yes	Yes	Yes

Source: Author's assessment based on country Fund Reports.

TABLE 7-7 Comparison of Investment Policy in Five Public Pension Funds

	Canada	*Ireland*	*Japan*	*New Zealand*	*Sweden*
Commercial investment mandate	Yes	Yes	Unclear	Yes	Yes
Statutory asset class restrictions	Yes, 30% limit on foreign securities	Yes, prohibition on holding domestic government bonds	Set by Minister, not in law	No	Yes, 40 percent limit on unhedged foreign securities
Statutory mandates (social/ETIs)	No	No	No	No	No
Minimum for government bonds	No	No	Yes, *de facto*	No	Yes, 30%
Shareholder voice policy	Allowed	Allowed, but limited by foreign investment	Delegated to manager but Minister can intervene	Allowed, limited by foreign investment	Allowed, but limits on individual firm shares

Source: Author's assessment based on country Fund Reports.

employee organizations. Again, there is a requirement that members should have relevant experience and background. Not included in the table is the fact that the Swedish system incorporates a unique feature of limited competition by distributing reserves among four separate funds.

The investment policy options available to each Board (and in Japan, to the MOHLW), are subject to quantitative restrictions in each country, except for New Zealand. The Irish reserve fund cannot be invested in domestic government bonds, while 30 percent of the portfolio in Sweden's AP funds must be in government bonds. Canada's main restriction is on foreign securities that cannot be more than 30 percent of the portfolio; this rule applies to private pension funds as well. The limits in Japan focus on the ratio of domestic to foreign securities and are more restrictive than the other countries in this regard. They are not statutory but rather have been determined by the Minister in the process of determining the long-term investment policy. Sweden also restricts foreign, unhedged investments to 40 percent.

Transition arrangements were necessary in the three countries that already had funds invested. Canada allowed a gradual weaning of the provinces off the automatic demand that the CPP reserves had provided, while Japan gave the FILP 7 years to unwind the old loan program that had financed public works for many years. The GPIF is required however, to continue to underwrite FILP bonds. Sweden included measures that would make the shift out of mortgage bonds more gradual, and limited foreign securities in the initial years after the reform in order to avoid pressure on their currency.

The Feasibility of Successful Centralized Funding

In each of the cases reviewed here, the decision to establish or reform a public pension system was preceded by a national debate. In that context, mandated individual account pensions were rejected in favor of centralized funding; operating on a strictly pay-as-you-go basis was also rejected. The underlying premise of the policy choice in each case was that, with the right safeguards in place, public pension plans could avoid the pitfalls of political pressure and perform at least as well as private plans. Whether public plans will be managed effectively in the future is a crucial question. There are at least sixty countries with public pension reserves equivalent to more than 1 percent of national income (see the Appendix). Globally, pension assets under public management are estimated at more than one-quarter of world GDP, although this impressive figure is driven primarily by United States and Japanese reserves. Nevertheless, a reasonable estimate for public pension fund assets excluding these two countries is probably around US$400 billion. The figure is likely to grow in the coming decades. In addition to the five initiatives already discussed, several European countries have introduced new reserve funds or are planning to do so. The Netherlands AOW Spaarfonds (savings fund) was introduced in 1998, financed by general tax revenues. Spain established a reserve fund in 1997, although the first contribution was made only in 2000. A small reserve fund was created in France in 1999 using privatization revenues and a Central Planning Commission report recommended a much larger fund be created (Leinert and Esche, 2000).

In several developing countries, public pension funds are already among the largest institutional investors. There is increasing recognition that this source of long-term savings has not been well utilized and that pension system sustainability has been compromised. This has led to heightened interest in reforming governance structures at existing funds. At the same time, many countries facing imminent demographic transitions are considering whether they should create or expand reserves, in order to cope with mounting pension obligations. China is an important example, given its size and projected rapid process, having established a national social security fund with the intention of partially funding its growing pension liability.

Risks and Mitigation Strategies

Next we look at the risks of a funding strategy and the mechanisms available to mitigate them; then we highlight the limitations imposed by country-specific factors; and finally, we revisit the debate over the two approaches to pension funding.

One obvious risk of funding public pensions is that state monopolies may not have the type of incentives that lead to good performance. Government pay scales may not attract good professionals. A lack of competition not only reduces pressure for higher productivity, but it also eliminates a set of benchmarks with which performance can be measured. These problems are not unique to public pension funds, and policies designed to align incentives for those running state monopolies have been tested with varying degrees of success in different countries (World Bank, 1995).

Another risk is that government access to pension funds may allow it to spend more than it would otherwise. Although difficult to prove empirically, the view is based on the plausible idea that the availability of these funds will lead to higher outlays. This is especially true when there is direct or even automatic access to borrowing from the fund, combined with a budgetary process that takes these resources into account when determining deficit targets.[26] In the case of Japan, for example, the FILP program is sometimes referred to as the "second budget" and it has clearly been a way to channel funds to housing and education. This situation is often reinforced by fiscal accounting standards that produce a lower net government debt figure when public pension funds purchase government bonds. To the extent that it occurs, the objective of funding may then be completely undermined.

A third and related risk involves pressures to invest pension funds in socially desirable or economically targeted projects. Mandates to invest in certain favored areas are observed in many countries, with a predictable negative impact on investment performance. In addition, there is the danger that certain investments would be excluded for reasons unrelated to maximizing risk-adjusted returns. Examples include investments in companies that produce tobacco or companies operating abroad that have labor standards that are unacceptable to unions (Mitchell and Hsin, 1997).

A fourth risk is that investment policy will lead to distortions where funds represent a large share of the potential investment pool. This is especially true where volumes traded are low and the market is illiquid. Small changes in the allocation of funds could move markets creating the potential for intervention for example, for the purpose of boosting stock markets or for supporting particular firms.

A fifth risk from having public funds investing in private securities arises from having governments become shareholders. Corporate governance could be compromised where a manager, influenced by other public policy priorities, exercised his power in a way that did not promote the interests of the firm or its shareholders. When the government is both owner and regulator of these firms, the best interest of the members of the fund and other public policy priorities may not be aligned.

The initiatives described in the last section included a number of safeguards designed to mitigate some of the specific risks associated with pension funds and political pressures. The most basic ones—the investment mandate and the governance arrangement—should also help to address the question of competence and performance incentives. All five of the schemes have a fairly clear commercial investment mandate that make them exceptional relative to the vast majority of public funds around the world. In addition, three countries—Canada, Ireland, and New Zealand—have what can be termed professional arms' length boards, while Sweden has a hybrid arrangement with a somewhat weaker professional criteria for membership. In Japan, decisions continue to be made by a government official, albeit under the tutelage of an expert advisory council. All five countries require high standards of reporting and disclosure, and except perhaps for Japan, all appear to be proactive in their efforts to increase public awareness. On the other hand, no country has been able to make those individuals responsible for key decisions personally liable or subject to the same supervisory regime as found in the private sector.

With respect to government consumption, the Irish fund prohibits investment in domestic government bonds.[27] In the case of Canada, its inherited portfolio was heavily weighted towards provincial bonds. As a result, the CPPIB was allowed to concentrate exclusively on equities. Commercial investments, combined with the arms' length governance structure, should provide some protection against pressures to finance deficits, although the Swedish 30 percent minimum rule runs counter to this objective. The Japanese fund seems the most susceptible to this problem because of its governance arrangement combined with its investment restrictions. According to its reference portfolio, it must hold a portfolio of around 70 percent in government bonds, compared to the 90 percent for the overall reserve.

It is interesting that all five funds examined here avoid mandates for targeted investments and adhere to a commercial investment policy in principle. However, as noted, there was some opposition to this in New Zealand and, along with Sweden, there are some conditions related to ethical investment included in the legislation. The situation is less clear in Japan, where there appears to be some discretion in this area left to the responsible Minister.

The danger that the funds might be used in a way that distorts capital markets is mitigated in Ireland and New Zealand through large foreign investment shares. In Sweden, limits on shares in individual firms, along with relatively high ceilings on foreign investment, would seem to provide good protection, especially if the four funds truly operate independently of one another. In all of the countries except Japan, the arms'-length Board arrangement, combined with the commercial investment mandate, is an important safeguard against a government that wants to prop up its market or direct investments to favored firms or instruments. Once again, the Japanese case is the most troubling in this regard. The size of the fund and its direct control by a government official have already led analysts to suspect that the government may intervene in financial markets.

In each of the five countries, the funds are instructed to employ passive investment techniques for a substantial proportion of the equity portfolio. applying a pure index fund strategy has not been adopted in any of the five countries. The CPPIB began with a pure index fund approach, but it moved to active management, partly to avoid overexposure to a specific firm, but also due to its decision to move into private equities.

One way around some of the potential problems involved in domestic investing, be it in private or public securities, is to invest abroad. Despite sound financial arguments for diversification, even low levels of foreign investment can be especially difficult for public pension funds if political pressures arise to "keep the capital at home." This has been true in Canada, where union pressure against foreign investment by the CPPIB was strong. It does not seem to have been an issue in Ireland or New Zealand, where investing abroad is an accepted practice. In Ireland, for example, more than two-thirds of Irish private pension fund assets are invested abroad. The relatively high proportion of Swedish investments allowed to go abroad was a sharp deviation from the past policy that had led to a foreign share of

TABLE 7-8 Subjective Assessment of Safeguards Against Political Interference

	Canada	*Ireland*	*Japan*	*New Zealand*	*Sweden*	*Mitigation Strategies*
Safeguards in system against						
Increased government borrowing	High	High	Low	High	Moderate	CIM, P-AL-B, Prohibition on public bonds
Social mandates and ETIs	High	High	Moderate	High	High	CIM, P-AL-B, Prohibition on ETIs
Capital market distortion	Moderate	High	Low	High	Moderate	CIM, P-AL-B, foreign investment
Corporate governance conflict	Moderate	High	Moderate	High	Moderate	CIM, P-AL-B, foreign investment

Note: CIM = commercial investment mandate.
P-AL-B = Professional, arms-length board.
Source: Author's computation.

only 9 percent. Japan's foreign exposure remains quite limited: 15 percent, according to the reference portfolio. Given the size of the fund, this target will make it difficult to avoid distortionary influence over fiscal policy or capital markets (or both). More importantly perhaps, it increases the exposure of the pension fund to Japanese country risk and reduces potential diversification gains.

To summarize this discussion, Table 7-8 provides a qualitative assessment of how well each of the five countries addresses the specific challenges for political insulation. The last column also lists some of the factors that can mitigate these risks. Based on previous studies, it seems safe to say that most other countries with public pension funds have not implemented these safeguards and would generally receive a "low" rating in all categories.

The Influence of Country-Specific Conditions

Time will tell whether the five reform plans discussed here will succeed. In addition to the governance arrangement, investment policy and process, disclosure and reporting rules, and other elements of design codified in the laws, success will also be influenced by conditions in which the public

TABLE 7-9 Indicators of Country-Specific Conditions for Public Pension Management

	Canada	*Ireland*	*Japan*	*New Zealand*	*Sweden*
Stock market cap. (% GDP, 1995)	64	43	72	56	78
Value traded (% GDP, 1995)	32	22	24	15	41
Foreign exchange restrictions	None	None	None	None	None
Accountability ranking (out of 173)	18	9	35	7	4
Rule of Law ranking (out of 166)	10	18	15	8	11

Source: See the Appendix.

pension scheme operates. Such country-specific conditions include the relative size of the capital market and its liquidity, the state of the asset management industry and related services available in the country, restrictions on foreign exchange conversion, and most importantly, the overall governance situation in terms of accountability of government, corruption, and the rule of law. The countries covered in this chapter are also an unusual set: they are rich, relatively well-governed countries, with certain favorable conditions for implementing key elements of a successful policy. Table 7-9 above quantifies some of these factors.

The conditions in other countries with significant public pension reserves are less conducive to success, especially poor and middle income countries. For example, among the more than 60 countries listed in the Appendix, we estimate that 36 have public fund reserves that exceed the value traded on their stock markets. An even larger proportion does not have a functioning bond market or does not issue government debt. The supply of debt and equities can be increased through parallel policy measures such as privatization, but the need to invest abroad in order to avoid the problems of capital market distortion and shareholder conflict of interest is often inescapable. For many developing countries with serious foreign exchange restrictions, this option may be limited.

Table 7-9 does not reveal the availability of domestic or foreign asset managers and other professionals. In the five countries of special focus here, actuarial and investment experts are relatively abundant due to a well developed private industry; however, these are scarce in most developing countries. Most public pension funds manage all of their investments in-house and with local personnel. It is important to adjust pay scales in order to attract these individuals and/or to hire foreign managers, but many poor countries are too small to attract much interest from providers. About one-third of the public funds have less than US$100 million while about half are probably below US$500 million.

There may be creative ways to deal with some of these issues and perhaps lower costs. Some experts have suggested asset swaps to deal with foreign exchange constraints in some countries (Bodie and Merton, 2002). The risk premium that would be involved in such a transaction could make the idea unattractive in some countries, and it remains to be attempted by any public pension fund. Regional initiatives such as among the Francophone countries may achieve economies of scale in several areas, including asset management and custodianship.

Finally, there is the overarching question of governance. Here we refer not to the Boards of public pension funds, along with their policies and processes, but rather to the broader question of accountability and transparency of government itself. In practice, even a well-designed system can be compromised by extralegal action. Moreover, the only discipline for public pension fund boards, not subject to any regulatory authority with limited personal liability, is the public accounting that must be demanded at the broad political level.

Some international evidence on the relationship between good national governance and public pension fund performance is available. Figure 7-4 plots long-term compounded rates of return for twenty public pension funds relative to bank deposit rates, against a measure of "voice and accountability"

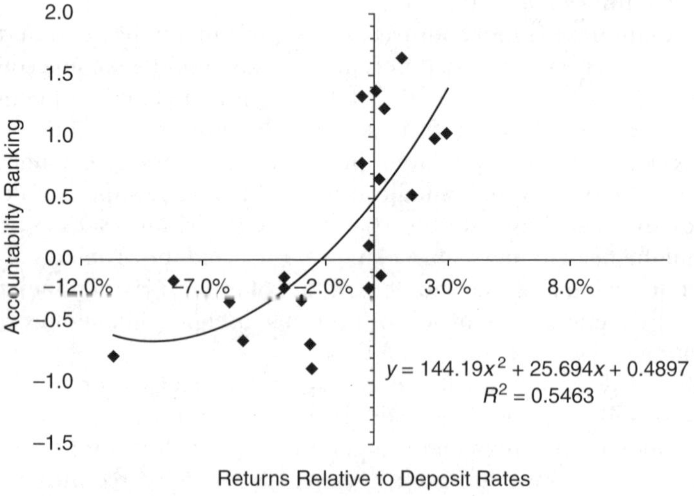

Figure 7-4. Accountability of government and public pension fund returns. (*Source*: Adapted from Iglesias and Palacios (2000) and Kaufmann et al. (2002).)

from the World Bank's database on governance indicators. With only one exception (Malaysia), countries with a negative ranking reported long-run returns below those they could have achieved if the money had been held in a bank deposit in the same country during the same period.[28]

Implications for the Debate over Publicly versus Privately-Managed Pension Assets

The main alternative to centralized funding of DB plans is to introduce privately-managed individual account defined contribution (DC) plans. Critics of the centralized approach, skeptical about the potential for shielding large public funds from government interventions, include Barro (1998), who argued that: "it is politically infeasible to have a public program that is funded to a substantial degree. Large-scale funding seems to be sustainable only in the context of privatized (though possibly publicly-mandated) social security".

Yet many of the challenges for public funds also apply to privately managed funds, including the general quality of governance. Only a public entity can supervise private funds and the task requires a certain level of competence and transparency. Also, in its role as supervisor and regulator, government can impose investment restrictions that may lead to the same distortionary consequences as might have prevailed under direct public management. Finally, decentralization and competition implies additional costs that can reduce the net investment returns perceived by the members.

The option to manage funds in a decentralized manner does appear to require a lower threshold of governance to operate, and it also introduces a number of disciplining features that are absent from even the best centralized model. One advantage is that moving from DB to DC creates a powerful incentive for members of the scheme to actively search out good management and reward or punish those making the investment decisions. In an open fund arrangement (where individuals have a choice of provider), this is achieved mostly through competition as individuals "vote with their feet." Malfeasance can be sanctioned by a supervisor entrusted with appropriate powers and/or the courts through the assessment of liability. This applies not only to the investment function, but also to recordkeeping and other services.

A second advantage of individual accounts is the creation of well-defined property rights. In a partially-funded DB scheme, the claims of members are to a large extent on future taxpayers, some of whom are not yet born. This muddles the meaning of the funding ratio, since returns may be less important than political lobbying to ensure that future fiscal priorities respect pension promises made earlier.

In addition, problems associated with the government's conflict of interest when it acts as shareholder and institutional investor are largely avoided through decentralization. There is still potential for a government to use its regulatory powers to channel funds to certain areas (e.g. minimum investment in socially-responsible projects or depressed regions), but it seems clear that this is more difficult to do if control of the funds is out of the hands of someone appointed by the government itself.

Cost pressures are likely to be higher in private DC schemes, although in many countries, public monopolies are massively overstaffed and inefficient. Marketing expenses can represent as much as half of the charges levied on members in decentralized schemes and much of this is unproductive for the economy as a whole. On the other hand, more efficient allocation of capital in the economy is a potentially large externality, difficult to replicate with a centralized model. There may even be a positive role for the private funds in corporate governance under certain conditions. Finally, what matters to the member of the scheme is the net investment return which is only partly determined by commissions.

While both approaches involve major design and implementation challenges, it is probably more feasible in most countries to succeed in funding through a private, competitive model than through centralized public management. One possible compromise solution would involve a centralized, low-cost, default scheme with an opt-out provision that allowed for the use of privately managed funds. This would impose some market discipline on the public fund while putting pressure on private managers not to pass along large marketing bills to participants. In countries with small memberships and/or assets, the private options could be limited and the firms selected through a tendering process. A key feature of this approach obviously, is the shift away from DB and partial funding.

Conclusions

Our survey shows that many countries have adopted a financing strategy that involves funding public pension promises. In addition to the normal challenges of pension governance, public plans face additional obstacles arising from the tendency of governments to interfere in the investment process. In the last few years, five countries passed legislation designed to mitigate these risks. Reviewing these cases, a number of "good practices" not commonly observed in most public funds were highlighted. These include (i) explicit funding targets and mechanisms to trigger action in the case of deviation from this objective; (ii) commercial investment policies flowing from these targets and aimed at maximizing risk-adjusted returns for members; (iii) professional boards selected through a process that maintains reasonable distance from government officials; (iv) prohibition on social investment criteria or ETIs; (v) significant share of investment done through external managers selected by explicit and objective criteria; (vi) avoidance of strict portfolio limits, especially on foreign investments; and (vii) high standards of reporting and disclosure including annual, independent audits, performance reviews, and codes of conduct for Board members, all made available to the public.

By adopting these practices, public plans can improve their performance, thus increasing the sustainability of their retirement promises and removing distortions. Country-specific conditions will always pose formidable challenges and may require difficult solutions, such as investing a very high proportion of assets abroad. The most important constraint, however, is likely to be the broader condition of national governance. Ultimately, even the most resilient and well-considered design for a national pension plan can be compromised if there is no way to hold the sponsor accountable.

Notes

1 For a review of the international evidence from many countries, see Iglesias and Palacios (2000).

2 For example, the press reported that Taiwan's government used "massive government intervention with large purchases by government pension and insurance funds" to prop up the stock market in 1999 (*Wall Street Journal*, 1999).

3 Of course, private management in a decentralized and competitive system need not guarantee good results. Private fund managers must be supervised closely, especially when contributions are mandated, thus raising the implicit (or sometimes explicit) liability of the state *vis-à-vis* their performance. In addition, the regulatory climate and in particular, investment rules and restrictions imposed on private managers can ultimately obviate the advantages of better incentives and competition. Finally, the cost of administration may be higher in a decentralized system.

4 Although not discussed in this chapter, an interesting exception to this rule is found in Costa Rica where the Superintendency of Pensions regulates both fully funded, private pensions and a partially-funded, public scheme. However, its role is still not clearly defined with respect to the latter.

5 Association of Canadian Pension Management (ACPM, 1997: 4).

6 In the United States, the Thrift Savings Plan (TSP), a DC scheme for Federal civil servants, provides an example of this problem in the case of a public scheme. Passage of the legislation creating the TSP was significantly delayed due to reluctance of potential trustees to assume liability. Ultimately, Congress granted exemptions from liability (Schreitmuller, 1998).

7 In the 1960s and 1970s, many developing countries in Latin America and Africa adopted the scaled premium approach where partial funding was aimed at maintaining target long-term contribution rates.

8 For a variety of real world examples, see Iglesias and Palacios (2000).

9 Useem and Hess (2001) and Mitchell and Hsin (1997) present empirical evidence of the influence of governance structure on asset allocation in US public pension plans at the state level.

[10] Another interesting example is the Norwegian Petroleum Fund. While not a pension fund *per se*, the assets have been explicitly earmarked to deal with the impact of population aging.
[11] Government of Canada (1998: 37).
[12] "Gender" representation was included among the criteria.
[13] The external auditor reviews internal controls every 6 months, although this is not required.
[14] Other services, such as custody, performance measurement, and investment accounting services are also provided externally by State Street Trust.
[15] CPPIB (2001).
[16] Most of this consisted of proceeds from a Telecom privatization earmarked for this purpose.
[17] Usuki (2002) points out that returns between 1995 and 2000 were slightly better than comparable market indices.
[18] This terminology is taken from Usuki (2001). Sakamoto (2001) refers to this as the Investment Fund of Social Security Reserves (IFSSR).
[19] In the future, bonds will be issued by FILP to support public projects.
[20] The idea of introducing a mandatory, funded retirement savings scheme was rejected in a referendum by what could fairly be termed a consensus of 97 percent of voters.
[21] Government of New Zealand (2000) (Executive Summary).
[22] The Government determined that transfers to the Fund would total 600 million NZ$ in 2001–02, 1,200 million in 2002–03, and 1,800 million in 2003–04. However, until the Fund is fully established and operating in 2002, it will earn the interest rate on short-term bank deposits.
[23] The nominating committee, appointed by the Minister of Finance in 2001, has members including the Chief Executive of the Investment Savings and Insurance Association, the Chairman of the First State Property Trust, a chartered accountant, a member of the Securities Commission, and the Executive Director of New Zealand Businesses for Social Responsibility.
[24] The new system also includes two more public funds. The first is a residual scheme from the old system that invests in small and medium sized enterprises in Sweden. It is relatively small. The second is the default fund for individuals who do not express their choice of private fund manager for their fully-funded, "Premium" pensions.
[25] Legislation for the three Anglophone countries can be found as follows:
Ireland: <http://www.ntma.ie/Publications/Pen_Res_Fund_Act_2000.pdf>.
New Zealand: <http://www.treasury.govt.nz/release/super/#15October>.
Canada: <www.cppib.ca/>.
[26] See Buchanan (1990) for a discussion in the US context.
[27] In its first year of its operation, critics asked to defer its mandated contribution to the fund. New Zealand's finance minister was also approached on this topic, even before the fund began to operate.
[28] To place this result in context, the accountability ranking is also included for the sixty-five countries listed in Appendix. Roughly half of the countries with public pension reserves, and about three-quarters of developing countries in the table, have negative rankings. In the global sample, the only non-OECD country among the top twenty (out of 173 countries) is Mauritius.

APPENDIX

TABLE A-1 Public Pension Reserves in Selected Countries

	Reserves Relative to			Reserves in US dollars (millions)	Board Composition	Voice and Accountability
	Year	GDP (%)	Traded Shares (%)			
SWITZERLAND	1998	5.7	5.9	15,000	Tripartite	1.73
FINLAND	2000	7.3	48	9,400	Tripartite	1.69
SWEDEN	2001	22.9	56.1	48,000	Tripartite	1.65
NETHERLANDS	2000	31	49.4		Tripartite	1.61
DENMARK	2000	18.8	124	30,483	Tripartite	1.60
NEW ZEALAND	2001	0.5	3.5	252	Professional	1.59
IRELAND	2001	5.3	24.4	6,600	Professional	1.57
COSTA RICA	2001	8.2		1,326	Tripartite	1.37
CANADA	2001	1.3	4.1	9,032	Professional	1.33
MAURITIUS	2000	17.5	971.4	686	Tripartite	1.27
UNITED STATES	2000	9.4	12.8	9,31,000	Government	1.24
SOUTH AFRICA	2000	19.2	153	27,573	Tripartite	1.17
JAPAN	2000	5.4	24	16,70,224	Government	1.03
KOREA, SOUTH	2000	12	29.5	54,866	Tripartite	0.98
GUYANA	2000	10.7				0.94
CAPE VERDE	2000	10		58	Government	0.92
BOTSWANA	2001					0.80
JAMAICA	1999	5.7	74	392	Tripartite	0.78
PANAMA	2000					0.77
INDIA	1998	4.1	97.6	17,515	Tripartite	0.66
TRINIDAD AND TOBAGO	1999	11.1	427	762		0.61
PHILIPPINES	1998	11.2	56.3	7,324	Tripartite	0.53
BENIN	2000		none		Tripartite	0.47
THAILAND	2000	2.8	8.2	3,000	Tripartite	0.37
NAMIBIA	2000	37.5		1,254	Tripartite	0.32
MALI	2000		none		Tripartite	0.32
MADAGASCAR	2000		none		Tripartite	0.28
SENEGAL	1998	1.3	none	59	Tripartite	0.12
MEXICO	2000	n.a.				0.12

TABLE A-1 *Continued.*

		Reserves Relative to		*Reserves in US dollars (millions)*	*Board Composition*	*Voice and Accountability*
	Year	*GDP (%)*	*Traded Shares (%)*			
SINGAPORE	2000	55.6	77	51,411	Government	0.11
NIGER	2000	n.a.	none		Tripartite	0.11
JORDAN	1996	16.9	164.1	1,186		0.10
GHANA	1995	9.4	3,142.2	371	Tripartite	0.02
PAPUA NEW GUINEA	2000	6.9		263		−0.03
HONDURAS	1994	3.4	104.2	118		−0.04
NEPAL	1997	4.7	1,169.8	226	Government	−0.06
NICARAGUA	1996	3.2	none	61		−0.06
TANZANIA	1995	0.9		37	Tripartite	−0.07
MALAYSIA	2000	54.4	60.4	48,591	Tripartite	−0.13
SRI LANKA	1998	15.8	930.3	2,498	Tripartite	−0.23
MOROCCO	1999	9.6	367.7	3,347	Tripartite	−0.23
LEBANON	2000	7.2		1,000	Government	−0.32
GUATEMALA	1995	1.7		249		−0.33
INDONESIA	2000	2.8	38.4	3,690		−0.40
COLOMBIA	2000	3.6	225	2,932	Tripartite	−0.41
NIGERIA	1998	1.2	1,233	160	Tripartite	−0.44
TUNISIA	2000	5.7	154.6	1,114	Tripartite	−0.61
YEMEN	1999	1	none			−0.63
EGYPT	1998	33.1	2,364.3	27,361		−0.65
KENYA	1995	12.1	1,732.8	929	Tripartite	−0.68
GAMBIA	1995	11.1		38	Tripartite	−0.73
UGANDA	2000	1		27	Tripartite	−0.79
MALDIVES	1999	1.5	none			−0.81
CAMEROON	2000				Tripartite	−0.82
ETHIOPIA	1997	1.4		98	Government	−0.85
CHAD	1999	0.3	none	4	Tripartite	−0.88
ZIMBABWE	1999	1.8	none	85	Tripartite	−0.90
SWAZILAND	1995	6.6	none	70	Tripartite	−0.93
SAUDI ARABIA	2000	135.2	none	2,34,000	Government	−1.07
CHINA	2001	2	27.6	21,135	Government	−1.11
COTE D'IVOIRE	2000				Tripartite	−1.19
BHUTAN	1999	9	none	39	Government	−1.27
PAKISTAN	2000	1.4	26.4	776	Tripartite	−1.43
BELIZE	2000	28.2		65	Tripartite	n.a.

Sources: World Development Indicators, Kaufmann et al. (2002), ISSA (1997), and country sources.

Note: For Canada, Japan, and Sweden, reserve figure is only for new scheme.

References

Angelis, Theodore J. 1998. “Investing Public Money in Private Markets: What are the Right Questions?” Presentation at the 1998 National Academy of Social Insurance Conference, January.

Association of Canadian Pension Management. (ACPM). 1997. “Governance of Pension Plans”. ACPM.

Barr, Daniel. 2001. “Reform of the Swedish National Pension Fund”. Presentation of the Ministry of Finance, Government of Sweden.

Barro, Robert. 1998. “Thoughts on Social Security”. Unpublished, Harvard University.

Bodie, Zvi and Robert Merton. 2002. “International Pension Swaps”. *Journal of Pension Economics and Finance* 1: 77–83, Cambridge University Press.

Brinson, Gary, Brian Singer, and Gilbert Beebower. 1991. “Determinants of Portfolio Performance II: An Update”. *Financial Analysts Journal* May/June.

Buchanan, James. 1990. In *Social Security's Looming Surpluses: Prospects and Implications*, ed. Carolyn Weaver. Washington: AEI Press, pp. 45–56.

Canada Pension Plan Investment Board (CPPIB). 2000–2001. “Annual Report”. <www.cppib.ca/>.

— 2002. “Investment Statement”. April 10. <www.cppib.ca/>.

Cullen, Michael. 2001. “Superannuation”. Speech to the Annual Conference of Life Broker's Association, July 25, Kilbirnie, New Zealand. <www.scoop.co.nz/mason/stories/PA0107/S00416.htm>.

Disney, Richard. 1999. “Notional Accounts as a Pension Reform Strategy: An Evaluation”. *Pension Reform Primer Series*, Social Protection Discussion Paper No. 9928. World Bank. <www.worldbank.org/pensions>.

Financial Bureau, Japanese Ministry of Finance. 2000. “FILP Report 2000”. Tokyo.

Government of Canada. 1998. “Final CPP Legislation: Briefing Book—Questions and Answers”.

Government of Ireland. 1999. “Report of the Budget Strategy for Aging Group”. July. <www.irlgov.ie/finance/pubbstag.htm>.

Government of New Zealand. 2000. “Pre-funding New Zealand Superannuation: Funding Arrangements”. Wellington, New Zealand: Office of Hon. Dr. Michael Cullen, Treasurer/Minister of Finance, Parliament Buildings, September 6.

Government of Sweden. 2001. “Sammanfanting—English Summary”.

Iglesias, Augusto and Robert Palacios. 2000. “Managing Public Pension Reserves: Evidence from the International Experience,” *Pension Reform Primer Series*, Social Protection Discussion Paper No. 0003. World Bank. <www.worldbank.org/pensions>.

Irish Pension Board. (IPB). 1998. “Securing Retirement Income: National Pensions Policy Initiative Report”. Dublin.

Kaufman, Daniel, Aart Kraay and Pablo Zoido-Lobaton. 2000. “Dataset from: ‘Aggregating Governance Indicators’ and ‘Governance Matters’ ”. World Bank. <www.worldbank.org/wbi/governance/datasets.htm>.

Kaufmann, R. K., L. Zhou, C. J. Tucker, D. Slayback, N. V. Shabanov, and R. B. Myneni. 2002. Reply to Comment on “Variations in Northern Vegetation Activity Inferred from Satellite Data of Vegetation Index During 1981–1999' by J. R. Ahlbeck”. *Journal of Geophysical Research* 107(D11), 10.1029/2001JD001516.

Leinert, Johanes and Andreas Esche. 2000. "Advance Funding of Pensions". *International Reform Monitor,* Special Issue, Bertelsmann Foundation, Gutersloh. October.

MacNaughton, John. 2001. "Principles and Practices of Governance for Public Pension Funds". Presentation at World Bank Conference on Public Pension Fund Management, Washington, September 25. <www1.worldbank.org/finance/html/presentations_ppfm.html>.

Maher, Anne. 2001. "National Pensions Reform Fund in Ireland". Presentation at the World Bank Conference on Public Pension Fund Management, Washington, September 25. <www1.worldbank.org/finance/html/ presentations_ppfm.html>.

McCulloch, Brian. 2000. "Funding New Zealand Superannuation". Working Document. Treasury, New Zealand.

— and Jane Frances. 2001. "Financing New Zealand Superannuation". Working Paper 1(20). Treasury, New Zealand.

Mitchell, Olivia S. 1998. "Administrative Costs in Public and Private Pension Systems". In *Privatizing Social Security,* ed. M. Feldstein. NBER, Chicago: University of Chicago Press, pp. 403–456.

— and Robert S. Smith. 1994. "Pension Funding in the Public Sector". *Review of Economics and Statistics,* May: 278–290.

— and Ping-Lung Hsin. 1997. "Managing Public Sector Pensions". In *Public Policy Toward Pensions,* eds. J. Shoven and S. Schieber. Twentieth Century Fund, Cambridge, MA: MIT Press, pp. 246–266.

Munnell, Alicia. 1983. "The Pitfalls of Social Investing: The Case of Public Pensions and Housing". *New England Economic Review,* September/October: 20–40.

— and Annika Sunden. 1999. "Economically Targeted Investments in Public Pensions". Pension Research Council Working Paper. Wharton School.

Pension Welfare Service Public Corporation (PWSPC). 1999. "Overview of Fund Investments". Mimeograph. Tokyo.

OECD. 2000. *Institutional Investors Yearbook 2000 Edition.* Paris: OECD.

OECD. 2001. *Social Expenditure Database,* 3rd edn (1980–1998). Paris: OECD.

Sakamoto, Junichi. 1998. "Pension Reform and the Funding Alternative". Paper Presented at the International Social Security Association, Second Seminar for Social Security Actuaries and Statisticians from Industrialized Countries. Tokyo, May.

— 2001. "Pension Reform and Funding Options". Paper Presented to the IAA International Pensions Seminar. Brighton, England, June 6–7.

Schreitmuller, Richard. 1998. "The Federal Employees" Retirement System Act of 1986'. *Transactions of the Society of Actuaries* 40(1): 543–602.

UK Treasury. 2000. "The Myners Review of Institutional Investment". London.

Useem, Michael and David Hess. 2001. "Governance and Investments of Public Pensions." In *Pensions in the Public Sector,* eds. Olivia S. Mitchell and Edwin Hustead. Pension Research Council, Philadelphia: University of Pennsylvania, pp. 132–152.

Usuki, Masaharu. 2001. "New Public Pension Fund Management System in Japan." Presentation at World Bank Conference on Public Pension Fund Management. Washington, September 25. <www1.worldbank.org/finance/html/presentations_ppfm.html>.

Usuki, Masaharu. 2002. "New Investment Management Scheme of Public Pension Fund in Japan." Unpublished Mimeo. Tokyo: NLI Research Institute.

von Furstenberg, George. 1979. *Social Security Versus Private Saving.* Cambridge, MA: Ballinger Press.

Wahal, Sunil. 1996. "Pension Fund Activism and Firm Performance." *Journal of Financial and Quantitative Analysis* 31(1): 1–23.

Wall Street Journal. 1999. "Taipei Signals Willingness to Discuss Unification if Beijing Accepts Taiwan as Diplomatic Equal." July 19: A10.

Weaver, Carolyn. 1990. *Social Security's Looming Surpluses: Prospects and Implications.* Washington: AEI Press.

World Bank. 1995. "Bureaucrats in Business: The Economics and Politics of Government Ownership." Policy Research Report.

—— 2002. Governance Indicators Website: <www.worldbank.org/wbi/governance/datasets.htm#dataset2001>.

Part II

Global Developments in Retirement Risk Transfer

Chapter 8

Understanding Individual Account Guarantees

Marie-Eve Lachance and Olivia S. Mitchell

Demographic aging is prompting workers everywhere to realize that they are vulnerable to the inherent uncertainty that arises from unfunded social security systems. This realization has prompted a global wave of social security reforms, resulting in over twenty countries setting up individual account (IA) plans. Interest in this movement has gained strength in the United States with the release of the President's Commission to Strengthen Social Security (CSSS) Final Report, in which voluntary IAs are proposed as a component of a reformed system.[1]

Key strengths of IAs are that participants gain ownership in their accounts and may diversify their pension investments. But in view of the recent demise of Enron, some have argued that access to capital market investments might impose new risk on IA participants.[2] Concern over capital market volatility has consequently prompted some policymakers to propose "guarantees" for defined contribution pension accumulations.[3] Abroad, such guarantees have already been adopted in several Latin American countries undergoing reform,[4] and more recently, in Japan and Germany.[5]

The purpose of this chapter is to illustrate how one might evaluate pension guarantees in the context of an IA component of a social security reform.[6] Plan designers and budget analysts should recognize guarantee costs and identify how they can be financed. Sensible public policy that proposes new guarantees must identify who will pay for them and why. In what follows, the first section, "An Overview of Pension Guarantees," surveys the major guarantee designs adopted or suggested in a social security context. The section entitled "Models for Costing Pension Guarantees," provides the background necessary to analyze guarantee costs. The third section on Illustrating Guarantee Costs, provides five examples of guarantee designs and

The authors are grateful for comments provided by Zvi Bodie, Neil Doherty, Alex Muermann, and Kent Smetters. They also benefited from research support provided by the Michigan Retirement Research Center, the Shannon Schieber Memorial Fund, and the Society of Actuaries (Lachance); the Pension Research Council (Mitchell); and the Department of Insurance and Risk Management at the Wharton School of the University of Pennsylvania (both authors).

their cost estimates, using the methodology and assumptions developed in the Appendix. A fourth section on Financing Pension Accumulation Guarantees, discusses alternative financing options for the pension guarantee, and a final section concludes.

An Overview of Pension Guarantees

While many alternative pension guarantee mechanisms could be envisaged, they may be classified into two general categories: minimum *rate of return* guarantees, and minimum *benefit* guarantees.

Under a minimum *rate of return* guarantee, plan participants would be entitled to receive payments at least equal to their lifetime contributions to the system plus some rate of return. One variant on this theme is a "principal guarantee," which is equivalent to guaranteeing a nominal rate of return of zero percent. This approach has been adopted in Germany and Japan, under which participants must receive at least their plan contributions at retirement (but not before). A more generous design proposed by Feldstein and Samwick (2001) involves a "real principal guarantee," under which participants would be guaranteed their lifetime contributions adjusted according to an inflation index. Still a more generous guarantee might promise participants their contributions plus some minimum rate of return. For example, participants could be told that they would always receive their contributions plus the return on a government bond (e.g. the 10-year Treasury bond).[7]

Irrespective of the particular guaranteed rate of return adopted, cost will depend in part on how often the guarantee threshold is tested. In many designs, as in the German and Japanese cases, the guarantee is evaluated only once, at the end of the plan participant's worklife. In other instances, the minimum rate of return is imposed annually. In Uruguay, for instance, the investment-based system provides pension participants a minimum *annual* real rate of return of two percent. In Chile, pension funds must pay an annual real rate of return that is a function of the average annual real rate of return earned by the entire set of pension funds and in Colombia, the guaranteed rate of return is evaluated over 3 year periods (Fischer, 1999; Pennachi, 1999).

A prominent alternative to a minimum *rate of return* guarantee is a minimum *benefit* guarantee. In this second approach, plan participants are promised that the benefits they will receive from social security at retirement will be at least as high as a minimum annuity, irrespective of their account's actual investment performance. For instance, the Chilean reform provides a "minimum annuity" to defined contribution participants, financed by a pay-as-you-go program (Zarita, 1994; Pennachi, 1999). Some social security systems have adopted a multi-pillar structure of benefits in which the participant receives the combination of a defined benefit annuity (first-pillar) and an IA (second-pillar). Under this design, evaluating possible program costs must take into account the sum of these benefits, and compare them to the minimum annuity. In the United States context, Feldstein and Samwick (2001) describe a "mixed" system where part of the participant's social security tax could be contributed to an IA while the remainder is used to finance the pay-as-you-go program. Their suggested model also includes a guarantee that participants would receive benefits at least as great as under the present law benefit formula.[8]

The Moral Hazard Issue

In addition to the guarantee formulas described above, another factor influencing the cost of the guarantee is the level of investment risk taken by the IA participant. Participants may boost the cost of the guarantee, if they elect to hold riskier investments in their portfolios. Naturally this can give rise to a moral hazard problem, as recognized by Bodie and Merton (1993) and Smetters (2002), among others.

Several tools are available to address the moral hazard problem. One would be to specify a *standard investment portfolio* and provide the guarantee only to those participants who elected that standard portfolio. Another approach would let participants invest in the portfolio of their choosing, but then guarantee payments would be computed using the standard portfolio as a benchmark, rather than the participant's actual investment returns. This second approach leaves participants with more investment flexibility, though it would not protect them against investment risk greater than experienced by the standard portfolio.

Models for Costing Pension Guarantees

This section models guarantee outcomes under the two approaches outlined above, and it further illustrates likely guarantee costs using financial techniques for determining the economic cost of guaranteed pension payments.

Guaranteeing Retirement Income

It is useful to develop a simple notation for costing both the minimum *rate of return* and minimum *benefit* guarantee approaches. Denote by T the number of years over which a plan participant contributes to his IA. For a young worker (i.e. a new system participant), the period T corresponds to the length of the full worklife. By contrast, when the system is first introduced, a more senior worker would have a much shorter window during which he could contribute to his IA. Further, let IA_T and G_T denote, respectively, the value of the IA and of a given guarantee formula at retirement.

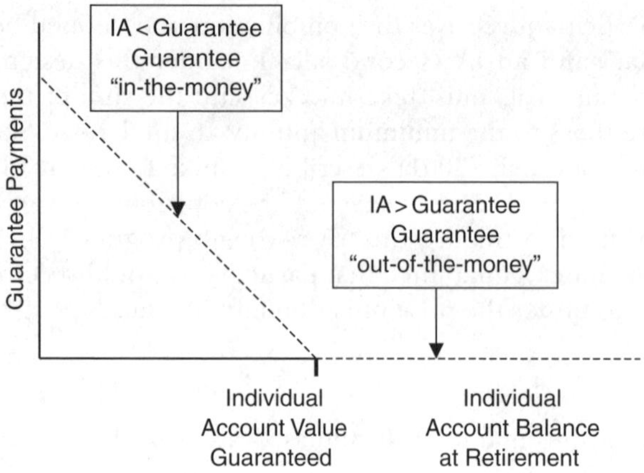

Figure 8-1. Guarantee payments as a function of the IA Value. (*Source*: Authors' calculations.)

The guarantee payments can then be specified depending on the account's investment result. No guarantee is paid at retirement if, at that time, the IA accumulation exceeds the value of the guarantee: $\mathrm{IA}_T > G_T$. But if the value of the IA is below the guaranteed minimum, then the guarantee payment must cover the difference (i.e. $G_T - \mathrm{IA}_T$). The guarantee payoffs, illustrated in Figure 8-1, may be represented as follows:

$$f_T = \max[0, G_T - \mathrm{IA}_T]. \tag{8.1}$$

It must be noted that equation (1) is applicable in the case of a newly created IA system, with no legacy commitment from a prior system. More generally, IA models sometimes develop after a partial or full conversion from a prior pay-as-you-go program. Under a full conversion, the participant would receive the sum of his IA and (possibly) an additional benefit reflecting his participation under the legacy system. Under a partial conversion (or "mixed" system), the participant would receive a combination of his IA and also a defined benefit component as specified under the old plan, perhaps subject to adjustment. Thus under a minimum *benefit* guarantee, it is necessary to adjust equation (1) by adding to the IA value any additional benefits.

To illustrate this point, we examine how one might adjust equation (8.1) for a "mixed" reform. Under the United States social security system, for instance, workers are promised a retirement annuity with present value, SS_T. If voluntary IAs were to be permitted, participants would likely be allowed to divert a portion (but not all) of their social security contributions to a funded defined contribution pension account. To compensate the Trust Fund for the loss in contributions, the promised social security annuity would have to be reduced by an offset amount. The President's Commission (2001) proposed to calculate such an offset by asking, in effect, how much IA contributions would be expected to accumulate under a given rate of return. Letting Offset_T and SS_T^{RED} represent, respectively, the offset and the reduced annuity, then a minimum *benefit* guarantee for a "mixed" social security system can be represented by:

$$f_T = \max\left[0, G_T - (\text{IA}_T + \text{SS}_T^{\text{RED}})\right], \tag{8.2}$$

or equivalently,

$$f_T = \max\left[0, G_T - (\text{IA}_T + (\text{SS}_T - \text{Offset}_T))\right]. \tag{8.3}$$

Finally, we note that in (8.2) and (8.3), social security benefits are assumed to be paid with certainty. Potential costs associated with the funding of social security benefits should be handled separately; that is, legacy system costs are properly attributed to the old system, and not to the guarantee.[9]

Costing Guarantee Payoffs with Option-Pricing Techniques

The discussion above shows that a pension guarantee can provide investors with a floor of protection against the chance of a capital market loss. In turn, the guarantee represents a liability to the sponsor, be it a private sector group—a plan sponsor, an insurer, a financial services firm—or a government entity. Over the last decade, as a result of experience with the Savings and Loan crisis as well as other government guarantee programs, the Congressional Budget Office (CBO) and the General Accounting Office (GAO) have increasingly taken the position that government guarantees should be evaluated and costed as to their budgetary impact. If a pension guarantee were to be included in an IA plan proposal, it would be necessary to estimate and recognize the financial cost of such a promise. That is, irrespective of whether guarantees are provided by a government entity or private sector firms, it is essential to account properly for their costs since real economic resources are required to finance them.

In practice, there is much confusion regarding how to compute the economic value of such guarantee payments. One reason is that the economic cost of providing the pension guarantee may not necessarily equal the recipient's valuation of the guarantee.[10] In this chapter, we focus only on the economic value of the pension guarantee for the provider,[11] referred to as "guarantee costs" below. Another reason is that more than one approach has been suggested to evaluate pension guarantee costs. The simplest approach is to project what pension guarantee payments might be according to a set of stochastic assumptions and take their expectation (cf. Feldstein and Samwick, 2001). This expectation approach has the merit of being easy to apply and explain; it is particularly useful when more sophisticated techniques cannot be adopted. On the other hand, this expectation approach does not incorporate an adjustment for the economic value of risk, so it would tend to underestimate guarantee costs.

An approach that does adjust guarantee costs for risk recognizes that the shape of the guarantee payments in Figure 8-1 conforms to a "put option." Indeed, the pension literature has long recognized that option-pricing techniques[12] can be used to value options related to pension obligations (e.g. Merton, Bodie, and Marcus, 1987). To apply this methodology, one must first detail the stochastic processes for the guarantee formula and the investment portfolio.[13] Then, risk-neutral valuation[14] is used to obtain the guarantee costs from this model. In the special case where the guaranteed portfolio consists of a single contribution that grows with investment returns over time and where the returns follow a lognormal distribution, the risk-neutral valuation technique corresponds to the well-known Black–Scholes formula. The obvious advantage of this approach, as illustrated by Bodie (2001) and Smetters (2002), is that it provides a closed-form solution for the guarantee costs.

More realism in the pension plan design can be introduced by permitting the pension investments to be deposited as a series of periodic contributions, rather than as a one-time investment. In this latter case, a closed-form solution for the guarantee costs is more difficult to find, but Monte Carlo simulations and the risk-neutral valuation technique can be used to model a wide variety of guarantee formulas and portfolio structures. Analysts who have used risk-neutral valuation techniques to value guarantees in this more complex pension framework include Pennachi (1999, 2000) who examined guarantees in Uruguay and Chile, Zarita (1994) who modeled guarantees in Chile, Fischer (1999) who evaluated Colombia's pension guarantee, and Feldstein and Ranguelova (2000) who explored the feasibility of pension collars for the United States.

In the present chapter we also adopt this technique to evaluate the types of pension guarantees that might be suggested in the context of a possible United States social security reform, one that combines a new defined contribution individual account component with a more traditional defined benefit structure. While specific model details are provided in the appendix for interested readers, it is useful to provide a short description of our application of this process. As a first step, it is necessary to risk-adjust the probability distributions of the underlying securities held in the pension portfolio. This probability adjustment is made such that risk-adjusted return processes are expected to yield the risk-free rate. Expectations taken with these risk-adjusted probabilities are represented by the operator $\hat{E}$. Second, the pension guarantee payments can be projected to time T and discounted back at the risk-free rate using the appropriate formulas. Third, the value of the pension guarantee is obtained by taking the risk-adjusted expected value of the discounted guarantee payments. The process may be summarized analytically in equation (8.4) below. Letting $\bar{r}$ represent the average risk-free rate over the period, the no-arbitrage value f of a derivative that pays f_T at time T is given by:[15]

$$f = \hat{E}[\exp(-\bar{r}T)f_T]. \tag{8.4}$$

Nature of the Downside Risk

As was shown above, having a pension guarantee is potentially valuable because of the "downside risk" inherent in IA investments. It is interesting that popular belief regarding the nature of this downside risk tends to downplay the cost of such guarantees. For instance, it is often recommended that investors with long investment horizons hold a larger proportion of stocks in their portfolios. This view is grounded in the argument that stocks are less risky in the long run or, putting it another way, that investors have more time to recoup their losses with longer investment horizons. Historically, stocks have outperformed bonds over long investment horizons,[16] so the belief is that this trend will repeat in the future, resulting in costless guarantees.

Empirical evidence on this point is provided in Figure 8-2, which graphs historical annual nominal returns payable to short-term investors in US stock and bond indexes over the period 1942–2000. The figure

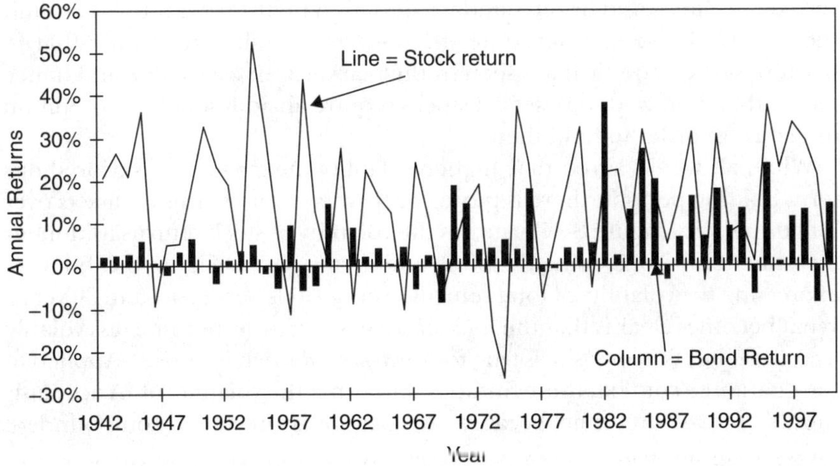

Figure 8-2. Annual returns for US Stock and Bond Markets, 1942–2000. (*Source*: Author's computations, data from CRSP; historical annual stock returns from S&P 500 index including dividends; bond returns from an index of 10-year Treasuries.)

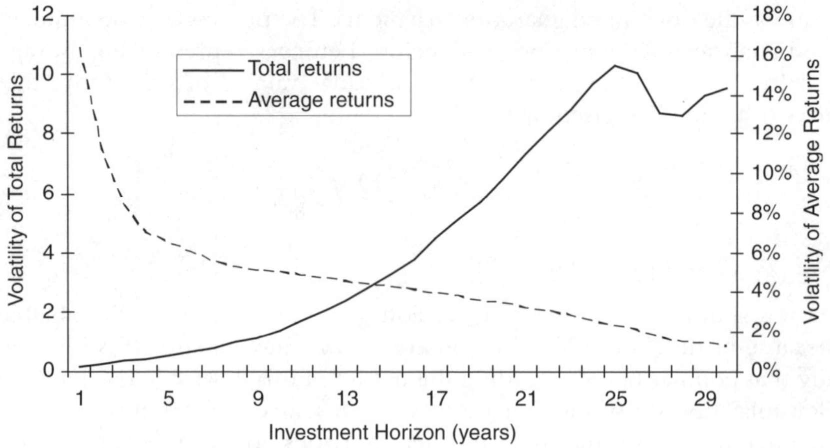

Figure 8-3. The effect of longer time horizons on the Volatility of Stock Returns. (*Source*: Authors' computations using data described in Figure 8-2.)

confirms that in the United States, at least, stock returns have historically exceeded bond returns, but with higher volatility. Over the period, the average annual (nominal) return was 14.6 percent on a stock index fund (S&P 500) compared to an average bond fund return of 5.8 percent. The volatility of the stock index over the same period was also higher, at 16.5 percent, compared to bond volatility of 9 percent. (Asset volatility is conventionally measured by the standard deviation of historical returns around the mean). These data illustrate the so-called "equity premium"—that is, because stocks (equities) are seen by the market as more volatile and hence riskier than bonds, purchasers of stocks require an additional risk premium or return in order to hold them.

While all would agree that higher volatility means more risk for short-term holding periods, there is more controversy over returns on assets over longer periods. Figure 8-3 illustrates the volatility of stock returns for longer investment horizons, using the same underlying data as Figure 8-2, but now expressing the volatility of total returns over periods between 1 and 30 years. What becomes clear is that the *annualized* stock returns become less volatile over time, but the opposite is true for *compounded* stock returns.[17] Applied to the guarantee context, these findings imply that the volatility of IA accounts should increase over time, because this volatility is affected by compounded, rather than annual, returns. Consequently, guarantee volatility rises over time, rather than being diversified away over longer investment periods.

A closer examination of Figure 8-3 reveals that, for investment periods longer than 25 years, volatility estimates become unstable, due to the paucity of return data for long investment periods. Over the post-WWII period, there are at best two independent observations for the 30-year period returns.[18] Clearly, data limitations weaken confidence regarding the claim that stocks outperform bonds over long-term investment periods. Experts using data from other countries also suggest that the US pattern is an exception, since other countries exhibit much smaller long-term equity premiums.[19] Further, past data may be a rather poor predictor of future performance, so extrapolating the potential costs of a guarantee from this data can be deceptive.

Illustrating Guarantee Costs

To provide a better understanding of the factors determining guarantee costs, this section presents and analyzes several examples. We show how pension guarantee costs depend on three key factors: the relation between the guarantee formula and the benefit structure, the volatility of the investor's portfolio, and the interaction between these two elements and the investor's investment horizon.

Five specific structures for guarantee designs help illustrate the interactions between pension guarantee formulas and benefit structures. The first three IA guarantee designs discussed are examples of a minimum *rate of return* guarantee, differentiated according to the rate of return guaranteed. Example 1 illustrates the cost of providing a *principal* guarantee, one that promises the participant the return of his contributions at retirement (equivalent to a zero nominal interest rate). Example 2 offers a *real principal* guarantee, one that promises the participant the return of his contributions with an adjustment for purchasing power at retirement (equivalent to a zero real interest rate). Example 3 provides the participant a guarantee that his individual account provides his principal plus a minimum interest rate equal to a *10-year Treasury bond* return.

Two additional examples are taken from the minimum *benefit* family of guarantees. Examples 4 and 5 consider a "mixed" system of social security benefits such as the one described in general terms in the second section.[20] In this context, we refer to SS_T as "present law benefits," or the benefits projected according to the formulas in effect under the traditional social security system. The social security benefit formula does not incorporate any minimum or floor benefit on its own. Hence the guarantees provided in Examples 4 and 5 ensure that the retiree receives a total payment equal to the larger of the *present law benefit* or the *poverty line*.[21]

It will be recalled that in a "mixed" system, the retirement benefit consists of the sum of the annuity SS_T^{RED} and a payment from the IA_T. In Example 4, as we have constructed it, the plan participant may invest 2 percent of his earnings to an IA, in lieu of paying social security taxes in that amount. Example 5 considers a larger IA system, where the participant can contribute 6 percent of his earnings to an IA. For both examples, in exchange for its participation in the IA, the participant's annuity is obtained by subtracting an "offset" from the present law benefits, that is, $SS_T^{RED} = SS_T - Offset_T$. This offset is equivalent to the participant's IA contributions accumulated at the 3-month *T*-bill rate of return.[22]

The current social security benefit formula is progressive, providing low earners a higher replacement rate though a lower dollar amount, as compared to higher earners. The guarantee formulas examined here promise different replacement rates by income level, as compared to present law. We illustrate this sensitivity to earnings levels in Example 4 by contrasting the guarantee costs for two hypothetical workers: one at *medium earnings* level corresponding to the Social Security system's Average Wage Index (AWI), and another at a *low earnings* level representing 45 percent of this amount. Guarantee costs are also influenced by how the participant invests his IA account. To show this, we develop guarantee cost estimates for three alternative IA portfolios: one fully invested in equities; a second one invested half in equities and half in bonds; and a third held all in bonds. The role of the investment horizon is depicted through the use of four different contribution periods, with IA contributions occurring over, respectively 10, 20, 30, and 40 years.

For each of the variations just listed, Tables 8-1–8-3 express the cost of providing the guarantee in question, for the specific investment mix, earnings level, and saving horizon illustrated. These costs are computed using the valuation method outlined in the second section of this chapter, and presented in a variety of units: as a percent of assets (Table 8-1), in present value dollars (Table 8-2), and as a percentage of lifetime contributions (Table 8-3). (The Appendix details the assumptions underlying the calculations.) Throughout this section, we refer mainly to Table 8-1's costs expressed in basis points (hundredths of a percent of assets) because it is conventional to refer to costs associated with managing retirement accounts in those terms. However, this measure does not readily reflect changes in costs associated with varying the contribution rate or the investment horizon. Hence, for some purposes, we explore present value dollar costs from Table 8-2.

Guarantee Formula and Benefit Structure

For ease of discussion, we take as the *base case* a participant with a 50/50 stock/bond portfolio and a 40-year investment horizon. For such an investor, Line 8 of Table 8-1 shows that the cost of guaranteeing the 10-year Treasury bond return (Example 3) would be 0.65 percent of assets annually, or 65 basis points (bps). Alternatively, this is worth \$3,406 in present value dollars (Table 8-2), or equivalently, 16 percent of total contributions (Table 8-3). To understand why the guarantee is expensive, it is

TABLE 8-1 Cost Estimates of Alternative Guarantees: Annual Charge as a percentage of IA Assets (in basis points)

Line	Years with Individual Account	Minimum Rate of Return			Minimum Benefit (with a "Mixed"[a] system)		
		Example 1: Principal (i.e. 0%)	*Example 2: Real Principal (i.e. inflation)*	*Example 3: 10-yr Treasury Bond Return*	*Example 4: Present Law Benefit w/ Poverty Line Minimum*[b] *(Contribution Rate = 2%)*		*Example 5: Present Law Benefit w/ Poverty Line Minimum*[b] *(Contribution Rate = 6%)*
			Any Earnings		*Low Earnings*[c]	*Medium Earnings*[c]	*Medium Earnings*[c]
I. Portfolio invested 100% in Equities							
1	10	60 bp	136 bp	267 bp	2946 bp	265 bp	265 bp
2	20	17	64	184	584	183	183
3	30	7	37	149	193	149	149
4	40	3	24	127	126	126	126
II. Portfolio invested 50% in Equities, 50% in Treasury 10-yr Bonds							
5	10	4	33	135	2940	133	133
6	20	0	10	93	523	93	93
7	30	0	4	76	118	76	76
8	40	0	2	65	65	65	65
III. Portfolio invested 100% in Treasury 10-yr Bonds							
9	10	0	0	0	2938	11	11
10	20	0	0	0	516	9	9
11	30	0	0	0	66	7	7
12	40	0	0	0	6	6	6

[a] In this example, a participant in a "mixed" system would be allowed to divert part of his social security contribution to an IA and his first-pillar benefit (social security annuity) would be reduced by an offset in return.

[b] This design guarantees that the combination of the first pillar benefits (annuity) and the IA is as least as much as the present law social security benefit. In addition, this benefit is subject to a minimum set equal to the poverty line for those who contribute to the first pillar benefits for at least 30 years.

[c] The income of the low and medium earners represent respectively 45% and 100% of the AWI. In 2000, they would have earned respectively 14,470 and 32,155.

Source: Authors' calculations.

TABLE 8-2 Cost Estimates of Alternative Guarantees (in present value dollars)

Line	Years with Individual Account	Minimum Rate of Return			Minimum Benefit (with a "Mixed"[a] system)		
		Example 1: Principal	Example 2: Real Principal (Contribution Rate = 2%)	Example 3: 10-yr Treasury Bond Return	Example 4: Present Law Benefit w/ Poverty Line Minimum[b] (Contribution Rate = 2%)		Example 5: Present Law Benefit w/ Poverty Line Minimum[b] (Contribution Rate = 6%)
			Medium Earnings[c]		Low Earnings[c]	Medium Earnings[c]	Medium Earnings[c]
I. Portfolio invested 100% in Equities							
1	10	$252	$576	$1,127	$16,781	$1,120	$3,361
2	20	258	964	2,782	10,656	2,776	8,329
3	30	214	1,173	4,681	4,150	4,677	14,030
4	40	163	1,240	6,613	2,971	6,602	19,087
II. Portfolio invested 50% in Equities, 50% in Treasury 10-yr Bonds							
5	10	16	141	570	16,775	564	1,692
6	20	4	153	1,408	10,557	1,406	4,219
7	30	1	134	2,390	3,144	2,390	7,171
8	40	0	106	3,406	1,531	3,401	10,204
III. Portfolio invested 100% in Treasury 10-yr Bonds							
9	10	0	0	0	16,771	46	137
10	20	0	0	0	10,560	130	389
11	30	0	0	0	2,804	227	681
12	40	0	0	0	147	328	983

[a] In this example, a participant in a "mixed" system would be allowed to divert part of his social security contribution to an IA and his first-pillar benefit (social security annuity) would be reduced by an offset in return.

[b] This design guarantees that the combination of the first-pillar benefits (annuity) and the IA is as least as much as the present law social security benefit. In addition, this benefit is subject to a minimum set equal to the poverty line for those who contribute to the first-pillar benefits for at least 30 years.

[c] The income of the low and medium earners represent respectively 45% and 100% of the AWI. In 2000, they would have earned respectively $14,470 and $32,155.

Source: Authors' calculations.

TABLE 8-3 Cost Estimates of Alternative Guarantees: as a percentage of Lifetime Contributions

Line	Years with Individual Account	*Minimum Rate of Return*			*Minimum Benefit (with a "Mixed"[a] system)*		
		Example 1: Principal (i.e. 0%)	*Example 2: Real Principal (i.e. inflation)*	*Example 3: 10-yr Treasury Bond Return*	*Example 4: Present Law Benefit w/ Poverty Line Minimum*[b] *(Contribution Rate = 2%)*		*Example 5: Present Law Benefit w/ Poverty Line Minimum*[b] *(Contribution Rate = 6%)*
			Any Earnings (%)		*Low Earnings*[c] *(%)*	*Medium Earnings*[c] *(%)*	*Medium Earnings*[c] *(%)*
I. Portfolio invested 100% in Equities							
1	10	3.6	8.2	16.1	531.9	16.0	16.0
2	20	2.0	7.6	21.9	186.2	21.8	21.8
3	30	1.2	6.7	27.0	53.2	27.0	27.0
4	40	0.8	5.9	31.3	31.3	31.3	31.3
II. Portfolio invested 50% in Equities, 50% in Treasury 10-yr Bonds							
5	10	0.2	2.0	8.1	531.7	8.1	8.1
6	20	0.0	1.2	11.1	184.5	11.1	11.1
7	30	0.0	0.8	13.8	40.3	13.8	13.8
8	40	0.0	0.5	16.1	16.1	16.1	16.1
III. Portfolio invested 100% in Treasury 10-yr Bonds							
9	10	0.0	0.0	0.0	531.6	0.7	0.7
10	20	0.0	0.0	0.0	184.5	1.0	1.0
11	30	0.0	0.0	0.0	35.9	1.3	1.3
12	40	0.0	0.0	0.0	1.6	1.6	1.6

[a] In this example, a participant in a "mixed" system would be allowed to divert part of his social security contribution to an IA and his first-pillar benefit (social security annuity) would be reduced by an offset in return.

[b] This design guarantees that the combination of the first-pillar benefits (annuity) and the IA is as least as much as the present law social security benefit. In addition, this benefit is subject to a minimum set equal to the poverty line for those who contribute to the first pillar benefits for at least 30 years.

[c] The income of the low and medium earners represent respectively 45% and 100% of the AWI. In 2000, they would have earned respectively $14,470 and $32,155.

Source: Authors' calculations.

helpful to look at the anticipated gap between the value of the guarantee and the benefits provided by the IA.[23] In the base case, the expected values of the IA and the guarantee are equal.[24] Therefore, guarantee payments will be generated as soon as the IA portfolio provides a below-mean return.

In the cases of Examples 1 and 2, the principal and real principal guarantees, the guaranteed amounts represent, respectively, only 30 percent and 52 percent of the expected IA value. Consequently the IA's investment performance would have to be significantly worse than expected before any guarantee would be paid; those payments will also be smaller in size as compared to Example 3. This translates into lower guarantee costs, as illustrated in Line 8 of Table 8-1: the guarantee costs drop to 0 and 2 bp, respectively. Of course guarantee costs this low indicates that such guarantees provide limited protection against investment risk. Although we have ignored administrative costs associated with the guarantee, in this case it is interesting to note that such fees could even exceed the guarantee payments themselves.

Continuing with the base case and moving along Line 8, we next consider the minimum *benefit* guarantees of Examples 4 and 5. Recall that for these examples, the minimum benefit is defined as the US present law benefit, plus a poverty line minimum income. Here the expected gap between the guarantee and the retiree's benefits is influenced by the participant's lifetime earnings level.[25] For the *low* earner, the guarantee represents from 100 percent to 120 percent of expected benefits under the mixed system, whereas this ratio is always 100 percent for the *medium* income earner. It is worth noting that the minimum benefit guarantee in this case introduces benefit improvements unrelated to the provision of investment risk protection. To see this, we note that the guarantee is costly even when the low earner invests his IA entirely in a bond portfolio: as indicated in Table 8-1, providing a minimum benefit for the *low* earner investing only in bonds still costs from 6 bp to 29.38 percent of assets.

Finally, costs are also influenced by the size of the IA. To illustrate this, Examples 4 and 5 compare two different systems, one with an IA contribution rate of 2 percent and the other with a contribution rate of 6 percent. A larger IA introduces more risk, which in turn results in higher costs for the guarantee. The guarantees cost the same amount in basis points (Table 8-1) but these are based on higher contributions and higher assets. To better judge the magnitude of the guarantee cost, dollar figures are presented in Table 4-2. Line 8 shows that as the contribution rate is tripled from 2 to 6 percent, the present value of guarantee costs is also tripled, rising from $3,401 to $10,204. This confirms that a minimum benefit guarantee in the context of a larger investment account is more costly.

Volatility of the Investment Portfolio

The illustrations also reveal that meeting a guarantee threshold is more likely if the IA is invested in more volatile assets; thus boosting the allocation in equities always results in greater guarantee costs. For instance, when we move from the base case with a 50/50 stock/bond mix to a portfolio invested all in equities, the cost of the guarantee doubles from 65 to 127 bp (Table 8-1, Example 3, Lines 4 versus 8). Reducing the fraction in equities to zero eliminates guarantee costs in the Example 3 case, of course, because the IA portfolio cannot do worse than the guaranteed benefit.

This implies that giving IA participants a choice over investment mix could be costly, in that they might boost the guarantee cost by selecting a riskier investment portfolio. In general, it would be dangerous to provide participants with an IA guarantee without placing restrictions on their portfolio mix. However, Table 8-1 reveals that, for some guarantee designs, the impact of the investment portfolio on costs is less than in the base case. When guarantees are either very likely or very unlikely to be exercised, their costs are less sensitive to the portfolio allocation.

Interaction with Investment Horizon

As mentioned above, some observers contend that lengthening the investment horizon might result in lower guarantee costs, because they believe that investment risk decreases over time. Nevertheless, Bodie (1995) showed that a put option guaranteeing the risk-free rate becomes more expensive as the investment horizon widens. In practice, the relation between guarantee costs and investment horizon proves to be fairly complex, as Table 8-2 reveals. This relation is determined by the evolution over time of the two factors defined in this section: the relation between the guarantee formula versus the benefit structure, and the IA volatility.

It will be recalled that, in the base case, the expected value of the guarantee formula and the IA are equal, which implies that the guarantee costs are only driven by volatility. As the investment horizon lengthens, so too does the size of the IA and its volatility. Since guarantee costs increase with volatility, the cost of the guarantee would be expected to rise with the investment horizon. Comparing Lines 5 and 8 of Table 8-2, we see that lengthening the investment horizon from 10 to 40 years in Example 3 results in costs rising more than proportionally, from $570 to $3,406. On the other hand, the cost of the principal guarantees (Examples 1 and 2) falls with time, rather than rising. This is because under the principal guarantee, the guarantee cost falls as a percent of the IA from 71 to 30 percent as the time period is extended from 10 to 40 years. The fact that the guarantee becomes less generous over time dominates the volatility effect and explains why the principal guarantee costs fall over time. Similarly, for the low earner in Example 4, the social security annuity grows over time at a faster rate than does the poverty line, which makes it less likely that the guarantee will pay off for the longer holding period.

Financing Pension Accumulation Guarantees

Proposals to include guarantees in an IA model must specify not only their costs, as outlined above, but also how they could be financed. Financing decisions include several aspects:

- Who will bear the guarantee costs? (e.g. participants, taxpayers)
- Who will manage the guarantee and how? (e.g. private sector, government agency)
- What will the price structure be? (e.g. one price for all, prices differentiated by earnings level, portfolio mix, time horizon, etc.)

This section examines several issues related to these three questions.

Guarantee Financing: Pay-as-you-go versus Self-Financed

Feldstein and Liebman (2001) have suggested that the risk associated with guarantees could either be shifted to future taxpayers or transferred to private markets.[26] One way to pay for an IA guarantee is to allow participants to elect self-financed guaranteed choices from a menu of investment options. Financial institutions could offer "guaranteed return accounts" in the set of investment choices for people willing to pay for them. In this case, participants desirous of a guaranteed investment product would pay the premium, irrespective of whether the government or the private sector managed the accounts. (In Germany and Japan, private financial service firms are slated to provide the guaranteed accounts.)

An advantage of the self-financing approach to guarantees is that those who most value the enhanced security would also be those who would pay for it. Less risk-averse people would not have to subsidize the more risk-averse. In addition, since guarantee costs rise with the size of the portfolio being guaranteed in this context, financing would be more expensive for higher earners with larger accounts. Having those who value guarantees most pay for them avoids the poor potentially having to subsidize the risk-averse rich.

A potential disadvantage of self-financing guarantees is that some low-wage earners might value a guarantee more highly, yet they would be least able to afford it. Financing guarantee costs for the poor, in this case, might require subsidizing low-income savers out of general revenue. This might be feasible, but it also might detract from the appeal of guaranteed accounts to the extent that additional revenue would have to be identified to pay for them. Even in this case, however, it is critical to note that guarantee costs do not disappear just because the federal government shoulders them. Failing to report economic costs and benefits of guarantees cannot avoid the reality that economic resources are still at risk under the guarantee, and value is being transferred to participants.

If guarantee costs were passed on to future taxpayers instead of having participants self-finance them, it would mean that future taxes would have to be devoted to the system when guarantees were "in the money." A major problem with this tactic is that the guarantor could be asked to pay out precisely when economic conditions were bleak. This could occur if the stock market and the economy collapsed at the same time, for instance. In such a circumstance, taxpayers might be unable or unwilling to raise taxes on themselves to cover the guarantees, even if promises had been made in the past. In other words, it is incorrect to assume that the federal government has "deep pockets" and can simply raise taxes on future workers to cover shortfalls whenever IA investments perform poorly.

Indeed, one might ask whether such guarantees could be any more reliable than present social security promises. The law has established that traditional social security benefit promises are payable only when revenues are sufficient to cover them (*Fleming v. Nestor*, 1960). A similar point could be made about any form of guarantee: in a massive economic downturn, the promises would be worth no more than could be paid. A related issue is that supporters of IAs often state that these accounts are useful in building wealth and reducing unfunded tax claims on our children and grandchildren. Instituting guarantees without making them self-financed represents a new entitlement likely inconsistent with the reform philosophy.

The Choice of a Guarantee Provider

Although a guarantee resembles an insurance contract, its underlying risk is not diversifiable; hence, it cannot be managed with traditional insurance "pooling" techniques. Figure 8-1 shows that the guarantee payments are asymmetric and this shape is preserved even when guarantee payments of all IA participants are aggregated. This shape cannot be replicated by simply depositing the premiums into an insurance fund. However if these premiums were used to purchase the appropriate financial instruments, it would be possible to obtain the desired structure of payoffs. As an example, Bodie (2001) discusses how investment accumulation products could be guaranteed with the use of a combination of capital market instruments.[27] In the eventuality that these products are not available in the capital markets,[28] their payoffs could be replicated by applying option-pricing techniques to a portfolio of appropriate securities.

When the guarantee payoffs can be replicated by the derivative strategy just described, either the government (or one of its agencies) or private providers would be able to offer the guarantee.[29] In practice, several elements of the guarantee contract cannot be hedged in capital markets (e.g. lifetime earnings, retirement age, etc.) To deal with this issue, one might imagine financial service firms offering contracts that are standardized in terms of earnings, portfolio mix, retirement age, and so forth. This approach has the advantage of reducing moral hazard, but it also subjects the participant to more risk due to the difference between his idiosyncratic situation and the standardized case (the "basis risk," in the options literature). If guarantees were not standardized, it would become more difficult for private providers to manage these contracts and it becomes more likely that the government would provide the guarantee. This is because the government may be better able to transfer losses to future generations, as compared to financial institutions. Such constraints could be mitigated if the private providers had access to reinsurance. Finally, if the guarantees featured some element of subsidy, private providers would be unable to manage the entire program without additional support.

Price Structure

The illustrations in the third section showed that the price of a guarantee is sensitive to the individual investor's characteristics and to his portfolio allocation. Consequently, a well-designed pricing strategy should avoid the creation of opportunities for adverse selection and moral hazard. In this context we have already mentioned the need to have the guarantee linked to a specific IA portfolio mix. Depending on the guarantee structure, providers too can be subject to moral hazard. Making the guarantee provider responsible for asset allocation provides an incentive to invest in safer assets (Jensen and Sorensen, 2000). In Colombia, for instance, the guarantee premium under the IA program is not adjusted for risk; partly as a result, only 0.3 percent of the funds were invested in shares (as of December 1996; Fischer, 1999).

Discussion and Conclusions

Opponents of IAs tend to understate the problems facing underfunded national pay-as-you-go social security systems, overlooking the fact that reductions in outlays and increases in revenues will be required to close the future financing gap. It is precisely the social security system's looming insolvency that makes current systems politically risky. Including IAs in a national social security reform plan can strengthen old-age economic security. These accounts can reduce the political risk confronting aging Americans when they assess the chances of actually receiving promised benefits under the insolvent social security system. These accounts also afford participants the opportunity to save in a cost-effective manner, and to diversify their investments in ways that they may not be able to at present.

Nonetheless, there may be concern among policymakers that IA participants will face capital market risk, particularly if they concentrate their accounts in stock market investments in the pursuit of higher returns. One approach to this problem is to restrict the extent of equities allowed in workers' accounts; another is to offer guarantees.

This chapter has explored several guarantee designs and assessed their likely costs. It shows that offering guarantees on defined contribution pension accounts could be costly, even when participants are restricted to holding no more than half their portfolio in stock and the rest in bonds. For instance, in this framework our model suggests that a 10-year Treasury bond return guarantee would still require increasing annual contributions by 65 bps, or 16 percent of contributions, for the long-term saver. This would likely be perceived as a substantial cost increase over and above the basic contribution by most plan participants. If these costs were not self-financed, substantial subsidies would be required. Subsidies of this sort must be measured, recognized, and their financing implications spelled out in detail for a full accounting of the economic costs and benefits of guarantees.

These cost estimates might seem high to people accustomed to the argument that stock returns are expected to outperform bond returns over time. We argue, however, that because of the paucity of independent observations in historical data on long holding periods, past returns are noisy predictors of future returns. In addition, guarantee costs are driven by stock and bond volatility rather than their expected returns.

Appendix: An Illustration of Option-Pricing Techniques Applied to Individual Accounts

This Appendix details the modeling assumptions used to derive cost estimates for the illustrative examples discussed in the text. We summarize guarantee costs for four workers who participate in the IA program for, respectively, $T = 10, 20, 30$, and 40 years. It is assumed that the IA starts in 2004 and economic variables are projected accordingly. Sections A and B of this Appendix describe the economic and demographic assumptions. The stochastic processes followed by the bills, bonds, and stocks are modeled separately in Section C. Section D details the elements necessary to compute the IA values as well as the social security annuity. Section E derives the cost of each guarantee formula while Section F shows how to generate numerical values for the guarantee costs using a Monte Carlo simulation.

A. Economic Assumptions

All projections are expressed in nominal values, with the inflation and real processes modeled separately. Assumptions for inflation growth, real wage growth, and real interest rates are taken from the OASDI Annual

Report (2001). In that report, the intermediate scenario assumes that real wage growth is $g = 1.0$ percent, while inflation grows at $i = 3.3$ percent. By combining these two assumptions, the result is a 4.3 percent nominal wage growth assumption. According to the intermediate scenario, the real interest rate assumption is $r^{\mathrm{REAL}} = 3$ percent. This fixed interest rate assumption is used for the annuity calculation in Section B, while the remaining calculations use the stochastic model of Section C.

At the inception of the IAs, earnings levels are denoted by W_0. In subsequent years, earnings W_t are obtained by projecting these initial earnings with a fixed rate of 4.3 percent. Two categories of wages are used in the simulations: the *medium* earner corresponds to the Social Security Actuary's AWI while a *low* earner represents 45 percent of this amount. For instance, the low and medium earners would have received \$17,785 and \$32,155, respectively in 2000.[30] Finally, according to the US Census Bureau, the poverty line for singles over 65 years old was \$8,494 in 2001, a level assumed to grow with the Consumer Price Index (CPI) over time.

B. Demographic Assumptions

The four illustrative cases are assumed to be, respectively, 22, 32, 42, and 52 years old at the inception of the IA system. Each participant is assumed to retire at the early retirement age of 62 years. At this age, the value of a \$1 annuity with payments indexed to inflation is denoted by the annuity factor $\ddot{a}_{62}$. To compute this annuity factor, it is necessary to define survival probabilities after retirement. The standard notation ${}_tp_{62}$ is used to denote the probability that an individual retiring at age 62 would still be alive at age 62+t. Post-retirement survival probabilities are derived from the Social Security 1997 period life table[31] (pre-retirement mortality is not included in the model). As for the real interest rate used to discount the annuity payments, it is taken from the Old age survivor and disability insurance (OASDI) intermediate scenario. Letting the last age (radix) of the mortality table be represented by ω, the value of the annuity factor is given by:

$$\ddot{a}_{62} = \sum_{t=0}^{\omega-1-62} (1 + r^{\mathrm{REAL}})_t^{-t}\, {}_tp_{62}. \tag{8.7}$$

C. Stochastic Processes (risk-adjusted)

Risk-Free Rate

The continuous risk-free rate is defined by Vasicek's (1977) mean reverting model:

$$dr_t = \kappa(\mu - r_t)dt + \sigma\, dW_t^r, \tag{8.8}$$

where dW_t^r is a standardized Wiener process and the initial risk-free rate is given by $r_0 = r$. According to Hull (1997), the current term structure should lead directly to the risk-neutral process for interest rates and the necessary risk-adjustments are incorporated in (8). For estimation and simulation purposes, it will be useful to take advantage of the fact that the Vasicek model leads to the following normal representation of the risk-free rate:

$$r_t|r_{t-1} = \mu(1 - e^{-k}) + e^{-k}r_{t-1} + \sigma\sqrt{(1 - e^{-2\kappa})/2\kappa\varepsilon_t} \\ \varepsilon_t \sim N(0, 1). \tag{8.9}$$

Equation (8.9) corresponds to a simple regression and its parameters can be estimated by online library system (OLS). For this estimation, the risk-free rate is represented by the 3-month T-Bill annual time series for the period 1980–2001. The period between World War II and October 1979 is excluded due to the Federal Reserve policy of stabilizing interest rates at the time. Using this data, the OLS parameters estimates are respectively $r_0 = 2$ percent, $\hat{\kappa} = 80$ percent, $\hat{\mu} = 3$ percent, and $\hat{\sigma} = 2$ percent. The annual risk-free rate values can then be simulated by generating a series of error terms ε_t and substituting them into equation (9).

Bond Returns

To compute the bond portfolio return, we take advantage of the direct relation between the movements of the risk-free rate and bond returns. The bond portfolio is invested in 10-year Treasury zero coupon bonds, assumed to be rebalanced annually. The same assumptions apply to the 10-year Treasury guarantee in Example 3. When it is computed with the Vasicek model, the price at time t of a bond with time to maturity τ can be represented as follows:

$$P(\tau, r_t) = e^{A(\tau)-B(\tau)r_t} \tag{8.10}$$

where,

$$A(\tau) = \big(B(\tau) - \tau\big)\left(\mu - \frac{\sigma^2}{2\kappa^2}\right) - \frac{\sigma^2 B(\tau)^2}{4\kappa}$$

$$B(\tau) = \frac{1 - e^{-\kappa\tau}}{\tau}.$$

Since it is assumed that the 10-year bond fund is rebalanced annually, its annual return B_t is given by the percentage increase in price after 1 year:

$$B_t = \frac{P(0, r_{t+1})}{P(10, r_t)} - 1, \tag{8.11}$$

where r_t and r_{t+1} are generated by (9). Note that there is no relation between the notations B_t and $B(\tau)$.

Stock Returns

Letting S_t^I represent the stock index level at time t, the continuous stock returns are modeled by the following geometric Brownian motion:

$$\frac{dS_t^I}{S_t^I} = r_t dt + \sigma dW_t^S, \tag{8.12}$$

where dW_t^S is a standardized Wiener process, which we assumed to be uncorrelated with the one in equation (8.8). Following the risk-neutral valuation technique, the drift of the return process in (8.12) is set equal to the risk-free rate. In addition, let S_t denote the annual stock return in year t. Then S_t is distributed according to a lognormal distribution and can be represented by:

$$\ln(1 + S_t) = r_t - \sigma^2/2 + \sigma\varepsilon_t, \quad \text{where} \quad \varepsilon_t \sim N(0, 1) \tag{8.13}$$

or, equivalently

$$S_t = \exp(r_t - \sigma^2/2 + \sigma\varepsilon_t) - 1. \tag{8.14}$$

To estimate the parameter σ, we note that equation (8.13) is normally distributed with standard deviation σ. The usual estimator can then be applied to obtain $\hat{\sigma} = 20$ percent. Stock return data for the estimation were taken from the S&P 500 Index (including dividends) during the period 1926–2000. Using this parameter estimate, the annual stock returns are simulated by generating a series of error terms ε_t and substituting them into equation (14).

Investment Returns for Individual Accounts

In this illustrative model, the worker is assumed to allocate his IA investments between two funds: an indexed stock fund and a bond fund (of 10-year Treasuries). Denote by α the proportion invested by the participant in the stock fund. Further, let S_t and B_t represent the total return at time t for each of the funds. It follows that the portfolio investment rate of return in year t is given by:

$$R_t = \alpha S_t + (1 - \alpha) B_t. \tag{8.15}$$

In Tables 4-1–4-3, the results are generated for three alternative portfolios with $\alpha = 0\%, \alpha = 50\%$, and $\alpha = 100\%$.

D. Retirement Benefits Structure: Social Security Benefits and Individual Account Payouts

Social Security Annuity

Denote by SSA_T the annuity payment that a participant would receive if he retired at age 62, under a stylized annuity benefit formula similar to, though not completely identical to, the existing law formulas. The first input to the benefit formula is the Average Indexed Monthly Earnings $(\text{AIME})_T$. Here we assume that the last thirty-five (annual) earnings are used in the AIME_T calculation. These are indexed with wage growth up to age 60, with the exception of the last two earnings values.

$$\text{AIME}_T = \frac{W_{T-1} + W_{T-2} + \sum_{i=T-35}^{T-3} W_t((1+i)(1+g))^{T-2}}{35} \tag{8.16}$$

The social security benefit formula involves the use of two "bendpoints," indexed to the AWI and referred to below as FBP_T and SBP_T. In 2002, the annualized bendpoints were \$7,104 and \$42,804, respectively. Present law benefits are computed by multiplying the AIME_T by 90 percent for the portion below the first bendpoint, and by 32 percent and 15 percent for the portions, respectively, below and above the second bendpoint. Finally, the retiree's benefits are subject to an early retirement reduction factor, denoted by ERR_T. According to SSA, $\text{ERR}_T = 75$ percent for the participant with $T = 10$ and $\text{ERR}_T = 70$ percent for the other participants. The following formula summarizes the benefit calculation.

$$\text{SSA}_T = \text{ERR}_T \left(\begin{array}{ll} 90\% \times \min(\text{AIME}_T, \text{FBP}_T) & \\ + 32\% \times (\min(\text{AIME}_T, \text{SBP}_T) - \text{FBP}_T) & \textit{if } \text{FBP}_T \le \text{AIME}_T \\ + 15\% \times (\text{AIME}_T - \text{SBP}_T) & \textit{if } \text{SBP}_T \le \text{AIME}_T. \end{array} \right. \tag{8.17}$$

The value of the first pillar social security benefit SS_T is then obtained by multiplying (17) by the annuity factor: $\text{SS}_T = \text{SSA}_T \cdot \ddot{a}_{62}$.

Individual Account Payouts

In all models considered but one, system participants are permitted to divert 2 percent of their taxable earnings to an IA. (The exception is Example 5 where participants are allowed to contribute 6% of taxable earnings.) Letting C represent the fixed contribution rate, then the dollar contribution in year t is given by $C_t = C \cdot W_t$. The value of the IA at retirement is represented by IA_T. This value is computed as:

$$\text{IA}_T = \sum_{t=0}^{T-1} C_t \prod_{j=t}^{T-1} (1 + R_j). \tag{8.18}$$

where R_j was defined in Section C.

Social Security Benefits for Individual Account Participants

Those who participate in the IAs reduce their contributions to the Social Security Trust Fund, so their first pillar benefits are offset in exchange. For the present case, we compute the offset by accumulating IA contributions with a stated rate of return R^O,

$$\text{Offset}_T = \sum_{t=0}^{T-1} C_t(1 + R_t^O)^{T-t}. \tag{8.19}$$

For this analysis we set $R_t^O = \exp(r_t) - 1$; i.e. the offset rate is defined as the risk-free rate. It follows that the expected present value of the reduced benefits, denoted by SS_T^{RED}, is given by the following formula:

$$\text{SS}_T^{\text{RED}} = \text{SS}_T - \text{Offset}_T. \tag{8.20}$$

The participant is then assumed to receive the sum of his IA and the reduced social security annuity, or $\text{IA}_T + \text{SS}_T^{\text{RED}}$.

E. Guarantee Formulas

Rate of Return Guarantees

Let R_t^G represent the guaranteed rate of return for any of the rate of return guarantees described in the text. Then G_T, the value of the guarantee at retirement, is given by:

$$G_T = \sum_{t=0}^{T-1} C_t \prod_{j=t}^{T-1} (1 + R_j^G). \tag{8.21}$$

For the principal guarantee and the real principal guarantee, we have $R_t^G = 0$ percent and $R_t^G = i$ percent, respectively. Letting B_t represent the bond return again, the 10-year Treasury guarantee is modeled using $R_t^G = B_t$. For each of these examples, the guarantee payments are obtained by comparing G_T and IA_T.

Minimum Benefit Guarantees

For Examples 4 and 5, let G_T represent the present value of the guaranteed annuity. Denoting by PL_T the value of a poverty line annuity at retirement, then $G_T = \max(\text{SS}_T, \text{PL}_T)$. The guarantee payments are obtained by comparing this amount to the "mixed" system benefit payment $\text{IA}_T + \text{SS}_T^{\text{RED}}$.

F. Risk-Neutral Valuation and Monte-Carlo Simulations

The results in the text are obtained by simulating the value of equation (8.4) using the appropriate definition of the guarantee payoffs f_T from equations (8.1) and (8.3). Cost estimates are obtained by using 10,000 Monte Carlo simulations. For Tables 4-1 and 4-3, these costs are divided, respectively, by $\sum_{t=0}^{T-1} \hat{E}[e^{-\bar{r}t}C_t]$ and $\sum_{t=0}^{T-1} \hat{E}[e^{-\bar{r}t}IA_t]$ to obtain the appropriate units.

Notes

[1] See President's CSSS 2001.

[2] See Jickling (2002) for an overview of the financial issues surrounding the Enron collapse, and Mitchell and Utkus (Chapter 3, this volume) on company stock in retirement plans.

[3] See, for instance, Benson (2001).

[4] Zarita (1994), Fischer (1999), and Pennachi (1999, 2000) discuss Latin American pension guarantees.

[5] See Clark and Mitchell (2002) for Japan, and Maurer and Schlag (Chapter 9, this volume) for Germany.

[6] Here we focus only on the accumulation phase of IAs, and not the decumulation phase.

[7] The DeMint-Armey plan, for instance, guarantees benefits for those who elect a balanced IA portfolio, but no additional value is assigned to either the guarantee or the cost of providing a minimum benefit under government cost estimates.

[8] Smetters (2001) analyses various alternative specifications for this type of guarantee, in the context of a complete conversion to IAs.

[9] The President's CSSS (2001) identified several alternative ways to handle legacy costs.

[10] This would arise if the provider of a guarantee has different circumstances from that of the recipient (e.g. differential access to the capital market, a broader range of investment choices, etc).

[11] How to value guarantees from the participant's point of view will be discussed in a future chapter. As a related issue, the approach we describe below makes no assumptions regarding any particular IA participant's risk aversion; in particular, workers are not required to be neutral in their preferences for risk for the cost estimates to hold.

[12] Standard references for option-pricing techniques include Duffie (1996) and Hull (1997). Option-pricing techniques require defining an economy, that is a set of market traded securities (e.g. a stock and a bond) along with their stochastic processes. If a consumption plan (in this case, the pension guarantee payments) can be strictly financed by a strategy involving only securities from the available set, then the cost of the guarantee must equal the cost of the replicating strategy in order to rule out "free lunches" (i.e. markets are dynamically complete and each consumption plan can be replicated). Typically, "incompleteness" problems arise when the consumption plan is a function of securities that are not market-traded. In the pension guarantee case, workers' earnings are likely to be problematic since their value cannot be replicated in the markets. Despite the loss of the "no-arbitrage" argument, if these non-replicable factors are relatively unimportant, option-pricing techniques can still provide insight.

[13] Specifically, the risk-free rate, workers' earnings, stock returns, and bond returns have to be modeled. In the appendix, we provide a model that is internally consistent and allows for replication of the guarantee payments. For instance, internal consistency requires that the relation between bond prices and discount rates be taken into account when modeling bond returns. Following Pennachi (1999), we assume that the risk-free rate follows a stochastic process represented by the Vasicek (1977) model. In contrast to prior work, we take advantage of the simple relation

between bond prices and the risk-free rate (under the Vasicek model) to derive the stochastic process followed by bond returns. Since the stock and bond returns are modeled separately, the total portfolio returns are simply obtained by adding the two processes. This permits an actual replication of the guarantee payments with market securities.

14 This technique is also referred to as "martingale pricing."

15 Deriving an analytical solution for (4) in the guarantee case requires an analytical expression for the probability distribution of the IA. In the Black–Scholes framework with a single purchase, the underlying stock growth process is assumed to be lognormal. In the IA framework, each year's contribution is assumed to grow according to a lognormal distribution, but the sum of these contributions is not lognormal nor does it have a meaningful analytical representation. Hence we evaluate equation (4) numerically using Monte Carlo simulation to illustrate the costs of alternative pension guarantee designs.

16 See for example Siegel (1998) on the relative historical performances of stocks and bonds.

17 Samuelson (1963) initially referred to this idea as the fallacy of large numbers; see also Bodie (1995).

18 When analysts use 30-year moving averages over the post-WWII period, these are not independent draws from the underlying distribution. This point has been made by various authors, including Bodie (2001).

19 For example Jorion and Goetzmann (1999) conclude that the US equity market had "the highest uninterrupted real rate of appreciation of all countries, at 4.3 percent annually from 1921 to 1996. For other countries, the median real appreciation rate was 0.8 percent. The high return premium obtained for US equities therefore appears to be the exception rather than the rule."

20 This analysis does not incorporate the financing required to move to a fiscally solvent system, since estimates of that cost are available elsewhere. Thus this exercise estimates the marginal cost of providing a guarantee for an IA program, rather than the cost of restoring the first pillar system to solvency. Details of the schematic model used to represent the first pillar system appear in the Appendix. These two cases are examples selected to identify the drivers of guarantee costs; neither coincides with proposals devised by the President's CSSS. In that group's report, the first pillar plan was assumed to be reformed with the advent of IAs, and IA contribution rates as well as offset rates were set to bring fiscal solvency to the system as a whole. Our goal here is not to establish costs of moving to solvency, but rather to outline the magnitude and sensitivity of guarantee costs to different guarantee designs.

21 To qualify for the poverty line minimum, the participant must contribute at least 30 years to the annuity component of the system.

22 Neither of these examples corresponds to specific plans outlined by the President's CSSS. In particular, the Commission included no guarantees in its proposed reforms. Our objective here is to describe generic alternatives that help think about guarantees, rather than to cost any specific proposal.

23 This concept is equivalent to the concept of "moneyness" in option pricing. When the strike price of an option is set equal to the stock price, the option is said to be "at-the-money" and its cost is solely driven by volatility. When the strike price of a put option is larger (smaller) than the stock price, the option is said to be "in-the-money"

("out-of-the-money"). In those cases, volatility is not the only factor driving value and these options can be very cheap or expensive, respectively.

[24] The term "expected value" refers to the risk-adjusted expected value used to determine the guarantee cost.

[25] In any mixed system, participants' earnings levels will influence guarantee costs; more generally, guarantee formulas and guaranteed benefits are likely to interact nonlinearly with earnings.

[26] As a variant, they also mention the "collar" strategy of Feldstein and Ranguelova (2000). With this strategy, the guarantee is financed by participants who give up some of the upside return potential of the IA's investment return. Smetters (2002) also describes a similar financing strategy.

[27] In this chapter, we describe the guarantee as a put option on the IA. By "put-call parity," the combination of this put option and of the IA is equivalent to Bodie's strategy of investing in bonds and call options.

[28] Alier and Vittas (2001) discuss some alternative strategies to reduce IA risk when it is not possible to manage this risk via the capital markets.

[29] Some private providers already offer guarantees with their investment accumulation products; see Francis (2001).

[30] No adjustment for age is made, since the AWI is an average measure for workers of all ages. Hence, earnings are likely overestimated for younger participants and underestimated for older ones.

[31] Available at <www.ssa.gov/OACT/STATS/table4c6.html>.

References

Alier, Max and Dimitri Vittas. 2001. "Personal Pension Plans and Stock Market Volatility." Development Research Group, World Bank. In *New Ideas about Old Age Security*, eds. R. Holzmann and J. E. Stiglitz. Washington: World Bank, pp. 391–423.

Benson, Miles. 2001. "Social Security Compromise Would Guarantee Benefit Levels." Newhouse News Services. <http://www.newhousenews:com/archive/story1b112001.html>

Black, F. and M. Scholes. 1973. "The Pricing of Options and Corporate Liabilities." *JPE* 81(3): 637–654.

Bodie, Z. 1995. "On the Risk of Stocks in the Long Run." *Financial Analysts Journal*, May/June: 18–22.

—— 2001. "Financial Engineering and Social Security Reform." In *Risk Aspects of Social Security Reform*, eds. J. Campbell and M. Feldstein. Chicago: University of Chicago Press, pp. 291–316.

—— and R. Merton. 1993. "Pension Benefit Guarantees in the United States: A Functional Analysis." In *The Future of Pensions in the United States*, ed. R. Schmitt. Philadelphia: University of Pennsylvania Press, pp. 194–234.

Clark, Robert L. and Olivia S. Mitchell. 2002. "Strengthening Employment-Based Pensions in Japan." *Benefits Quarterly* Second Quarter: 22–43.

Commission to Strengthen Social Security. (CSSS). 2001. *Strengthening Social Security and Creating Personal Wealth for All Americans.*

Duffie, Darrell. 1996. *Dynamic Asset Pricing Theory.* Princeton, NJ: Princeton University Press.

Feldstein, Martin and Jeffrey B. Liebman. 2001. "Social Security." NBER Working Paper 8451, September.

— and Elena Ranguelova. 2000. "Accumulated Pension Collars: A Market Approach to Reducing the Risk of Investment-Based Social Security Reform." NBER Working Paper 7861, August.

— and Andrew Samwick. 2001. "Potential Paths of Social Security Reform." NBER Working Paper 8592, November.

Fischer, Klaus P. 1999. "Pricing Pension Fund Guarantees: A Discrete Martingale Approach." *Canadian Journal of Administrative Sciences* 16(3): 256–266.

Francis, Theo. 2001. "Guaranteed Funds Give Skittish Security." *Wall Street Journal*, June 8.

Hull, J. 1997. *Options, Futures, and Other Derivatives*, 3rd Edn. Prentice-Hall.

Jensen, Bjarne Astrup, and Carsten Sorensen. 2000. "Paying for Minimum Interest Rate Guarantees: Who Should Compensate Who?" Working Paper 2000–1. Copenhagen Business School.

Jickling, Mark. 2002. "The Enron Collapse: An Overview of Financial Issues." *Congressional Research Service*, February 4.

Jorion, Philippe and William Goetzmann. 1999. "Global Stock Markets in the Twentieth Century." *Journal of Finance* 54(3): 953–980.

Maurer, Raimond and Christian Schlag. This volume "Money-Back Guarantees in Individual Account Pensions: Evidence from the German Pension Reform."

Merton, Robert C., Zvi Bodie, and Alan J. Marcus. 1987. "Pension Plan Integration As Insurance Against Social Security Risk." In *Issues in Pension Economics*, eds. Z. Bodie, J. B. Shoven, and D. A. Wise. Chicago: University of Chicago Press, pp. 147–174.

OASDI Board of Trustees. 2001. Annual Report of the Board of Trustees of the Federal Old-Age and Survivors Insurance Trust Funds, March 19.

Pennachi, George G. 1999. "The Value of Guarantees on Pension Fund Conversion." *Journal of Risk and Insurance* 66(2): 219–237.

— 2000. "Methodology to Assess Fiscal Risk of Pension Guarantees." Working Paper. University of Illinois, May.

Samuelson, Paul. 1963. "Risk and Uncertainty: A Fallacy of Large Numbers." *Scientia* 98: 1–6.

Siegel, Jeremy. 1998. *Stocks for the Long Run*. McGraw Hill.

Smetters, Kent. 2001. "The Effect of Pay-when-needed Benefit Guarantees on the Impact of Social Security Privatization." In *Risk Aspects of Social Security Reform*, eds. J. Campbell and M. Feldstein. University of Chicago Press, pp. 91–112.

— 2002. "Controlling the Costs of Minimum Benefit Guarantees in Public Pension Conversions." *The Journal of Pension Economics and Finance* 1(1): 9–34.

Vasicek, O. 1977. "An equilibrium characterisation of the term structure." *Journal of Financial Economics* 5: 177–188.

Zarita, Salvador. 1994. "Minimum Pension Insurance in the Chilean Pension System." *Revisita de Analisis Economico* 9(1): 105–126.

Chapter 9

Money-Back Guarantees in Individual Pension Accounts: Evidence from the German Pension Reform

Raimond Maurer and Christian Schlag

The German Retirement Saving Act ("Altersvermögensgesetz"[1]) which passed the German legislative body in May of 2001 instituted a new funded system of supplementary pensions coupled with a general reduction in the level of state pay-as-you-age pensions. The goal of this new pension system is to cap and to stabilize the contributions of German employees to the state pension system, which cost 19.1 percent of salary. For compulsory members of the state pension systems not already in retirement, the maximum "first pillar" state pension level will be gradually cut from 70 to 67 percent of the last net salary before retirement by 2030.[2] To compensate for the cut in state pension payouts, individuals will be able to invest voluntarily and on a pre-tax basis a part of their income in individual pension accounts ("Altersvorsorgevertrag," called here IPAs).[3] Additional incentives to invest into the IPAs are given by the government in the form of a tax relief on pension contributions, direct subsidies for low income earners, and extra contributions for children. In order to get the full benefits, households will have to invest about 1 percent of their income (up to the social security ceiling) into the pension system in 2002, increasing every 2 years by 1 percent reaching a maximum of 4 percent in 2008. The investment income during the accumulation period is not subject to income tax, whereas the payments from the IPA during the distribution phase will be fully subject to income tax.

In general, individuals are free to make IPA pension investments in a wide array of products offered by private sector financial institutions. This allows participants to choose an investment portfolio that is consistent with their individual preferences for risk and return. In order to qualify for a tax credit, however, the IPA products have to satisfy a number of criteria.

This research is part of the Research Program "Institutional Investors" of the Center for Financial Studies, Frankfurt/M. This chapter was written in part during Dr. Maurer's time as the Metzler Visiting Professor at the Wharton School's Pension Research Council. The authors would like to thank Manfred Laux, David McCarthy, Olivia S. Mitchell, Alex Muermann, Rudolf Siebel, Wolfgang Raab, and Kent Smetters for helpful comments. Opinions and errors are solely those of the authors.

These conditions are codified in a special law concerning the certification of individual pension products ("Altersvorsorge-Zertifizierungsgesetz") and supervised by a special authority ("Zertifizierungsstelle") belonging to the German Federal Financial Supervisory Agency. The intention of the certification requirements is twofold:

1. First, the government wants to ensure that individuals only use the (tax-supported) accumulated savings for a lifelong income stream in the post-retirement phase, and not for consumption during pre-retirement.
2. Second, private (and often uninformed) investors paying into the new individual pension plans should be protected against the risk of making "too bad" investment decisions.

In the spirit of the first intention, investments in the personal pension accounts must be preserved until employees reach the age of 60,[4] and no distributions may be made during the accumulation period. When the age of retirement is reached, the accumulated assets must be drawn down in the form of a lifelong annuity or a capital withdrawal plan which must (partly) revert into an annuity at the age of 85.[5] To provide transparency, the providers of IPAs must disclose the nature and level of fees (e.g. to cover distribution and/or administrative costs). If distribution fees are not charged as a percentage of the periodic contribution into the plan, they must be spread equally over a period of at least 10 years.[6] During the accumulation phase, the policyholder has the right to suspend the contract as well as to terminate the contract by switching the cash value of the policy to a new provider.

In line with a certain minimum level of investor protection, only regulated financial institutions, like banks, life insurance companies, and mutual fund companies, are allowed to offer IPAs. In principle, these providers are free to design their IPA. In particular, the Certification Act imposes no restrictions concerning the assets in which the providers invest the contributions that back the pension accounts.[7] In addition, the supervisory authority does not check whether the risk and return characteristics of an IPA are "economically feasible." Yet, the provider of an IPA must promise the plan participant that the contract cash value at retirement is at least equal to contributions made to the IPAs, including all extra payments by the government.[8] This "money-back" guarantee, which was the core of an intense and controversial debate during the social security reform in Germany, is the focus of this chapter. Advocates of the guarantee argue that it protects plan participants against a portion of the downside volatility of capital market returns, by providing them with a minimum rate of return with respect to their lifetime contributions. However, the guarantee shapes the design of saving products offered by the providers and raises a question about the economic costs of such a promise.[9] Depending on the assets used to back the pension accounts, providers may be exposed to shortfall risk due to adverse movements in capital markets. If, at retirement, the value of the pension assets is lower than the sum of the contributions paid into the plan, the IPA provider must fill the gap with its own equity capital. The problem faced by money managers is therefore to find a product design, in conjunction with an appropriate investment strategy, that protects the credibility of the guarantee in scenarios of negative investment returns (hedging effectiveness), while still allowing for sufficient upside potential if capital markets are booming (and thus avoiding excessive hedging costs). In addition, the guarantee has important implications for regulators who must find an effective and efficient solvency system for such saving schemes, especially for mutual funds.

The objective of this chapter is to explore how this money-back guarantee works for products offered by the German mutual fund industry. We evaluate alternative designs for guarantee structures including a life cycle model (dynamic asset allocation), a plan with a pre-specified blend of equity and bond investments (static asset allocation), and some type of portfolio insurance. We use simulation to compare hedging effectiveness and hedging costs associated with the provision of the money-back guarantee.

Long-Term and Shortfall Risks, and Return of Saving Plans

In order to make appropriate investment decisions under uncertainty, individuals must be able to compare the risk and rewards of different asset classes. Yet policymakers, regulators, and providers are also interested in the long run performance of financial assets that back the new pension products. The impact of the investment horizon on the risk of the various financial assets is still a subject of intense and controversial debate within the academic community and among investment professionals.[10] For example, a popular statement is that stocks have a lower downside risk in the long run than in the short run. A practical guideline based on this argument is that people should invest a higher fraction of their money in stocks the younger they are, independent of preferences.[11] If the time horizon is long enough, this approach would imply that people should invest 100 percent in stocks. To justify this view, proponents call on the law of large numbers which (seemingly) forces a phenomenon called "time diversification." Intuitively, this means that over a sufficiently long investment horizon, losses resulting from the high downside fluctuations will be compensated by gains resulting from the high upside fluctuations of short term stock returns. Some investment advisors press this argument by pointing to historical returns and demonstrating that stocks have outperformed bonds for every 10-, 15-, or 20-year period on record.

Nevertheless, it is well known in the academic literature that this is a misleading argument. For example, Samuelson (1963) uses utility theory, Levy and Cohen (1998) use stochastic dominance, and Bodie (1995, 2001) applies option pricing theory to demonstrate the logical flaw in this conjecture. In addition, the use of historical return series implies that the 10-, 15-, or 20-year periods used are strongly overlapping, so the resulting rollover multiperiod returns have a high degree of correlation, both of which result in a serious estimation bias.

Shortfall Risk Measures

This section provides additional evidence concerning the impact of the time horizon on the risk of the major financial asset classes in the German context, that is, stocks and bonds. To do so, we use alternative shortfall risk measures. The concept of shortfall risk is associated with the possibility of "something bad happening," in other words, falling short compared to a required target (benchmark) return.[12] Returns below the target (losses) are considered to be undesirable or risky, while returns above the target (gains) are desirable or non-risky. In this sense, shortfall risk measures are called "relative" or "pure" measures of risk.

A popular measure to examine the downside risk of different investment vehicles is the *shortfall probability*. Formally, let R denote the cumulative (multiyear) return of an investment at a specific point in time. Then the shortfall probability is given by

$$\mathrm{SP} = \mathrm{Prob}(R < z), \tag{9.1}$$

where z is the target (benchmark) which translates the total investment returns into gains or losses. In the special case of a money back guarantee, the target is set equal to zero; that is, the shortfall occurs when the cash value of the policy is lower than the premiums paid into the saving plan. Despite the popularity of this risk measure in the investment industry, it has a major shortcoming. As Bodie (2001: 308) points out it "completely ignores how large the potential shortfall might be." If the same investment strategy can be repeated many times, the shortfall probability only answers the question "how often" a loss might occur, but not "how bad" such a loss might be.

To provide information about the potential extent of a loss, we calculate the Mean Excess Loss (MEL), also known as the *conditional shortfall expectation*, as an additional measure to evaluate the long-term and shortfall risk of financial assets. Formally, this risk index is given by

$$\mathrm{MEL} = \mathrm{E}[z - R | R < z], \tag{9.2}$$

and it indicates the expected loss with respect to the benchmark, under the condition that a shortfall occurs. Therefore, given a loss, the MEL answers the question "how bad on average" the loss will be.[13] In this sense, the MEL can be considered a worst case risk measure, since the measure only considers the consequences of the mean shortfall-level assuming that a shortfall happens.

A shortfall risk measure which connects the probability and the extent of the conditional shortfall in an intuitive way is the *shortfall expectation* (SE):

$$SE = E[\max(z - R, 0)] = SP \times MEL \tag{9.3}$$

The shortfall expectation is the sum of losses weighted by their probabilities, and hence it is a measure of the unconditional "average loss." As equation (9.3) shows, the mean shortfall level is simply the product of the shortfall probability and the mean level of shortfall, given the occurrence of a shortfall. In addition, the SE is, in a certain way, related to the price of an insurance contract which would cover the shortfall. For example, the provider may have the possibility of transferring the shortfall risk to the capital market by using appropriate arbitrage-free put options. Then the shortfall expectation between the cash value of the pension assets and the guarantee payment with respect to the risk adjusted ("martingale") probabilities discounted back at the risk-free interest rate, results in the (modified) Black and Scholes (1973) option pricing formula.[14] If the provider transfers the shortfall risk to a reinsurance company, the shortfall expectation could be seen as an important element of an appropriate premium.

Calibration

Next we quantify and compare the shortfall risk (in the sense defined above) with respect to the preservation of principal of two saving plans. The first invests the contribution into stock index fund units, represented by the German stock index (DAX). The other saving plan is based on bond index fund units, represented by the German bond index (REXP). The DAX stands for an index portfolio of German blue chips, and the REXP represents a portfolio of German government bonds. Each of these indices is adjusted for capital gains as well as dividends and coupon payments (on a pre-tax basis). We assume a series of equal contributions paid at the beginning of each month up to the end of the accumulation period, which ranges from 1 to 20 years.

To gain information about the relevant risk measures, we employ an *ex ante* approach by imposing an exogenous structure on the probability distribution governing the uncertainty of future asset returns. With such a model, it is possible to look into the future and compute the risk measures in which we are interested. Due to the complexity of the underlying payment structure of saving plans, there are no analytical closed form expressions for these risk-measures.[15] Therefore we use Monte-Carlo simulation to generate a large number of paths for the evolution of the saving plans.

The relevant statistics for the shortfall risk measures are then evaluated on the basis of these scenarios. The stochastic dynamics of the (uncertain) market values of investment fund units are posited to follow geometric Brownian motion, a standard assumption in financial economics that may be traced back to Bachelier (1900). This implies that the log-returns of each type of index fund are independent identically and normally distributed. For the estimation of the process parameters (drift/diffusion), we use the historical monthly log-returns of the DAX and REXP over the period January, 1973–December, 2001. The mean log rates of return for stocks (bonds) are 0.7967 percent per month (0.5683 percent p.m.) and the corresponding standard deviation 5.58 percent p.m. (1.12 percent p.m.). To take potential administration costs into account, we subtract the equivalent of 0.5 percent per annum (p.a.) from the monthly average return on the investments.[16] Compatible with the prevalent German mutual fund fee structure, we take marketing costs into consideration by assuming front end sales charges of 5 percent for the stock and 3 percent for the bond fund units.

With respect to these parameters and consistent with the model of a geometric Brownian motion, we generated 3,000,000 random paths for the development of the pension plan with an investment horizon of 20 years (240 months).[17] For each simulation path $i(i = 1, \ldots, 3{,}000{,}000)$ we compute for each month $t(t = 1, \ldots, 240)$ the (uncertain) compounded (multiyear) return, that is,

$$R_{i,t} = \frac{V_{i,t} - P_t}{P_t}. \tag{9.4}$$

Here $V_{i,t}$ stands for the cash value of the IPA in month $t(t = 1, \ldots, T)$ in simulation run $i(i = 1, \ldots, n)$ and P_t for the sum of contributions paid until month t. According to the money-back guarantee, we set the benchmark return equal $z = 0$. With respect to this target, the relevant risk parameters are then determined on the basis of the spectrum of possible future developments.

Results

We start with the results for the development of the expected (multiyear) return and the shortfall probability of the stock and bond index fund over time. The graphs in Figure 9-1 indicate that a German investor would have the potential to receive a substantially higher expected return by investing in stocks instead of bonds. For example, in the case of stocks at the end of a 20-year accumulation period, the investor can expect a compounded return with respect to his contributions of 270 percent. For a saving plan based on bond index funds, the expected return is only 109 percent. However, purchasing such an investment exposes the plan participant to the volatility and therefore the downside risk of financial markets.

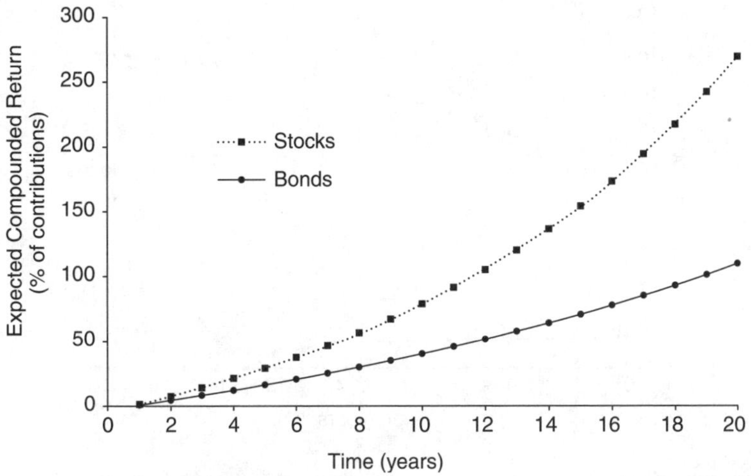

Figure 9-1. Expected compounded return of saving plans in stocks and bonds. (*Source*: Authors' computations.)

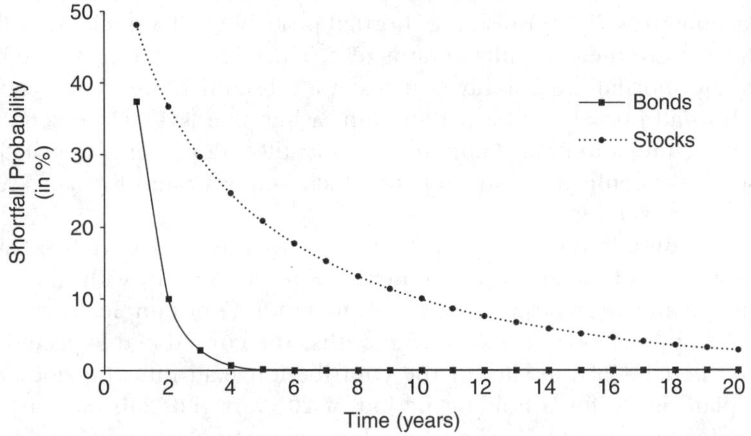

Figure 9-2. Shortfall probability against a (nominal) zero percent target rate of return in stock and bond saving plans. (*Source*: Authors' computations.)

Next we illustrate the results for the development of the shortfall probability of a saving plan using stock and bond index funds over time. Figure 9-2 shows the well-known effect of time diversification, implying that the risk of not maintaining nominal capital decreases monotonically with an increasing investment period for bonds and stocks. Yet the rate and the extent of the risk reduction differ notably between the two investment vehicles. For bond index funds, the shortfall probability is 37 percent for a yearly investment,

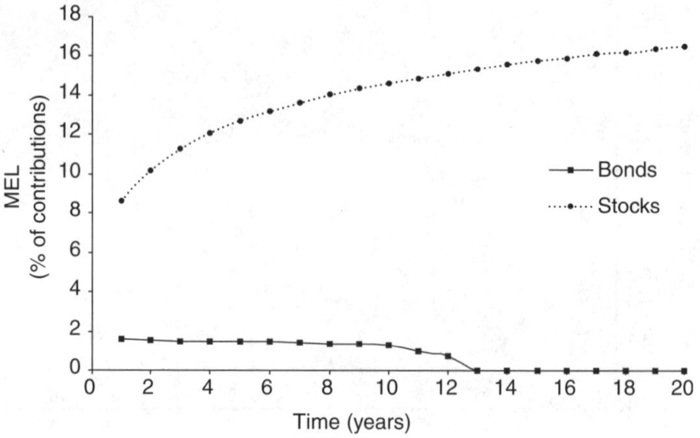

Figure 9-3. Conditional mean expected loss (MEL) against a (nominal) zero percent target rate of return in stock and bond saving plans. (*Source*: Authors' computations.)

and close to zero (i.e. lower than 0.1 percent) with an investment horizon of 7 years onwards. By contrast, the shortfall probability of a stock index fund does not converge as rapidly towards zero. Thus, even for longer time horizons, the shortfall probability remains at a substantial level. For example, the shortfall probability for a 12-month saving plan is 48.09 percent, and for an accumulation period of 20 years it is still 2.72 percent. In principle, these results confirm a characteristic which Leibowitz and Krasker (1988) call *persistence of risk.*

Corresponding results for the MEL are presented in Figure 9-3. Saving plans in stocks have an MEL that increases monotonically with the length of the accumulation period, in contrast to bonds. For example, for an accumulation period of 1 year (i.e. 12 months) the conditional expected loss is 8.62 percent of the sum of the contribution paid into the stock pension plan, while for a holding period of 20 years (i.e. 240 months) this risk index increases to 16.53 percent. For a pension plan using bond index funds, the MEL is 1.63 percent after 1 year, while for accumulation periods of 13 years onwards, none of the 3,000,000 simulation paths produces a shortfall. Hence, with respect to the magnitude of a potential shortfall, the popular argument that stocks become less risky in the long run is not true.

This result is in line with Samuelson's (1963) finding concerning the fallacy of the law of large numbers. In addition, these results make clear that the use of the shortfall probability alone is a misleading risk measure of stock investments in the long run. The worst-case aspect of a long-term investment in stocks is partly hidden by only taking the shortfall probability into consideration. Bodie (2002) provided the following very intuitive explanation for this result "the probability of a bad thing happening is only part of the risk

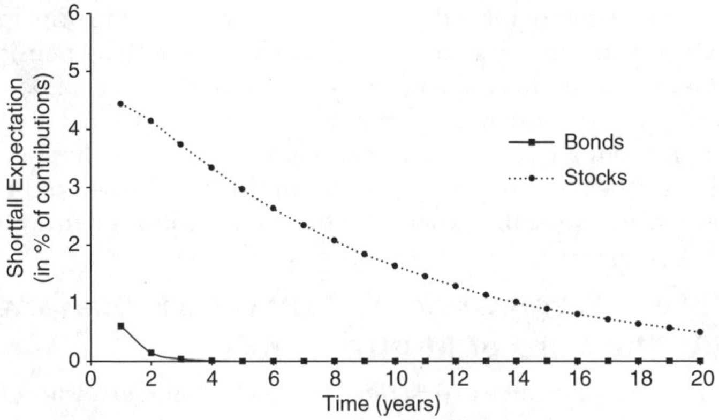

Figure 9-4. Expected shortfall against a (nominal) zero percent target rate of return in stock and bond saving plans. (*Source*: Authors' computations.)

equation. The other part is the severity of that bad thing, and the further out you go, the more severe it could be." Thus, the elucidation of the worst-case risk embodied in a long-term investment in stocks represents an additional piece of information that might be essential for investors.

Figure 9-4 shows how the unconditional shortfall expectation develops over time. For a saving plan in bond index funds, both the probability of loss and the mean excess loss decrease with the length of the time horizon. Because the shortfall expectation measures the net effect of both risk components, it is also decreasing in time. For a stock-based saving plan, this risk measure is also decreasing, that is the decreasing shortfall probability overcompensates the increasing MEL, to a certain extent. However, in contrast to bonds, we can observe a risk persistence-characteristic in the stock fund: even for very long time horizons, the shortfall expectation remains at a substantial level.

In summary, even for long investment horizons, a pure stock investment is not free of the downside risk of losing money. Hence it is not possible to perfectly smoothen the negative short-run fluctuations of stock returns over long horizons and simultaneously, to keep expected excess returns with certainty. Consequently, assets with low volatility and low expected returns, like bonds, are not superfluous in the design of long-term saving products. Insurance contracts covering the shortfall of a principal guarantee are not costless for a pure stock investment, even for long investment horizons (see Lachance and Mitchell, Chapter 8, this volume).

For low volatility assets like a portfolio of government bonds, the probability and the severity of losing money decreases over time. Over long investment horizons, the price to insure the downside risk of a principal guarantee for a pure bonds investment is very low (close to zero). Hence bond pension plans are very effective vehicles for producing principal guarantees. Of course, this does not mean that with a pure bond pension plan, the economic cost of downside protection is zero. Providers of bond-based IPAs must give up a substantial part of the upside returns that are possible with stocks. From an *ex ante* point of view, a measure of these economic (hedging) costs—in the sense of a smaller upside potential—can be seen as the difference between the expected return of both investment vehicles.[18]

Regulatory Framework of Money-Back Guarantees for IPA: The Case of Mutual Funds

The money-back guarantee as described in the German Certification Act can be represented as a fixed liability of the provider, when it issues the IPA. If the cash value of the financial assets backing the liabilities at the beginning of the retirement phase is lower than the sum of the contributions paid into the policy, the provider must fill the gap with equity capital. From this point of view, it is clear that the money-back guarantee should be subject to solvency regulation.

Saving products offered by commercial banks (e.g. saving accounts) or insurance companies (e.g. life insurance products) in Germany are usually designed (at least in part) with fixed interest rates. Nevertheless such is not the case for mutual funds. The fundamental idea of a collective investment scheme such as a mutual fund is to collect money from many private investors via the offering of fund units, and to invest this money in a well-diversified portfolio of stocks, bonds, and/or real estate. The units of the mutual fund are liquid in the sense that they are traded on an active secondary market (e.g. for so-called exchange-traded-funds) or investors can ask for redemption of their holdings at net-asset value prices, at any point in time. The investment management company usually assumes no obligation other than that of investing the funds in a reasonable and prudent manner, solely in the interest of the investors. It provides no guarantees with respect to a rate of investment return. Hence, the investor bears all capital market risk and receives the full reward of the financial asset that backs the mutual fund units. Because the balance sheets of mutual fund providers are not exposed to financial market fluctuations, they are excluded from risk-based solvency capital regulation requirements in Germany, in contrast to insurance companies and commercial banks.[19]

By contrast, if the provider of an IPA is an investment management company which uses its own mutual funds, the German Federal Banking Supervisory Authority (BAKred)[20] requires (conditional) solvency capital because of the statutory "money back" guarantee. This solvency requirement, published in December 2001, can be modeled in the following way. Let V_t denote the cash value of an IPA at time t, and let P_t be the sum of the contributions (including all extra payments by the government) paid into the policy until time t. Furthermore, let $r_f(t, T) =: r_{f,t}$ be the yield at time t on a zero coupon bond maturing at time T (i.e. the planned age of retirement), taken from the current term structure of German interest rates.

For each IPA, the investment management company must build solvency capital equal to 8 percent of the total contributions paid into the plan,[21] in each period t in which the risk-adjusted cash value of the policy is lower than the present value of the contribution:

$$\frac{V_t}{\exp(2.33\sigma)} \leq \frac{P_t}{(1 + r_{f,t})^{T-t-1}}. \tag{9.5}$$

In this formula,[22] σ stands for the monthly volatility of the mutual fund units backing the pension account. The volatility must be estimated from historical time series returns of the fund unit prices using a window between 2 and 5 years. If the policy consists of more than one type of mutual fund (e.g. equity and bond funds), σ is computed as the weighted sum of the individual fund volatilities according to the asset allocation of the policy.

The economic rationale behind this formula is as follows. At every point in time, the IPA issuer has the safe investment alternative of investing some part of the contributions in zero bonds, so that at the end of the investment period at time T the proceeds would equal the participant's contributions during the accumulation phase. The necessary amount to meet the total contribution guarantee of P_t at time t is $P_t/(1 + r_{f,t})^{T-t-1}$, which is the right hand side of formula (9.5). If the provider does not use zero bonds, but instead employs only stocks to back the IPA, nothing happens as long as the cash value of the policy is "substantially" higher than the present value of the contributions. "Substantially" higher means, under the German solvency rule, that given a current cash value of V_t there is a probability of only 1 percent (note 2.33 is the 99 percent quantile of the standard normal distribution) that the uncertain cash value of the policy one month later V_{t+1} is lower than the present value of the contributions. This explains the risk adjustment on the left hand side of the solvency formula.

Hence, without capital requirements, an underfunding of the principal liability during the accumulation period is possible. The amount to which such an underfunding is allowed depends on the volatility of the pension assets and the time remaining to the end of the accumulation period. For example (see Table 9-1), if the monthly returns of the pension assets have a volatility of 7.22 percent per month, which when annualized is about 25 percent per year (a typical value for German stock funds), the risk free interest rate is 4 percent p.a., and the remaining accumulation period is 30 years (360 months), then the critical level is only 35.8 percent. This means that as long as the cash value of the policy exceeds 35.8 percent of the contribution paid into the plan, no risk-based-solvency capital is necessary. If the

TABLE 9-1 Critical Level of Under Funding (as Percent of Contributions) with respect to the Solvency Formula (9.5)

	Volatility (% per month)							
End of plan (Years)	0.29	0.58	0.87	1.15	1.44	2.89	5.77	7.22
30	30.5	30.7	30.9	31.1	31.3	32.4	34.6	35.8
25	37.2	37.5	37.7	38.0	38.2	39.5	42.3	43.7
20	45.4	45.8	46.1	46.4	46.7	48.3	51.6	53.4
15	55.5	55.9	56.2	56.6	57.0	59.0	63.1	65.2
10	67.8	68.2	68.7	69.1	69.6	72.0	77.0	79.6
5	82.7	83.3	83.8	84.4	85.0	87.9	94.0	97.2
3	89.6	90.2	90.8	91.4	92.0	95.2	101.8	105.3
2	93.3	93.9	94.5	95.2	95.8	99.1	106.0	109.6
1	97.1	97.7	98.4	99.0	99.7	103.1	110.3	114.1

Source: Authors' computations.

time to retirement is only 5 years (60 months), the critical level increases to 97.2 percent. However, the provider has the possibility of reducing the volatility of the IPA and the possible amount of underfunding by investing more of the pension assets in low volatility assets such as bonds.

In summary, with an appropriate asset allocation and depending on the age of the participant, it is possible for the provider of mutual fund-based IPA to avoid capital requirements without jeopardizing the credibility of the principal guarantee. However, the burden of such a conditional solvency system is the implementation of an efficient risk monitoring system for each IPA.

Hedging Costs and Hedging Effectiveness of Mutual Fund Products

In view of our results concerning the long-run risks of pure stock investments, and given the regulatory environment placing a significant capital charge on a fund with too much shortfall risk, it is clear that a sensible strategy for a mutual fund must contain some element of risk management or hedging. As mentioned above, the problem is to provide sufficient credibility for promised payments (hedging effectiveness), while at the same time reducing the upside potential of the investment as little as possible, to keep hedging costs low. Note that the term "hedging costs" refers neither to the regulatory capital the mutual fund company has to provide, nor to potential expenditures for the purchase of derivative contracts. The only source of hedging costs for the products considered below is a reduction in average expected wealth or, equivalently, in the total return on the contributions paid into the IPA.

Because of the substantial positive correlation of the financial assets backing the pension plans, an IPA provider cannot manage the risk resulting from guarantees by using traditional insurance pooling techniques.[23] Hence it is necessary to manage underlying risk of the principal guarantee for each IPA individually.

Methodology

Focusing on products currently offered by German mutual fund companies, we compare them to the simple strategies of investing in stocks or bonds exclusively. In total, we analyze five strategies with respect to their long-run risk-return profile.

Pure Stock Strategy

This strategy was discussed above with respect to its long-run risks. Given the parameter values used in our simulation study, this strategy is likely to produce the highest expected wealth at the end of the investment period. On the other hand, this strategy can be quite costly for the mutual fund company if it must put up substantial solvency capital to render credible its payment promises.

Pure Bond Strategy

A pure bond strategy follows the opposite approach. To reduce the risk of falling short of the promised wealth at the end of the accumulation period, this strategy invests only in bonds or broadly diversified government bond portfolios. One might expect that this reduces or even completely eliminates the shortfall risk, but this benefit also comes at the cost of lower expected returns.

Static Portfolio Strategy

This strategy is a mixture of the pure bond and the pure stock strategy. The portfolio remains unchanged over the whole period, and it contains both stocks and bonds from the start. With reference to the typical asset allocation of German retirement funds (AS-Funds),[24] our simulations for the 15-year horizon use an equally weighted stock and bond portfolio, whereas for the 30-year investment period we use 75 percent stocks and 25 percent bonds.

Life Cycle Strategy

Popular advice often given to investors is to alter the portfolio composition with age. People are usually advised to hold a larger share of the portfolio in stocks when young, and then to shift into bonds later on. The idea behind this strategy is that it would be hard to compensate unfavorable movements on the stock market occurring late in the accumulation period, since little time is left, so that this type of risk could be avoided by investing in bonds. The life cycle strategy is an unconditional "hedge" in the sense that more volatile return opportunities are generally considered too dangerous late in the investment period, irrespective of the performance of stocks before the rebalancing date. We implement this strategy by defining fixed points in time at which the portfolio composition is changed, with more and more weight on bonds instead of stocks. The exact dates and compositions are as follows: For an investment horizon of 15 years, the plan is assumed to start with 40 percent of the allocations going into equity and 60 percent into bonds. After 5 years this allocation changes, and for the remaining time 10 percent go into stocks and 90 percent into bonds. In the case of a 30-year plan, there is an initial period of 10 years with pure stock investment, followed by 5 years with an allocation of 70 percent equity and 30 percent bonds. After another 5 years, the allocation of the contributions is again changed to 40 percent equity and 60 percent bonds. Over the remaining 10 years, 90 percent of the contributions go into bond funds and the remaining 10 percent into stocks.

Conditional Hedging Strategy

This strategy aims at combining the performance advantage of a pure stock strategy with the risk-reducing effect of a pure bond strategy. As opposed to the life cycle strategy, however, the decision to shift from one investment into the other is not driven by an exogenous variable like age, but rather by the performance of the respective investments. For this reason, such a strategy represents a "conditional hedging" approach. Usually one starts out with a pure stock investment and shifts to bonds as soon as a certain critical level of wealth is reached. In this case, subsequent contributions go in bonds until the safety level is again exceeded, when the strategy switches back to a 100 percent stock investment. An important parameter for this type of strategy is the critical level of wealth at which the investment rule (for subsequent contributions) changes. To link this critical value to the intervention line set by the regulatory authorities in Germany (see equation 9.5), we set the critical level of wealth (as an example) to 75 percent above the intervention value defined according to the solvency equation (9.5).

A possibility not discussed up to now is the use of derivative assets to protect the value of an investment plan against shortfall risk. The appropriate instrument here would be a put option on the value of the plan, with a strike price equal to the sum of the nominal payments. However, the application of put options in this context is not without problems. First of all, due to the very long maturity of the savings plans, any option would be very expensive, and the cost would have to be paid up front (at the beginning of the accumulation period) which raises financing questions. Second, it seems unlikely that a put with such a long time to maturity would be offered at all, so that a roll-over strategy would become necessary with all the risks involved in terms of prices and liquidity. Third, for the put option to be of real value to the institution holding it, the seller would have to demonstrate that it could actually cover its liabilities at the end of the accumulation period. In practice, there would always be doubts concerning the actual risk-reduction potential of such an option. Finally, there is a significant operational problem in using put options, since all the accounts have to be protected individually. This means that for every IPA, the provider would have to hold a put option with the appropriate strike price and time to maturity. This seems too costly and complicated for the typical institution, so that hedging strategies using "physical" financial derivatives will not be considered further in the following analysis.

We analyze the five strategies described above in terms of wealth levels (or total returns) and required regulatory capital. Since there are no closed-form expressions for the statistics of interest, we use Monte Carlo simulation to generate a large number of paths for the evolution of the savings plans. The relevant statistics for total returns (relative to a benchmark) and regulatory capital are then evaluated on the basis of these scenarios. The key ingredient in such a simulation is a suitable model to describe the dynamics of the relevant funds and the short rate of interest. For the funds we use the standard capital market model, representing asset price movements by means of correlated Wiener processes. The dynamics of the short rate are given by the one-factor model suggested by Cox, Ingersoll, and Ross (1985). While we assume constant correlations between the risk factors, the covariances will vary due to the fact that the conditional standard deviation for the short rate will in general not be equal to the unconditional value.

The time series used to estimate the process parameters (mean returns, volatilities, correlations) are the monthly log returns of the German stock index DAX representing the stock index fund, the log returns of the bond performance index REXP as the bond index fund as well as the 1-year interest rate as a proxy for the short rate. Parameters were estimated via a maximum-likelihood approach, the estimates are presented in Tables 9-2 and 9-3. As discussed above we subtracted the equivalent of 0.5 percent p.a. from the monthly average return on the investments to take potential administration costs into account.

The CIR process is very popular in interest rate modeling. This is mainly due to the fact that it is able to generate both mean-reversion in interest rates as well as non-negative rates with probability one. Since the process exhibits mean-reversion, the sign of the drift component (i.e. the expected change in the short rate over the next time interval) depends on whether the process is currently above or below its long-run mean. How quickly the process reverts back to this long-run mean is determined by the speed of mean-reversion. In Table 9-3, κ (kappa) represents this speed of mean reversion, θ (theta) stands for the long-run mean of the interest rate, while

TABLE 9-2 Descriptive Statistics for Risk Factors in Germany from January, 1973 to December, 2001

Asset	*Mean (% p.m.)*	*Volatility (% p.m.)*	*Correlations*	
			Stocks	*Bonds*
Stocks	0.7967	5.5800	1	0.2051
Bonds	0.5683	1.1200		1

Source: Authors' computations.

TABLE 9-3 Descriptive Statistics for the German Short Rate Process from January, 1973 to December, 2001

κ	θ	σ	*Correlations Innovations with*	
			Stock Returns	*Bond Returns*
0.1494	0.0539	0.0511	0.1417	−0.7009

The process estimated is the CIR process $dr_t = \kappa(\theta - r_t)dt + \sigma\sqrt{r_t}dW_t$, where κ is the speed of mean-reversion, θ is the long-run mean of the short rate, and σ is the volatility of changes in the short rate. dW_t is the increment of a standard Wiener process.

Source: Authors' computations.

σ (sigma) denotes the volatility of changes in the short rate. The market price of interest rate risk was set equal to zero for reasons of simplicity.

To ensure stability of the simulation results, we base our analysis on 3,000,000 simulations for each of the respective strategies. We then compute:

(1) statistics related to hedging costs: the mean of the total return generated by the respective strategies for the different points in time (months);

(2) statistics related to hedging effectiveness: the shortfall risk and the required regulatory capital for the respective strategies.

The model assumes equal contributions into the plan occurring at the beginning of each month, and a front-end load of 5 percent proportional to the unit price for the stock fund and 3 percent for the bond fund. These loads are comparable to the current German mutual fund fee structure. $V_{i,t}$ denotes the uncertain total wealth of the IPA in month $t(t = 1, \ldots, T)$ in simulation run $i(i = 1, \ldots, n)$, and $z_{i,t}$ represents the critical level of wealth in month t according to formula (9.5) determined by the BAKred.[25]

If P_t represents the sum of payments into the plan until time t, the average compounded (multiyear) return (EW_t) of the IPA at the end of month t is given by:

$$EW_t = \frac{1}{n}\sum_{i=1}^{n} \frac{V_{i,t} - P_t}{P_t}. \tag{9.6}$$

The probability of a solvency capital charge (CP_t) in month t is estimated by:

$$CP_t = \frac{1}{n}\sum_{i=1}^{n} I_{(-\infty, z_{i,t})}(V_{i,t}), \tag{9.7}$$

where the indicator variable $I_{(a,b)}(X)$ is equal to one if $X \in (a, b)$ and zero otherwise. The mean solvency capital charge (MC_t) at time t month after the beginning of the plan normalized by the sum of the contributions P_t paid into the IPA, is given by

$$MC_t = \frac{1}{n}\sum_{i=1}^{n} \frac{C_{i,t}}{P_t}. \tag{9.8}$$

According to the regulatory authorities, the solvency capital charge $C_{i,t}$ depends on how far the mutual funds based IPA wealth falls short of the critical level. The rule says that the capital charge is at least 8 percent when wealth falls below the critical level. If the amount of the shortfall exceeds 8 percent, the capital charge is increased accordingly to cover the gap. Hence $C_{i,t}$ must be calculated according to the following formula:

$$C_{i,t} = \begin{cases} 0.08 \cdot P_t & 0 < 1 - V_{i,t}/z_{i,t} \leq 0.08 \\ (1 - V_{i,t}/z_{i,t}) \cdot P_t & 1 - V_{i,t}/z_{i,t} > 0.08 \\ 0 & 1 - V_{i,t}/z_{i,t} < 0 \end{cases}. \tag{9.9}$$

The mean conditional capital charge (MCC_t) at month t given that a capital charge has occurred is computed according to:

$$MCC_t = MC_t / CP_t. \tag{9.10}$$

Results

Our results for the expected total return of savings plans based on the different investment strategies are given in Table 9-4. It is no surprise that the pure stock strategy does best in terms of this measure, since stocks have the highest expected monthly return. This also causes the differences between the respective strategies to increase with time. Nevertheless, it is interesting to note how close the conditional hedge strategy comes in terms of expected total return. Even after 30 years, the difference to the pure stock strategy

TABLE 9-4 Expected Total Return in Germany (in % of contributions)

Year	1	5	10	15	30
100% bond	0.80 (0.80)	16.26 (16.26)	40.17 (40.17)	70.67 (70.67)	225.38 (–)
100% stock	1.38 (1.38)	29.09 (29.09)	78.78 (78.78)	154.06 (154.06)	731.60 (–)
Static	1.72 (1.08)	26.31 (22.44)	68.79 (58.03)	130.38 (107.36)	554.59 (–)
Life cycle	1.38 (1.03)	29.09 (21.39)	78.78 (46.73)	140.13 (81.36)	384.93 (–)
Conditional hedge	1.38 (1.33)	29.09 (26.07)	78.77 (67.40)	153.93 (126.54)	728.06 (–)

The table gives the expected total compounded return for the different IPA plans at different points in time for a 30-year accumulation period (numbers in parentheses are for an accumulation period of 15 years). For example, an entry of 16.26 for the 100 percent bond strategy in year 5 means that the value of an IPA with an investment horizon of 30 years is after 5 years on average 16.26 percent higher than the sum of the contributions over the first 5 years.

Source: Authors' computations.

is only about 3.5 percent of the contributions paid. This can be taken as a first indication that this type of strategy might be an interesting compromise between the return potential of a pure stock strategy and the risk-avoiding property of a pure bond approach.

Nevertheless, expected wealth is just one measure to be considered; any sensible comparison of the given products must also focus on risk measures. The risk of the different strategies is measured by the regulatory capital charge that the mutual fund company adopting these strategies would face. Table 9-5 indicates that, for an investment horizon of 30 years, no regulatory capital is needed over the first 5 years for any of the strategies. The pure bond strategy can even be regarded as entirely risk-free with respect to regulatory capital charges. The life cycle approach also exhibits very low capital charges on average. This strategy seems to be an interesting alternative to a pure bond investment, given its advantage in terms of expected return.

As expected, the pure stock strategy balances its high return potential with an "expensive" regulatory capital level. It requires more than three times the regulatory capital than the conditional hedge strategy, which is in second place with respect to this criterion. Furthermore, Table 9-5 provides insight into the impact of the investment horizon. Long-term strategies generally exhibit lower risk than the 15-year plans with the only exception being the life cycle strategy. The fundamental reason for

TABLE 9-5 Mean Regulatory Capital Charge in Germany (as % of Contributions)

Strategy	*Year*				
	1	*5*	*10*	*15*	*30*
100% bond	0 (0)	0 (0)	0 (0)	0 (0)	0 (0)
100% stock	0 (0)	0 (0.07)	<0.01 (0.68)	0.01 (1.67)	0.28 (–)
Static	0 (0)	0 (0)	0 (0.01)	0.01 (0.08)	0.04 (–)
Life cycle	0 (0)	0 (0)	<0.01 (0)	<0.01 (<0.01)	0 (–)
Conditional hedge	0 (0)	0 (<0.01)	<0.01 (0.01)	<0.01 (0.06)	0.08 (–)

The table gives the average regulatory capital that has to be put up for the different IPA plans at different points in time for a 30-year accumulation period (numbers in parentheses are for an accumulation period of 15 years). For example, an entry of 0.04 for the static strategy in year 30 means that in this year on average 0.04 percent of the contributions made over 30 years have to be provided as regulatory capital.

Source: Authors' computations.

longer-term strategies requiring less regulatory capital than shorter-term strategies is the discounting embedded in the critical solvency ratio set by the regulatory authorities. This means that the required minimum wealth level of a plan is lower, when the remaining time to maturity of the plan is longer. For the life cycle strategy, however, there are two effects to be considered. For the shorter horizon plan, the period of pure stock investment is rather short, so the risk in general decreases. To take the most pronounced example for the usual impact of the investment horizon, consider the pure stock strategy. The average capital increases dramatically compared to the 30-year plan, so that this approach looks very costly when it is implemented over this short investment horizon.

The probability that the mutual fund company will be required to put capital aside is given in Table 9-6, and the results are qualitatively similar to Table 9-5. The pure bond strategy never forces the provider to put up capital, whereas the pure stock does with a significant likelihood. Again, time is an important factor here. For the 30-year horizon, the probability of a capital charge for any strategy never exceeds 1.4 percent, but for a 15-year pure stock plan, this probability is almost 9 percent at the end of the investment period. For the other strategies, the ratios of 15- to 30-year probabilities are also quite high, so that if a plan actually exhibits the risk of a capital charge, this risk tends to increase for shorter horizons.

TABLE 9-6 Probability of a Regulatory Capital Charge in Germany (in %)

Strategy	*Year*				
	1	*5*	*10*	*15*	*30*
100% bond	0	0	0	0	0
	(0)	(0)	(0)	(0)	(0)
100% stock	0	0	<0.01	0.07	1.40
	(0)	(0.67)	(4.78)	(8.98)	(–)
Static	0	0	0	<0.01	0.25
	(0)	(0)	(0.06)	(0.74)	(–)
Life cycle	0	0	<0.01	<0.01	0
	(0)	(0)	(0)	(<0.01)	(–)
Conditional hedge	0	0	<0.01	0.01	0.64
	(0)	(<0.01)	(0.08)	(0.62)	(–)

The table gives the average frequency (or probability) of the event that regulatory capital has to be put up for the different IPA plans at different points in time for a 30-year accumulation period (numbers in parentheses are for an accumulation period of 15 years). For example, an entry of 0.07 for the 100 percent stock strategy in year 15 means that in this year in 0.07 percent of the cases regulatory capital had to be provided. Numbers in parentheses represent results for an investment horizon of 15 years.

Source: Authors' computations.

We also note that there is an important difference between shortfall probability and the probability of a regulatory capital charge. As shown above, the shortfall probability of a pure stock investment actually falls with a longer investment horizon, whereas the probability of a capital charge goes up. Again this is due to the fact that the critical level of wealth set by the German regulatory authorities contains a discounting component. Thus this critical level will go up with decreasing time to maturity, thereby causing a higher likelihood for a capital charge.

The average conditional regulatory capital charge depicted in Table 9-7 shows how much capital will be needed given that the cash value of the IPA falls below the critical BAKred value. Note that when the empirical probability of a capital charge is zero, this measure is not defined. The Table shows results qualitatively similar to the general long run risk-return profile of the various asset classes. The risk of a pure stock strategy becomes obvious, since if regulatory capital is needed, it will probably be a significant amount. For example, at the end of 30 years the mutual fund company would need on average almost 20 percent of the contributions as regulatory capital in those scenarios where wealth falls below the critical BAKred value. The benefits of flexibility become obvious when the static strategy is compared with the conditional hedge. The conditional hedge produces, on average,

TABLE 9-7 Mean Conditional Regulatory Capital Charge in Germany (as % of Contributions)

Strategy	*Year*				
	1	*5*	*10*	*15*	*30*
Pure bond	n.def. (n.def.)	n.def. (n.def.)	n.def. (n.def.)	n.def. (n.def.)	n.def. (n.def.)
Pure stock	n.def. (n.def.)	n.def. (9.92)	9.46 (14.31)	11.59 (18.63)	19.90 (—)
Static	n.def. (n.def.)	n.def. (n.def.)	n.def. (8.75)	9.31 (10.17)	14.71 (—)
Life-cycle	n.def. (n.def.)	n.def. (n.def.)	9.46 (n.def.)	8.04 (8.00)	n.def. (—)
Conditional Hedge	n.def. (n.def.)	n.def. (8.06)	8.00 (8.90)	9.00 (9.95)	13.29 (—)

The table gives the average conditional regulatory capital that has to be put up for the different IPA plans at different points in time for a 30 year accumulation period (numbers in parentheses are for an accumulation period of 15 years), that is, the average amount of regulatory capital that is necessary, given that regulatory capital has to be put up at all. For example, an entry of 9.00 for the conditional hedge strategy in year 15 means that in this year on average 9.00 percent of the sum of contributions over the first 15 years had to be provided as regulatory capital in those cases where capital had to be put up at all. Note that this number is not defined ('n.def.'), if the empirical probability of having to provide regulatory capital is equal to zero.

Source: Authors' computations.

higher wealth over the whole investment period and the average conditional regulatory capital is also lower. So if one were to compare the different products on the basis of these two measures only, the static strategy would be dominated. Note, however, that the probability of a capital charge is lower for the static strategy.

The analyses thus far focus on the statistical output, but it is also important to assess the administrative costs generated by each plan. Cost will not be major for the strategy products such as the pure bond, the pure stock plans, the static, and the life cycle strategies. However, for the conditional hedge, the need to shift incoming distributions across asset classes depending on how much wealth has been accumulated in the plan, might imply considerable administrative effort. It is therefore of interest to examine the relative frequency of shifts from one asset class to the other, when a conditional hedge strategy is run. Here again, time is an important factor, since for the 15-year plan the mutual fund company must change the asset class in 98 percent of the paths generated by the simulation, whereas this need arises in only 26 percent of the cases for the longer horizon. In any case, costs must be taken into account when strategies are compared with respect to their practical application.

In summary, it is not possible to identify the overall dominating investment product or strategy. With a few exceptions, higher potential in terms of average wealth usually comes at the cost of higher regulatory capital. It is important in this context to look at the average amount of regulatory capital conditional on the event that capital actually has to be put aside. Here it becomes obvious that strategies with a fixed stock investment can produce significant risks. This risk is mitigated when the conditional hedge strategy is employed. Nevertheless, additional administrative cost must be considered.

Conclusions

Due to the severe financing problems of standard pay-as-you-go pension systems in many countries, alternative vehicles for retirement financing have to be developed. In Germany, such a new system was installed when the German Retirement Saving Act was passed by the legislative body. The government offers significant tax relief for investment products meeting certain requirements, the most important of these being a guarantee promising that the cash value of the IPA at the end of the accumulation period will be at least as high as the nominal sum of the contributions. To lend sufficient credibility to the payment promises made by institutions providing investment products for these savings plans, the regulatory authorities in Germany have imposed a capital charge in case the value of the savings plan falls below a certain critical level.

At first sight, it seems that in order to implement such a principal guarantee, complicated and expensive financial products like derivatives are needed. However, as we have shown, there are other ways of achieving a sometimes practically risk-free position without using options or similar instruments. We analyze in detail various strategies aimed at combining the potentially return-increasing properties of equity investment with the risk-reducing characteristics of bond investments. These strategies offer a real-world application of the tools and methods of capital market theory. Of course, the trade-off between return and risk is always at the core of the analysis. Yet in the context of this chapter it is important to recognize that variance is not the most important measure of risk. As opposed to a more traditional approach we consider shortfall and the need of regulatory capital as the two most important types of risk.

The strategies analyzed here range from simple pure bond or equity investments, to mixed equity-bond funds and products offering a change in portfolio composition at pre-defined points in time, to highly sophisticated products with conditionally changing investment styles. One of the key results of our study is that these dynamic strategies, switching from stocks into bonds whenever the value of the savings plan falls below some critical solvency ratio set by regulatory authorities, perform rather well in terms of expected total returns for long investment horizons. They come close to pure stock investments with respect to the average value they generate for the investor. However, it is also very important for the financial institution to keep an eye on the expected amount of regulatory capital required by a certain investment strategy. Due to the conditional change in allocation when the critical regulatory value is reached, the expected capital charge is significantly smaller than in the case of a pure equity investment.

Besides the basic type of strategy, the length of the investment horizon is an important factor for the risks and rewards of alternative strategies. In general, the longer the maturity of the plan, the lower the expected capital charge, since the critical level set by the authorities in Germany contains a discount factor, the higher the expected total return. Nevertheless, it is important to consider other risk variables as well in this. We are far from claiming that one of the strategies discussed here should be seen as uniformly superior to any other. Rather we seek to point out the benefits and risks offered by the different types of products, to provide a basis for a thorough discussion of the issues involved in product design and regulation.

Appendix

Derivation of the Solvency Formula

Consider an investment plan where payments into an IPA are made at equally spaced points in time $t = 0, 1, \ldots, T$ (e.g. months). Let P_t denote the sum of payments up to time t, T the planned terminal date of the plan (equal to the beginning of the payout phase), and $q(r_{f,t}, T - t) = (1 + r_{f,t})^{t-T}$ the discount factor with risk-free rate $r_{f,t}$ and remaining time to maturity $T - t$. Without loss of generality we assume that the investor holds exactly one share of the fund at time t. We are interested in the solvency ratio V_t/P_t at time t, which makes sure that the uncertain market value of the shares V_{t+1} at time $t + 1$ is less than the sum of payments P_t into the plan discounted up to time T, that is, less than $P_t \cdot q(r_{f,t}, T - t - 1)$, with a probability of at most ε.

To be able to quantify this shortfall risk, we have to specify a model for the random evolution of the value of the investment shares. Here we make the standard assumption that the dynamics of this value can be described by a geometric Brownian motion. This implies that the relative change in value (i.e. the log-return) $\ln(V_{t+1}) - \ln(V_t)$ is normally distributed with mean μ und variance σ^2. Formally we obtain the desired solvency ratio as the solution of the following inequality:

$$\begin{aligned}\text{Prob}[V_{t+1} &< P_t \cdot q(r_{f,t}, T - t - 1)]\\ &= \text{Prob}[\ln(V_{t+1}) < \ln(P_t \cdot q(r_{f,t}, T - t - 1))] \leq \varepsilon \qquad (9.\text{A1})\end{aligned}$$

Using the above distributional assumption inequality (9.A1) is equivalent to

$$\ln(V_t) + \mu \geq \ln(P_t) + \ln[q(r_{f,t}, T - t - 1)] + \mathrm{N}_{1-\varepsilon} \cdot \sigma, \qquad (9.A2)$$

where $\mathrm{N}_{1-\varepsilon}$ is the $(1 - \varepsilon)$-quantile of the cumulative standard normal distribution. Under the additional (conservative) assumption[26] that the one-period expected return is equal to zero (i.e $\mu = 0$) inequality (9.A2) can be written as

$$V_t / \exp[\mathrm{N}_{1-\varepsilon} \cdot \sigma] \geq P_t \cdot q(r_{f,t}, T - t - 1). \qquad (9.A3)$$

Setting $\mathrm{N}_{1-\varepsilon} = 2.33$, which implies a tolerated shortfall probability of not more than 1 percent, this represents the equation (9.5) for the solvency ratio presented in the main text.

Notes

[1] This Act is also known as "Riester Reform." Walter Riester was the German Labor Minister responsible for the reform of the pension system in the year 2001. More formally, the reform as a whole alters several existing laws including (among others) the social security law, the income tax law, the occupational pensions law, the social welfare law, the civil law, the law governing investment management companies, and the law governing insurance companies.

[2] Similar to that, the maximum pension for civil servants is being reduced from 75% to 71.75% of the last salary.

[3] In addition, the government also promotes the "second pillar" occupational pension system, for example, by establishing a new funding vehicle called "Pensionsfonds."

[4] An exemption is, that a part of the pension plan (min €10,000 and max. €50,000) can be withdrawn during the accumulation phase to finance own house. This amount must be paid back (at a zero interest rate) into the IPA before the beginning of the distribution phase.

[5] In the case of a life annuity the provider must promise lifelong constant or increasing (monthly) payments to the annuitant. In the case of a capital withdrawal plan (typically offered by mutual fund and/or bank providers) at least 60% of the accumulated assets (but not less than the contributions paid into the IPA) must be used for constant or rising periodic payments. At latest at the age of 85 the balance must revert into a life annuity, whereas the benefits cannot be less than the last payment received before that age. In addition, not more than 40% of the accumulated assets can be used for a withdrawal plan with variable pension payments (reflecting the return of a specific asset portfolio).

[6] Especially for traditional life insurance policies, it is conventional (until now) that distribution costs are charged as front end loads on the first premiums (via the so-called zillmer-adjustment) resulting in no or low early cash values for the policyholder.

[7] An exemption are financial derivatives (e.g. option, futures, swaps), which can be used within an IPA for hedging purposes only.

[8] Not more than 15% of total contributions can be deducted from the principal guarantee level, if the IPA include insurance coverage against disability. In the case

of a switch to a new provider during the accumulation phase, the policyholder gets from the new provider a guarantee on the policy's cash value at the time of transfer plus new premiums.

[9] See also Lachance and Mitchell (Chapter 8, this volume).

[10] For surveys cf. Albrecht, Maurer, and Ruckpaul (2001) and Kritzman and Rich (1998).

[11] Cf. Bodie (2001) and Bodie (2002) for a critique of these simple arguments.

[12] The concept of shortfall risk was introduced in finance by Roy (1952) and Kataoka (1963), expanded and theoretically justified by Bawa (1975), and Fishburn (1977, 1982, 1984). It is widely applied to investment asset allocation by Leibowitz, Bader, and Kogelman (1996) and used by Albrecht, Maurer, and Ruckpaul (2001), Asness (1996), Butler and Domian (1991), Leibowitz and Krasker (1988) and Zimmermann (1991) to judge the long term risk of stocks and bonds.

[13] The MEL is closely connected with the tail conditional expectation, which is given by TCE $= E(R \mid R < z) = z -$ MEL. The TCE has some favourable features, for example, it is (in contrast to the shortfall probability) a coherent risk measure with respect to the axioms developed by Artzner et al. (1999). In addition the MEL is a suitable version of the mean excess—respectively mean excess loss-function $E(X - z \mid X > z)$ considered in extreme value theory. For extreme-value methods in financial risk management cf. Borkovic and Klüppelberg (2000) and Embrechts, Resnick, and Samorodnitsky (1999). Very early, Gürtler (1929) introduced the MEL as "Mathematisches Risiko" to evaluate the underwriting risk of insurance companies.

[14] The Black and Scholes formula follows directly only for a single lump sum pension payment and not for a series of contributions; see also Lachance and Mitchell (Chapter 8, this volume).

[15] As shown by Albrecht, Maurer, and Ruckpaul (2001) the risk measures can be derived analytically in the case of a lump-sum investment.

[16] Feldstein, Ranguelova, and Samwick (2001: 60) use a similar procedure to account for potential administration costs.

[17] The large number of simulation paths is necessary to receive a precise picture of the worst case risk measure MEL, especially when the shortfall probability is low.

[18] Despite the fact that the expected return is the most common measure of the "reward," "return," or "value" of financial investments it is—especially in a downside risk context—possible to measure the upside potential more directly, c.f. Holthausen (1981) or Albrecht, Maurer, and Möller (1999).

[19] According to German Investment Company Law (KAGG), the minimum equity capital for investment fund management companies (i.e. the provider of the pension products) is €2.5 millions.

[20] Since May of 2002 the BAKred is a Department of the new German Federal Financial Supervisory Agency.

[21] In addition to the solvency equity capital, investment management companies must build supplementary reserves if the difference between the present value of the contributions and the risk adjusted cash value of the policy exceeds 8% of the total contributions.

[22] The formula is explained in more detail in the Appendix.

[23] See also Lachance and Mitchell (Chapter 8, this volume).

[24] AS-Funds (Altersvorsorge-Sondervermögen) are special mutual fund products regulated in the Investment Management Company Act, which the German

government introduced in 1998 for retirement saving. In contrast to usual balanced funds, AS-Funds can invest into real estate, require a saving plan of at least 18 years, and are subject to some quantitative investment restrictions. For more details see Laux and Siebel (1999).

[25] C.f. BAKred (2001).

[26] This assumption is indeed conservative, since it increases the shortfall probability compared to the common case $\mu > 0$. Furthermore it is no longer necessary to estimate expected returns (e.g. from historical time series), which are subject to much larger estimation risks than volatilities. See, for example, Merton (1980).

References

Albrecht, Peter, Raimond Maurer, and Matthias Möller. 1999. "Shortfall-Risiko/Excess-Chance-Entscheidungs-Kalküle: Grundlagen und Beziehungen zum Bernoulli-Prinzip." *Zeitschrift für Wirtschafts- und Sozialwissenschaften* 118: 249–274.

——— and Ulla Ruckpaul. 2001. "The Shortfall-Risk of Stocks in the Long Run." *Journal of Financial Market and Portfolio Management* 4: 427–439.

Ammann, Manuel and Heinz Zimmermann. 2000. "Evaluating the Long-Term Risk of Equity Investments in a Portfolio Insurance Framework." *Geneva Papers on Risk and Insurance* 25: 424–438.

Artzner, Philippe, Fredy Delbaen, Jean-Mar Eber, and David Heath. 1999. "Coherent Measures of Risk." *Mathematical Finance* 9: 203–38.

Asness, Clifford S. 1996. "Why Not 100% Equities?" *Journal of Portfolio Management*, Winter: 29–34.

Bachellier, Louis. 1900. "Théorie de la Spéculation", *Annales de l'Ecole Normale Superieure*, Paris: Ganthier–Villars.

Bawa, Vijay S. 1975. "Safety First, Stochastic Dominance and Optimal Portfolio Choice." *Journal of Financial and Quantitative Analysis* 13: 255–271.

Benartzi, Shlomo and Richard H. Thaler. 1999. "Risk Aversion or Myopia? Choices in Repeated Gambles and Retirement Investment." *Management Science* 45: 364–381.

Bernstein, Peter L. 1996. "Are Stocks the Best Place to be in the Long Run? A Contrary Opinion." *Journal of Investing* 5: 9–12.

Bodie, Zvi. 1975. "Common Stocks as a Hedge Against Inflation." *Journal of Finance* 31: 459–470.

— 1995. "On the Risks of Stocks in the Long Run." *Financial Analysts' Journal*, May–June 18–22.

— 2001. "Financial Engineering and Social Security Reform." In *Risk Aspect of Investment-Based Social Security Reform*, eds. J. M. Campbell and M. Feldstein. National Bureau of Economic Research Conference Report, pp. 291–320.

— 2002. "Time Horizon Does Not Reduce Risk." *Financial Times*, January, 26.

Bundesaufsichtsamt für das Kreditwesen, BAKred. 2001. "Rundschreiben 12/2001 zur Bankaufsichtsrechtlichen Berücksichtigung der Leistungszusage nach §1 Abs. 1 Satz 1 Nr. 3 des Gesetzes über die Zertifizierung von Altersvorsorgeverträgen."

Cox, John C., Jonathan E. Ingersoll, Jr, and Stephen A. Ross. 1985. "A Theory of the Term Structure of Interest Rates." *Econometrica* 53(March): 385–407.

Embrechts, Paul, Claudia Klüppelberg, and Thomas Mikosch. 1997. "Modelling Extremal Events." Berlin: Springer.

—— Sidney Resnick, and Gennandy Samorodnitsky. 1999. "Extreme Value Theory as a Risk Management Tool." *North American Actuarial Journal* 3: 30–41.

Fishburn, Peter C. 1977. "Mean Risk Analysis Associated with Below Target Return." *American Economic Review* 67: 116–126.

—— 1982. "Foundations of Risk Measurement. II. Effects of Gains on Risk." *Journal of Mathematical Psychology* 25: 226–242.

—— 1984. "Foundations of Risk Measurement. I. Risk as Probable Loss." *Management Science* 30: 396–406.

Gürtler, Max. 1929. "Das Risiko des Zufalls im Versicherungsbetrieb." *Zeitschrift für die gesamte Versicherungswissenschaft* 29: 209–236; 292–326.

Holthausen, Duncan H. 1981. "A Risk-Return Model with Risk and Return Measured as Deviations from a Target Return." *American Economic Review* 71: 182–188.

Kritzman, Mark. 1994. "What Practitioners Need to Know About Time Diversification." *Financial Analysts' Journal*, January–February: 14–18.

—— and Don Rich. 1998. "Beware of Dogma: The Truth About Time Diversification." *Journal of Portfolio Management*, Summer: 66–77.

Laughhunn, Dan J., John W. Payne, and Roy Crum. 1980. "Managerial Risk Preferences for Below-Target-Returns." *Management Science* 26: 1238–1249.

Laux, Manfred and Rudolf Siebel. 1999. "The AS-Fund: A Modern Pension Fund for Everyone." Working Paper. Frankfurt/M.

Leibowitz, Martin L. and William S. Krasker. 1988. "The Persistence of Risk: Stocks Versus Bonds Over the Long Term." *Financial Analysts' Journal*, November–December: 40–47.

—— Stanley Kogelman, and Lawrence N. Bader. 1996. "Asset Allocation under Shortfall Constraint." *Journal of Portfolio Management*, Winter: 18–23.

Levy, Haim and Allan Cohen. 1998. "On the Risk of Stocks in the Long Run: Revisited." *Journal of Portfolio Management*, Spring: 60–69.

Libby, Robert and Peter C. Fishburn. 1977. "Behavioral Models of Risk Taking in Business Decisions: A Survey and Evaluation." *Journal of Accounting Research* 15: 272–292.

Merton, Robert. 1980. "On Estimating the Expected Return on the Market." *Journal of Financial Economics* 8: 323–361.

Navon, Jacob. 1998. "A Bond Manager's Apology." *Journal of Portfolio Management*, Winter: 65–69.

Roy, Andrew. 1952. "Safety First and the Holding of Risky Assets." *Econometrica* 20: 431–449.

Samuelson, Paul A. 1963. "Risk and Uncertainty: A Fallacy of Large Numbers." *Scientia*, April–May 1–6; reprinted in: Collected Scientific Papers of P. A. Samuelson, Vol. 1, Chapter 17, Cambridge, MA: MIT Press, pp. 153–158.

Siegel, Jeremy. 1998. *Stocks for the Long Run*, 2nd edn. Irwin, Burr Ridge, II.

Thaler, Richard H. and Peter J. Williamson. 1994. "College and University Endowment Funds: Why Not 100% Equities?" *Journal of Portfolio Management*, Fall: 27–38.

Wirch, Julia L. 1999. "Raising Value-at-Risk." *North American Actuarial Journal* 3: 106–115.

Zimmermann, Heinz. 1991. "Zeithorizont, Risiko und Performance: Eine Übersicht." *Finanzmarkt und Portfolio Management* 5: 164–181.

Chapter 10

Hedging Segregated Fund Guarantees

Peter A. Forsyth, Kenneth R. Vetzal, and Heath A. Windcliff

Segregated funds have become a very popular investment instrument for self-directed pension plans in Canada. Essentially, these are mutual funds that have been augmented with additional insurance features that provide a guarantee on the initial principal invested after a specified time horizon. These investment products offer investors the upside potential of the equity market, while providing a protective floor should the market fall and have been particularly attractive to risk averse investors nearing retirement. The purpose of this chapter is to develop quantitative tools so that institutions can make informed decisions about the risks associated with offering guarantees on mutual funds, and their ability to mitigate this risk through hedging strategies.

Segregated funds are similar in many respects to variable annuities in the United States. However, segregated funds often have complex embedded optionality. For instance, many contracts provide a "reset provision" that allows investors to increase their guarantee level as the value of the underlying mutual fund goes up. From the viewpoint of the investor, the motivation for the reset feature is easy to see. For example, if the investor starts with an initial investment of $10,000 and the market value of his mutual fund portfolio subsequently increases to $16,000, then the guarantee of recovering his initial principal is unlikely to seem very valuable. This is because, on paper, the investment is worth much more than the guarantee level. If the guarantee contract offers a reset provision, the investor can lock in a new guarantee set at the existing market value of the account. Typically, the maturity of the new guarantee is 10 years from the date at which the guarantee level was set. These contracts also offer features such as mortality benefits, where the guarantee is paid off immediately upon the death of the investor. Research has indicated that these guarantees can be very valuable (Windcliff et al., 2002). As a result, the payment for the guarantee is usually amortized over the life of the contract. This introduces additional complexity due to the

This work was supported by the Natural Sciences and Engineering Research Council of Canada, the Social Sciences and Humanities Research Council of Canada, and RBC Financial Group. Opinions remain those of the authors.

fact that investors can lapse, and avoid paying any remaining fees, if they deem that the guarantee is not very valuable.

The rationale for financial services firms offering these products is somewhat more subtle. To illustrate, we reconsider our example of an investor who started with an initial investment of $10,000, which has grown to $16,000. If the guarantee does not offer a reset provision, the investor may be better off lapsing out of the guarantee contract in order to avoid paying the remaining proportional fees. Thus, the reset provision can help retain customers. The back end fees used to penalize investors for lapsing often only apply during the first few years of the contract. In fact, in the absence of back end fees, the investor can synthetically create reset opportunities by lapsing and immediately re-entering a new guarantee contract, effectively resetting the guarantee level to the current market value of the account.

In Canada, the Office of the Superintendent of Financial Institutions (OSFI) has recently imposed stricter new regulations for these contracts, requiring that insurers set aside a substantial amount of capital to back the guarantees. These capital requirements may be reduced if appropriate hedging strategies have been put in place. This chapter describes hedging strategies that would allow underwriting companies to reduce their risk exposure to these contracts, techniques that incorporate the strengths of both actuarial and financial approaches. We investigate the performance of these types of hedging strategies using stochastic simulation. We also study their impact on the capital requirements used to back these guarantees.

A contract with a maturity guarantee attached to it can be thought of as an investment in the underlying asset combined with a put option, which may have very complex features such as mortality benefits or reset provisions. Hedging strategies that reduce downside risk for put options typically involve short positions in the underlying asset. Since the underlying mutual fund can be under the management of the insurer providing the guarantee, it may not be possible for the underwriting company to take short positions in the underlying mutual fund. One alternative is to hedge using other actively traded securities, such as index participation units, stock index options, or stock index futures contracts, whose behavior is close to that of the underlying mutual fund. This can create basis risk, due to the mismatch between the hedging instrument and the underlying mutual fund. If hedging is performed using short-term derivative contracts such as futures or index options, there will be further risk when the hedging positions are periodically rolled over. Using stochastic simulation we can quantify the risk associated with selling these contracts in a more realistic setting which includes non-optimal investor behavior and basis risk.

We emphasize that the decision of whether or not to hedge these contracts in many situations is a risk-management issue. In some cases, hedging may be necessary to reduce the capital requirements due to regulations. The hedging strategies described here are capable of reducing the downside risk associated with writing such contracts, though they come at an expense, as the expected profit of the hedged position is lower than the expected profit of the unhedged position.

Description of the Segregated Fund Contract

The term "segregated fund" often refers to a mutual fund combined with a long-term maturity guarantee (typically 10 years) with additional complex features. One popular provision included with many of these contracts is a reset feature. When investors reset, they exchange an existing guarantee for a new 10-year maturity guarantee, set at the current value of the mutual fund. Hence, the reset feature allows them to lock in market gains as the value of the underlying mutual fund increases. The contracts offered in Canada typically allow investors to reset the guarantee level up to a maximum of two or four times per calendar year. This introduces an optimization component to these contracts, where investors must decide when they should reset and lock in at the higher guarantee level.

In addition to the reset option, many other exotic features may be included in segregated fund guarantees. For example, many segregated funds include a death benefit, so that the guarantee is paid out immediately if the investor dies before the maturity date of the guarantee. As the investor ages, these mortality benefits may become more valuable, so resets are often disallowed after the investor's 70th birthday. More complex variations of the reset feature can also be introduced, as the investor becomes older. For example, after the investor's 70th birthday, the guarantee level upon reset may be some fraction of the value of the underlying mutual fund at the time of the reset.

In practice, the investor is not charged an initial fee for the segregated fund guarantee. Instead the investor pays a higher management expense ratio (MER) over the life of the contract to cover the cost of providing the guarantee. The total MER can be considered to be the sum of a proportional fee, r_m, allocated to the management of the underlying mutual fund, together with a proportional fee, r_e, allocated to finance the guarantee portion of these contracts.

It may be optimal for an investor to lapse and avoid paying the higher MER, if the guarantee is unlikely to be in-the-money at maturity. For these and other reasons, such as a need for liquid assets, investors may sometimes withdraw their investment from the segregated fund contract. The reset feature described above will help to reduce the amount of investor lapsing, since the guarantee can be reset to a new at-the-money guarantee. Further, a proportional deferred sales charge (DSC) is often applied if the investor withdraws his/her investment during the first several years. Communications with vendors of these contracts suggest that this fee is paid to the underlying mutual fund, and in practice none of it is allocated to finance the guarantee portion of the contract. It should be reiterated that investor lapsing is not always beneficial to the insurance company writing the guarantee portion of these contracts. Specifically, since the payment of the guarantee is deferred over the life of the contract, any hedging costs incurred by the insurer may not be recovered if the investor lapses prematurely.

The numerical experiments presented in this chapter are based on two contracts depicted in Table 10-1. The first contract is a simple 10-year maturity guarantee with no reset provisions, while the second contract incorporates a reset feature. These contracts were chosen to be representative of current guarantees offered on mutual funds, and to illustrate the effect of attaching reset provisions to these guarantees. Both contracts provide mortality benefits, so that the guarantee is paid out immediately upon the death of the investor. No initial fee is charged to enter into these contracts; the investor pays for these guarantees by the increased MER as described in Table 10-1, with the sliding scale DSC to mitigate investor lapsing. Table 10-1 also describes the key market parameters used in the simulations, such as the assumed risk-free interest rate and volatility of the underlying mutual fund.

Due to the complexity of these contracts, it is difficult to draw general conclusions from individual numerical experiments. The numerical results in this chapter are therefore intended to illustrate the behavior of a realistic contract.[1]

The Distribution of Returns for Unhedged Positions

To quantify the risk involved with writing segregated fund guarantees described above, we can investigate the distribution of returns for an unhedged position. At this point, we do not assume optimal investor behavior, but instead we presume that investors use heuristic rules for the reset feature and optimal lapsing. We will find that there can be a substantial amount of downside risk to the insurer when writing segregated fund guarantees with a reset provision, even when investors act nonoptimally.

Let S represent the value of the underlying mutual fund and let K be the current guarantee level. In this section we will use two rules for applying the reset feature and lapsing:

- *Heuristic reset rule*: Investors will reset the guarantee level if there are reset opportunities remaining and $S > 1.15K$; that is, if the value of the underlying mutual fund has risen so that the current guarantee level is 15 percent out-of-the-money.
- *Heuristic lapsing rule*: Investors will lapse out of the contract at time t^*, and thereby avoid paying the remaining proportional fees, if there are no reset opportunities available at time t^* and $S > 1.4K$; that is, if the

TABLE 10-1 Specification of the Guarantee Contracts and Market Information Used in the Numerical Experiments Provided in this Chapter

Feature	*Description*
Investor profile	50 year old Canadian female (from www.soa.org)
Deterministic lapse rate	5% per annum
Optimal Lapsing	Investors will lapse out of the contract if the value of the guarantee becomes less than the value of the remaining fees that will be deducted to maintain the guarantee
Initial investment	\$100
Maturity term	10 years, with a maximum expiry on the investor's 80th birthday
Resets	Contract 1: No resets Contract 2: Two resets per year permitted until the investor's 70th birthday. Upon reset, the guarantee level is set to the value of the underlying mutual fund and the maturity is extended by 10 years from the reset date
Mortality benefits	Guarantee is paid out immediately upon the death of the investor
MER	For both contracts, a proportional fee of $r_m = 1\%$ is allocated to the manager of the underlying mutual fund. In addition, to finance the guarantee portion of these contracts, additional fees are deducted at the following rates Contract 1: (no resets) $r_e = 50$ bp is allocated to finance the guarantee for a total MER of 1.5% Contract 2: (two resets p.a.) $r_e = 90$ bp is allocated to finance the guarantee for a total MER of 1.9%
DSC	A deferred sales charge is levied upon early redemption using a sliding scale from 5% in the first year to 0% after 5 years. This fee is paid to the management of the underlying mutual fund and none of it is allocated to the guarantee portion of the contract
Volatility	$\sigma = 17.5\%$
Risk-free interest rate	$r = 6\%$
Drift rate (before fees)	$\mu = 10\%$

Source: Authors' computations.

value of the underlying mutual fund has risen so that the guarantee level is 40 percent out-of-the-money.

Investigation of the optimal reset region shows that resetting the guarantee when the underlying asset has risen by 15 percent can be a reasonable approximation to the optimal exercise boundary during the first few years of the contract, or during the first few years after a reset has taken place (Windcliff et al., 2002). In fact, this heuristic rule has been adopted by a Canadian Institute of Actuaries task force on segregated funds (CIA, 2000) for its assessment of risk management strategies. If investors do not have the ability to reset, they may be better off lapsing out of the contract to avoid paying the proportional fees, since the guarantee is unlikely to be in-the-money at maturity. In fact, even if reset features are not explicitly offered, investors can synthetically create them by lapsing and re-entering the contract, thereby obtaining a new at-the-money guarantee (Windcliff, Forsyth, and Vetzal 2001).

In the Monte Carlo simulations provided below, it is assumed that the investor makes decisions regarding the reset feature and optimal lapsing 100 times per year, or approximately twice per week.[2] To quantify the risk associated with writing an unhedged segregated fund guarantee, we consider the 95 percent conditional tail expectation (CTE) and the annualized rate of return on an initial capital requirement. The 95 percent CTE is the expected value of the outcomes that lie in the worst case 5-percent tail. In other words, the 95 percent CTE is the mean value of the worst case outcomes that are ignored by a 95 percent value at risk (VaR) measurement. In comparison with VaR measures, the CTE is much more conservative when setting aside capital for contracts such as segregated fund guarantees, which exhibit a long tail of values that occur with relatively low probability.

Recent regulatory changes from the Canadian regulatory agency OSFI have introduced stricter capital requirements for companies offering these contracts to ensure that sufficient resources are available to back these guarantees. Specifically, if no hedging strategy is put in place, OSFI requires that the insurer set aside the 95 percent CTE in liquid, risk-free instruments. If the insurer implements a hedging strategy, the OSFI capital requirement can be reduced by up to a maximum of 50 percent of the reduction in the 95 percent CTE indicated by the proposed hedging strategy. The capital must be invested in safe, liquid instruments; here we will assume that the capital investment grows at the risk-free rate. It should be pointed out that, for these numerical experiments, we have chosen the proportional fee r_e so that the cost of hedging, net of future incoming fees for these contracts, is initially zero; in other words, the reserve amount is zero. As a result the total balance sheet requirement and capital requirements are identical.

We estimate the required capital by generating simulations of the mutual fund path, thereby generating a profit and loss (P&L) distribution for the writer of the guarantee as shown in Figure 10-1(a). The P&L for a particular stock price path generated during a simulation is given by:

$$\text{P\&L} = (\text{hedge value} - \text{payoff value})\big|_{t^*} \times e^{-\bar{r}t^*},$$

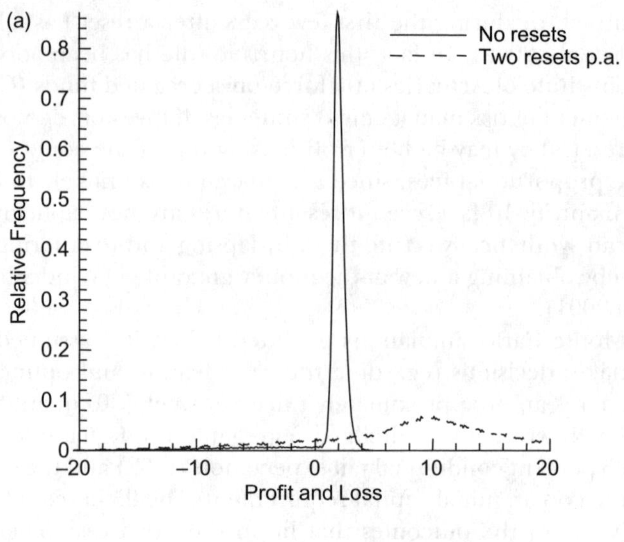

Figure 10-1. (a) The profit and loss distribution for unhedged segregated fund guarantees that offer no resets and two resets per annum.
Note: We assume that investors utilize the heuristic rules described in the accompanying text to determine their use of the reset feature and anti-selective lapsing.
(b) The return on investment for a 95% CTE capital requirement for unhedged segregated fund guarantees which offer no resets and two resets per annum. (*Source*: Authors' computations.)
Note: Model assumes that investors utilize the heuristic rules described in the accompanying text to determine their use of the reset feature and anti-selective lapsing.

where $\bar{r}$ is the discounting rate used and t^* is the time that the contract is terminated. In this formula, "hedge value" refers to the value of the hedging portfolio at the time the contract is terminated, and "payoff value" refers to the contractual payment made to the investor at the contract termination. If we use the risk-free rate as the discounting rate, $\bar{r} = r$, then the P&L distribution can be used to estimate the 95 percent CTE. This is the amount that must be set aside in risk-free instruments so that the insurer has sufficient resources to back up the guarantee in the average of the worst-case situations.

Table 10-2 gives statistics for the P&L distributions. It is difficult to draw useful comparisons between these P&L distributions since there are many risk/reward tradeoffs to consider and the duration of the contract is uncertain due to investor lapsing, mortality, and the investor's use of the reset feature. However, one common observation is that the capital requirement, given by the 95 percent CTE, is quite large for any of these contracts. This is the case for both contracts that offer reset provisions, and to a somewhat lesser extent, contracts that offer no resets. We also see that the capital requirement is not substantially reduced by assuming that investors act non-optimally when they make decisions regarding lapsing and when to reset the guarantee level.

We use the distribution of the annualized return on the capital set aside for these guarantees as a measure of the profitability of offering these products. The outlay of capital to satisfy the OSFI requirements can be thought of as introducing an associated cost with selling these guarantees, and we are

TABLE 10-2 Statistics for the Profit and Loss Distribution and the Return on Investment for a 95 percent CTE Capital Requirement for an Unhedged Segregated Fund Guarantee

Investor	*Contract*	*Profit and Loss*		*Return on Initial Capital*		
		Mean ($)	*95% CTE ($)*	*Capital ($)*	*Mean ARC (%)*	r_{eff} *(%)*
Heuristic	No resets	1.89	8.65	8.65	13.1	9.6
	Two resets p.a.	8.66	13.46	13.46	21.2	8.5
Optimal	No resets	1.90	8.72	8.72	13.1	9.5
	Two resets p.a.	6.80	13.40	13.40	20.2	8.5

Note: The contract with no resets charges a proportional fee of $r_e = 50$ bp to finance the guarantee while the contract with two reset opportunities per annum charges a proportional fee of $r_e = 90$ bp. The heuristic rules used by investors to determine their use of the reset feature and anti-selective lapsing are described in the accompanying text.
Source: Authors' computations.

interested in studying the rate of return on this investment. We define the annualized return on capital (ARC) as:

$$\text{ARC} = \frac{1}{t^*}\left(\frac{(\text{capital value} + \text{hedge value} - \text{payoff value})\big|_{t^*}}{\text{initial capital}} - 1\right).$$

In this formula, "capital value" refers to the value at contract termination of an initial capital outlay of "initial capital" made by the provider of the guarantee. This capital was placed in a risk-free investment to back the guarantee. The quantities "hedge value" and "payoff value" are as described above. This can be regarded as the return on the initial capital per year for the writer of the guarantee.[3]

It should be noted that the ARC cannot be thought of as a compounded rate of return. We have chosen this specification of the return on the initial investment since the final value of our position at maturity can be negative, and cannot be quantified as a compounded rate of return on the (positive) initial investment. In order to facilitate comparisons with compounded rates of return we define an effective continuously compounded rate,

$$r_{\text{eff}} = \frac{1}{t^*} \times \ln(1 + \text{ARC} \times t^*),$$

where t^* is the average duration of the contract during the simulation and we use the mean ARC in this calculation. This definition of the effective rate r_{eff} incorporates the fact that upon selling these contracts, the insurer is locked into this position for a duration of time, which depends upon the investor's actions. We find that t^* is approximately 6.3 years for the contract with no resets and is approximately 21.2 years for the contract with two resets per year, when investors use heuristic rules described in this section to determine their use of the reset feature and anti-selective lapsing behavior. When the investors act optimally, the average duration of the contracts become 6.4 and 17.9 years, respectively.

The results in Table 10-2 indicate that when no hedging strategy is in place and investors act nonoptimally, the expected effective return on a 95 percent CTE capital requirement is approximately 9.6 percent for the guarantee that offers no resets, and is about 8.5 percent for the guarantee which offers two resets per annum. Many segregated funds are currently offered with substantially lower proportional fees. Of course, with a lower proportional fee charged to cover the cost of providing the guarantee, the return on capital will be reduced. Note that in Table 10-2, when no hedging strategy is implemented, investor nonoptimality does not significantly increase the rate of return on the insurer's initial capital investment. Below we show that when a dynamic hedging strategy is in place, investor nonoptimality can result in a significant increase in the effective rate of return on capital.

Although the expected return indicates that writing these contracts and leaving them unhedged can be profitable, the capital requirement may be prohibitive. For the numerical examples provided in this chapter, 8.65 percent of the underlying mutual fund is required for the contract with no resets, and 13.46 percent of the underlying mutual fund value is required for the contract with two resets per annum. As mentioned above, the OSFI capital requirements for these products can be reduced if appropriate hedging strategies have been put in place. Furthermore, in Figure 10-1 (b) we see that there is a substantial amount of variability in the ARC, particularly for the contract that offers two resets per annum, with many outcomes generating losses. Next we investigate the statistical performance of various hedging strategies for segregated fund guarantees.

Hedging Risk Exposure for Segregated Fund Guarantees

The hedging strategies we investigate incorporate the strengths of both actuarial and modern financial theory approaches. An insurer offering a segregated fund guarantee is exposed to several sources of risk. For example, due to the mortality benefits offered by many of these contracts, the value of the contract will depend upon the demographic profile of the investor who is purchasing the contract (e.g. female, aged 50 years, non-smoker). If a large number of these contracts have been sold to investors from a similar demographic profile, we can assume that mortality risk is diversifiable. We can consider hedging an aggregate contract from which a fraction of the investors die during each year at a rate specified by a standard mortality table.

Another source of uncertainty that may be considered to be diversifiable is deterministic investor lapsing. Here we may be able to treat the fraction of the investors that withdraw their accounts (for nonoptimal reasons) each year as a deterministic function.[4] The insurer is also exposed to risk due to the uncertain movements of the underlying mutual fund since the guarantee will only have positive value to the investor if the fund is below the guarantee level at maturity. It is well known that market risk exposure is not readily diversifiable. In this case, techniques from modern financial theory can be applied (Wilmott, 1998; Hull, 2000).

Let $V(S, K, U, T, t)$ be the value of the segregated fund guarantee, which depends upon the value of the underlying mutual fund S, the current guarantee level K, the number of reset opportunities used this year U, the current maturity date T, and time t. In this work we consider simple dynamic hedging strategies which create delta-neutral positions for the insurer over brief time intervals. To create a delta-neutral position, the insurer will purchase

$$\Delta = e^{(r_m+r_e)t} V_S$$

index participation units in order to make the value of the hedged portfolio immune to small changes in the value of the underlying mutual fund over short intervals of time. The exponential factor, which makes this appear different from the typical delta hedge ratio seen in introductory finance texts, is due to the proportional management fees, which are deducted from the underlying mutual fund, while it is assumed that no fees are paid on the index participation units.

If it is not optimal to utilize the reset feature or lapse, then the value V satisfies the partial differential equation:

$$V_t + (r - r_m - r_e)SV_S + \frac{1}{2}\sigma^2 S^2 V_{SS} - rV - R(t)r_e S + M(t)\max(K - S, 0) = 0,$$

where $R(t)$ denotes the number of investors remaining in the contract (who have not perished or lapsed) at time t and $M(t)$ is the mortality rate at time t. This equation is very similar to the classical Black–Scholes equation from option pricing theory, but it contains two additional terms. The final two terms of this equation represent the rate of incoming proportional fees collected from investors remaining in the contract at time t, and the rate of payments made to deceased investors at time t, respectively. Also, the drift coefficient (in front of the V_S term) is slightly different from that in the classical Black–Scholes model. This is because we have assumed that hedging is performed with a perfectly correlated asset that does not have management fees deducted. Recall that we are imagining hedging a guarantee on an index tracking mutual fund by trading index participation units. Below, we generalize these techniques to allow for hedging with an imperfectly correlated asset.

If we let $U_{\max}$ denote the maximum number of resets permitted per annum by the segregated fund contract, then if $U < U_{\max}$ there are reset opportunities remaining and the guarantee value must satisfy the constraint:

$$V(S, K, U, T, t) \geq V(S, S, U + 1, t + T_{\text{ext}}, t),$$

where T_{ext} is the amount that maturity is extended by upon resetting the guarantee level. Effectively, this models the fact that the investors can receive a new guarantee with guarantee level $K = S$ and maturity $T = t + T_{\text{ext}}$, and that one more reset opportunity has been used.

It will be optimal for investors to lapse if the value of the guarantee, net of the proportional fees required to maintain the contract, is more negative than any deferred sales charges that must be paid upon terminating the contract. As a result, the writer cannot allow the value of the hedging position to become negative in anticipation of future incoming fees. We can model optimal investor lapsing by imposing the additional constraint:

$$V(S, K, U, T, t) \geq 0.$$

Finally, at maturity, the value of the contract is:

$$V(S, K, U, T, T) = R(T)\max(K - S, 0),$$

which states that only investors remaining in the contract at maturity receive the final guarantee payoff.

Typically, the investor is not charged an initial premium or front end load to enter into these contracts. As a result, their fair value is determined by the expense ratio, r_e, that makes the value of the contract initially zero. The fair proportional fee rate for various contracts and various models for the underlying fund is described in Windcliff et al. (2002). Here, we assume that the expense ratios are fixed at the levels given in Table 10-1 and our focus is to investigate the ability to hedge the risk exposure due to price movements by the underlying security. Other sources of risk, such as interest rate risk and implied volatility risk, basis risk, liquidity risk, etc., will affect the value and hedging of these contracts. The new actuarial reserving guidelines and OSFI's new capital standards require insurers to explicitly provide for these risks if they intend to take credit for hedging strategies.[5]

Statistical Results for Dynamically Hedged Positions

An insurer may wish to implement a hedging strategy for several reasons. First, by implementing such a strategy, the downside risk associated with writing these contracts may be reduced. Second, if the insurer implements a hedging strategy, the OSFI capital requirement can be reduced by up to a maximum of 50 percent of the reduction in the 95 percent CTE indicated by the proposed strategy. For the numerical results provided in this chapter the required capital for a dynamically hedged position is given by:

$$\text{Required OSFI Capital} = \text{CTE}_{\text{hedge}} + \tfrac{1}{2}(\text{CTE}_{\text{no hedge}} - \text{CTE}_{\text{hedge}}),$$

where the conditional tail expectations are taken with a 95-percent confidence level. This current capital requirement policy is conservative and does not offer a full credit for insurers that dynamically hedge their positions. We will also study the effect of variations in this capital requirement policy that allow for a full reduction when hedging is implemented.

Table 10-3 provides numerical results from implementing a delta-neutral hedging strategy, which is re-balanced fifty times per year (i.e. approximately on a weekly basis). Comparing these results with those for unhedged positions contained in Table 10-2, we see that the 95 percent CTE is reduced dramatically due to the hedging strategy, resulting in much smaller capital requirements. Of course, this reduction in downside also comes with lower expected profits from the contract, but since less capital is required when a hedging strategy is implemented, the rate of return on the initial capital

TABLE 10-3 Statistics for the Profit and Loss Distribution and the Return on Investment for a Segregated Fund Guarantee that is Hedged 50 Times per Year

Investor	*Contract*	*Profit and Loss*		*Return on Initial Capital*		
		Mean ($)	*95% CTE ($)*	*Capital ($)*	*Mean ARC (%)*	r_{eff} *(%)*
Heuristic	No resets	0.42	1.02	4.83	9.8	7.6
				2.93	11.4	8.6
				1.02	19.3	12.6
	Two resets p.a.	1.30	0.46	6.96	15.7	6.9
				3.71	18.6	7.5
				0.46	62.1	12.5
Optimal	No resets	0.42	1.02	4.87	9.8	7.6
				2.95	11.5	8.6
				1.02	19.4	12.6
	Two resets p.a.	0.28	1.04	7.22	11.8	6.3
				4.13	12.4	6.5
				1.04	16.1	7.6

Note: The three capital amounts shown for each scenario represent a maximum 50% reduction, a 75% reduction and a 100% reduction from the unhedged 95% CTE. The contract with no resets charges a proportional fee of $r_e = 50$ bp to finance the guarantee while the contract with two reset opportunities per annum charges a proportional fee of $r_e = 90$ bp.

Source: Authors' computations.

outlay is only moderately affected. For the contract with no resets, the rate of return on the initial reserve is approximately 7.6 percent, whereas for the contract with two resets per annum the return is between 6.3 percent and 6.9 percent, depending upon the degree of optimality displayed by investors in their use of the reset feature.

It should be noted that when this dynamic hedging strategy is implemented, nonoptimal investor behavior could lead to additional profits by the insurer, which was not the case when no hedging strategy was implemented. This indicates that the insurer is not penalized for hedging the worst-case situation, which assumes that the investor acts optimally, and additional profits accrue as non-optimal decisions occur. Although it may be safe to assume that the majority of investors will act suboptimally, it would be dangerous to build this assumption into the long-term pricing and hedging of these products.

The effective rate of return on the initial capital outlay by the insurer is quite low due to the fact that the capital requirement is only reduced by a maximum of 50 percent of that indicated by the proposed hedging strategy. The guidance note issued by OSFI (2001) specifying this maximum capital offset due to hedging states that "as the industry and OSFI gain confidence in implementing such strategies, this limitation will be reviewed." In Table 10-3 we also provide numerical results in the cases when the capital requirement can be reduced by up to a maximum of 75 percent and 100 percent of the reduction in the 95 percent CTE indicated by the proposed hedging strategy. When it is profitable to offer these contracts, as in the case when investors act suboptimally, the return on capital can improve quite dramatically when the capital requirements are reduced. As a result, this modified policy may entice more institutions offering these products to implement strategies in order to receive the hedging credit. The risk in allowing for a full capital requirement reduction is that the hedging strategy may prove to be less effective than the model indicates. Below we study the impact of basis risk on the effectiveness of simple dynamic hedging strategies.[6]

Figure 10-2(a) assesses the relative strengths and weaknesses of the hedged position. This figure depicts the annualized return on capital for a standard OSFI capital requirement, which allows the initial capital outlay to be reduced by up to a maximum reduction of 50 percent as a result of the proposed hedging strategy. For the hedged position, the initial capital is \$7.22 per hundred dollars of underlying mutual fund, while for the unhedged position, the initial capital is \$13.40 per hundred dollars of underlying mutual fund. We see that for the hedged position the ARC is always positive (to the resolution of the figure). If the ARC is positive, this indicates that the payment made to the investor at the contract's maturity was fully covered by the hedging strategy and capital allocation. In other words, the provider was not required to infuse any additional capital to back the guarantee at the termination of the guarantee contract. On the other hand, the simulation of the unhedged position results in many outcomes where the ARC is negative. It should be noted that hedging, which reduces the downside risk associated with providing these guarantees, also reduces the upside potential. We see that the hedged position also has relatively fewer outcomes that generate large profits when compared with the simulations of the unhedged guarantee.

Figure 10-2(b) compares the effects of optimal and heuristic investor behavior for a hedged position. We see that the profit for the writer increases when the investor does not act optimally. Notice that non-optimal investor behavior introduces a positive skew in the distribution and the downside risk is not dramatically affected by the heuristic investor behavior.

Hedging with a Correlated Asset

Classical hedging strategies mitigate the insurer's downside risk by taking a short position in the underlying mutual fund. Since the underlying mutual

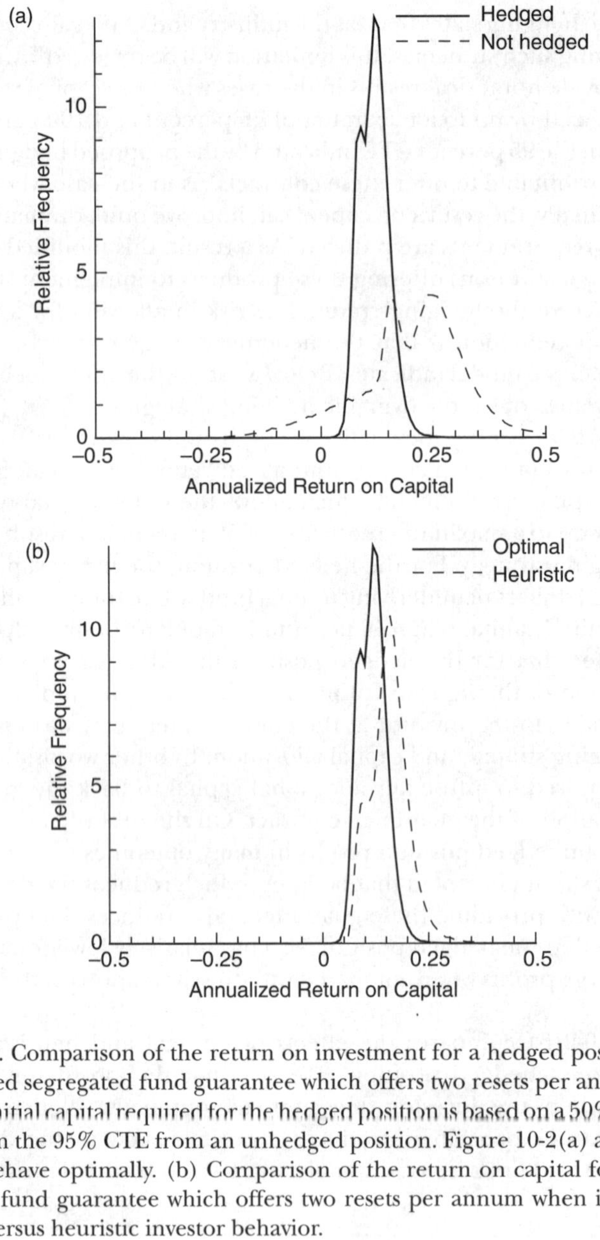

Figure 10-2. Comparison of the return on investment for a hedged position versus an unhedged segregated fund guarantee which offers two resets per annum.
Note: The initial capital required for the hedged position is based on a 50% maximum reduction in the 95% CTE from an unhedged position. Figure 10-2(a) assumes that investors behave optimally. (b) Comparison of the return on capital for a hedged segregated fund guarantee which offers two resets per annum when investors act optimally versus heuristic investor behavior.
Source: Authors' computations.

fund is often under the management of the insurer providing the guarantee, taking short positions directly in the underlying asset is not always possible. We have mentioned above that a guaranteed investment can be viewed as holding the underlying asset and having a put option on that asset. Alternatively, the insurer can back this contract by setting aside a bond with a face value equal to the guarantee level, and dynamically hedging a variation of a call option position. The advantages of this formulation are that the insurer can easily take long positions in the underlying mutual fund and downside risk has been completely hedged. On the other hand, now the insurer is exposed to a considerable amount of upside risk if the replication of the call option is not effective.

If the mutual fund is tracking an actively traded index, then one can use index participation units to accurately hedge risk exposure. The numerical results provided thus far in this chapter have assumed this. Yet, it is often the case that the mutual fund is not constructed to closely track an index, and hedging must be performed using a basket of securities that closely replicate the performance of the fund. In general, the price movements of this basket will not be perfectly correlated with the underlying fund. Another possible motivation for studying hedging with a partially correlated asset is illiquidity in the underlying asset (Sircar and Papanicolaou, 1998). In this situation, the positions taken by the hedging strategy can affect the price of the underlying asset. Sufficient illiquidity may make hedging with a correlated liquid asset the preferred choice. With the exception of a brief note on minimum variance cross hedging strategies (Seppi, 1999), very little research has apparently been done in the mathematical modeling of hedging strategies utilizing a partially correlated asset.[7]

In the Appendix, we extend the Black–Scholes framework to allow for the pricing and hedging of option contracts when it is not possible to establish a hedging strategy which trades directly in the underlying asset. The basic idea is that, given an asset that has price increments, which are correlated with the underlying (with correlation coefficient ρ), we determine a hedging strategy using this secondary asset. The position held in the secondary hedging asset is chosen to minimize the variance of the partially hedged position. The option pricing model in the Appendix includes, as special cases, the Black–Scholes model, as well as discounted cash flow valuation models which use the actual drift rate and a risk-adjusted discounting rate.

Numerical Experiments

Table 10-4 provides estimates for the risk-adjusted discounting rate r^* for these contracts. In this work, we cannot estimate r^* using market prices, since these exotic long-term options are not traded on exchanges. Instead, we estimate r^* by determining the discounting rate so that the present

TABLE 10-4 Risk Adjusted Discounting Rates, r^*, for the Segregated Fund Guarantees Studied in this Chapter

Contract	r_e	*Lapse penalty*	r^* (%)
No resets	50 bp	DSC	−14.5
		No DSC	0.0
Two resets per annum	90 bp	DSC	−7.8
		No DSC	−7.0

Note: The discounting rate, r^*, was obtained by determining the discounting rate that makes the present value of these contracts zero initially using the real world (P-measure) drift rate for the underlying mutual fund. The deferred sales charge (DSC) used to mitigate investor lapsing utilizes a sliding scale from 5% to 0% during the first 5 years of the contract.
Source: Authors' computations.

expected value of these contracts (using the real drift rate for the underlying security) is initially zero. In other words, we determine an upper bound on the discounting rate that the customer must implicitly be using to warrant entering into these contracts.

Since the drift rate of the underlying asset is greater than the risk-free rate, taking into account the fees required to maintain the guarantee, on average the holder of a long position in the guarantee will encounter a loss. The results shown in Table 10-4 are consistent with the findings in Coval and Shumway (2001) where, using market prices for exchange traded options, the authors find that put options have returns that are both statistically and economically negative. In our case, this refers to the rate of return on the proportional fees paid by the customer to maintain the segregated fund guarantee.

Again referring to Table 10-4, we see that the deferred sales charge has a dramatic impact on the expected rate of return for a contract with no reset features but has very little impact for the contract with two resets per annum. If there are no reset opportunities, the investor should optimally lapse out of the contract if the guarantee becomes out-of-the-money, thereby avoiding the remaining fees required to maintain the guarantee. On the other hand, if the contract offers the customer the ability to reset the guarantee level, then anti-selective lapsing does not play as large a role. This indicates that the reset feature may be an effective way for financial institutions to retain customers in these accounts in a rising market.

Table 10-5 provides results for a partially hedged position when ρ, the correlation between the underlying mutual fund and the hedging assets

TABLE 10-5 Performance of Hedging Strategies, which use Hedging Assets with Varying Levels of Correlation, ρ, with the Underlying Mutual Fund

Rehedge Frequency (p.a.)		*Profit and Loss*			*Return on Initial Capital*	
	ρ	*Mean ($)*	*95% CTE ($)*	*Capital ($)*	*Mean ARC (%)*	r_{eff} *(%)*
50	1.0	1.30	0.46	6.96	15.7	6.9
	0.9	2.86	9.27	11.37	15.6	6.9
	0.75	8.61	18.99	18.99	15.8	6.9
	0.0	8.66	13.46	13.46	21.2	8.5
50	0.9	2.86	9.27			
10	0.9	2.90	9.60			

Note: The guarantee offers two resets per annum and it is assumed that investors use the heuristic rules as described in the accompanying text for their use of the reset feature and anti-selective lapsing.
Source: Authors' computations.

varies between 0 and 1. When $\rho = 0$, the hedging asset and underlying asset are uncorrelated and we are unable to hedge using this asset. In this case, the outcome is identical to that of the unhedged position described in Table 10-2. When $\rho = 1$, the hedging asset and underlying asset are perfectly correlated and there is no basis risk. In this case, the results are identical to the hedged positions described in Table 10-3. When the assets are partially correlated the performance of the hedging strategy degrades rapidly. When $\rho = 0.9$, the 95 percent CTE when hedging with the partially correlated asset is $9.27 compared with $13.46 for the unhedged position. Consequently, the reduction in the required capital may not be sufficient to warrant attempting to hedge these contracts when basis risk is present. In fact, the 95 percent CTE is even worse when $\rho = 0.75$, increasing from $13.46 for the unhedged position to $18.99 for the position which hedges using the imperfectly correlated asset. This indicates that when hedging with a partially correlated asset, the correlation must be very high. Otherwise, the hedging strategy may, in fact, increase the risk associated with providing these contracts.

The re-balancing interval does not significantly affect the performance of the dynamic hedging strategy when using a non-perfectly correlated asset. In Table 10-5 we see that with a correlation of $\rho = 0.9$, adjusting the hedging position 50 times per year only marginally reduces the 95 percent CTE when compared with hedging 10 times per year, from $9.60 to $9.27 per hundred dollars of underlying mutual fund. This is because the majority of the risk is due to basis risk between the underlying and hedging instruments. In the absence of basis risk, it is possible to dramatically improve the performance of the classical Black–Scholes delta-neutral hedging strategy by matching the option's curvature using a gamma hedge. Gamma-neutral hedging strategies reduce the risk exposure to large asset price movements by trading in other option contracts written on the same underlying asset. As noted above, the majority of the risk is due to basis risk and consequently we expect that gamma-neutral strategies would do little to improve the performance when hedging with an imperfectly correlated asset.

Figure 10-3 plots the profit and loss distributions and distributions of return on capital when hedging with assets which have various degrees of correlation with the underlying mutual fund. We see that even for quite a high correlation of $\rho = 0.9$, the distributions are very broad and much of the downside risk is not effectively reduced. Interestingly, when using a hedging asset with $\rho = 0.75$, the lower tail of the profit and loss distribution shown in Figure 10-3(a) is actually thicker than the unhedged case (corresponding to $\rho = 0$).

It must be noted that many segregated fund guarantees are offered on mutual funds that are actively managed. In this case, it may be quite difficult to determine a basket of securities that has a very high degree of correlation with the underlying mutual fund. The hedging strategy described in this section is in some sense an optimal one, in that the position in the hedging asset, Δ_h, is chosen to minimize the variability. As a result, we contend that the management of basis risk is of extreme importance when hedging with a partially correlated asset and should be approached with care.

Conclusion

Recent market volatility has spurred interest in attaching guarantees to pension investments. In this chapter, we look at maturity guarantees offered on mutual funds in Canada. The guarantees embedded in these products are often much more complex than a simple maturity guarantee that insures the initial investment. In addition to offering mortality benefits, these contracts typically allow the investors to lock in market gains by resetting the guarantee level to the existing value of the account. Even if such provisions are not explicitly offered, investors can synthetically create reset opportunities by lapsing and re-entering the contract. Hence, institutions offering even simple maturity guarantees must carefully consider the effects of anti-selective investor lapsing when they are quantifying their risk exposure.

A guarantee is only valuable to the consumer if the financial institution offering the product is able to back the guarantee in the event of a market downturn. In order to ensure solvency, regulatory agencies require that institutions offering these products set aside capital in a risk-free, liquid investment. This introduces an associated cost with providing these guarantees. These capital requirements can be quite onerous, but they can be reduced if a suitable hedging strategy is implemented.

The decision of whether or not to actively hedge guarantees offered on mutual fund investments is a management issue. In essence, hedging can

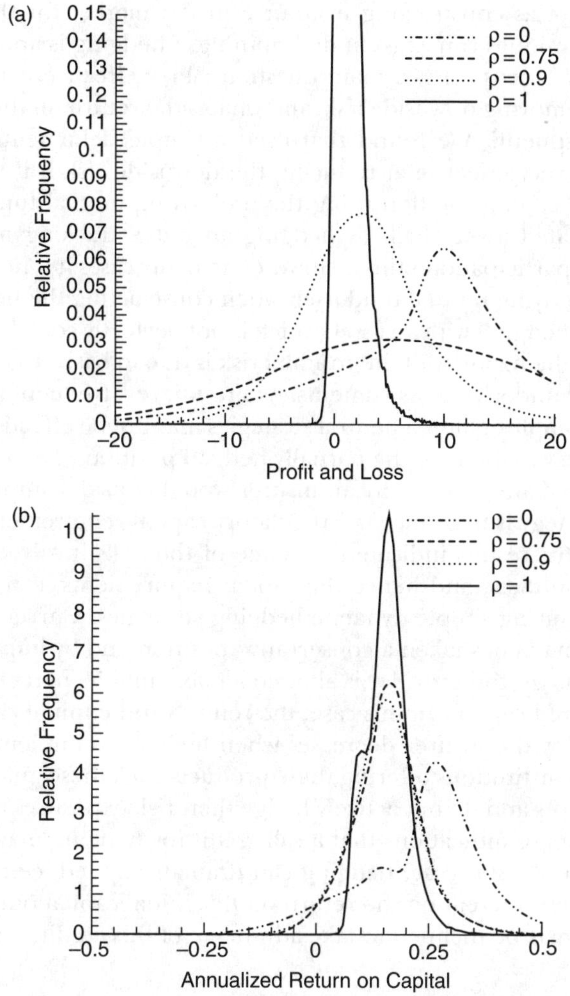

Figure 10-3. The profit and loss distribution. A segregated fund guarantee which offers two resets per annum when hedging using an asset which has correlation ρ with the underlying mutual fund: (a) Profit and loss* distribution, (b) The return on capital**.

Notes:

*Model assumes that investors utilize the heuristic rules described in the accompanying text to determine their use of the reset feature and anti-selective lapsing. (*Source*: Authors' computations.)

** We assume that investors utilize the heuristic rules described in the accompanying text to determine their use of the reset feature and anti-selective lapsing.

Source: Authors' computations.

be thought of as constructing insurance in the market for the provider, and our techniques can assist in determining if hedging is appropriate. In particular, we focus on two main questions: how effective is the hedging strategy at removing downside risk, and what is the return on the regulatory capital investment? We found that even a simple delta-neutral hedging strategy was very effective at reducing the downside risk if it was possible to set up a hedging position using the underlying mutual fund, or a perfectly correlated asset (such as hedging an index tracking mutual fund using index participation units). However, in many cases it is not possible to use the underlying mutual fund itself when constructing the hedging portfolio. When hedging with an asset, which is not perfectly correlated with the underlying, the majority of the residual risk is due to basis risk between the hedging and underlying instruments. As a result, very frequent re-balancing and more complex gamma-neutral strategies may not be effective at further reducing the variability of the partially hedged position.

The other main reason why an insurer would consider implementing a hedging strategy is to reduce the regulatory capital requirements for these contracts. Our results indicate that some of the risks involved with offering these contracts, and hence the capital requirements, can be reduced dramatically using simple dynamic hedging strategies. Current regulatory policy in Canada has taken a conservative position and by implementing a hedging strategy, the provider is allowed a maximum 50 percent reduction in the required capital. In this case, the return on the initial capital investment made by the insurer decreases when hedging is implemented. As a result, many institutions offering these products back these guarantees with capital reserves and do not actively hedge their risk exposures to these contracts. There are indications that a full credit for hedging may be granted in the future. In this case, hedging can dramatically reduce the required capital, thereby increasing the return on this initial capital outlay, so more institutions may be inclined to take advantage of this credit.

Appendix

Hedging with Basis Risk

For expositional simplicity, we develop the model for hedging with a partially correlated asset in the context of a simple vanilla put option. In particular, we ignore exotic features associated with segregated fund guarantees such as mortality benefits, the deferred payment of these contracts through proportional fees, the reset feature, and lapsing. Yet, the numerical results provided in this chapter are based on a generalized model that incorporates these effects.

Consider an option written on the underlying asset with price given by S_u, which satisfies the stochastic differential equation:

$$dS_u = \mu_u S_u dt + \sigma_u S_u dz_u.$$

Here μ_u is the drift rate and σ_u is the volatility of this asset and dz_u is an increment from a Wiener process.

If it is not possible to trade directly in the underlying asset S_u, we can try to establish a hedge for this option by trading in another asset with price process S_h, which satisfies

$$dS_h = \mu_h S_h dt + \sigma_h S_h dz_h,$$

where μ_h is the drift rate and σ_h is the volatility of the asset S_h. The Wiener increment dz_h is correlated with the increment for S_u with $\mathrm{corr}(dz_u, dz_h) = \rho$.

Following standard techniques as described by Wilmott (1998) we establish a portfolio that contains the option, whose value is given by $V(S_u, t)$, and a short position of Δ_h shares of the second asset S_h,

$$\Pi = V(S_u, t) - \Delta_h S_h.$$

Using Ito's Lemma we can estimate the change in value of this portfolio over small increments of time. The choice of Δ_h, which minimizes the variance of the returns on this portfolio is given by

$$\Delta_h = \rho \frac{S_u}{S_h} \frac{\sigma_u}{\sigma_h} V_{S_u}.$$

We may loosely think of this model as hedging as much of the risk exposure to underlying price movements in light of the basis risk introduced by hedging with a non-perfectly correlated asset.

If this partially hedged portfolio earns the rate of return $\bar{r}$ (which we discuss below) then we find that the value of the option satisfies the partial differential equation:

$$V_t + \left(\mu_u - \rho \frac{\sigma_u}{\sigma_h} (\mu_h - \bar{r}) \right) S_u V_{S_u} + \tfrac{1}{2} \sigma_u^2 S_u^2 V_{S_u S_u} - \bar{r} V = 0.$$

In order to determine an appropriate specification for the discounting rate $\bar{r}$ we consider this equation under several special circumstances.

- $\rho = \pm 1$: In this case we are in a standard Black–Scholes setting and holding Δ_h shares of the hedging asset eliminates all risk from the portfolio Π to leading order. In this case we should discount at the risk-free rate, r.
- $\rho = 0$: If $\rho = 0$ then $\Delta_h = 0$ and the portfolio Π consists only of a long position in the option. In this case we should discount the portfolio Π by

the expected rate of return on the option, r^*, which can be empirically estimated using market option prices and the real-world (P-measure) drift rate.

A simple way to model the discounting rate, $\bar{r} = \bar{r}(\rho)$, which is consistent with the cases described above is to specify

$$\bar{r}(\rho) = (1 - |\rho|)r^* + |\rho|r,$$

where r is the risk-free rate and r^* is the expected rate of return on the option. We remark that when $\rho = 1$ we recover the Black–Scholes model and when $\rho = 0$ we recover expected valuation methods using the real drift rate of the underlying security and a risk-adjusted discounting factor.

Notes

1 Small changes in the contractual details or variations in the market settings such as the volatility and risk-free interest rate may affect the pricing and hedging of these contracts. Interested readers are referred to Windcliff et al. (2002) for a discussion of the effects of these and other parameters such as the level of investor optimality used in making reset decisions on the valuation of segregated fund guarantees.
2 Numerical experiments indicate that more frequent exercise decisions by the investor do not appreciably affect results.
3 The ARC is similar to the risk adjusted return on capital (RAROC) described in Jameson (2001), but it has been converted to an annualized rate of return to facilitate comparisons between contracts of different durations.
4 We emphasize that pricing these contracts under the assumption that investors will act non-optimally may be dangerous and may result in mis-pricings by the insurer. Although the majority of individual investors may not have the expertise to utilize these complex features efficiently, we have heard of incidents where financial planners have assisted their customers in doing so as an additional service.
5 Interested readers are referred to Windcliff, Forsyth, and Vetzal (2001) for a detailed description of the mathematical model and computational techniques used to obtain the hedging strategies for the numerical experiments in this chapter.
6 For the impact of other modeling assumptions such as volatility, interest rates, investor profile, as well as the impact of variations in the product design, interested readers are referred to Windcliff et al. (2002).
7 Another method that can be applied when hedging with a partially correlated asset formulates the option-pricing problem in an incomplete market setting and uses a utility maximization approach (Davis, 2000).

References

Canadian Institute of Actuaries (CIA). 2000. "Report of the CIA Task Force on Segregated Fund Investment Guarantees." <www.actuaries.ca/publications/2000/20020e.pdf>.

Coval, Joshua D. and Tyler Shumway. 2001. "Expected Option Returns." *Journal of Finance* 56(3): 983–1009.

Davis, Mark. 2000. "Optimal Hedging with Basis Risk." Working Paper. Financial and Actuarial Mathematics Group, Technische Universitat Wien, Vienna, Austria.

Hull, John. 2000. *Options, Futures and Other Derivative Securities*, 4th edn. New Jersey: Prentice Hall.

Jameson, Rob. 2001. "Between a RAROC and a Hard Place." *ERisk*, February: 1–5.

Office of the Superintendent of Financial Institutions of Canada. 2001. *Capital Offset for Segregated Fund Hedging Programs (MCCSR)*. Toronto.

Seppi, Duane J. 1999. "Mathematical Finance: Class Notes." Graduate School of Industrial Administration, Carnegie Mellon University.

Sircar, K. Ronnie and George Papanicolaou. 1998. "General Black–Scholes Models Accounting for Increased Market Volatility from Hedging Strategies." *Applied Math Finance* 5(1): 45–82.

Wilmott, Paul. 1998. *Derivatives*. West Sussex, England: John Wiley and Sons.

Windcliff, Heath A., Peter A. Forsyth, and Kenneth R. Vetzal. 2001. "Segregated Funds: Shout Options with Maturity Extensions." *Insurance: Mathematics & Economics* 29(1): 1–21.

—— Martin K. Le Roux, Peter A. Forsyth, and Kenneth R. Vetzal. 2002. "Understanding the Behaviour and Hedging of Segregated Funds Offering the Reset Feature." *North American Actuarial Journal* 6(2): 107–125.

Chapter 11

Retirement Guarantees in Mandatory Defined Contribution Systems

Jan Walliser

Risk protection for retirees has become one of the centerpieces of the debate on how to organize retirement systems. The global push for a larger role for defined-contribution (DC) plans has raised the question how retirees should be protected from capital market risk. Proponents of individual investment pension accounts often consider these risks to be as easily manageable and far outweighed by the opportunities offered by a DC system. Opponents contend that the risks of individual investment are large and that defined-benefit (DB) pension systems are more appropriate for mandatory public systems.

Notwithstanding the merits of both arguments, all implementations of mandatory public DC plans around the world in fact feature some form of guarantee. In some cases, the government maintains a public benefit independent of past contribution and wage history ("flat benefit"); in others, it tops up retirement savings. Some systems also offer guarantees on the rate of return of retirement savings.[1] Protecting retirees from poverty is a driving force behind the discussion on appropriate retirement guarantees.

Guarantees are neither free nor cheap. From an economic viewpoint, the guarantor faces the costs of these guarantees *ex ante*, even though they may only rarely require outlays. The allocation and management of risks crucially affects the extent to which retirement income can be effectively prefunded and the extent to which taxpayers are exposed to changes in the size of retiree cohorts (Smetters, 2001). Hence, the risk aspect has macroeconomic implications. Moreover, interventions by the guarantor may have behavioral impacts because participants have the tendency to expand their risk exposure if a third party guarantees these risks. Providing as much up-front information as possible to policymakers about macroeconomic and behavioral implications guarantees is therefore an important task for economists.

Kent Smetters provided helpful comments and advice. The opinions expressed in the chapter are those of the author and should not be attributed to the World Bank.

This chapter discusses guarantees offered under mandatory public pension systems around the world.[2] To set the stage, the next section outlines interactions between guarantees and strategies to limit governments' risk exposure. The important conclusion is that the evaluation of these guarantees must go hand in hand with the regulation and design of the underlying public DC system. Next we compare a number of actual implementations of guarantees and analyze their particular risk allocation and risk management mechanisms. A final section concludes.

Retirement Guarantees: Understanding their Costs and Managing their Risks

Retirement guarantees come in two basic forms: contingent payments, and noncontingent payments. The first category includes benefits based on an income or means tests as well as minimum rate of return guarantees. The second category includes benefits that are paid independent of incomes and rates of return, such as the so-called flat pension.

The financial impact of noncontingent payments can be more easily assessed, because the process does not involve evaluating risks that the government may be assuming on behalf of the individual. To take the universal flat benefit as an example, its costs depend largely on fairly easily predictable demographic developments, since everybody above a certain age would receive an identical benefit. If an inflation-protected flat benefit is set sufficiently high, it also automatically protects people from poverty. However, it would be poorly targeted and would require pending considerable resources on people who are far above any notion of the poverty line. The economic impact of noncontingent payments is similar to giving people an additional safe asset. This additional safe asset would entice people to increase their holdings of risky assets and to increase their risk exposure. However, if the government could credibly commit to not increase its assistance in case of poor investment outcomes, these behavioral adaptations would have no repercussion on the cost of the income guarantee, since payments are independent of outcomes.

The case is more complicated for contingent payments. A danger of such guarantees is that their cost is not at all or only partially recognized by policymakers, since "on average" guarantees are not being called. It may therefore appear that the costs of these guarantees would be negligible. However, Smetters (1998, 2001, 2002) has demonstrated, a market-based evaluation of the value of guarantees along the line of the Black Scholes (1973) option price formula can imply large unfunded liabilities. These calculations exploit the fact that a guarantee can be interpreted as an option to receive a payment if the value of retirement assets or the rate of return falls below a certain threshold. Lachance and Mitchell (Chapter 8, this volume) provide an overview of the costs of guarantees and the implications of alternative financing strategies.

The intuition for this result derives from the observation that economic agents are generally averse to risk. Even though the probability to be penniless during retirement may be virtually zero, many people would probably pay a considerable amount of money to have a guarantee against that outcome. It would therefore be wrong to equate the expected value of the payments made under the guarantee with the *ex ante* value of providing the guarantee.

Merton and Bodie (1992) provide a useful framework for the management of risks generated by guarantees. They discuss three tools to manage these risks: monitoring risks, pricing guarantees, and imposing restrictions on assets. In the case of government retirement guarantees, these tools are of different applicability. Monitoring risks involves reviewing portfolios on a regular basis, marking them to market, and seizing assets or intervening in the activity of the guaranteed entity when the asset level moves dangerously close to one at which the guarantee will be activated. In the case of relatively small individual portfolios, it is virtually impossible for the government to monitor performance. Moreover, monitoring is subject to considerable arbitrariness. An agency charged with monitoring performance could acquire considerable power through its ability to intervene when risks are considered to be too large for the guaranteed entity (i.e. the pension fund or individual investor) to continue making decisions on its portfolio.

It would also be difficult to move to the *ex ante* pricing of guarantees, i.e. in form of an insurance premium paid to the government, since the latter would need to be based on individual circumstances given that each individual has a different portfolio and risk exposure.[3] In view of the difficulties with individual monitoring and pricing of risks, a third way to limit exposure is to restrict portfolio investments. By regulating the composition of investment portfolios, the government can reduce the volatility of outcomes, limit moral hazard, and reduce the risk that guarantee payments must be made. At the same time, the exact specifications of asset restrictions will have ramifications on investment choices and thus may involve efficiency losses. The same problem of choice arises if the government decides to specify a "benchmark portfolio" with "acceptable" risk exposure to be covered by the government guarantee, but additional risk must be borne by the individual.[4]

What are the practical implications of the above? First, guarantees are costly and their costs play an important role in designing DC pension systems. Second, government risk exposure can be limited through applying one or several instruments of risk management. Third, the ultimate mix between individual risk exposure, government guarantees, and government regulation, determines the viability of the pension system in the long term. On the one hand, exposing too many retirees to the risk of poverty in old age will erode participant support for the pension system. On the other hand, too generous government guarantees or lack of appropriate risk management for guarantees can undermine government finances, and in the end they may lead to the same problem of sustainability faced by many pay-as-you-go systems.[5]

Retirement Guarantees around the World

What can retirement guarantees promise? The short answer is as much or as little as can be credibly committed to pay in case the guarantees are being called. The combination of promise and risk-management mechanism differs by country, but in looking at a variety of countries, some general patterns emerge. Table 11-1 summarizes key aspects of guarantees in national mandatory DC schemes. Next, we discuss three broad arrangements, along with more detailed reference to a few specific country cases.

The British Model and its Derivatives

The British pension model is characterized by a relatively high level of individual responsibility and the concomitant fairly high level of risk that remains with individual investors. Income support from the government is limited to a flat payment, conditional on the worker satisfying an extended period of coverage and contributions. The individual is largely left to fend for himself while retaining a large variety of investment choice. The addition of a second DB layer to the flat benefit dates only from 1975 (the so-called state earnings related pension scheme (SERPS)), and people can opt out through funded occupational or personal pension plans. Neither occupational nor personal pensions are subject to strict investment regulations, with most regulatory efforts concentrated on ensuring that people receive accurate investment advice.[6]

As a result of the UK government's commitment to a limited and noncontingent floor of protection, its risk exposure is limited to demographic change. Therefore, the freedom to invest that was left to workers does not create a contingent government liability. In this respect, the guarantee would appear to be a minimum pension promise, which the government could probably afford to keep. But, under current projections, the flat benefit is projected to decline from about 15 percent of average earnings in the mid-1990s to about 9 percent of average earnings by 2030, largely on account of a lack of adjustment for productivity growth (Budd and Campbell, 1998). By reducing the size of the benefit in relative terms and thus reducing the generosity of the guarantee in terms of average earnings, the British government seeks to encourage more funding and risktaking, while simultaneously reducing the relative size of the noncontingent guarantee. The main challenge for this strategy flows from uncertainty over the political consequences of shifting most of the responsibility to prepare and invest for retirement

TABLE 11-1 Guarantees and Portfolio Restrictions on Mandatory DC Pensions

Country	*Noncontingent Payments*	*Contingent Payments*	*Portfolio Restrictions*
Argentina	Flat benefit	Relative rate of return guarantee for pension funds (absolute rate of return guarantee for state-owned pension fund)	Yes
Australia	No	Means-tested flat benefit	No. "Prudent-man rule" for investment managers
Chile	No	Topping-up of phased withdrawals from retirement accounts (relative rate of return guarantee for pension funds)	Yes
Colombia	No	Topping-up of phased withdrawals from retirement accounts (relative rate of return guarantee for pension funds)	Yes
Croatia	DB pension	Minimum rate of return for pension accounts	Yes
El Salvador	No	Topping-up of phased withdrawals from retirement accounts (relative rate of return guarantee for pension funds)	Yes
Hungary	DB pension	Topping-up of annuity from mandatory DC pension (relative rate of return guarantee for pension funds, set annually)	Yes
Kazakhstan	No	Topping-up of low account balances	Yes
Mexico	No	Topping-up of phased withdrawals from retirement accounts.	Yes
Poland	Notional DC system	Topping-up of combined benefits from notional DC system and individual accounts (relative rate of return guarantee for pension funds)	Yes
Singapore	No	Absolute rate of return guarantee	Government makes investment decisions
Sweden	Notional DC system	No	Yes
Switzerland	Public and occupational DB plans	Means-tested flat benefit (absolute rate of return guarantee for pension funds)	Yes
United Kingdom	Flat benefit	No	No. "Prudent-man rule" for investment managers
Uruguay	DB pension	Topping-up of DB pension (absolute and relative rate of return guarantee for pension funds)	Yes

to individuals. It may happen that people making poor investment choices end up with lower retirement income than under SERPS and pressure the government to raise guaranteed benefits.

The Australian Superannuation System

The Australian system also originally limited old-age support to a relatively low government benefit and largely left individuals to prepare for their own retirement. In contrast to the United Kingdom, the income guarantee was means-tested and thus contingent on investment returns and labor earnings. This basic pillar is financed out of general revenue and not as a result of a contributory scheme, as under the British system. A mandatory funded second pillar was introduced in the 1990s, which relies mostly on employer-controlled "superannuation" funds. Most of these funds are run by employers and many do not allow individuals to control investment decisions, so their investment choices tend to be fairly conservative. As a result, even though the government provides a contingent payment, the lack of portfolio limits for pension funds does not appear to entice more risk-taking or pose a serious threat to government finances. Nevertheless, the means-testing provisions of the Australian system combined with the possibility to withdraw retirement savings in a lump sum could lead people to run down assets or invest in assets that are not fully considered for the means test, such as housing. The interaction of the different pillars in the Australian pension system is discussed in more detail by Piggot and Doyle (Chapter 5, this volume). Prior to the expansion of superannuation plan coverage, more than 80 percent of Australian retirees were eligible for a full or partial government pension. If this trend continues, the mandatory funded second pillar may not have the expected salutary effects on future retirement income, in which case the means-tested benefit may need to be scaled back or unfunded spending on old-age support may crowd out other government spending.

Provident Funds

Many countries with historical ties to the United Kingdom also adopted the so-called provident funds, among them, Kenya, Malaysia, and Singapore. These pool contributions in a mandatory DC fund, managed by the government and subject to government investment decisions, and the government often guarantees a minimum rate of return with its budgetary resources. At first sight, this may appear to resolve the bulk of the risk management problem, since the government as guarantor also controls the asset allocation in the pension fund. But if the minimum rate of return is sufficiently low, the government may prefer to use provident fund income to finance government operations (by selling government bonds to the fund), or investing assets in projects and sectors receiving preferential treatment. The lack of transparency and exclusion of accountholders from investment decisions hampers their ability to evaluate investment risks and management acuity, and it also reduces the responsiveness of investment choices to rate of return differentials. As a result, provident fund performance has generally been poor compared with other investment funds, and some provident funds, for example, in Kenya, have been an almost continuous burden to the budget. When the government's financial position is weak, the governments may take larger risks with fund assets or to finance operations by borrowing from the fund, and the probability rises that the government may not be able to make good on its promises. In the extreme case, a provident fund system can become a pay-as-you-go system, where benefit promises depend entirely on the government's overall financial situation. In provident funds, therefore, the risk is that the government may change the generosity of guarantees.

Reforms in Latin America

A wave of pension reforms started in the 1980s, beginning with the Chilean reform, and followed by a number of Southern and Central American countries in the early 1990s.[7] Under the Chilean model, workers newly entering the labor force and those opting out of the old system contribute to a privately managed pension fund selected from among several competitors. Workers who chose the new system receive so-called "recognition bonds" for their accrued claims under the old system.

The national Chilean system offers two types of guarantees. The first is a relative rate of return guarantee for pension investments. In this case, every participant is guaranteed a minimum annual rate of return no less than 2 percentage points below the average of other pension funds, or less than half the average rate of return of all pension funds, whichever is greater. If a pension fund cannot cover the minimum rate of return from its reserves, the government makes the payment and the pension fund is liquidated. To minimize the risks from the rate of return guarantee, the government not only protects investors from downside risks, but it also mandates that excess returns be held in a profitability reserve. In particular, returns exceeding the average return earned by other funds by more than 2 percentage points or exceeding twice the average return, whichever is smaller, are not allocated to individual accounts but kept in reserve. By protecting investors against downside risks but limiting their participation in upside risks, the government reduces its own risk exposure. As Smetters (2002) shows, taxing away good returns is an efficient way to reduce the *ex ante* value of government guarantees. Combined with the asset restrictions placed on portfolios (described below), this relative rate of return criterion tends to lead insurers to choose similar portfolios and thus produces limited portfolio choices for workers in the Chilean system.

The second form of guarantee in Chile is a minimum pension benefit payment for those who contribute to the pension system for at least 20 years, and for whom their individual accounts are too small to finance a minimum pension of roughly 75 percent of the minimum wage. Thus, long-term workers with too little pension saving receive a topping-up of their pension from the government, financed out of general government revenue. To reduce moral hazard, the government has imposed fairly stringent restrictions on the pension plan portfolio composition, limiting the level of equities and investments abroad.

As a result of these guarantees and regulation, the Chilean government participates in both upside and downside risks. By design, all fund managers have strong incentives to invest in similar portfolios, making large deviations from the mean a relatively rare outcome. The fact that returns in pension funds are fairly similar also limits the number of cases with low levels of retirement savings to those who had low labor incomes during their working lives, rather than those who made poor investment choices. The major risk exposure remaining is country-specific risk, in view of the limits imposed on foreign investments. In particular, the small size of the Chilean economy combined with the limited portfolio diversification implies that all pension funds will be exposed in case of national economic difficulties. This would not trigger the relative rate of return guarantee, but it could eventually require more topping-up under the minimum pension guarantee.[8] The government could therefore be simultaneously exposed to poor economic performance and financial pressures generated from the minimum pension guarantee.

Variations on a theme: Argentina and Mexico

The Argentine system features a minimum rate of return guarantee similar to the Chilean setup. The main difference is that the relative rate of return guarantee is asymmetric, such that the provisions are triggered if a fund outperforms the average by 30 percent or falls short of the average by 70 percent. This asymmetry leads to larger government participation in upside risks and lower exposure to downside risk as compared with the Chilean case. The Argentine system also imposes similar portfolio constraints as the Chilean system, leading to similar herding behavior in pension funds.

In contrast to the Chilean case, the Argentine government offers a noncontingent basic pension floor for those having contributed to the mandatory system for 30 years or more. Worth about 25 percent of the average wage, this pension floor represents about the same level of income as the Chilean minimum pension guarantee. Pension portfolio choices therefore do not expose the government to additional risks and the costs of the flat benefit are not exposed to country-specific shocks. To the extent that the participation in upside risks already limits exposure to the minimum rate of return guarantee, portfolio restrictions in the Argentine case may be redundant as compared to Chile. The anticipated costs of the universal benefit, however, may raise doubts about the government's ability to finance the benefit in the long term. Hence, while the government's contingent liability may be smaller than in the Chilean case, its overall unfunded liability appears to be larger, generating larger political uncertainty about the long-run viability of the benefit.

Recent economic difficulties in Argentina underscore the worry that the national funded pension system has not insulated pensions from the overall financial position of the government. In 2001, the government drastically reduced payroll taxes from 11 to 5 percent, which significantly cut pension savings inflows. More importantly, the government also obliged pension funds to buy short-term bonds with long-term deposits and exchanged public bonds for short-term loans. It then proceeded to convert dollar-denominated government debt at a rate of Peso 1.40 per US$ compared with the then-current exchange rate of around Peso 3.5 per US$ (Oxford Analytica, 2002). These transactions resulted in massive wealth losses for the pension plans and undermined confidence in the system, resulting in a sharp decline in contribution rates. As a result of these developments, the government's long-run liabilities to pensioners remain high and perhaps are unsustainable.

In Mexico, the individual account system introduced in 1997 features a minimum pension guarantee similar to the Chilean setup. By contrast, however, there is no minimum rate of return guarantee for pension funds and thus there is no government participation in any upside risk. Nonetheless, the government is potentially exposed to risky behavior by workers and pension funds because the Mexican minimum guarantee of about 40 percent of the average wage is substantially more generous than in Chile. In the Mexican case, as in Chile and Argentina, the investment risks are limited through portfolio restrictions imposed on pension fund assets.

It is noteworthy that the differences across systems in Chile, Argentina, and Mexico—even if they may appear slight—are significant in terms of the risk distribution between the government and workers, as well as the scope of reducing government restrictions on investment choices. The Chilean solution contains government liabilities through participation in upside risks, self-insurance, and portfolio restrictions, as well as a means test on pension assets. The Argentine system, while using similar risk management tools, kept a first-pillar DB program not contingent on investment outcomes, rather than opting for a means-tested topping-up. Therefore, the unfunded liability of the system is likely larger than in Chile and the rationale for portfolio restrictions less clear. By contrast, in Mexico, portfolio restrictions are a crucial element to limit government risk exposure in light of the absence of self-insurance against rate of return fluctuations and fairly generous government minimum benefit guarantees.

Reforms in Transition Economies

A second generation of pension reforms took place after the transition of Eastern and Central European countries to market-based economies in the mid-1990s. These reforms faced different circumstances than in many Latin American countries, as a result of larger retiree populations and larger formal labor markets with more substantial unfunded pension liabilities. As a result of the transition costs involved in moving to funded pension schemes, most of these countries opted to maintain a larger pay-as-you-go financed pillar than Latin American reformers (a notable exception is Kazakhstan).

In Hungary, the 1997 reform revised the existing unfunded DB system and instituted a mandatory DC pillar, with a contribution rate of 6 percent of salary. The DB plan continues to provide a replacement rate of about 50 percent, after 40 years of work. In addition to the benefit promised by the DB system, the Hungarian system offers a rate of return guarantee for the accounts maintained under the mandatory DC plans, along with a minimum benefit guarantee equivalent to 25 percent of the DB pension. This benefit guarantee would be called if pension accounts generate less than an average annual real rate of return of about 2 percent over a 40-year horizon.

The rate of return guarantee is specified annually by the supervisory board for private pension funds and, as in the Chilean case, provides for both upper and lower limits on returns. This setup implies that the government is guarantor of last resort and participates in upside as well as downside risks. When the rate falls short of the minimum, the difference is made up from pension fund reserves and further backed by an industry-wide guarantee fund, financed by mandatory contributions from pension funds and backstopped by the government. Returns exceeding maximum rates set by the supervisory board serve to boost pension fund reserves. The industry-wide guarantee fund also backs the minimum benefit guarantee. As elsewhere, the portfolio composition of Hungarian pension funds is subject to regulation.

The guarantees for the DC portion of the Hungarian pension system impose fairly limited risks on the government, due to the self-insurance mechanism for pension funds against return fluctuations and the modest returns necessary to generate sufficient wealth in pension accounts to avoid calling the minimum benefit guarantee. Of course, the government maintains its commitment to the fairly large DB pillar. In light of the retirement income derived from the first pillar, it would appear that the DC guarantees are intended to instill confidence in workers unfamiliar with an investment-based pension system.

In Poland, the unfunded DB first pillar was replaced with an unfunded notional DC system. Under a notional DC system, retirement accounts are credited with a fictitious rate of return, although no assets are actually accumulated. The second pillar of the Polish system is a mandatory DC system financed with a payroll tax worth 7.3 percent of salary. The government guarantees a minimum pension of around 30 percent of the average wage from both pillars. In addition, the second pillar is covered by a relative rate of return guarantee similar to Chile's, except that restrictions regarding deviations from average rates are less stringent. Similar to the Hungarian case, the minimum rate of return guarantee is backed by a guarantee fund, which in turn is backed by the government, the ultimate guarantor. Polish law also imposes restrictions on pension fund portfolios.

As in Hungary, the ultimate rationale for multiple guarantees is unclear. Although these guarantees do not expose the government to excessive risks, given the participation of the government in upside risks, they seem unnecessary given the importance of the first pillar. Put differently, since the first pillar prevents people from being exposed to very low retirement income, one might ask whether the second pillar guarantees and the related portfolio restrictions to limit risk exposure are necessary. It is worth noting that Sweden, which served as an example for several Baltic and Eastern European states, did not add further guarantees to the promises made under the first pillar when it designed its mandatory second pillar DC plan.

Conclusion

Our review has identified a wide variety of pension systems with a mandatory DC component, and most of these include guarantees. In many cases, governments have opted for multiple guarantees, limiting the fluctuation of returns in individual accounts and setting a minimum for the benefits paid in retirement. The minimum income promises are in some countries contingent on pension fund performance, while in others they simply derive from the pay-as-you-go DB tier.

DC guarantees must be affordable in order to be credible. Too generous guarantees on investment returns or minimum benefits expose retirees to the political risk that governments may have to scale back payments if financial pressures rise in later years. In that respect, DC plans with guarantees may begin to look similar to traditional DB systems.

When guarantees are contingent on the investment outcomes, such as minimum rate of return guarantees and topping-up of investment accounts, governments have generally implemented risk management tools to limit their risk exposure. These tools include reserves, mandatory pension self-insurance, and restrictions placed on the composition of pension investment portfolios. Safeguarding public resources has tended to imply that rate of return and minimum pension guarantees come at the cost of limitations on portfolio choices.

Notes

[1] The World Bank (1994) has proposed a three-pillar system. The first pillar is a pay-as-you-go financed benefit and it provides some basic retirement income or income guarantee. The second pillar is a mandatory DC plan, and the third pillar comprises voluntary savings plans. More generally, the first pillar includes not only standard DB pensions but encompasses all kinds of guarantees, means-tested benefits etc. that the government may offer to keep people above a certain minimum level of retirement income.

[2] Pension guarantees in voluntary pension systems are discussed by Turner and Rajnes (Chapter 12, this volume).

[3] Charging a premium should not be confused with those reform proposals attempting to reduce risk exposure by simply raising the contribution rate to individual accounts. In the latter case, the expected account balances and payouts will increase because higher contributions generate higher retirement savings. By contrast, an insurance fee paid to the government is paid in return for the insurance provided and thus would not increase available retirement savings.

[4] Smetters (2002) discusses risk management through limiting guarantees to the returns of a standardized portfolio rather than offering a blanket minimum return guarantee. As a result, the insurance value of the guarantee declines and moral hazard to increase risk exposure is reduced because the guarantor participates in only some of the downside risks.

[5] Smetters (1998) shows that guarantees can be exactly equivalent to unfunded liabilities. The economic argument relies on the *ex ante* value of guarantees, which can be evaluated with the options pricing formula. Under certain specifications, the value of the insurance against downside risks of pension account protfolios can be exactly equivalent to the promise made under a pay-as-you-go system. In that case, even though notionally the government may have shifted from a DB to a DC system, the value of its promise has not declined and future taxpayers remain exposed to the same financial risks.

[6] See CBO (1999) for a more detailed overview of the British system and the reforms introduced in the 1980s.

[7] Diamond and Valdés-Prieto (1994) provide a detailed overview of the features of the Chilean system. Mitchell and Barreto (1997) discuss successor reforms in other Latin American countries.

[8] This risk is akin to the risk of a large corporation whose workers have invested most of their retirement savings in company stocks, with the important difference that sovereign government default is much less likely than the failure of a private enterprise. For a discussion of risk exposure in company pension plans see Mitchell and Utkus (Chapter 3, this volume).

References

Black, Fischer and Myron J. Scholes. 1973. "The Pricing of Options and Corporate Liabilities." *Journal of Political Economy* 81(3): 637–654.

Budd, Alan and Nigel Campbell. 1998. "The Pensions System in the United Kingdom." In *Privatizing Social Security*, ed. Martin Feldstein. Chicago: University of Chicago Press, pp. 99–127.

Congressional Budget Office. 1999. *Social Security Privatization: Experiences Abroad.* CBO Paper, January.

Diamond, Peter and Salvador Vadés-Prieto. 1994. "Social Security Reforms." In *The Chilean Economy: Policy Lessons and Challenges,* eds. Barry P. Bosworth, Rudiger Dornbusch, and Raúl Labán. Washington: The Brookings Institution. pp. 257–357.

Merton, Robert C. and Zvi Bodie. 1992. "On the Management of Financial Guarantees." *Financial Management,* Winter.

Mitchell, Olivia S. and Flávio Ataliba Barreto. 1997. "After Chile, What? Second-Round Social Security Reforms in Latin America." *Revista de Analisi Economica* 12: 3–36.

Oxford Analytica Brief. 2002. *Argentina: Pension Problems,* May 3.

Smetters, Kent. 1998. "Privatizing versus Prefunding Social Security." Mimeo. University of Pennsylvania.

— 2001. "The Effect of Pay-When-Needed Benefit Guarantees on the Impact of Social Security Privatization." In *Risk Aspects of Investment-Based Social Security Reform,* eds. John Campbell and Martin Feldstein. Chicago: University of Chicago Press, pp. 91–112.

— 2002. "Controlling the Costs of Minimum Benefit Guarantees in Public Pension Conversions." *The Journal of Pension Economics and Finance* 1(1): 9–34.

Srinivas, P. S., Edward Whitehouse, and Juan Yermo. 2000. *Regulating Private Pension Funds' Structure, Performance and Investments: Cross-Country Evidence.* World Bank Pension Reform Primer. The World Bank. <www.worldbank.org/pensions>.

World Bank. 1994. *Averting the Old Age Crisis.* Oxford University Press.

Chapter 12

Retirement Guarantees in Voluntary Defined Contribution Plans

John A. Turner and David M. Rajnes

A key feature of most defined contribution (DC) pension plans is that the participant bears the financial market risk of plan investments. This risk can be reduced in a number of ways. It can be reduced by means of an investment strategy, where diversified portfolio can limit the investment of pension funds to relatively low risk portfolios. Alternatively, investing in guaranteed products can reduce capital market risk exposure. It can also be limited by government oversight and regulation of pension funds and financial markets (see Walliser, Chapter 11, this volume). In addition, DC arrangements can be developed to credit workers a different, less volatile rate of return than the rate actually received on the workers' DC accounts. A rate of return guarantee is one way of delinking the rate of return received on the workers' portfolios from the rate of return credited to workers.

This chapter explores the conceptual basis for a rate of return guarantee as an option for voluntary DC plans. It does so by analyzing different possible features of rate of return guarantees. In considering possible features, the analysis is not limited to features that would be allowed for Employee Retirement Income Security Act of 1974 (ERISA) plans in the United States,[1] but rather it also considers a range of possible features. Rather than attempting a complete catalog of guarantees operating in voluntary DC plans around the world, we discuss the guarantees in selected countries.[2] We draw several conclusions as to possible lessons learned for countries considering a rate of return guarantee in either a voluntary or a mandatory DC system.

Types of Guarantees

The definition of a "voluntary" plan is not completely straightforward. The definition used here is that voluntary plans are those which are not mandated by government. These plans include, however, plans that workers must participate in if they work for a particular employer, in a particular industry, or belong to a particular union. Thus, we include plans that are mandated by labor agreements between trade unions and employers.

Our focus is on rate of return guarantees in DC plans during the accumulation phase, before the worker retires. To better understand how guarantees work, we consider a simple two-period model where in the first period, the worker contributes C_1 to his DC pension account. This is used to purchase A_1 shares of assets at a price of p_1 per share. It is useful to separate the effects of capital value changes, through changes in the asset price p_1, from rate of return changes, because guarantees often treat these differently. The worker receives a nominal rate of return of i per share, so at the start of the second period he has assets worth p_2A_2, where the price of assets in period 2 is p_2:

$$C_1 = p_1A_1 \tag{12.1}$$

$$p_2A_2 = (1+i)p_1A_1 + (p_2 - p_1)A_1 + C_2 \tag{12.2}$$

$$= (ip_1 + p_2)A_1 \tag{12.3}$$

In a DC plan without a guarantee, the worker receives the value of his account balance as determined solely by investment earnings and capital gains or losses on his initial purchase of assets.

Financial market variables that may be guaranteed in this context consist of the nominal rate of return i, and the initial asset price p_1. Alternatively, the two variables may be jointly guaranteed. For example, if the rate of return includes capital gains and losses, the value $(1+i)p_1$ is guaranteed. Expressing the nominal rate of return as approximately equaling the real rate of return r plus the inflation rate π,

$$p_2A_2 = [(r+\pi)p_1 + p_2]A_1 \tag{12.4}$$

Here the rate of return guarantee may be tied to the inflation rate π, or it can be set at a real rate of π plus a constant.

In practice, guarantees tend to be expressed three ways. First are rate of return guarantees, which typically are a guarantee jointly of the asset price and rate of return, since they incorporate capital gains and losses in the calculation of the rate of return. Second are minimum benefit guarantees. Here the guarantee is over the terminal value of the account. Third are capital value guarantees. These are guarantees that the rate of return will not fall below zero and the initial asset price will not change.

The Structure of Rate of Return Guarantees

Further clarification of the structure of rate of return guarantees focuses on four aspects of guarantees:[3] the rate of return that is guaranteed; the risk management technique used to control rate of return risk; the characteristics of the guarantee; and the institution providing the capital that backs the guarantee. Understanding these aspects of rate of return guarantees is important both for analyzing existing guarantees and for creating alternative designs as part of a pension or social security reform. These aspects are summarized in Table 12-1.

The rate of return to be guaranteed may be classified according to various characteristics. First, it may be real or nominal; a real guarantee is indexed

TABLE 12-1 Structure of Rate of Return Guarantees in Voluntary DC Plans

Aspect of Guarantee	*Options*	*Discussion*
Rate of return	Real or nominal	Adjustment for inflation
	Fixed or relative	Particular rate or index
	Timing	Reference period
Method of risk management	Hedging	Sacrificing gain
	Insuring	Insurance premium
The guarantee	Point versus minimum	Risk and expected return faced by worker
	Catastrophic versus smoothing	
	Voluntary versus mandatory	
	Longevity	
Institutional backing	Employer PAYG or funded	Explicit sources of financing
	Associated reserve fund	
	Associated DB fund	
	Fund management company	
	Guaranteed product	

Source: Authors' compilation.

for inflation. Second, it may be fixed or relative. A fixed guarantee is linked to a particular rate, while a relative guarantee is linked to a capital market index. Third, it may be for a calendar year, a rolling multi-month period (ranging typically 12 to 36 months), or cumulative from a set date.

There are three methods of managing risk—hedging, insuring, and diversifying (Bodie, Hammond, and Mitchell, 2002). Rate of return guarantees typically involve either hedging or insuring, or both. Hedging involves eliminating the risk of a loss by sacrificing some or all of the potential for gain. Insuring involves paying an insurance premium to eliminate the risk of losing a larger amount. The insurance premium may be not readily observable, such as the reduced wage the worker presumably receives in exchange for working for an employer that provides a guarantee for a DC plan. The method used affects the type of guarantee provided.

The guarantee can be analyzed in terms of the risk and expected return the worker faces when the guarantee is in place. First, the guarantee can be a point guarantee or a minimum guarantee with income participation. With a point guarantee, the worker receives a specified rate of return, either nominal or real. The employer or the institution providing the guarantee receives the entire rate of return above the guarantee level when the actual rate of return exceeds the guarantee level. A point guarantee is similar to a cash balance plan. For the period of the guarantee, the rate of return the worker receives bears no relationship to the rate of return received on the underlying investments. Alternatively, with a minimum guarantee, the worker can receive the entire rate of return above the guarantee level or the employer or the institution providing the guarantee may receive part of it. This type of guarantee may also specify a maximum.

The guarantee may provide catastrophic protection, or it may provide rate of return smoothing. The guarantee can be set for a low rate of return so that it only provides "catastrophic" protection and rarely affects the rate of return received by the participant, or it can be set fairly high so that it provides rate of return smoothing over time.

The guarantee may be voluntary or mandatory. The voluntary or mandatory aspect can apply differently to employers and employees. For example, it could be voluntary for employers, but employers that provide it could make it mandatory for their employees. Alternatively, it could be mandated that employers offer a guarantee as an option, but it would be voluntary for employees to choose that option.

The guarantee may contain some risk that it will be changed. The guarantee may be viewed as an enduring promise or the guarantee may have a set period for which it applies, such as a year, with the expectation that it would be reset. The risk that the guarantee will be changed is greater the higher is the guarantee and the lower the capital backing the guarantee. It is also greater for fixed nominal guarantees than it is for real guarantees or guarantees that are set relative to an index because those guarantees have greater built in flexibility.

The guarantee can be provided by different institutions. It can be provided by the employer out of the employer's operating funds on a pay-as-you-go or funded basis. It can be provided by a DC pension fund through an associated reserve fund. It can be provided by an associated defined benefit (DB) fund, which operates as a reserve fund. It can be provided by a pension fund management company. It can be provided through the purchase of a guaranteed product from an insurance company or the government. In a voluntary system, the ultimate financing source of the guarantee may be the employee, who may finance the guarantee indirectly through receiving lower compensation in other respects to offset the cost of the guarantee.

Rate of Return Guarantees in Voluntary DC Plans Around the World

The format just developed is useful for classifying the types of rate of return guarantees provided across a sample of voluntary DC pension systems around the world. The survey covers the range of types of guarantees provided, but it is not exhaustive in terms of countries covered. The guarantee provided is discussed first, followed by a discussion of the financial backing for the guarantee. The countries are listed in alphabetical order.

Table 12-2 provides a list of these countries and the associated plan features of interest described below.

Belgium

Belgium has a draft law in process that would guarantee a return of 3.25 percent on employer contributions and 3.75 percent on employee contributions. It is expected that most contributions would be employer contributions. The guarantee would not be on annual rates of return, but rather it would apply over the period that the worker participated in the plan (Payne, 2002).

Brazil

The majority of pension assets in voluntary pension plans in Latin America is held in Brazil (Turner, 2002). Here, financial service providers offer pension funds that are available to any worker or firm, called "open" pension funds. These plans may be either group or individual plans. When they are DC plans, they have been required to provide a guaranteed real rate of return of 6 percent annually (Kane, 1998). A portion of the excess return that varies across plans is also paid into the worker's account. This portion increases with worker tenure up to 5 years on average and reaches a maximum of 50–75 percent. The excess return can be received as an annual payment to the worker or allowed to accumulate in the worker's account (World Bank, 2000). Thus, the guarantee g is for a 6 percent real rate of return, with the rate of return b the worker receives, being higher if the actual real rate of return r on the portfolio is higher:

$$g = 6\% \text{ real} \tag{12.5}$$

$$b = \max(6\% \text{ real}, 6\% \text{ real} + \alpha[r - 6\% \text{ real}]) \tag{12.6}$$

where α is the sharing rate (or participation rate) for rates of return above 6 percent real, which varies by worker tenure.

Fixed rate guarantees backed by financial market investments are limited by the rates of return available in the market. Because Brazil historically has had high real rates of return, it has been possible for pension funds to meet the real rate of return guarantee by investing in Brazilian securities markets. But real rates of return have declined recently, so these guarantees are no longer provided on new accounts.

Denmark

In Denmark, more than 80 percent of all employees are members of trade unions and they are covered by pensions that are mandated by labor agreements with employers (Herbertsson, Orszag, and Orszag, 2000). Danish

TABLE 12-2 Voluntary DC Plan Guarantees Surveyed, by Country

Country and Plan Design	*Noteworthy Features*
Brazil	
Open pension funds	Required real rate of return 6% per annum; portion of excess return paid into workers' account based on tenure; unavailable on new accounts
Denmark	
Occupational plans	Insurance contracts provide guaranteed rate with maximum set by government and further restricted by European Union; participant may receive excess yields above allocation to reserve funds; maximum guaranteed rate declining with fall in market interest rates
Germany	
Supplementary scheme	New system (2001) must guarantee nominal value of total principal contributed by retirement to receive favorable tax treatment
Existing occupational plans	Guaranteed minimum rate of return available in some plans
Japan	
New supplementary plans	New system (2001) mandates have three investment options, including guarantee of total principal contributed
New Zealand	
National Provident Fund	Primarily for employee of local governments, now closed to new entrants; fund credits member accounts with nominal return equal to 4% per annum financed through conservative asset allocation and use of reserve fund; government backs shortfall
Sweden	
Supplementary plans	Specific to blue-collar workers as negotiated by their trade union and employers; minimum guarantee is one option with the return set historically in a range of 3–4% by the Financial Supervisory Board
United Kingdom	
Investment option for DC plans	Investment banks and mutual funds (unit trusts) may offer funds that purchase put options to guarantee a certain return
Combined DB–DC plan	Worker receives the higher of the two benefits calculated

Source: Authors' compilation.

occupational pension plans are almost exclusively DC plans that purchase insurance contracts, which generally provide a guaranteed rate of return.

While the government sets a maximum on the guaranteed rate allowed, participants may receive a higher rate of return if the fund's investment experience permits paying such a rate. Excess yields above the guaranteed rate, however, are first allocated to reserve funds. The reserve funds are used to meet the guarantee when the rate of return falls below the guarantee level, and they also pay for bonuses above the guarantee level, depending on the reserve fund level. Following stock market declines precipitated by the terrorist attacks of September 11, 2001, the Danish insurance group PFA announced that its bonus reserves had been completely depleted and that it was no longer able to comply with the capital requirements under Danish law (Wheelan, 2001).

For many years, the maximum guarantee rate was set at 4.5 percent nominal for many years; it was lowered to 3.5 percent between 1994 and 1999; and since 1999, it has been 1.5 percent on new insurance policies. In 2001, the guaranteed rate on old policies was lowered from 4.5 percent to 2.0 percent (Jarvenpas, 2001). It was reduced because lower market interest rates have made it difficult to provide a higher guarantee. Contracts written before 1994 still provided the 4.5 percent guarantee through 2001. When the rate of return received on pension funds exceeded 4.5 percent, however, all participants received a similar rate. This created an inequity between holders of old and new contracts when the actual market rate is less than 4.5 percent.

The level of the guaranteed rate is restricted by the European Union (EU) 3 Directive on Life Assurance. That Directive limits an interest guarantee to no more than 60 percent of the return gross of taxes on government bonds. Because Denmark has a 26 percent tax on the interest income received by life insurance companies and pension funds, the low guaranteed rate provided to participants in the late 1990s could not be higher given the low market interest rates. The tax reduces the amount of investment income received that is available for paying to workers.

Germany

Germany launched a new system of supplementary pensions in 2001. In order to receive preferential tax treatment, these pensions must guarantee the nominal value of contributions at retirement. The guarantee is thus equivalent to a guarantee of a 0 percent nominal rate of return (see Maurer and Schlag, Chapter 9, this volume). Some pension funds in Germany provide a higher guarantee. For example, the pension for the construction industry, called ZukunftPlus, guarantees a minimum return of 3.5 percent (EIRO, 2001). Volkswagen has introduced a plan that guarantees a minimum return of 3 percent.

Japan

Japanese law permitted companies to offer DC plans in 2001 (see Clark and Mitchell, 2002). These require that workers have three investment options (IBIS, 2002). One of these options must provide a guarantee of the contributions made, as in Germany. This guarantee can be expressed as

$$g = 0\% \text{ rate of return} \tag{12.7}$$

$$b = \max(0\%, i) \tag{12.8}$$

New Zealand

The National Provident Fund in New Zealand has guaranteed to credit members' accounts with a minimum annual rate of return of 4 percent nominal. This fund was established primarily for the employees of local governments, and it is now closed to new members. To manage this guarantee, the Fund Board adopted an asset allocation strategy that is conservative by New Zealand standards. It has invested 60 percent in fixed interest bearing assets and cash, and 40 percent in equities and property.

The Board operates a reserve fund, as in Denmark, whereby in good investment years, part of the investment returns are placed in the reserve fund, which can be drawn on when investment returns fall below 4 percent. The objective is to build the reserve fund up to 10 percent of the members' account balances. The government acts as the ultimate guarantor if the pension fund exhausts its assets but still has benefit obligations.

Because of difficulty in meeting the guarantee due to lower market interest rates, the Board managing the National Provident Fund changed the guarantee to a minimum of a 4 percent nominal per year, compounded from April 1, 2000 to the date a member elects to receive his or her benefit from the scheme. The longer the period used to calculate the rate of return that is guaranteed, the less costly is the guarantee because a shortfall in some months can be compensated for by a higher return than the guarantee level in other months. With this guarantee, the actual rate received in any year could be less than 4 percent. Each year, the actual rate of return received is credited to the account.

When the worker exits the plan, the actual amount in the plan is compared to the amount that would have been in the worker's account if the worker had received a rate of 4 percent during the entire period. If the actual amount is less, the government will make up the difference. Thus, the guarantee and the actual rate received can be expressed as:

$$g = 4\% \text{ from April 1, 2000} \tag{12.9}$$

$$b = \max(g, i) \tag{12.10}$$

where i represents the actual average rate received since April 1, 2000. This change requires maintaining a shadow account for each member to track the minimum 4 percent rate. The annual statement received by the member shows the performance of the actual account and that of the 4 percent minimum account.

Sweden

Sweden's supplementary pension for blue-collar workers is negotiated between the national trade union confederation and the Swedish employers' confederation. Since 1998, it has offered a guaranteed rate of return as an option. That option is an insurance fund that provides a stable rate of return with a guaranteed minimum rate of return, which is set by the Financial Supervisory Board. The minimum rate of return is set in the range of 3–4 percent (EIRO, 1998).

United Kingdom

Private sector DC plans in the United Kingdom have been much less prevalent than DB plans, covering only 1 percent of employees in 1994–95 (Whitehouse, 1998). There has been some movement, of late, towards DC plans, with many DB plans being closed to new entrants (*The Economist*, 2002; Reid, 2002). As an investment option for DC plans, some UK investment banks or mutual funds (unit trusts) offer funds that purchase put options to guarantee their return (Valdés-Prieto, 1998). Barclay's Bank marketed a guaranteed rate of return fund using put options, but it has stopped doing so because of little demand for the product at the price it was able to offer it.

Some employers offer a DB and DC plan in combination, like a floor-offset plan in the United States. The worker receives the higher of the two benefits. If the DC plan receives a low rate of return, the worker will receive the benefit promised by the DB plan. Thus, the guarantee is that the worker will receive the benefit provided by the DB plan, with the worker receiving the benefit from the DC plan if that is higher:

$$g = \text{DB benefit} \tag{12.11}$$

$$b = \max(\text{DB benefit, DC benefit}) \tag{12.12}$$

A few companies, such as the pharmaceutical company Zeneca, offer a DC plan for younger employees but then allow them to transfer, at guaranteed rates, into a DB plan at some specified age.

As in a number of other countries, life insurance companies provide products with guaranteed rates of return in the United Kingdom. Government-issued inflation indexed bonds have been available for nearly two decades, and these can be used to provide a guaranteed real rate of return. Because of the availability of these bonds, participants in occupational DC plans can purchase insurance company products from at least nine insurance companies that provide a guaranteed real rate of return (Brown, Mitchell, and Poterba, 2000).

United States

In the United States, pension plans not governed by the ERISA, which covers most private sector plans, have greater latitude in structuring rate of return guarantees. These non-ERISA plans include church plans, plans for government employees, and non-qualified plans for top executives. This section provides information on some of the types of guarantees that are used in the United States. Table 12-3 provides a summary of these features.

Church Plans

Church plans and other non-profit plans in the United States are subject to fewer constraints than are most other private sector plans, since they are exempt from parts of the ERISA. A plan sponsored by the United Methodist Church offers a guarantee called the "base interest credit," the level of which is set annually by the Church's General Board of Pension and Health Benefits (General Board, 2002). The guarantee for this DC church plan is backed by a reserve fund financed by part of the rate of return received on the fund in years when the rate of return exceeds a fixed amount (6.5 percent for many years, reduced to 3 percent in 2001). If the actual rate of return exceeds the guaranteed rate of return, the excess rate of return goes into the reserve fund. Twice a year, the reserve fund is evaluated, and if it exceeds the target level, an extra distribution is made to the accounts of participants. The plan may credit a rate of return higher than the guarantee even if the actual return received in a year is lower if the reserve fund is sufficiently large. Thus, the guarantee and actual rate of return received are as follows:

$$g = 3\% \tag{12.13}$$

$$b = \max[3\%,\ 3\% \text{ plus bonus if reserve fund greater than minimum}] \tag{12.14}$$

The reserve fund consists of assets of the pension fund not allocated to participant accounts. They are assets that exceed the known obligations of the plan. The target level of the reserve fund is set as a percentage of the assets to be guaranteed and is higher, the greater is the volatility of the guaranteed assets. The reserve fund is set so that in most years it will be adequate to compensate for a fall in the value of the assets in the portfolio of the pension fund, though there is a small probability that the reserve fund will not be large enough to fund the guaranteed rate of return in a year.[4] In the Methodist Church plan, if the reserve fund is completely depleted, as happened in 2002, the plan can generate an unfunded liability. That situation arises when the reserve fund has been exhausted and the

TABLE 12-3 Descriptive List of Plans Surveyed in the United States

Tax Code/Sector and Plan Design	*Noteworthy Features of the Guarantee*
Church plans	
United Methodist Church	Base interest credit set annually by oversight board and backed by reserve fund financed by portion of returns in better-than-average years
YMCA section 401(a) plan	Guarantee set annually by board of trustees for following year and backed by reserve fund; if fund reserves warrant, trustees may declare extra interest credits to active participants and even retirees
Public sector retirement systems	
State of Indiana guaranteed fund	DC plan option available to all state employees; backed by DB plan in which all employees are required to participate; guaranteed under Indiana state law; principal growth based on interest credit rate determined each year by the board of trustees
Ohio STRS section 401(a) plan	New plan option (2001) offering a 7.75 return per annum backed by DB plan; initial entrants must remain in option for 5 years, whereas future participants may receive a higher or lower guaranteed return; excess returns on investment placed in the DB plan
TIAA traditional annuity	Primarily for college and university professors. Guarantees principal and specified interest rate, while offering opportunity for greater growth through dividends.
Texas' counties alternate plans	Investments in fixed income marketable securities provide guaranteed minimum nominal rate of 4% with workers and insurer sharing excess returns
Private for-profit sector plans	
Cash balance plans	Technically hybrid form (DB with DC features); provides fixed rate of return on notional individual accounts unrelated to underlying plan assets; available for both private and public sector plans.
Floor offset plans	Provide guaranteed minimum benefit by linking returns from DB and DC plan; often structured so that workers bear more of the financial risk

Source: Authors' compilation.

total asset amount credited to workers' accounts exceeds the total assets in the fund. This is not a problem for short periods, so long as the fund has sufficient assets to meet its cash flow requirements for benefit payments.

When a plan sets a fixed nominal interest rate as the guarantee rate, its ability to guarantee that rate is affected by the level of rates of return in financial markets, which is affected by the inflation rate. Thus, a higher level of guarantee has been deemed appropriate during periods of relatively high inflation and high nominal rates of return as compared to times of lower inflation. A nominal guarantee that is adjusted with respect to the level of financial market returns thus can resemble a real guarantee.

For younger workers, the effect on participant account balances of a rate of return guarantee provided by a reserve fund is unclear over the long term. The total credits paid to participants depend on the investment returns received by the pension plan. Over the short term, the guarantee does affect the level of credits, and it may be a particularly valuable feature for workers nearing retirement, who are assured that they will have a guaranteed minimum asset account balance at retirement.

The Young Men's Christian Association (YMCA), which meets the Internal Revenue Code requirements for a church plan, provides a different form of guarantee for its DC pension plan, one that also makes use of a reserve fund. Every November, the plan Board of Trustees meets to set the 1-year rate of return to be credited to participants' accounts for the following year. While the Methodist Church attempts to avoid changes in its guarantee, the YMCA guarantee varies from year to year. If the Board of Trustees decides that the Fund's reserves are sufficiently large, it can declare extra interest credits to active participants, in addition to the amount that it guarantees for the year, and it makes extra payments to retirees.

Reserve funds, such as those used by the Methodist Church and the YMCA, can allow for rate of return smoothing over time. The guarantee is financed by the participants of the pension fund, since the reserve fund in these two plans is made up entirely of investment earnings on the plan assets that have not been allocated to the accounts of individual workers. Nonetheless, in the corporate sector, reserve funds are not permitted under the ERISA. This is because the law stipulates that all investment earnings must be allocated to the accounts of individual participants.

US State Retirement Systems

Public sector plans in the United States are exempt from many of the substantive requirements of ERISA which provides them greater opportunity to offer DC guarantees. One option available to public employees of the State of Indiana is a guaranteed return tied to the actuarially assumed rate used for the associated DB fund, with the guarantee (after fees and expenses) fixed at 8.25 percent (Turner, 2000). The Guaranteed Fund is backed by the funds of the DB plan in which all state employees are required to participate. The principal amount of an investment in the DC plan does not fluctuate but grows based upon an interest crediting rate determined annually by the Board of Trustees.[5] This investment option is guaranteed under Indiana law, and the crediting rate is applied to the balance of the member's pension account at the end of each fiscal year. Guaranteed Fund investments include bonds, large capitalization stocks, small capitalization stocks, and other types of diversified investments. The guarantee is one of several options that workers participating in the plans can select.

Along similar lines, the DC (401(a)) plan of the Ohio State Teachers' Retirement System (STRS) in 2001 began providing a guaranteed 7.75 percent annual rate of return backed by the system's DB plan (Kennedy and Jacobius, 2001). This total guaranteed return choice is one of the options provided by the plan. Participants choosing the option in future years may be offered a higher or lower guaranteed return. The guarantee is offered to participants who leave their money in the fund for 5 years. Workers who withdraw from the option before 5 years must pay a 10 percent penalty. Thus, the guarantee and penalty provide an incentive for workers not to change their investment options and, instead, to stay in the plan for at least 5 years. The asset allocation of the Ohio investment portfolio parallels that of the system's $55 billion DB plan. Shortfalls are to be made up from the funds of the DB plan, and any excess must be placed in the DB plan. This approach combines a hedge and insurance. The hedge aspect is that the workers give up returns above the guaranteed level in exchange for not getting returns below that level. The insurance aspect is provided by the DB plan, on the view that there will be sufficient funds to pay the guaranteed rate of return. Since workers are free to choose this option or alternative options, those choosing the option presumably pay no implicit (and clearly no explicit) insurance premium.

TIAA-CREF (the Teachers Insurance and Annuity Association College Retirement Equities Fund) offers the TIAA Traditional Annuity. TIAA-CREF covers 12,000 nonprofit institutions, including government and private universities, other educational institutions, and some museums. The TIAA traditional annuity guarantees the participant's principal and a specified interest rate, plus it offers the opportunity for a higher return through dividends.

Government employees of three Texas counties—Galveston, Mattagorda, and Brazora—withdrew from Social Security in 1981.[6] These counties replaced the Social Security program benefits for their workers with a system of individual DC accounts known as the Alternate Plans.[7] These plans offer employees a guaranteed minimum nominal rate of return of 4 percent, with workers and the insurance company sharing returns above that benchmark. To do this, managers of the Alternate Plans purchased Group Fixed

Annuity Contracts from a private insurance company, the American United Life Insurance Company. The portfolios holding plan contributions are invested only in fixed-rate marketable securities (government bonds, corporate bonds, and preferred stocks) as well as bank certificates of deposit (GAO, 1999). The annual interest rate earned on Galveston's investments averaged 4.6 percent real, or 8.6 percent nominal, for the years 1981–98 (Wilson, 1999).

Guarantees in the Private For-Profit Sector

US private sector employers have provided DC guarantees financed through the purchase of insurance products. These offer participants relatively safe low-yield investments which are ultimately covered by some type of state solvency system, but these funds typically cap the amount of coverage. Stable-value instruments include guaranteed investment contracts (GICs) offered by insurance companies, as well as banking investment contracts (BICs) offered by banks. BICs marketed by the banking industry are insured by the Federal Deposit Insurance Corporation (FDIC), whereas GICs are covered by state-regulated solvency funds. A 1992 survey of large employers sponsoring 401(k) plans in the United States found that over half of the assets of these plans were invested in GICs (Wyatt, 1993). A more recent study found a lower prevalence of these contracts, with 20 percent of thrift and savings plans in medium and large private establishments offering GICs as an option for the investment of employee contributions (US Department of Labor, 1999).

In the United States, cash balance plans provide a fixed rate of return on the individuals account, but are financed like DB plans. With a cash balance plan, workers have an individual account but it is not funded. Instead, the worker's account is credited with the contribution made on behalf of the worker and the guaranteed rate of return; it is unrelated to the underlying assets held by the plan. These plans are hybrids in that they have features of both DB and DC plans, and are legally DB plans for solvency fund purposes.

Floor offset plans are hybrid plans that provide a guaranteed minimum benefit. A floor offset plan is actually a combination of a DB plan linked with a DC plan. Often, the two are structured so that retirees tend to receive only a benefit from the DC plan, but if that plan fails to provide the guaranteed minimum benefit, the DB plan makes up the difference. Floor offset plans are generally structured so that the worker bears most of the financial market risk, with the floor plan taking over only in the case of a serious market downturn (Robinson and Small, 1993).

Evaluation

In most cases, guarantees in voluntary DC plans offer fixed nominal rates of return over a calendar year. In some countries, the guarantees are provided by insurance companies, while in other cases, the guarantees are backed by a reserve fund or an associated DB plan. In several instances, guarantees of a fixed nominal rate have had to be revised to a lower rate because of declining rates of return in capital markets. There have also been cases where reserve funds have proved to be inadequate and have been exhausted, creating unfunded liabilities for the guarantors.[8]

The rate of return guarantees discussed would appear to have relatively few behavioral effects on workers, since typically the participant does not determine investments in his pension account, reducing the potential for moral hazard. The guarantee could affect the extent that workers take on risk in their nonpension investments, since it makes their investment in their DC plan relatively low risk. In terms of labor market effects, guarantees may affect the timing of job change and retirement. This is because workers can have greater certainty as to the level of their account balance in the future and thus are better able to plan for a specific retirement date.

Defined contribution plans are growing in importance in retirement income systems around the world. Thus, it is important to investigate ways that these plans might be improved. Rate of return guarantees are one approach to reduce the financial market risk that workers bear in them. The rate of return guarantees used by voluntary plans may provide useful experience for structuring mandatory DC systems, as well as for reform of voluntary DC systems.

Notes

[1] The ERISA requires most private-sector retirement plans in the United States to satisfy minimum coverage, participation, vesting, funding, and fiduciary requirements as a means of improving retirement income security for plan participants.

[2] An earlier survey of rate of return guarantees for mandatory DC plans is described in Turner and Rajnes (2001).

[3] See Turner (2001).

[4] In the Chilean mandatory pension system, if the reserve fund of a pension fund management company is completely exhausted, the company is declared insolvent and is disbanded (Gillion et al., 2000).

[5] See Public Employees' Retirement Fund of Indiana (2002) at <www.state.in.us/perf/glossary/index.html>.

[6] Before the Social Security Act was amended in 1983, state and local governments that had previously participated in Social Security were permitted to opt out.

[7] The Alternate Plans are a secondary source of retirement income for these workers in the three Texas counties. Their primary retirement benefit is provided under the Texas County and District Retirement System, another DC plan, which also provides disability and survivor benefits (GAO, 1999).

[8] One important area not addressed in this chapter involves the costing of these guarantees. For recent research see Hansen and Miltersen (2002), Jensen and Sorensen (2000), Feldstein and Ranguelova (2000), and Lachance and Mitchell (Chapter 8, this volume).

References

Clark, Robert and Olivia S. Mitchell. 2002. "Strengthening Employment-Based Pensions in Japan." Pension Research Council Working Paper No. 2002–1. The Wharton School, University of Pennsylvania. <prc.wharton.upenn.edu/prc/prc.html>.

The Economist. 2002. "Survey: A Matter of Definition." February 16.

European Industrial Relations Observatory On-line (EIRO). 2001. "First Sectoral Agreement on Private Pensions Signed in Construction." April. <www.eiro.eurofound.ie/2001/04/inbrief/DE0104216N.html>.

Feldstein, Martin and Elena Ranguelova. 2000. "Accumulated Pension Collars: A Market Approach to Reducing the Risk of Investment-Based Social Security Reform." NBER Working Paper 7861, August.

— 1998. "New Scheme Enables Employees to Choose How Their Pension Contributions are Invested." November. <www.eiro.eurofound.ie/1998/11/feature/SE9811120F.html>.

General Accounting Office (GAO). 1999. "Social Security Reform: Experience of the Alternate Plans in Texas." GAO/HEHS-99-31, February.

General Board of Pension and Health Benefits of the United Methodist Church. 2002. On-line documents available at <www.gnophb.org>.

Gillion, Colin, John Turner, Clive Bailey, and Denis Latulippe. 2000. *Social Security Pensions: Development and Reform.* Geneva, Switzerland: International Labor Office.

Hansen, Mette and Kristian R. Miltersen. 2002. "Minimum Rate of Return Guarantees: The Danish Case." Paper Presented at the Quantitative Methods in Finance Conference. Sydney, Australia, April 28.

Herbertsson, Tryggvi Thor, J. Michael Orszag, and Peter R. Orszag. 2000. "Retirement in the Nordic Countries: Prospects and Proposals for Reform." Prepared for the Nordic Council of Ministers, May 10.

Indiana Public Employees' Retirement Fund. 2002. On-line document describing the Guarantee Fund option at <www.state.in.us/perf/glossary/index.html>.

International Benefits Information Service. (IBIS). 2002. "Japan: First of the Defined Contribution Plans Are Up and Running." *IBIS Report* 3(2).

Jarvenpas, Perttu. 2001. "Denmark's DKr250bn ATP fund set for overhaul." *I&PE Newsline,* May 15. <www.ipe-newsline.com/article.asp?article=11335>.

Jensen, Bjarne Astrup and Carsten Sorensen. 2000. "Paying for Minimum Interest Rate Guarantees: Who Should Compensate Who?" SSRN Electronic Library. November 3.

Kane, Cheikh. 1998. "Reforming the Brazilian Pension System." In *Do Options Exist? The Reform of Pension and Health care Systems in Latin America,* eds. Maria Amparo Cruz Saco and Carmelo Mesa-Lago. Pittsburgh: University of Pittsburgh Press, pp. 293–309.

Kennedy, Mike and Arlene Jacobius. 2001. "New Ohio Teachers' 401(k) Plan Promises a 7.75% Rate of Return." *Pensions & Investments,* June 11: 3, 34.

Lachance, Marie-Eve and Olivia S. Mitchell. This volume. "Understanding Individual Account Guarantees."

Maurer, Raimond and Christian Schlag. This volume. "Money-Back Guarantees in Individual Account Pensions: Evidence from the German Pension Reform."

Payne, Beatrix. 2002. "Belgian Plan Participants Will Get Guaranteed Returns on Investments." *Pensions and Investments,* March 18: 241.

Reid, Dickon. 2002. "Less than 40% of UK DB schemes remain open." *I&PE-Newsline*, June 18. On-line news service available at <www.ipe-newsline.com>.

Robinson, Patti and William S. Small. 1993. "The Floor Offset Retirement Plan: Versatile and Tested, It Merits More Attention." *Compensation and Benefits Review* 25(May–June): 25–29.

Turner, John. 2000. "Guaranteed Defined Contribution Plans." *Contingencies* July–August: 77–80.

—— 2001. "The Design of Rate of Return Guarantees for Defined Contribution Plans." *Journal of Pensions Management*, September: 55–63.

—— 2002. "Extending Pension Coverage in a Middle Income Country: The Case of Brazil." *Journal of Aging and Social Policy* (forthcoming).

—— and Rajnes, David. 2001. "Rate of Return Guarantees for Mandatory Defined Contribution Plans." *International Social Security Review*, October–December: 49–66.

US Department of Labor, Bureau of Labor Statistics. 1999. *Employee Benefits in Medium and Large Private Establishments 1997*. US Government Printing Office, September.

Valdés-Prieto, Salvador. 1998. "Risks in Pensions and Annuities: Efficient Designs." Human Development Network, Social Protection Group. Washington DC: The World Bank, February.

Wyatt, Watson. 1993. "Investing for the Future in Defined Contribution Plans." *Wyatt Comparison*. Washington, May.

Wheelan, Hugh. 2001. "Danish Pension Insurers in Bonus Reserve Wipeout." *IP&E Newsline*, September 28. <www.ipe-newsline.com/article.asp?article=11972>.

Whitehouse, Edward. 1998. "Pension Reform in Britain." World Bank Social Protection Discussion Paper No. 9810. June.

Wilson, Theresa M. 1999. "Opting Out: The Galveston Plan and Social Security." Pension Research Council Working Paper No. 99–22. Available on-line at <prc.wharton.upenn.edu/prc/prc.html>.

World Bank. 2000. "Brazil: Critical Issues in Social Security." Report No. 19641-BR. Brazil Country Management Unit, Latin American and the Caribbean Region. Washington, June 19.

Chapter 13

Securitized Risk Instruments as Alternative Pension Fund Investments

J. David Cummins and Christopher M. Lewis

Financial innovation has dramatically expanded the variety of assets available to investors over the past two decades. Assets that formerly were held on-balance-sheet by banks, insurers, other financial institutions, and industrial firms, are now actively traded in securities markets. Moreover, the types of cash flows that are traded in financial markets have expanded significantly beyond traditional categories and now encompass many new asset-backed securities and derivative instruments.[1] Other chapters in this volume have focused on the integration of capital market instruments into traditional pension and annuity contracts as a means of expanding *individual investor* investment opportunities (Maurer and Schlag, Chapter 9; Turner and Rajnes, Chapter 12; Vetzal, Forsyth, and Windcliff, Chapter 10; Walliser, Chapter 11) and the difficulty that many individual investors have in understanding these contracts (Bodie, Chapter 2). This chapter focuses on the potential opportunity that these new securities offer for more sophisticated *institutional investors* charged with optimally investing pension fund assets on behalf of individual investors.

The expansion in the number and types of assets traded in the marketplace provides unprecedented opportunities for institutional investors to improve the risk-return performance of their pension portfolios. Securities have been introduced to trade the risk in "exotic underlyings," including catastrophic property losses (CAT bonds and options), temperature risk (weather derivatives), and other unconventional risks. Yet, many of the new securities are unfamiliar and complex, and they may expose investors to risks that are not fully understood.[2] As a result, investment managers, concerned about fiduciary responsibilities and beating market index benchmarks, have a disincentive to take positions in these assets unless they can be convinced that they clearly help their portfolio performance. With little price transparency and few tools for analyzing the risks inherent in the new assets,

The authors would like to thank John Kalamarides, Olivia Mitchell, and Kent Smetters for helpful comments on the chapter. The authors accept responsibility for all errors or omissions.

investment managers often pass on these securities and forego the material diversification benefits offered by these structures.

The purpose of this chapter is to help resolve some of the uncertainty associated with the innovative securitized products available in today's financial markets by providing information on some of the most promising new assets that have emerged from the securitization process. We outline the characteristics of these new securities, analyze their advantages and disadvantages, and provide a simplified approach for valuing these deals in the context of the familiar linear capital asset pricing model (CAPM). We focus primarily on asset-backed securities (ABS), which are the securitized products most likely to be of interest to institutional investors. We also comment on some particularly promising non-asset-backed derivative securities recently introduced.

Our primary focus is to evaluate ABS from the perspective of enhancing portfolio diversification within the pension fund, as opposed to developing new hedging instruments for pension liability risks. From an asset-liability management perspective, our analysis can be generalized to incorporate the purchase of structured products that "hedge" the risk of pension liabilities or pension asset concentrations. The practical problem of analyzing pension fund hedging strategies with structured notes is that, short of a few emerging mortality-linked notes that may be used to hedge pension mortality risk, few structured products offer acceptable hedging benefits for individual defined benefit pension funds as currently structured. Thus, while our approach is sufficiently general to incorporate liability-motivated structured note purchases, we defer a formal discussion of pension fund hedging strategy to future research.

Background on the Development of Securitization

Securitization involves the repackaging and trading of cash flows that traditionally would have been held on-balance-sheet by financial intermediaries or industrials. Securitizations generally involve the agreement between two parties to trade cash flow streams to manage and diversify risk and/or to take advantage of arbitrage opportunities. The cash flow streams to be traded often involve contingent payments as well as more predictable components that may be subject to credit and other types of counterparty risk. Securitization provides a mechanism whereby contingent and deterministically scheduled cash flow streams arising out of a transaction can be unbundled and traded as separate financial instruments that appeal to different classes of investors. In addition to facilitating risk management, securitization transactions also add to the liquidity of financial markets, replacing previously untraded on-balance-sheet assets with tradable financial instruments.

Securitization has been driven by both demand and supply factors. Demand-driven securitization occurs when new risks emerge or when existing risks become more significant, rendering traditional hedging techniques inadequate or obsolete. For example, the increasing levels and volatility of interest rates during the late 1970s led to a demand by banks to liquidate the mortgage loans on their balance sheets. Precedent for this type of securitization had arisen during the late 1970s and early 1980s when government institutions such as the Federal National Mortgage Association began to issue securities backed by pools of mortgage loans. These mortgage-backed assets were initially unattractive to many investors due to prepayment risk. A breakthrough in mortgage securitization was the development of collateralized mortgage obligations (CMOs) that unbundled the cash flows arising from mortgage portfolios and repackaged the cash flows into various tranches of bonds with different risk characteristics. This process provided securities with greatly reduced prepayment risk that appealed to relatively risk averse investors as well as riskier tranches that appealed to investors willing to take more risk to earn higher returns. As a result, the market for US agency mortgage backed securities grew from about $100 billion in 1980 to more than $2.8 trillion by 2001.[3]

The emergence of new risks and the increasing magnitude of existing risks on the demand side have led to a significant expansion in the markets for interest rate, foreign exchange, commodity price, and credit derivatives. The increasing property exposure in geographical areas prone to property catastrophes such as hurricanes and earthquakes has led to the development of securities designed to finance catastrophic risk, including CAT bonds and options, which are discussed below. The exposure of energy companies and other firms to risk from temperature fluctuations has led to the development of an active market in weather-linked securities. Other innovations, such as products that securitize cash flows from life insurance and annuities, also have begun to emerge.

Supply side factors also have influenced the growth of the market for securitized financial instruments. The development of modern financial theory, including option pricing models and models of the term structure of interest rates, provided the basis for standardizing the pricing of many financial products, facilitating the development of liquid markets. Simultaneously, rapid advances in computing and communications technologies have enabled financial engineers to develop sophisticated new products at an unprecedented rate.

Although the market for securitized financial products has experienced remarkable advances, there are still obstacles to be overcome in order for the more innovative and complex securitizations to be fully successful. To a significant extent, the ability of markets to supply securitized financial products has outrun the existing demand. In part, this is due to a lack of

TABLE 13-1 Asset-Backed Securities: New Issuance Market Share by Asset Type, 2001 (Volume in $ US Billions)

Asset Type	*$ Volume*	*Number of Deals*	*Market Share (%)*
Residential mortgage	142.9	374.0	18.9
Commercial mortgage	97.0	171.0	12.8
Credit cards	80.4	127.0	10.6
Corporate bonds	76.0	223.0	10.0
Sub-prime mortgages	65.2	134.0	8.6
Non-US home loans	59.9	123.0	7.9
Auto loans (prime)	52.0	57.0	6.9
Home-equity loans	38.5	78.0	5.1
Auto loans (sub-prime)	21.7	34.0	2.9
Equipment leases	17.0	53.0	2.2
Other	105.8	260.0	14.0
Total	756.4	1634	100.0

Source: Authors' computations derived from asset-backed alert <www.abalert.com>.

understanding by investors of the parameters of the available contracts and the role that such contracts can play in improving portfolio performance. However, there is also uncertainty about how to price the new products, and there is still perhaps insufficient standardization within some of the new classes of securities to permit the development of more liquid markets. These problems can be expected to recede as issuers and investors gain experience with the contracts and the market continues to mature.

During 2001, more than $756 billion in ABS was issued worldwide, a 34 percent increase over the $566 billion in ABS issued during 2000. An additional $55 billion in ABS was issued during January and February of 2002. While almost $600 billion of the ABS issued in 2001 was placed in the United States and benchmarked to US collateral, non-US ABS activity represents a growing share of overall issuance—accounting for approximately 21 percent of issuance volume in 2001.[4]

Not surprisingly, a majority of the new issuance volume, both in the United States and overseas, continues to be backed by traditional assets. This is shown in Table 13-1, which reports the 2001 worldwide ABS issuance by asset type. The securitization of receivables backed by real estate, credit cards, automobile loans, and corporate bonds, continues to represent over 80 percent of all new issuance in terms of dollar volume (83 percent) and number of deals (81 percent):

1. The securitization of real estate assets, including prime residential and commercial mortgages, sub-prime mortgages, non-US mortgages,

home-equity loans and home-equity lines of credit (i.e. HELOC's), represented over half (53 percent) of all securitization activity in 2001 ($403 billion).

2. The securitization of credit card assets was $80.4 billion or 10.6 percent of new issuance volume in 2001, maintaining a relatively constant market share despite the deteriorating credit conditions in the US economy and the problems faced by large issuers like Providian Financial.
3. The securitization of corporate bonds through collateralized debt obligation (CDOs) or collateralized loan obligations (CLOs) dropped in 2001 to $76 billion or 10.1 percent of the total issuance volume—down from $78.5 billion (13.9 percent) in 2000.
4. Automobile loan securitizations totaled $73.7 billion in 2001 for a market share of just under 10 percent. Issuance volume in 2000 was $67.3 billion, or just under 12 percent of the market.

Given the size of the market for traditional ABS, pension investment managers usually have access to mark-to-market or mark-to-model pricing, to value structures backed by traditional asset collateral. As such, pension fund managers have a level of comfort in dealing with traditional ABS. The focus of this chapter, however, is non-traditional ABS and innovative non-asset backed products that have been introduced and where fund manager familiarity is often less certain.

The Non-traditional ABS Market

How should pension fund managers evaluate non-traditional ABS securities? With names like Act-of-God bonds, Bowie bonds, Tobacco bonds, and Kelvin Weather Derivatives, these structures have often gained considerable public attention and interest in the market. Moreover, non-traditional ABS represents a growing share of the overall ABS market. According to Standard & Poor's (S&P), non-traditional ABS (as defined herein), which represented 15 percent of the public ABS market in the United States in 1995, had grown to 25 percent of the public ABS market by 2001 (Hu, Coyne, and Elengical, 2002).

What are the risk-return dynamics of these securities? Are non-traditional ABS an appropriate investment for pension fund managers? To address these questions, we must first understand the structure of non-traditional ABS, and then develop the tools needed to measure the risk-return dynamics of these securities in the context of how pension fund managers measure risk.

While often equipped with catchy marketing names, non-traditional ABS are structured using the same format as traditional ABS. In any ABS structure, a company that is exposed to the risks associated with an uncertain set of cash flows is looking to sell some or all of these risks to third-party investors

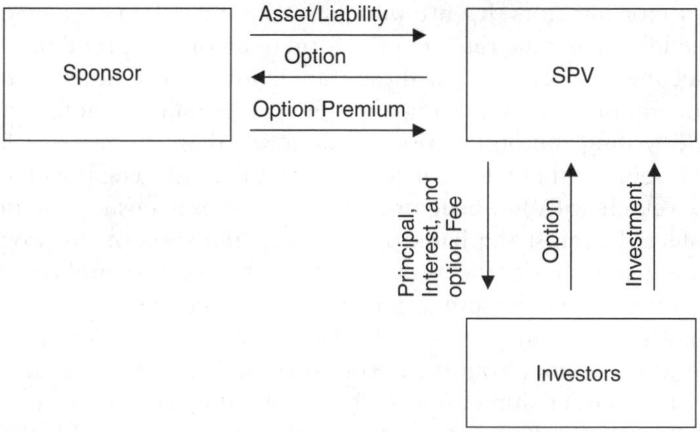

Figure 13-1. Basic ABS structure. *Source*: Authors' derivation.

in exchange for the risk-adjusted return available on these cash flows. The motivations of the seller can range from regulatory arbitrage, to the need to manage a concentration of risk on the balance sheet, to sourcing a lower cost of funds for origination activity.

For example, the market for mortgage-backed securities developed in the late 1970s and early 1980s as banks and thrifts—caught in the vice of high funding costs and low yielding long-term mortgage assets—explored options for reducing asset concentrations and lowering the funding costs associated with mortgage origination. In a similar fashion, foreign competition and record delinquencies on automobile loans enticed the automobile companies in the early to mid-1980s to use the automobile installment credit as collateral and issue securitized car loans to obtain a cheaper source of funding (Fink, 1998). Credit card issuers followed the same model, providing banks and financial companies with a lower cost alternative to retail funding.

In the non-traditional ABS market, the range of underlying asset types and risks can vary widely, and each deal merits individual attention. However, as depicted in Figure 13-1, the basic structure for most ABS and structured notes is the same. The sponsor of the program is looking to transfer a risk associated with an asset or a liability to private sector investors. The underlying asset could be the right to future income streams, the value of a loan portfolio, or an insurance portfolio. The corresponding risk that the sponsor is looking to transfer, which can be viewed as a financial option, could be the risk of economic downturns on cash flows, credit deterioration in a loan portfolio, or catastrophic property claims from an insurance portfolio. In each of these cases, the sponsor is looking to sell these risks or options to private sector investors that are willing to take the risk in exchange for an enhanced fixed-income return in the form of an option premium.

The economic rationale for these transactions is as follows: If investors value the option as a diversifying asset, the risk premium that they demand for underwriting the option risk will be lower than the internal funding costs of a sponsor that has a concentration of this risk. The use of a special purpose vehicle (SPV) in structuring the deal helps to ensure that investors are protected against the bankruptcy risk of the sponsor, to provide for transparent servicing of the assets/liabilities, to structure and collateralize various tranches of debt, and to provide tax and accounting benefits to the sponsor. All of these functions tend to be deal-specific. In addition, the SPV insulates the investors from the agency costs and risks of the issuing firm's other operations, creating a "pure play" in the subject cash flows.

For a pension fund manager to evaluate a non-traditional ABS, therefore, he must address three core questions:

1. Do I understand the dynamics of the risk being transferred in the deal?
2. What is the expected value of the loss being transferred and am I being compensated for this expected loss?
3. Is this a diversifying asset in my portfolio and what is a fair risk premium for underwriting this exposure?

To address these issues across a wide variety of asset classes would require an entire volume. To keep the discussion manageable and to provide maximum value-added for institutional investors, we instead review the process of evaluating non-traditional ABS in the context of the main growth areas in asset-backed securitization.

Important Types of Non-Traditional ABS

An important challenge in the study of non-traditional ABS is that these new structures are primarily privately placed, either directly or as a US Rule 144a security.[5] As such, obtaining a full list of transactions and obtaining accurate information on any one transaction is difficult.[6] Therefore, we focus here on evaluating the five broad categories of non-traditional ABS that have garnered the most attention in the market: credit linked notes, insurance linked notes, aircraft securitizations, stranded cost securitizations, and future cash flow securitizations.

Credit-Linked Notes

As the use of credit derivatives to buy and sell credit risk has expanded over the past 5–8 years, some institutions have started issuing instruments that combine traditional fixed income securities with an embedded credit derivative within the same structured note. While these credit-linked notes have come in many forms, the basic premise behind the structure is simple: a credit-linked note provides investors with an indirect opportunity to invest in the return associated with a particular entity's credit risk performance.

One of the principal drivers of the market for credit-linked notes is investor demand for bypassing regulatory restrictions on credit risk underwriting and risk-taking. For example, participation in the bank loan market is restricted to regulated financial institutions within the United States. Therefore, until the creation of the credit-linked note market, investors in other industries could not diversify their risk exposure to the bank credit market. With the advent of credit-linked notes, a wide variety of institutional investors now can invest in bank loan credit risk.

There are two basic forms of credit-linked notes (Das, 1998):

1. Traditional structured notes where the coupon or principal is indexed to the credit risk performance of an underlying reference credit. These traditional structures include a variety of product variations, including returns based on the total return of the reference credit, returns based on the spread between the reference credit and a market return (e.g. AA bond curve), and a return indexed to a credit default event.
2. Synthetic bonds that entail the use of embedded credit derivative structures to replicate the fixed income security characteristics and credit exposure of the underlying reference credit. Under this type of structure, the investor receives a fixed income return provided that the reference credit does not experience a "credit event" (e.g. bankruptcy). However, if the reference credit does have a default event, the investor's return would be adjusted to reflect the recovery value of the reference credit's debt.

To illustrate, an investor in a *total return credit-linked note* is essentially entering into two simultaneous transactions (see Figure 13-2). First, the investor invests in a floating rate note (FRN) indexed to a market return like the London-Interbank-Offer Rate (LIBOR). Then, at the same time, the investor matches the terms of the FRN with a total return swap whereby the investor pays the FRN LIBOR and earns a rate of interest tied to the underlying reference credit. As such, the return earned by the investor matches the total return associated with the reference credit. In simple terms, the investor swaps his/her floating rate return for the return of the reference credit.

Credit spread structured notes mirror the total return structured notes with the exception that the investor enters into a credit derivative linked only to the basis risk between the reference credit and an underlying index. As such, the investor is only exposed to the relative credit performance of an underlying reference credit to the market index. In both the total return swap and credit-spread structures, the investor is able to leverage his return and to short the underlying index.

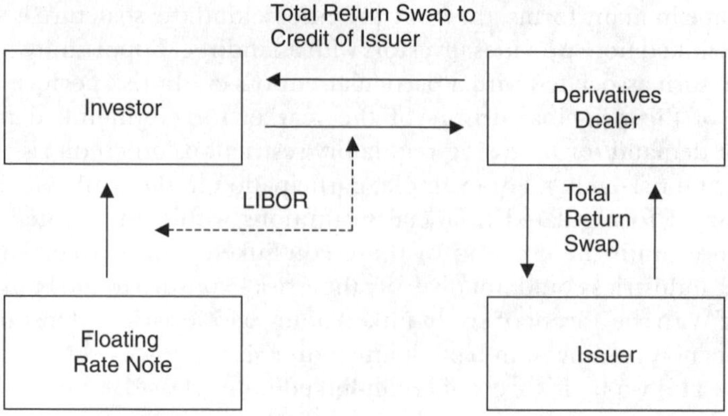

Figure 13-2. Credit-linked note. *Source*: Authors' derivation.

In a *credit-linked note with a credit default swap*, the investor purchases a portfolio of assets and then simultaneously enters into a credit default swap agreement with respect to a referenced credit asset. In this case, the return to the investor matches the portfolio of assets held in the trust of the structured note trust until such time that the reference credit experiences a credit default event. When this occurs, the trust has the right to substitute the "impaired" debt of the reference credit for the assets in the trust and the investor earns a return linked to the defaulted reference credit.

For example, in one credit default swap structure, investors ostensibly were investing in the bonds of the large California utility providers (i.e. trust assets). Actually, the structured note included a credit default swap whereby a default by a reference credit (i.e. Company ABC) would trigger the substitution of the defaulted company's debt into the trust in exchange for the utility company's debt–which presumably would be liquidated to help cover losses at the defaulted company. As such, the investors' return was based on the return of the utility company debt up until the occurrence of a reference credit default, at which time the returns switched over to the return on the impaired reference credit assets. Of course, if the reference credit never defaulted the investors could earn a return equal to the utility companies' debt plus the option premium for underwriting Company ABC's credit risk.

Synthetic bond structures are designed to allow an investor to replicate an investment in a given company's debt instrument without having to purchase that company's debt. For example, JP Morgan structured a synthetic bond structured note that paid investors a return (Treasury + 65 basis points (bps)) that was designed to replicate the return on WalMart's debt. The advantage of purchasing a synthetic bond, as opposed to the direct purchase of WalMart's debt, is that WalMart never actually had to issue any debt to be purchased. In addition, the investor can obtain structuring advantages (e.g. enhanced credit rating of the structure) through the design of the structured note (Das, 1998).

Another good illustration of the value of synthetic bond structures and credit default swap structured notes, is the Sparc's Trust that was issued in the late 1990s. Under this structure, investors were able to purchase a pool of assets with a credit default swap linked to Uruguayan debt. For investors wanting to take a long position on Uruguayan debt but not having the international infrastructure to support cross-border investments, this structured security provided an ideal investment vehicle with a return of LIBOR + 250 bps.

To date, a large share of the credit-linked note market has focused on bank loans and public debt securities. However, there is growing interest in formulating a secondary market for emerging market trade receivables (EMTRs), which are letters of credit supporting international trade flows. To date, EMTR securitizations have been limited to more traditional bank-specific portfolios sales. However, growing interest on the part of exporters and export financiers should help push this market forward in the near future.

Insurance-Linked Notes: Property-Liability Risks

Paralleling the securitization of bank loans, several types of insurance-linked securities have been developed over the years. Many of these have been designed to provide additional risk capital to finance property catastrophes from natural hazards such as hurricanes and earthquakes. The development of securitized instruments linked to property catastrophes was primarily motivated by demand side considerations. Hurricane Andrew in 1992 and the Northridge earthquake in 1994 resulted in $30 billion in insured property losses and led insurers to drastically increase their estimates of potential losses from property catastrophes. In fact, these dramatic events were the most prominent manifestation of a sharp increase in the frequency and severity of catastrophic loss events that began in the 1980s. During the period 1970–86, the number of catastrophes averaged about 35 per year. Beginning in 1987, however, the number of catastrophes increased sharply, and from 1990 to 2001, the number of catastrophes exceeded 100 in every year (Swiss Re, 2002).[7] From 1970 to 1986, insured losses from natural catastrophes exceeded $5 billion in only 1 year, and the average annual catastrophe loss for this period was $2.6 billion. From 1987 to 2001, however, insured catastrophe losses exceeded $8 billion in all but 2 years, and catastrophe losses averaged $14.3 billion per year (Cummins, Lalonde, and Phillips, 2002*a*).

As catastrophic losses continued to rise, it became increasingly apparent that international reinsurance markets were not adequate for financing this type of loss. Insurance and reinsurance markets operate most successfully in diversifying relatively small, frequent events, but are not well equipped to handle large, infrequent events. Moreover, events that are large relative to the capacity of the insurance and reinsurance industries are small relative to securities markets. For example, the $100 billion "Big One" in Florida or California would represent approximately 75 percent of the equity of the global reinsurance industry but would amount to less than half of 1 percent of the value of stocks and bonds traded on US securities markets. Moreover, because the occurrence of natural catastrophes is not linked to economic events, catastrophe-linked securities would be "zero-beta" assets and hence very valuable to investors for diversification (Cantor, Cole, and Sandor, 1996; Litzenberger, Beaglehole, and Reynolds, 1996). These factors led to the recognition that securitization is likely to offer the most logical and efficient solution to the catastrophic loss financing problem.

CAT-risk securities also are interesting because there is no traded underlying asset or commodity that can be used to trigger payment under the securities. In the absence of a traded underlying asset, CAT-risk securities have been structured to pay-off on three types of variables: issuer-specific catastrophe loss criteria, insurance-industry catastrophe loss indices, and *parametric* indices based on the physical characteristics of catastrophic events. The choice of a triggering variable involves a trade-off between moral hazard and basis risk (Doherty, 1997). Securities based on insurer-specific (or hedger-specific) losses have low basis risk but expose investors to moral hazard, whereas securities based on industry loss indices or parametric triggers greatly reduce or eliminate moral hazard but expose hedgers to basis risk.[8] Additionally, index-linked securities are more easily standardized than issue-specific instruments, thus providing the potential for the development of a more liquid market in index-linked contracts.

The first catastrophe insurance derivative contracts were introduced by the Chicago Board of Trade (CBOT), which began listing catastrophic loss futures contracts in 1992. The CBOT contracts eventually evolved into option spreads that settled on insurance-industry loss indices compiled by Property Claims Services (PCS), an insurance industry statistical agent.[9] Although the CBOT options are no longer traded due to low trading volume (mainly due to lack of interest in the options by insurers), they represent an important innovation and are likely to provide the model for exchange traded options that almost certainly will be developed in future years.[10]

Currently, catastrophe bonds account for the greatest amount of risk capital raised in the catastrophe securities market. Unlike the CBOT options, the CAT bonds issued to date are ABS analogous to the credit-linked products discussed above. The first successful CAT bond was an $85 million issue by Hannover Re in 1994 (Swiss Re, 2001). The first CAT bond issued by a non-financial firm, occurring in 1999, covers earthquake losses in

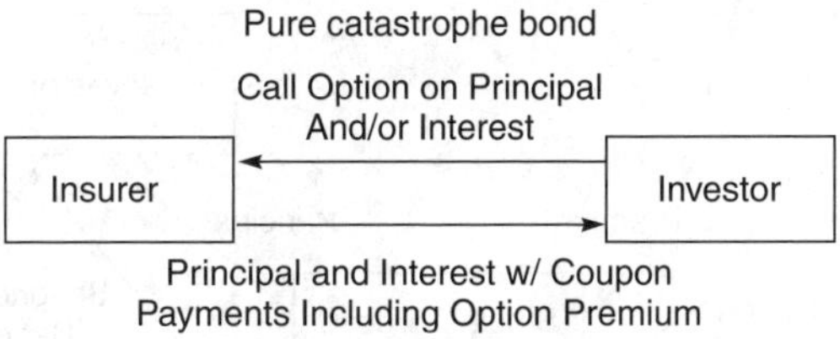

Figure 13-3. Pure catastrophe bond. *Source*: Authors' derivation.

the Tokyo region for Oriental Land Company Ltd., the owner of Tokyo Disneyland.

Under a very general catastrophe bond structure, shown in Figure 13-3, investors purchase debt securities from an insurer (or an insurance trust) in exchange for a nominal interest yield that compensates investors both for the use of their funds and for an embedded option that allows the insurer to reduce the yield (either through a reduction in principal and/or interest payments) if a predefined disaster event occurs during a preset exposure period. Stated differently, catastrophe bonds expose investors' principal and/or interest to loss in the event of a pre-specified natural disaster event. In return, investors receive a higher yield reflecting the embedded call option (on principal and/or interest payments) held by the insurer. In principle, this structure is no different from a credit default swap except that the underlying reference portfolio is a basket of insurance risks instead of loans and the triggering event is a natural disaster loss instead of a credit default.

A good illustration of a CatBond structure is the catastrophe bond program established in 1997 by the US property-liability insurer USAA to transfer the risk of large-scale hurricane losses from the insurer to investors. USAA structured the CatBond so that investors earned an above market-yield on the notes, but were exposed to losing principal and/or interest if hurricane losses for USAA exceeded $1 billion (Lewis and Davis, 1998). If hurricane losses for USAA exceeded $1 billion, investors would have to cover 80 percent of USAA's hurricane losses in excess of $1 billion through foregone interest or principal payments on their notes.[11] The total payout by investors was capped, however, at $400 million. USAA retained the risk of hurricane losses below $1 billion, losses above $1.5 billion, and the 20 percent of losses not covered by investors in the $1.0–1.5 billion layer of protection provided by the CatBond.[12]

In implementing CatBond structures, however, insurers and investors often prefer to segregate the underlying liabilities in an insurance-linked note through the use of a special purpose reinsurer (SPR). Insurers prefer the use of a SPR to capture the tax and accounting benefits associated with traditional reinsurance. The SPR also keeps the transaction off the insurer's

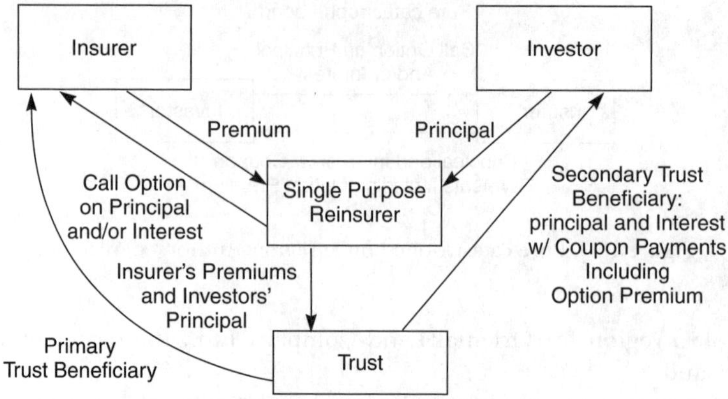

Figure 13-4. CatBond with SPR. *Source*: Authors' derivation.

balance sheet and hence does not change its capital structure. Investors prefer the use of a SPR to isolate the risk of their investment in the secured assets or liabilities from the general business and insolvency risks of the insurer. As a result, the issuer of the securitization can realize a higher return from the sale of assets or liabilities through segregation. The transaction also is more transparent than a debt issue by the insurer, because the funds are held in trust and are released according to carefully defined criteria.

The structure of a CAT bond with a SPR and trust is shown in Figure 13-4. Once established, the SPR provides traditional reinsurance to the insurer for the pre-specified insurance risks being "securitized." The insurer also retains a residual interest in the SPR to ensure that the arrangement is fully recognized as reinsurance for regulatory and tax purposes. However, unlike traditional reinsurance firms, the SPR is financed through the placement of catastrophe bonds issued directly to investors. Proceeds from the sales of the securities to the investors and the insurer's premium payments for the catastrophe coverage are then placed in a trust, usually established in the United States. Funds from the trust can be released only to pay the issuing insurer's claims or to make payments on the bonds. This structure assures investors that they are not exposed to other risks inherent in the issuing insurer's book of business that would prevent it from repaying the bond were it issued direct by the insurer rather than the SPR.

The funds in the trust are invested in safe securities such as Treasury bonds. The investors receive the interest on the assets in the trust and a risk premium paid into the trust by the insurer. The risk premia on most CAT bonds issued to date have been in the range of 400–600 bps, and it is not unusual for the risk premium to be five or six times the expected value of the covered catastrophe loss (Cummins, Lalonde, and Phillips, 2002*b*). These high premia, which have made the bonds very attractive to investors, pose a pricing puzzle: that is, if CAT risk is truly "zero-beta," then the bonds should yield approximately the expected loss plus the risk-free rate of interest, not several times the expected loss. Possible explanations for the high premia include investor unfamiliarity with the contracts (a "novelty" premium), the low liquidity of the contracts issued to date (a liquidity premium), and investor uncertainty about the accuracy of the models used to estimate expected losses (a "modeling risk" premium). In addition, although the catastrophic events observed in the United States to date have been uncorrelated with returns in securities markets (Litzenberger, Beaglehole, and Reynolds, 1996), it is not clear that this lack of correlation also would exist for a $100 billion plus "Big One." It is possible that such a large event might have repercussions that could drive down securities prices, creating systematic risk for CAT securities. An extra premium for this type of risk might be characterized as a "hidden-beta" premium.

The CAT bonds that have been issued to date are summarized in Table 13-2. The table shows forty-two securitizations that account for over $5.5 billion in risk capital. Most of the transactions are limited to coverage of hurricanes and/or earthquakes, although fifteen are multiline, indicating that they could be triggered by events from other lines of insurance. The issues have ranged in value from $10 to $500 million, and nearly all have been privately placed.

Insurers also have hedged property-liability risk using other types of securitizations, including contingent capital/surplus note financings and option/swap contracts. A contingent capital transaction is structured similarly to a CAT bond, except that the financing event triggered by the contingency is an equity capital issue. For example, assume that an insurer issues contingent capital securities to investors. As in the case of a CAT bond, the funds from the capital issue are placed in a trust and invested in safe securities. If the triggering event occurs, the insurer is permitted to withdraw funds from the trust and to replace the funds with contingent capital certificates or surplus notes.[13] There is usually a provision for retiring the surplus notes according to a specified schedule. Thus, investors are exposed to the ultimate credit risk of the issuer (i.e. the risk that the notes will not be retired as promised) but otherwise will not lose their principal as the result of the occurrence of the covered event. The contingent capital transactions to date are summarized in Table 13-3. There have been sixteen transactions, raising a total of $4.5 billion in risk capital. All contingent capital transactions to date have been privately placed.

There also have been several option/swap securitizations covering property-liability risks. One model for this type of securitization is the catastrophic equity put option, where an insurer purchases a catastrophe put option from investors in return for an option premium. This derivative gives the insurer the right to issue a specified number of shares (usually

TABLE 13-2 Natural Disaster Catastrophe Bonds ($ US Millions)

Issue	*Issuer*	*Year*	*$ Millions*	*Risk*
Georgetown Re	St. Paul Re	1996	69.0	Multi-line
AIG	AIG	1996	25.0	Multi-line
Winterthur	Winterthur Re	1997	282.0	Wind
SLF I	Reliance	1997	20.0	Multi-line
SLF II	Reliance	1997	20.0	Multi-line
Residential Re I	USAA	1997	477.0	Wind
SR Earthquake	Swiss Re	1997	137.0	EQ
Parametric Re	Tokio Marine & Fire	1997	100.0	EQ
Trinity Re I	Centre Re	1998	84.0	Wind
SLF III	Reliance	1998	25.0	Multi-line
Pacific Re	Yasuda Fire & Marine	1998	80.0	Wind
Residential Re II	USAA	1998	450.0	Wind
Mosaic Re I	F& G Re	1998	54.0	Multi-line
Trinity Re II	Centre Re	1998	57.0	Wind
Mosaic Re II	F& G RE	1999	46.0	Multi-line
SLF IV	Reliance	1999	10.0	Multi-line
Domestic Re	Kemper	1999	100.0	EQ
Halyard Re	Sorema SA	1999	17.0	Multi-line
Concentric Re	Oriental Land Co.	1999	100.0	EQ
Residential Re III	USAA	1999	200.0	Wind
Juno Re	Gerling	1999	80.0	Wind
Namazu Re	Gerling	1999	100.0	EQ
Golden Eagle Re	AmRe	1999	182.0	Multi-line
Seismic	Lehman Re	2000	145.5	EQ
Atlas Re	SCOR	2000	200.0	Multi-line
Halyard Re	Sorema SA	2000	17.0	Multi-line
Alpha Wind	Arrow Re/State Farm	2000	90.0	Wind
Residential Re IV	USAA	2000	200.0	Wind
NeHi	Vesta	2000	50.0	Wind
Mediterranean Re	AGF	2000	129.0	Wind/EQ
Prime Capital	Munich Re	2000	300.0	Wind/EQ
Western Capital	Swiss Re	2001	100.0	EQ
Golden Eagle Re II	American Re	2001	120.0	Wind/EQ
Halyard Re	Sorema SA	2001	17.0	Multi-line
SR Wind	Swiss Re	2001	120.0	Wind
Trinom Ltd	Zurich Re	2001	161.9	Multi-line
Mediterranean Re	AGF	2001	129.0	Wind/EQ
Redwood Capital	Lehman Re	2001	160.5	EQ
Atlas II	SCOR	2001	N/A	Wind/EQ
Munich Re	Open	2002	500.0	Multi-line
CEA	Open	2002	100.0	EQ
Swiss Re	Open	2002	300.0	–
		Total	5554.9	

Sources: Swiss Re (2001), Lane (2000, 2001).

Note: EQ = Earthquake, Wind = Hurricane/Windstorm.

TABLE 13-3 Contingent Capital/Surplus Notes (Volume in $ US Millions)

Issuer	*Year*	*$ Millions*	*Risk*
Nationwide	1995	400.0	N/A
Hannover Re-Kover	1995	85.0	Multi-line
Arkwright	1995	100.0	N/A
FWUA	1995	1,500.0	Wind
Hawaii Hurricane	1995	500.0	Wind
RLI	1996	50.0	Multi-line
Horace Mann	1996	100.0	Multi-line
LaSalle Re	1997	100.0	Multi-line
CEA	1997	700.0	EQ
Lloyds	1998	40.0	Multi-line
Oriental Land Co.	1999	100.0	EQ
Pacific Electric	2000	120.0	Credit
Michelin	2000	170.0	GDP
US Consulting	2000	250.0	N/A
Royal Bank of Canada	2000	200.0	Credit
Countrywide	2000	100.0	Credit
	Total	4,515.0	

Sources: Authors' computations from Swiss Re (2001), Lane (2000, 2001).

Note: EQ = Earthquake, Wind = Hurricane/Windstorm.

preferred stock) at an agreed upon price contingent on the occurrence of a specified catastrophe event. If the insurer's stock price drops below the option strike price as the result of a catastrophe, the insurer can replenish its equity capital by issuing shares at the strike price. Options have an advantage over CAT bonds in that they do not tie up pools of capital in trust. However, options expose the insurer to counterparty credit risk, and the issue of shares following an event dilutes the insurer's equity capital. For investors, these options should be attractive as long as the option premium is sufficient to compensate for the risk. However, because they are off-balance sheet transactions, investing in options/swaps may create regulatory problems for some types of institutional investors.

The option/swap contracts issued to date are shown in Table 13-4. There have been twenty transactions, raising $4.8 billion in risk capital. Aggregating the CAT bonds, contingent capital, and options/swap transactions in Tables 13-2, 13-3, and 13-4 gives a total of seventy-eight transactions that have raised nearly $15 billion in risk capital. Clearly, these securities have been viewed as attractive by both issuers and investors, and there is significant potential for the future development of this market.

TABLE 13-4 Property-Liability Linked Options/Swaps (Volume in $ US Millions)

Issuer	*Year*	*$ Millions*	*Risk*
Hannover Re (K2)	1996	100.0	Multi-line
CAT LTD	1997	35.0	Wind
Mitsui Marine	1998	35.0	EQ
AXA	1998	40.0	EQ
XL Mid-Ocean	1998	200.0	Multi-line
Constitution Re	1998	10.0	Wind
CNA	1998	115.0	Wind
FIFA World Cup	1998	3,000.0	EQ
Societe Generale	1998	45.0	EQ
Societe Generale	1998	100.0	EQ
Reliance National	1998	40.0	Multi-line
AXA	1998	21.0	EQ
Allianz	1998	150.0	Wind
Hannover Re (K2+)	1998	50.0	Multi-line
CNA	1999	50.0	EQ
Lehman Re	1999	111.0	EQ
Tokio Marine/Arrow Re	2000	200.0	EQ
WestLB	2000	45.0	N/A
Tokio Marine/Swiss Re	2001	450.0	EQ/Wind
FIFA/ Munich Re	2001	50.0	EQ
	Total	4,847.0	

Sources: Authors' computations from Swiss Re (2001), Lane (2000, 2001).

Note: EQ = Earthquake, Wind = Hurricane/Windstorm.

Insurance-Linked Notes: Life Insurance/Annuity Risks

Unlike the property-liability insurance industry, securitization in the life insurance industry has been relatively rare. To date, we are aware of only five successful securitization transactions involving life insurance assets (see Table 13-5), and four of these were "closed block" securitizations completed by one reinsurance company, Hannover Re.[14] Under a "closed block" securitization, an insurance company segregates the life insurance policies and the associated assets of a given volume of business. The assets and liabilities are then sold to investors through an ABS structure. Through this mechanism, an insurance company can effectively originate a block of business and then "sell" that business block directly to investors through a securitization structure.

Life insurance securitizations are motivated by insurer needs to recapture funds expended in writing new life insurance. The need arises because the expense of writing new life insurance policies is generally incurred by the

TABLE 13-5 Life Insurance and Annuity Securitizations (Volume in $ US Millions)

Issue	*Issuer*	*Year*	*$ Millions*	*Risk*
ASLAC Funding Trust I	American Skandia	1996	42.0	Annuity fees
Prudential	Prudential	1996	175.0	Mutual fund fees
ASLAC Funding Trust II	American Skandia	1997	158.0	Annuity fees
Interpolis Re	Hannover Re	1998	57.0	Closed life block
Mutual Securitization	National Provident Life	1998	438.0	Open life block
ASLAC Funding Trust	American Skandia	1998	111.0	Annuity fees
Interpolis Re	Hannover Re	1999	250.0	Closed life block
Whiterock	Hannover Re	1999	49.0	Closed life block
L4 Securitization	Hannover Re	2000	182.0	Closed life block
		Total	1,462.0	

Sources: Authors' computations from Swiss Re (2001), Lane (2000, 2001).

insurer in the first policy year and then amortized over the term of the policy. Thus, writing new business can create liquidity problems for life insurers. In addition, regulatory accounting requirements usually result in an increase in insurer leverage associated with new business. Consequently, one motivation for life insurance securitizations is to reduce leverage and obtain immediate access to the "profits" expected to emerge from a block of life insurance policies. The advantage for the insurance company is access to cheaper financing and the ability to bypass regulatory capital requirements associated with keeping the business on the company's balance sheet. In a series of transactions (known as L1–L4) dating back to 1998, Hannover Re has used "closed block" securitizations to sell four large blocks of life, health, and personal accident reinsurance in the market. The latest sale involved $182 million of life, health, and personal accident in December of 2000.

A more innovative life insurance securitization approach is the direct sale of interests in "open blocks" of life insurance policies underwritten by an insurance company. In an open block securitization of life insurance policies, a SPV is established to make a loan to the operating unit of an insurance company in return for the right to the surpluses expected to "emerge" on a specified block of life insurance policies. Emerging surpluses constitute the residual value within a block of life insurance policies at the end of each policy year, after subtracting dividends to policyholders. The present value of these emergent surpluses across future policy years represents the present value of future profits from the life insurance block. The SPV, therefore, is funded through the issuance of floating and fixed rate structured notes placed directly in the capital markets with investors interested in taking a position in the present value of future profits on these life insurance policies (Standard & Poor's, 2001).

In May of 1998, National Provident Insurer (NPI), a UK life insurance company, became the first company to successfully securitize an open block of life insurance policies. In this structure NPI, sold $438 million of life insurance policies through an SPV called Mutual Securitization PLC. The limited recourse bonds used to fund the SPV were rated A by S&P and divided into Class A1 and A2 securities that carried terms of 14 and 24 years, respectively. Similar to the securitization of mutual fund asset fees, the main profit driver of emerging surplus in this transaction was the management fee levied by NPI on the portfolio fund backing these policies.[15]

While NPI remains the only open block life insurance securitization that has been successfully placed in the market, interest in life insurance securitization is once again drawing the attention of leading investment banks. In fact, it has been reported that Prudential Financial is exploring the opportunity to securitize up to $1.5 billion in portfolio life insurance policies.[16] Unlike closed block transactions, the direct securitization of life insurance emerging surplus enables insurance companies to "sell"—and investors to buy—the pure risk of adverse mortality and morbidity developments in its underwriting. Of course, mortality rates tend to remain extremely stable over time. Thus, the interest in life insurance securitization centers around the desire of life insurance companies to find capital-saving approaches to manage the risk of "catastrophic" changes in mortality rates, presumably from plagues, famine, large scale conflagrations, or terrorist attacks. In this context, the motivational factors behind the insurer demand for open block securitizations of life insurance are analogous to factors underlying the CatBond market for property–casualty insurance.

Credit-Insurance

Parallel to the development of credit-linked notes, insurance companies have been exploring strategies for securitizing the risks associated with portfolio credit insurance. In the market for alternative risk transfer, reinsurance companies have spent the last few years developing a wide variety of innovative products to insure the portfolio credit risk exposures of both corporates and financial services firms. Examples of these innovative new policies include the $200 million in contingent capital protection against portfolio credit risk to the Royal Bank of Canada in January of 2001; the

$260 million of surety bond protection provided to ResidenSea Ltd; and the $159 million excess-of-loss policy provided to the Paris Bourse in the event that member defaults and losses exceed $180 million. Coupled with traditional credit risk insurance products, this growth of insurance company credit exposure also has increased the demand for insurance companies to develop new approaches for securitizing the resulting concentrations of credit risk in their portfolios.

To find a precedent for the securitization of portfolio credit risk from an insurance company, however, we must once more look to Europe. In April of 1999, Gerling Financial successfully placed $455 million worth of credit-linked notes in the market through a novel structure called SECTRS. In the SECTRS transaction, Gerling was able to lay off large concentrations of European credit risk exposure associated with the firm's credit insurance operations through an indexed structure similar to JP Morgan's Bistro Credit-linked notes. The transaction allowed investors to participate directly in the credit risk performance of small-to medium-sized European companies through an indexed measure of industry default experience based on the default experience of 92,000 European firms. Arranged in the sequential layers, the SECTRS transaction exposed investors to varying levels of risk pegged to the annual and 3-year cumulative default experience of an index of European company defaults.

- Tranche A: totaled $245.5 million, was rated AA2, and carried a yield of Euribor + 45 bp.
- Tranche B: totaled $127.5 million, was rated AA2, and carried a yield of Euribor + 82.
- Tranche C: totaled $ 82.0 million, was rated BBB, and carried a yield of Euribor + 170.

The payoff of principal and interest in each tranche was tied to a specific set of default rates based on a European default rate index. The trigger points for annual default rates on Tranche A, B, and C were set to 3.3, 2.6, and 2.1 percent, respectively. Cumulative default rate trigger points for Tranches A, B, and C were set at 6.6, 5.9, and 5.4 percent, respectively. Gerling was left with the responsibility for managing the basis risk between the European industry index and the firm's portfolio exposure, as well as bearing the first layer of loss associated with defaults for the portfolio up to a level of a 2.1 percent annual default loss (approximately $325 million in exposure).

The structure of the transaction was similar to a credit-linked structured note with an embedded portfolio credit default swap. Proceeds from the sale of the structured notes were used to purchase US Treasury securities and AAA-rated German Agency bonds to collateralize and meet the interest and principal payments on the underlying notes. Gerling then purchased an interest rate swap to convert the fixed-rate collateral bonds into a floating rate payment for investors. In the event that a default trigger was pierced, Gerling would be able to liquidate some of the underlying collateral in the trust to cover credit insurance losses within its portfolio. As a result, the reduction in the underlying collateral within the trust would reduce the principal and interest payments to the affected investors of the SECTRs securities.

Weather-Linked Securities

Another developing market is the market for weather derivatives and for structured notes that embed weather derivatives in an ABS structure. Weather derivatives are another example of derivatives on "exotic underlyings." Although various weather-related indices could undoubtedly be constructed, most contracts traded to date settle on indices of the number of heating degree days (HDD) for contracts hedging against relatively warm temperatures (e.g. a natural gas producer) or cooling degree days (CDD) for contracts hedging against relatively low temperatures (e.g. an electricity producer hedging against low demand for air conditioning). Weather derivatives have been sold over-the-counter, and the Chicago Mercantile Exchange (CME) now offers HDD and CDD futures and options on ten US cities, although transactions volume has been low to date.

As an example of a weather derivative consider a HDD futures contract on the Philadelphia weather index purchased on the CME. The CME HDD index is an accumulation of HDDs over a calendar month, valued at $100 per tick (day). A daily HDD is defined as Max[65° Fahrenheit-daily average temperature, 0]. If the number of HDDs during November in Philadelphia accumulated to 600, the nominal value of a futures contract on the index would be $60,000. A natural gas company might decide to hedge using put options on the index. If it bought December puts with a strike price of 900 (approximately the average HDDs in Philadelphia in December), it would collect the following amount on each option: $P = 100 \times \text{Max}[900 - I^{HDDP}, 0]$, where I^{HDDP} is the realized value of the Philadelphia HDD index for that month. For example, if the actual number of HDDs was 750, the hedger would collect $15,000 per put option. Of course, many other types of derivatives, including swaps, caps, floors, etc., could be traded based on weather related risks.

Asset-backed securities also can be structured with embedded weather derivatives. Similar to the development of the credit-linked note and the CatBond market, weather-linked ABS could be beneficial to both the issuing company and the investor. For the issuer, the note can be structured using a SPV that allows the ceding company to obtain the favorable tax and accounting advantages of insurance. For investors, the structured note would provide a low cost means for taking positions in the weather market that are currently not feasible given the limited market infrastructure for weather derivatives. A market-leader in this area is Koch Energy Trading. In a two-tranche structured note dubbed Kelvin, Koch was able to securitize a $50 million portfolio of weather derivatives tied to degree-day measures in the United States in December of 1999.

- Tranche A: totaled $21.6 million, provided first event coverage, carried a B-rating, and was priced at LIBOR + 1570.
- Tranche B: totaled $23.0 million, provided second event coverage, was rated BBB, and was priced at LIBOR + 870.

Other deals that have been examined but withdrawn or held back include insurance-linked notes tied to rainfall precipitation (e.g. Nicaraguan drought or deluge) and snowmelt and/or river water level exposure (e.g. United Kingdom or Bangladesh).

Aircraft-backed Debt and Lease Securitization

An interesting class of investments that has flourished recently represents securities backed by aircraft assets and aircraft lease programs. Aircraft-backed securities now come in a variety of forms for investors, but for convenience, we can classify these securities within four basic structures: Equipment Trust Certificates (ETCs), Enhanced Equipment Trust Certificates (EETCs), Aircraft Lease Portfolio Securitizations (ALPS), and securitized pools of aircraft loans. The risks associated with aircraft-backed loans are very unique from other types of loan structures. However, the basic structure of a securitized pool of aircraft loans is the same as a traditional CLO. Our discussion focuses on the first three types of aircraft ABS.

Equipment Trust Certificates

For airline companies, a substantial portion of their debt funding capacity historically has been tied up in the financing of aircraft purchases (e.g. Boeing 747s). Furthermore, the funding costs of aircraft purchases have been tied directly to the credit rating of the airline company. The question for the airline companies, therefore, was whether there was a means to leverage the residual value of a purchased aircraft to reduce the debt funding costs associated with the purchase? The answer was ETC.

In issuing ETCs, an airline company uses an arms-length SPV to issue secured debt to private investors to finance the purchase of aircraft assets. In the transaction, however, the airline company transfers its interest in the property rights of the aircraft and all related property rights (e.g. lease returns) to the SPV trust as security for repayment of the limited-recourse notes.[17] Investors are then granted a first priority perfected security interest in the aircraft and any associated collateral, and are entitled to secure the benefits of favorable payment treatment in the event of a bankruptcy by the airline.[18] The investor interest in the aircraft collateral translates into enhanced recovery rate prospects on the debt in the event of a default by the sponsoring airline. As such, the secured debt is usually rated 1–2 notches above the corporate rating of the airline and the airline benefits from a lower-cost financing of the aircraft purchase. Northwest was one of the first airlines to issue ETCs in 1994, but several large deals followed the Northwest deal as more airlines took advantage of this lower cost funding mechanism.

Enhanced Equipment Trust Certificates

Given the funding cost savings that were realized through the issuance of ETCs, the airline companies started to explore alternative structuring options in an attempt to further enhance the credit rating of the debt securities and lower the acquisition costs of aircraft assets. What evolved out of this exploration was a more highly levered secured debt structure known as EETCs. While the basic premise behind the EETCs remained consistent with the original ETCs, these new structures used tranching and flexible payment terms to convert the collateral of the aircraft into a reduced probability of default–as opposed to an improved recovery rate in the event of default. This approach yielded more favorable credit ratings and lower funding costs.

The main features that were added to EETCs to effect this trade-off of collateral enhanced ratings were as follows:

1. Debt tranching–providing various levels of over-collateralization.
2. Dedicated liquidity facilities that could continue debt service (usually just interest only) payments during the time required for the trust to repossess and sell aircraft collateral to pay off the debt obligations in the event of a default–up to a maximum of 18 months.
3. Soft amortization terms that allowed an extension in the repayment of principal up to a maximum final maturity date.
4. Reliance on improved legal mechanisms for assuring access to the underlying collateral.

The basic advantage of the last three features listed above was to give the trust sufficient flexibility to determine the optimum timing of selling repossessed assets into the market place. Early ETC and portfolio securitization transactions that resulted in asset repossession and liquidation demonstrated the risk associated with trying to accomplish a forced asset sale during a down market in the value of airline assets. The flexibility accorded to the trust in an EETC was an attempt to avoid an asset "fire sale," thereby recognizing greater value in the transaction.

Aircraft Lease Portfolio Securitization

While airline companies were looking for novel ways to lower their cost of aircraft acquisition, aircraft manufacturers and aircraft leasing companies also were exploring ways to securitize leasing programs. In an aircraft lease program, the aircraft manufacturer leases a plane to an airline for commercial use over a fixed period of time on an operating lease basis. During this period, the airline company has an option to put the plane back to the aircraft manufacturer before the end of the lease term under conditions of financial stress. As a result, aircraft lease programs carry significant contingent market risks for the manufacturer, especially since the development of adverse circumstances for lessees is likely to be correlated with airline industry recessions when releasing and residual aircraft values are lower. With roughly 2,500 of the 12,500 total outstanding commercial aircraft worldwide being financed through lease programs, the extent of this risk–and the opportunity for cost savings with a new ABS structure–was substantial. As a result, the industry developed ALPS (Bowers, 2002).

Under an ALPS, the aircraft manufacturer issues securities through a SPV that grants investors rights to the lease receivables of a portfolio of leased aircraft, as well as the net residual value of the aircraft in the lease portfolio at lease termination. In the transfer, the special purpose trust retains the property rights to the lease income and the residual value of the aircraft to support the payment of debt service to investors. Meanwhile, the investors accept the contingent liability of the lease program. The main risk to investors, therefore, is the joint event where airlines default on their lease obligations during a period in which the value of the leased aircraft falls below a level needed to meet debt service obligations.

A key distinction between ALPS and ETCs, however, is that the credit quality of the transaction is not tied to a rating of the underlying sponsor, but instead it is based on the level of diversification in the lease portfolio (i.e. number of airlines, aircraft types, and countries), the robustness of the aircraft technology, the reputation of the manufacturer, the quality of the lease servicer, and the expected market liquidity for the aircraft assets. Furthermore, while the trust has the authority to sell the aircraft to support debt service payments to investors, the presumption in a lease securitization is that lease terminations will be replaced with new leases. Other structuring options have evolved in a similar fashion to EETCs.

The first portfolio securitization of airplane receivables was a $521 million issue in June of 1992 that was called Aircraft Lease Portfolio Securitization Limited 92-1 ("ALPS 92-1"). In this transaction, the sponsor (the GPA Group) securitized the lease receivables associated with fourteen different planes, fourteen different lessees, and twelve countries. The aircrafts were sold to ALPS 92-1 in "true-sale" format and the SPV issued $417 million in senior (three classes) and mezzanine debt. The ALPS 92-1 debt was to be repaid from aircraft sales in the last 18 months of the program, but failure to meet aircraft sales goals eventually forced a refinancing of the debt in 1996 (ALPS 96-1) (Bowers, 2002). The experience of ALPS 92-1 was important in illustrating the risks in an aircraft securitization structure based on the residual value of the aircraft—the risks that the market value of the leased aircraft will fall below a level required to finance the payment of the securities financing the structure.

A second major ALPS issuance in 1994, Aircraft Lease Portfolio Securitization 94-1, presented an important improvement on the original aircraft lease securitization model. ALPS 94-1 was a $854 million issue backed by a lease portfolio of twenty-seven aircrafts, with twenty-two lessees in fourteen countries. Legally, the structure was similar to ALPS 92-1. However, in the event that low market valuations of the leased aircraft did not support the scheduled retirement of the trust's debt, the trust had the authority to extend the maturity of the debt at a higher interest rate. This feature allowed the trust to avoid a forced sale of the leased aircraft in a down market—exacerbating the decline in the residual value of the aircraft and forcing a restructuring of the debt.

Another major hurdle in aircraft securitization was crossed in 1997, with the $4.1 billion securitization issued by Airplanes Trust Delaware and Airplanes Limited Jersey ("Airplanes Group"). This deal, which marked the largest to date, involved the lease securitization of 229 aircrafts on lease to 83 lessees in 40 countries. The novelty in this transaction was that the structure involved the transfer of bankruptcy-remote SPVs that held the aircraft as opposed to the physical transfer of the aircraft themselves. (Similar deals are also taking place with respect to automobile leasing programs.)

In terms of the yield opportunity for investors, we can look at the 1997 ALPS issued by Pegasus Aircraft Lease Securitization and the June 2001 issue by Triton-ABD.

1. Pegasus issued $119 million in 7-year securities backed by airplane lease receivables in May of 1997. The issue was divided into a BBB-rated tranche of $99 million and a BB-/Ba3-rated tranche of $20 million. The BBB-rated tranche carried a fixed rate of interest of 8.6 percent; while the junior tranche had a rate of 11.76 percent. The interesting aspect of the Pegasus transaction was that fortunate circumstances in the timing of lease terminations and aircraft sales in a strong aircraft market actually generated unexpectedly strong returns for investors. Unfortunately, the prospect of these high returns is also informative of the potential for strong negative returns in down markets.
2. Triton issued $805 million in 25-year securities backed by airplane lease receivables. The transaction covered a geographically diverse portfolio of lease receivables with the top 5 markets being France (15 percent), the United Kingdom (14.4 percent), the United States (14.3 percent),

Canada (10.6 percent), and China (5.2 percent). The transaction was divided into six rated classes ranging from AA-rated paper to Ba2/BB-rated paper, along with an un-rated equity piece worth $85 million. In terms of yield opportunity, the AA-rated securities carried a return of LIBOR + 70 bps, the AA-rated securities offered LIBOR + 150 bps, and the Ba2/BB-rated paper had a stated return of 300 bps over LIBOR.

Insurance-linked Aircraft Receivables

In 1998, the first insurance-linked structure based on the residual value of aircraft leases was completed. In this transaction, BAE (formerly British Aerospace) purchased $3.8 billion worth of financial risk insurance to cover two key aspects of the company's risk exposure:

- Lease Portfolio Cover—the risk that the actual lease income on a fixed portfolio of aircraft leases, adjusted for costs, is less than a predetermined target level of income: and
- Aircraft Portfolio Cover—the risk that the residual value of repurchased aircraft under the lease contracts is less than BAE's contractual price for aircraft repurchase.

The insurance protecting this exposure was then securitized through the issuance of structured notes privately placed in the market through an SPV similar to an ALPS structure. The structure used by BAE was later replicated by both SAAB and Rolls Royce. The SAAB deal was a 15-year transaction covering $1.3 billion worth of portfolio lease protection where investors were given a stated return of LIBOR + 367 bps.

Stranded Cost Securitization

One area that is quickly becoming a main ABS product is the securitization of the "stranded costs" of public utilities. Stranded costs refer to power producer costs that were historically built into the traditional regulatory cost-plus system, but currently cannot be passed on to consumers due to the competitive marketplace created by industry deregulation. Before deregulation, power producers undertook significant investments in a wide variety of capital expenditures designed to improve baseline production. These expenditures included investments in high-cost nuclear and fossil plants, deferred and capitalized operating costs, conservation and economic development, nuclear decommissioning costs, and long-term contractual obligations with high cost non-utility generators. Under the traditional cost-plus regulatory system, these investments were encouraged and passed on to consumers in the form of higher energy costs (Standard & Poor's 1998).

With the passage of the National Energy Policy Act of 1992 (NEPA), the United States began a national program of deregulation in the energy sector with the goal of creating a competitive marketplace in the production or generation of power. The introduction of a competitive marketplace, along with falling power generation costs, caused the wholesale price of power to fall well below the traditional mark-up pricing rates used historically. As a result, existing power plants had little ability to immediately recoup the costs of their capital expenditure investments—leaving them saddled with "stranded costs" that threatened their profitability and even solvency. State utility regulators passed legislation that enabled the utilities to set rates to recover stranded costs (and any interest, servicing, or issuance costs of debt used to finance stranded costs) from customers, but only when amortized over a 30–40 year period. As a result, utilities looking to remain competitive in the wholesale generation market turned to securitization to expedite the recovery of these costs.

In a securitization of stranded assets, the utility company transfers both its stranded cost liability and its interest in the state regulatory fees designed to cover stranded costs (and associated financing charges) to a SPV. The SPV then issues secured fixed-rate debt to investors, with the principal proceeds being used to repay the utility company. In exchange for their investment, investors receive an overcollateralized interest in the nonpassable, usage-based, per kilowatt hour charges payable to the utility by residential and commercial customers for the amortization of the stranded costs. As structured, the fees supporting the secured debt are designed to yield sufficient revenue to amortize the notes funding the SPV after adjusting for any servicing and issuance fees.

Of course, the actual retirement of the collateralized notes depends on the actual usage and fee rates earned by the utility during the term of the note. Lower usage rates than projected (e.g. warmer winters or cooler summers) or lower overall revenue (e.g. adverse demographic changes) could result in total collections falling below levels needed to support the repayment of the structured debt. To mitigate this risk, the securitization structure incorporates a "true-up" mechanism whereby the utility must go to the state regulatory commission to secure an adjustment in the regulatory tariffs charged to power consumers to cover any shortfall. As such, the risk to investors associated with insufficient tariff revenue is minimized. At the same time, if revenues exceed projections, the "true-up" mechanism could lower tariffs for energy customers and mitigate the prepayment risk of the debt. These structures also attempt to protect investors against sponsor insolvency—requiring that any company acquiring the sponsor assume responsibility for meeting the terms of the securitization. Given the true-up mechanism, the bankruptcy protection, and the collateralization of the debt service payments, stranded cost securitizations consistently have been rated AAA.

The securitization of stranded costs was initiated when the three big Southern Californian Public Utility Companies (Southern California

TABLE 13-6 Other Noteworthy Securitizations (Volume in $ US Millions)

Issuer	*Year*	*$ Millions*	*Risk*
PGE, SCE, SDGE	1997	6,000.0	Stranded costs
Bowie Bonds	1997	55.0	Music royalties
FHLMC–MODERN's	1998	243.0	Mortgages
Toyota–Gramercy Place	1998	566.0	Residual value
Toyotal Motor Company	1998	4,000.0	Auto residual value
British Aerospace	1998	3,770.0	Plane lease residual value
Gerling–SECTRS	1999	455.0	Credit
ResidenSea LTD	1999	260.0	Surety bond
Swiss Re–ELF	1999	330.0	Credit
Koch Energy–Kelvin	1999	50.0	Weather
PEAK	1999	106.0	Trade receivables
Criterion Healthcare	1999	100.0	Health care receivables
Swiss Re–ELF II	2000	330.0	Credit
SAAB	2000	1,300.0	Plane lease residual value
Triarc Companies	2000	290.0	Franchise royalty
Rolls Royce	2001	N/A	Plane lease residual value
	Total	17,855.0	

Sources: Authors' computations from Swiss Re (2001), Lane (2000, 2001).

Edison, Pacific Gas and Electric, and San Diego Gas and Electric) effectively securitized $6 billion of their estimated $28 billion in stranded costs. In this securitization, each utility issued multiple AAA-rated tranches of secured debt with varying maturity dates and fixed rates of interest. Southern California Edison, for example, issued seven classes of debt with maturities ranging from 3 years to 12 years and fixed rates of interest ranging from 5.98 to 6.42 percent. Following this transaction, the securitization of utility stranded costs quickly spread across the United States and now serves as a key financing strategy for public utilities in a variety of states, including Washington, Pennsylvania, Connecticut, and Massachusetts. The California stranded cost securitization and some other noteworthy transactions are summarized in Table 13-6.

Future Cash Flow Securitization

Other important ABS structures that have been successfully placed in the market over the past several years include structured notes linked to firm royalties, tobacco settlement payments, and tax lien receivables.

Royalty Bonds

Whether backed by revenue from future record sales (e.g. Bowie Bonds), franchise profits (e.g. Triarc's Arby's Revenue), ticket sales (e.g. UK football clubs), or sports stadiums, a variety of ABS coming to the market are structured based on the valuation of future cash flows. In each of these cases, the issuer is attempting to monetize a future flow of rental income through the use of a securitization–effectively transferring the economic risk of cash flow variability to the investor.

1. In the case of the "Bowie Bonds," investors purchased the rights to the future flow of David Bowie's royalty payments from song and record catalog copyrights for $55 million. In exchange, investors will receive all royalty payments owed to David Bowie until the principal plus 8 percent interest is repaid (Benz, 2001). From the issuance of these securities to June 2001, approximately $210 million in similar deals were structured and issued into the market.
2. In the case of Triarc, Swiss Re was able to help the firm securitize $290 million worth of future franchise royalties associated with Triarc's Arby's fast-food restaurants through an SPV vehicle Triarc Franchise Trust. In the transaction, which was settled in December 2000, Triarc issued 20-year non-recourse fixed rate notes at a rate of 7.44 percent. The notes were credit enhanced by a first loss insurance policy issued by Swiss Re and an excess-of-loss insurance policy provided by Ambac Assurance Corporation. With the insurance, the notes carried a AAA-rating from both Moody's and S&P.[19]

Government Revenue Securitization

Starting in the early 1990s, state and local municipalities started exploring the securitization market as a means to monetize receivables associated with outstanding tax collections (e.g. tax liens). Early success in this market has since encouraged the spread of this public sector financing strategy to other types of receivables, ranging from the tobacco settlements in the United States to social security receivables in Italy.

Tax Lien Securitization–Starting in 1993, New York City started securitizing tax lien receivables in an effort to monetize the expected recovery value of these tax receivables. Over the period 1996–2001, New York City successfully completed seven deals with an average annual volume of approximately $138 million. Each deal also included several differently rated classes, typically ranging from a AAA-rated layer to a BBB-rated layer. For example, the 2001 transaction included four separate classes ranging from AAA-rated to BBB-rated with fixed rates of interest ranging from 5.59 percent (AAA) to 6.29 percent (BBB). Given New York's success, many other states and localities have followed suit. In fact, in 1997, several private companies were established to facilitate multistate tax lien securitizations, opening up the market for smaller states and localities.

Tobacco Settlements–With large liability awards granted to the states as part of the US tobacco company settlements, states had a new annuity stream of cash flow payments. Before long, states were again looking for an inexpensive financing mechanism for monetizing their interest in these tobacco settlement payments. Recognizing their success in tax lien securitizations, states quickly turned to the ABS market with tobacco settlement bonds, issuing over $4 billion in tobacco settlement payment ABS through the end of 2001. These tobacco settlement bonds were securitized using a variety of structures with ratings on senior tranches ranging from A1-Aa3 depending on the rating of the underlying tobacco firm and the level of collateralization.

Evaluating Non-Traditional ABS and Other New Securities

This section discusses the advantages and disadvantages of holding non-traditional ABS and other new assets. We also consider the important related issue of how to evaluate the risk-adjusted return of these securities.

The Advantages and Disadvantages of ABS

Non-traditional ABS have two principal advantages for investors. First, by securitizing cash flow streams that have not previously been traded in securities markets, ABS can create a non-redundant security that provides a new source of diversification for investors–improving portfolio efficiency. Second, particularly in the early stages of the market, non-traditional ABS can offer superior risk-adjusted returns in comparison with comparably rated conventional securities. As the market develops, however, one would expect arbitrage trading to eliminate any abnormal returns from holding these investments. Nevertheless, the diversification benefits of these assets would persist even if arbitrage opportunities were not present. Most ABS are also structured in such a way that investors can choose the risk-return tranches that are most appealing in terms of their investment strategies or can obtain access to opportunities not available in conventional securities.

Non-traditional securities also have some potential disadvantages, which can be expected to diminish in importance as the market continues to develop. Because most ABS and non-traditional securities issued to date have been privately placed, secondary market trading has been limited, exposing investors to liquidity risk. In addition, because such securities are often complex relative to conventional assets, they are more difficult to evaluate, raising transactions costs and exposing investors to an additional source of uncertainty.

Another key risk that investors have to evaluate with non-traditional ABS is the potential for moral hazard, adverse selection, and other forms of risk-shifting within the transaction. In addition to the potential for risk shifting in the underlying assets (e.g. making loans to customers in a credit transaction), the potential exists for the actual structure to induce risk shifting by the issuer. For example, a bank that securitizes its credit risk exposure to a specific sector through a structured note in order to obtain additional lending capacity may then expand lending activities within this same sector–increasing the overall debt burden and riskiness of that sector. Moreover, if the bank can "substitute" assets into a structured pool, the bank may have the incentive to substitute "bad loans" into the securitized pools and keep the higher-performing loans on the bank's balance sheet. The same process can occur in the area of property insurance, where the structured note payouts are closely linked to the insurance company's insured properties (i.e. the insurer may place higher risk properties into the pool). As a result, investors must be careful to evaluate, control, and price for moral hazard opportunities in each ABS structure.

The limited experience so far in trading some types of cash flow streams incorporated in ABS also suggests that such securities may be subject to risks that are presently unforeseen by issuers and investors. Non-traditional swaps and options, which are not asset-backed, are subject to all of these potential disadvantages as well as the additional regulatory and market risks of undertaking off-balance sheet exposures. Finally, because of the types of cash flows covered by some of these securities and the fact that they usually contain embedded options, conventional valuation methods are not likely to be adequate to evaluate the risk-return trade-offs provided by many of these securities. The next section proposes a valuation methodology that may overcome this last limitation.

Evaluating the Risk-Adjusted Returns of Non-traditional ABS

With an understanding of the dynamics underlying non-traditional ABS and other new products, we now turn to the issue of how pension fund managers should value these securities. As discussed above, the first objective in evaluating any security with an embedded option is to ensure that the security's return at least compensates the investor for the expected value of the loss being transferred. While few would argue with this presupposition, prospective investors often find the process of evaluating the expected loss transferred under these transactions challenging.

Measuring the Expected Loss Transfer

The rating agencies have tried to bring some clarity to the process of measuring expected losses on non-traditional ABS in their assignment of ratings. Specifically, the rating agencies generally apply the same "probability of default" methodology to structured transactions as applied to credit transactions. As an example, we consider the corporate bond default rates from 1990 to 2001, shown in Table 13-7. Since a BB-rated corporate credit is expected to have an average annual default rate of approximately 1.2 percent, a Ba-rated ABS should be expected to have an average probability of loss of 1.2 percent. Moreover, since most of the options embedded in non-traditional ABS represent low frequency/high severity risks, market participants often assume a 100 percent severity and use this approach to examine the expected loss of each transaction. As such, a ratings-based approach, while not a substitute for a full analysis of the underlying risk, provides a good first approximation in evaluating the return structure of an ABS deal.

Although bond ratings provide guidance when evaluating non-traditional ABS, they need to be supplemented by other sources of information that allow the investor to understand the financial, economic, and physical processes underlying the potential losses on each contract. For example, if we look at the estimated annual expected losses of five BB-rated CatBonds issued during 1999, the estimated annual expected loss on each transaction ranged from 0.30 to 0.75 percent, with three of the deals estimated pegged to the 0.42–0.45 percent range (Lane, 2000). Thus, the pricing of these securities implies that either the probability of an event or the expected loss given an event occurs is less than for comparably rated securities with different underlying risks. A straight application of a ratings-based approach would have overestimated the actual amount of loss transfer in these securities, understating the true expected return on the bonds.

Within a given asset-class, ratings provide a more uniform standard. Nonetheless, investors need to understand the underlying risk dynamic of each risk. Investors in CatBonds need to understand the dynamic processes underlying catastrophe risk; investors in weather-linked securities need to understand the physical processes associated with degree-days; and investors in credit-linked notes need to be comfortable with evaluating the financial and economic conditions that influence defaults. As such, investing in non-traditional ABS involves a significant investment in education and risk measurement tools by the investor—an investment that often forces investors to concentrate their expertise into just a few non-traditional markets.

Fortunately, since the early 1990s, significant advances have been made in the modeling of non-traditional risks. During this period, considerable research has been devoted to the development of pricing models for catastrophe risk (e.g. Dong, Shah, and Wong, 1996; Cummins, Lewis, and Phillips, 1998; Aase, 2001), weather risks and power risks (e.g. Lucia and Schwartz, 2002), and mortality-linked securities (e.g. Blake and Burrows, 2001). Moreover, firms such as Applied Insurance Research, Risk Management Solutions, and EQECAT have entered the

Table 13-7 Annual Default Rates on Corporate Bonds: By Rating

Rating Class	*1990*	*1991*	*1992*	*1993*	*1994*	*1995*	*1996*	*1997*	*1998*	*1999*	*2000*	*2001*	*Average 1990–2001*
Aaa	0	0	0	0	0	0	0	0	0	0	0	0	0.00
Aa	0	0	0	0	0	0	0	0	0	0	0	0	0.00
A	0	0	0	0	0	0	0	0	0	0	0	0.17	0.01
Baa	0	0.29	0	0	0	0	0	0	0.12	0.11	0.39	0.3	0.10
Ba	3.37	5.43	0.31	0.57	0.24	0.7	0	0.19	0.64	1.03	0.91	1.19	1.22
B	16.18	14.56	9.05	5.86	3.96	4.99	1.49	2.16	4.15	5.88	5.42	9.35	6.92
Caa-C	53.33	36.84	27.91	30	5.26	12.07	13.99	14.67	15.09	20.05	18.15	32.5	23.32
Investment grade	0	0.07	0	0	0	0	0	0	0.04	0.04	0.14	0.17	0.04
Speculative grade	9.9	10.47	4.98	3.61	1.99	3.41	1.7	2.09	3.43	5.65	5.88	10.2	5.28
All corporate	3.73	3.45	1.42	1.02	0.61	1.1	0.54	0.68	1.26	2.2	2.34	3.77	1.84

Source: Derived from Moody's Investor Services, Default and Recovery Rates of Corporate Bond Issuers (February 2002).

market with simulation models to evaluate the risks being transferred within securities backed by a variety of natural phenomena. Historical weather data are available to help develop prices for weather-linked securities. However, the fact that non-traditional methodologies and databases must be used in evaluating these securities and the absence of traded market prices for these securities increases the costs of valuing their risk-return trade-offs and imposes a steeper learning curve on investors in comparison with securities based on more familiar cash flows.

The learning curve is less steep for institutional investors entering the credit-linked ABS market. Significant progress has been made in evaluating credit risk and pricing credit-linked securities. The credit risk pricing methodologies are available to address a wide variety of asset-types and pricing requirements. For traded assets, these credit risk tools include simple rating migration models, term structure models of credit-spread risk, reduced form term structure models of default risk, and structural models of default risk. Furthermore, these models are readily available from commercial vendors such as CreditMetrics, Kamikura Corp., and KMV Inc. For non-traded assets, statistical hazard rate models, discriminant analysis, and neural network techniques have been applied to evaluate the credit risk profile of a portfolio of assets classes. Thus, while no one credit risk pricing model has been accepted as the dominant methodology, sufficient technology exists today for pricing a wide variety of credit-risk sensitive products. For the interested reader, Kao (2000) provides a brief overview of these different credit risk methodologies.

Estimating Risk-Adjusted Returns

Once the pension fund manager understands the portion of the return in excess of the risk-free rate going to compensate for the expected loss transferred, he can analyze the risk-adjusted return for underwriting this type of risk. To analyze the risk-return trade-offs of alternative investment strategies, most pension fund managers look to the traditional one-factor CAPM to assess the risk-adjusted return required for investing in any particular asset class. Based on the assumption that either all asset returns are normally distributed or that investors have mean–variance preferences, the CAPM model shows that, in equilibrium, all assets will yield the same equilibrium *risk-adjusted* rate of return. As a result, the expected return on any asset or portfolio can be computed as a simple combination of the risk-free rate of interest and a market risk premium based on the asset's estimated beta:

$$E(r_a) = r_f + \beta_a[E(r_m) - r_f] \qquad (13.1)$$

where r_a = the return on a given security or portfolio; r_f = the risk-free rate of interest; r_m = the return on the market portfolio; and

$$\beta_a = \frac{Cov(r_a, r_m)}{Var(r_m)} \tag{13.2}$$

The significance of the traditional CAPM model in the pension investment world is highlighted by the fact that fund manager performance is regularly evaluated based on the ability to consistently outperform specific market benchmarks. "Outperform" is usually measured directly in terms of the fund manager's ability to generate α-return, defined by.

$$\alpha_a = E(r_a|\Theta) - \beta_a[E(r_m) - r_f] - r_f \tag{13.3}$$

In Equation (13.3), $E(r_a|\Theta)$ represents the expected return on a given asset/portfolio based on the information set used by the investment manager (Θ). Hence, in equilibrium, the α-performance of any investment fund manager should be zero unless the manager has superior information on investments. Alternatively, positive indicates that a given pension investment fund manager is adding value in comparison to passively-managed index investment strategies.

The assumptions underlying the traditional CAPM model, however, generally do not hold with respect to assets like ABS, whose return distributions are often highly skewed. First, the return distribution of ABS are usually a function of a collateral pool and a short call option that allows the issuer to transfer losses to the holder of the ABS under certain low frequency/high severity events. Portfolios with embedded options of this type generally are not normally distributed. Secondly, as highlighted by Kraus and Litzenberger (1976), investors value positive skewness in evaluating alternative investment strategies. As such, assuming that investor preferences are completely defined using a simple mean–variance framework will lead to asset mispricing for assets with non-symmetric return distributions.

Leland (1999) highlights the importance of this asset mispricing and demonstrates that any mispricing ultimately manifests in biased estimates of the investment fund manager's α-return. Thus, measuring a fund investment manager's performance under a traditional CAPM model will lead to biased estimates of excess returns. More importantly, the traditional CAPM measure could provide incentives for the investment manager to purchase too much or too little non-traditional ABS for the pension portfolio, moving the fund return away from the efficient security market return line. Fortunately, Leland (1999) also demonstrates how a correction to the traditional CAPM model can provide unbiased estimates of investment fund performance without the need to develop more sophisticated valuation

TABLE 13-8 Estimated Excess Returns Representative ABS (1999)

Issuer/Asset Class	*Term (Years)*	*Security Rating*	*Volume ($ US Millions)*	*Estimated Excess Return*
CatBonds				
Domestic Re (Kemper)	3	BB+	80	3.24
Concentric Re (Oriental)	5	BB+	100	2.72
Residential Re	1	BB	200	3.27
Golden Eagle CatBond	2	BBB−	50	2.28
Credit Risk				
Gerling SECTRS–C	3	BBB	82	1.00
Weather Risk				
Kelvin 2nd Event	3	BBB−	23	4.52

Source: Lane (2001).

Note: Excess return represents spread over risk-free rate and premium for expected loss.

models. Specifically, he shows that the discrete time asset-pricing model developed by Rubinstein (1976) can be used to adjust the traditional CAPM model to account for investor preferences for higher moments of the return distribution. The key assumptions for making this adjustment are that the return on the market portfolio is independent and identically distributed at any moment in time and that the market is complete in the sense that the law of one price holds and all relevant risks are traded in the market. Both assumptions are consistent with assumptions used in conducting empirical research on market returns and the notion that a representative investor values higher moments of any given return distribution (e.g. skewness and kurtosis).[20]

Following Leland, we can evaluate the risk-adjusted returns of alternative asset classes like non-traditional ABS by evaluating the return dynamics of the underlying asset portfolio and adjusting for a modified measure of the market price of risk. Using this approach provides a better criterion for evaluating the attractiveness of these assets within a portfolio for a pension fund. It also provides a better measurement framework for assessing the performance of fund managers relative to benchmark returns.[21]

Table 13-8 provides a useful illustration of the value of this approach. Here we examine six different ABS deals that include three traditional catastrophe bonds, the catastrophe bond issued for the Oriental Land company, Gerling's European credit risk structure, and the Kelvin Weather derivatives structure. With the exception of the USAA transaction, all of these deals were multi-period, carried ratings between BB+ and BBB, and had a notional value in the range of $23–$100 million. Moreover, using information from Lane (2001), we computed the excess return over the estimated expected loss associated with each transaction. What is striking about this comparison is that the excess returns built into the CatBonds and weather derivatives are 250–450 bps in excess of the expected loss, whereas our pricing approach would suggest that these zero-b securities should be priced at or near the expected loss being transferred. At the same time, the excess return offered on the Gerling transaction—a transaction with significant systemic risk (positive b)—is relatively thin as compared with other ABS structures. This result, which is consistent with other studies, illustrates the value in correctly pricing these securities and the potential benefits of including a portion of these securities in a pension fund's asset allocation strategy.

Conclusion

Financial innovation has led to the creation of several new classes of securities that provide opportunities for institutional investors to improve the efficiency of their portfolios. Our objective here has been to provide information on the design and valuation of some of the more promising and innovative securities that have been introduced. We focus primarily on non-traditional ABS and also discuss several innovative derivative securities on non-traditional underlying assets and cash flows.

Securitization of non-traditional cash flows and risks has been driven by both demand and supply factors. Demand for new securities arises when new risks appear and when existing risks become more significant in magnitude. Risk expansion helps to explain the development of mortgage backed securities during the 1970s and 1980s, catastrophic risk bonds and option in the 1990s, and many other financial innovations. Supply factors driving the market include the development of modern financial models, which enable investors to price and value the new securities, as well as technological and communications advances that give more flexibility and modeling power to financial engineers. These factors have combined to permit the securitization of cash flows that were previously held on-balance sheet by financial intermediaries and industrial firms as well as the securitization of cash flows that were not previously considered viable candidates for financing or trading.

The development of non-traditional ABS and derivatives on non-traditional underlyings provides significant opportunities for pension fund investment managers. These securities provide a new source of diversification, often have attractive yields in comparison with comparably rated conventional securities, and enable managers to take positions in risk-return tranches that are consistent with their investment objectives to a greater extent than in the past.

Some caution is in order in approaching this market because some of the securities are complex and may be subject to unforeseeable risks.

In addition, at the present time, many of these new derivatives are relatively illiquid. Most of these non-traditional ABS and the new derivative contracts also are characterized by highly skewed returns such that the traditional CAPM benchmarking techniques are likely to give misleading results.

Fortunately, relatively straightforward models have been developed that generalize the CAPM to give meaningful risk-adjusted return valuations for the new financial instruments. Investment managers who make the commitment to learn how to evaluate and price these contracts will be well positioned to take advantage of this important market as it continues to evolve and expand. Investment managers can expect to have access to a growing volume of privately placed contracts as well as more standardized and liquid publicly traded contracts on non-traditional cash flows.

Notes

[1] The volume of financial transactions also has increased significantly, reflecting economic growth as well as the process of moving many assets and liabilities off-balance sheet. For example, the value of international debt instruments outstanding quadrupled during the 1990s to nearly $7.5 trillion, and the notional value of outstanding derivatives (open interest) rose from less than $1 trillion in 1986 to nearly $25 trillion at the end of 2001 (Bank for International Settlements).

[2] The collapse of Long-Term Capital Management in 1998 and Barings Bank in 1995 provide object lessons in types of disasters that can occur when various types of risks are not foreseen or appreciated.

[3] The Bond Market Association, <www.bondmarkets.com/research/mbsdat2.shtml>.

[4] Data based on "Summary of Worldwide Securitization in 2001," *Asset-Backed Alert*, <http://www.abalert.com>.

[5] Only about 60 percent of all ABS are publicly traded securities and the bulk of these are residential (RMBS) or commercial mortgage-backed securities (CMBS).

[6] Readers should be cautioned that, while we have taken extreme caution in ensuring quality of the information reported in this chapter, the information is limited in breadth and depth to what was obtainable from reliable sources. Actual deal lists and transaction detail may differ from the information reported herein.

[7] These figures are based on the definition of a catastrophe devised by Swiss Re, which defines losses as catastrophic if they exceed specified dollar valued thresholds that vary by type of catastrophe. For insured property catastrophes other than marine and aviation, Swiss Re defines a catastrophe for 2001 as an event causing at least $35.1 million in insured property loss (Swiss Re, 2002).

[8] In fact, the perception among insurers that CAT index securities are subject to unacceptable levels of basis risk has been identified as the primary obstacle to the more rapid development of the CAT-loss securities market. For an analysis of the basis risk of index-linked CAT-loss derivatives, see Cummins, Lalonde, and Phillips (2002*b*).

[9] Nine indices were available—a national index, five regional indices, and three state indices (for California, Florida, and Texas). The indices were based on PCS estimates of catastrophic property losses in the specified geographical areas during

quarterly or annual exposure periods. The indices were defined as the total accumulated losses divided by $100 million. For example, a 20/40 Eastern call spread would be in the money for a catastrophic loss accumulation in the Eastern region of more than $2 billion (20 points). Each index point was worth $200 on settlement so that one 20/40 call would pay a maximum of $4,000 (20 points times $200 per point).

[10] Over-the-counter options also have been traded, although these usually settle on insurer-specific loss criteria (Swiss Re, 2001).

[11] To better target investor appetites, USAA's notes were actually divided into an A-1 Class of $164 million that was principal protected, rated AAA, and priced at LIBOR + 273 bps; and an A-2 Class of $313 million that had both principal and interest at risk, was rated BB/BB-, and priced at LIBOR + 575 bps.

[12] USAA actually purchased private reinsurance to cover a large portion of these "retained" exposures.

[13] Surplus notes are a quasi-debt security issued by insurers in the United States that are treated as equity capital for regulatory purposes, provided that they satisfy the appropriate regulatory criteria.

[14] In addition to these deals, American Skandia has entered into a series of transactions (e.g. ASLAC Trust I and II) designed to securitize their interest in money management fees from managed mutual fund portfolios. While American Skandia is entitled to earn these fund management fees at the inception of an account, the recognition of the fee income must be accrued over the life of the fund. To expedite the recognition of these fees, Skandia has effectively sold its interest in this fee income.

[15] See for example, Capital Markets Report, Dow Jones & Company, May 1998.

[16] See, for example, BondWeek, November 19, 2001.

[17] Technically, the ownership of the aircraft assets are transferred to the SPV trust to secure the interest of investors. The trust then enters into a lease agreement with the airline for the use of the aircraft assets and provides the airline sponsor with an equity interest sized by the initial deposit for the aircraft being purchased.

[18] For more information on Aircraft Securitizations, see S&P rating criteria for aircraft securities.

[19] "Arby's Completes Innovative Securitization of Franchise Royalty Payments," TRIARC Press Release, November 22, 2000.

[20] Under these assumptions, Leland shows that the expected return formula can be re-specified as follows:

$$E(r_a) = r_f + \beta'_a[E(r_m) - r_f] \qquad (13.4)$$

where

$$\beta'_a = \frac{Cov[r_a, -(1+r_m)^{-b}]}{Cov[r_m, -(1+r_m)^{-b}]} \qquad (13.5)$$

The parameter b is the market's price of risk when the return on the market portfolio is lognormally distributed (as implied by the first model assumption), and can be determined from observable market factors:

$$b = \frac{in[E(1+r_m)] - in(1+r_f)}{Var[in(1+r_m)]} \qquad (13.6)$$

where $in[\bullet]$ refers to instantaneous parameter estimates. Thus, the coefficient b is the market's instantaneous excess rate of return divided by the variance of the market's instantaneous rate of return. Parallel to the traditional CAPM model, Leland shows how to derive an adjusted α-estimate that differs only in the specification for the market's price of risk.

$$\alpha'_a = E(r_a|\Theta) - \beta'_a[E(r_m) - r_f] - r_f \qquad (13.7)$$

[21] This approach also is superior to the comparison of Sharpe ratios since Sharpe ratios–like the traditional CAPM model–are only relevant when investors have mean–variance preferences.

References

Aase, Knut K. 2001. "A Markov Model for the Pricing of Catastrophe Insurance Futures and Spreads." *The Journal of Risk and Insurance* 68(1): 25–49.

Benz, Matthew. 2001. "Bowie Bonds: One-off or a Sound Vision for the Future." *BillBoard Magazine* June 20.

Blake, David and Williams Burrows. 2001. "Survivor Bonds: Helping to Hedge Mortality Risk." *The Journal of Risk and Insurance* 68(2): 339–348.

Bowers, William C. 2002. "Aircraft Lease Securitization: ALPS to EETCs." <www.winstim.com>.

Cantor, Michael S., Joseph B. Cole, and Richard L. Sandor. 1996. "Insurance Derivatives: A New Asset Class for the Capital Markets and a New Hedging Tool for the Insurance Industry." *The Journal of Derivatives* Winter: 89–104.

Cummins, J. David, David Lalonde, and Richard D. Phillips. 2002*a*. "Managing Risk Using Index-Linked Catastrophic Loss Securities." In *Alternative Risk Strategies,* ed. Morton Lane. London: Risk Books.

—— —— —— 2002*b*. "The Basis Risk of Index-Linked Catastrophic Loss Securities." Working Paper. Philadelphia: Wharton Financial Institutions Center.

—— Christopher M. Lewis and Richard D. Phillips. 1998. "The Pricing of Excess-of-Loss Reinsurance Contracts Against Catastrophic Loss." In *The Financing of Property/Casualty Risk,* ed. Kenneth Froot. National Bureau of Economic Research, University of Chicago Press, pp. 93–148.

Das, Satyajit. 1998. *Credit Derivatives: Trading and Management of Credit and Default Risk.* New York: John Wiley & Son.

Doherty, Neil A. 1997. "Financial Innovation in the Management of Catastrophe Risk." *Journal of Applied Corporate Finance* 10: 84–95.

Dong, Weimin, Haresh Shah, and Felix Wong. 1996. "A Rational Approach to Pricing Catastrophe Insurance." *Journal of Risk and Uncertainty* 12: 201–219.

Fink, Laurence D. 1998. "The Role of Pension Funds and Other Investors in Securitized Debt Markets." In *A Primer on Securitization,* eds. Leon T. Kendall and Michael J. Fishman. MIT Press, pp. 117–127.

Hu, Joseph, Patrick Coyne, and Jay Elengical. 2002. "Commentary: Rating Transitions 2001: U.S. ABS Credit Ratings Endure the Test of Recession." Standard & Poor's. <www.standardandpoors.com>.

Kao, Duen-Li. 2000. "Estimating and Pricing Credit Risk: An Overview." *Financial Analysts Journal* July/August: 50–66.

Kraus, Alan and Robert H. Litzenberger. 1976. "Skewness Preference and the Valuation of Risk Assets." *Journal of Finance* 31: 1085–1100.

Lane, Morton N. 2000. "Pricing Risk Transfer Transaction." Lane Financial LLC, Keynote speech at the AFIR 2000 Colloquium in Tromso, Norway.

— 2001. "Analyzing the Pricing of the 2001 Risk-linked Securities Transactions." Presented at the IIASA-DPRI Meeting on Integrated Disaster Management, Laxenberg, Austria.

— and Roger G. Beckwith. 2001. "Current Trends in Risk-Linked Securitizations: March 2000–March 2001, Trade Notes." <LaneFinancialLLC.com>.

Leland, Hayne E. 1999. "Beyond Mean-Variance: Performance Measurement in a Nonsymmetrical World." *Financial Analysts Journal* 55: 27–38.

Lewis, Christopher M. and Peter O. Davis. 1998. "Capital Market Instruments for Financing Catastrophe Risk: New Directions?" *Journal of Insurance Regulation* 17(2): 110–133, NAIC Press.

Litzenberger, Robert H., David R. Beaglehole, and Craig E. Reynolds. 1996. "Assessing Catastrophe Reinsurance-Linked Securities as a New Asset Class." *Journal of Portfolio Management* Special Issue, December: 76–86.

Lucia, Julio J. and Eduardo S. Schwartz. 2002. "Electricity Prices and Power Derivatives: Evident from the Nordic Power Exchange." *Review of Derivatives Research* 5: 5–50.

Maurer, Raimond and Christian Schlag. This volume "Money-Back Guarantees in Individual Account Pensions: Evidence of German Reform."

Rubinstein, Mark. 1976. "The Valuation of Uncertain Income Streams and The Pricing Of Options." *Bell Journal of Economics* 7: 407–425.

Standard & Poor's. 1998. *New Assets.* <www.standardandpoors.com>.

— 2001. "Interest in Life Insurance Securitization Heats Up." October 2001 Commentary. <www.standardandpoors.com>.

Swiss Re. 1997. "Too Little Reinsurance of Natural Disasters in Many Markets." *Sigma* 7: 3–22.

— 2002. "Natural Catastrophes and Man-Made Disasters in 2001: Man-Made Losses Take on a New Dimension." *Sigma* 1: 1–25.

— 2001. "Capital Market Innovation in the Insurance Industry." *Sigma* 3: 35–37.

Turner, John, and David Rajnes. This volume "Retirement Guarantees in Voluntary Defined Contribution Plans."

Vetzel, Kenneth, Peter Forsyth, and Heath Windchff. This volume "Hedging Segregated Fund Guarantees."

Walliser, Jan. This volume "Retirement Guarantees in Mandatory Defined Contribution Systems."

Chapter 14

Credit Implications of the Payout Annuity Market

Arthur Fliegelman, Moshe Arye Milevsky, and Scott A. Robinson

As baby boomers gradually shift from the asset accumulation to the distribution phase of their lifecycle, competition between insurance companies, mutual funds, and banks to control these substantial assets will intensify. The penalty for not offering products that meet retirees' demands is the potential loss of sizable asset pools. To offset this risk, US life insurers can take advantage of their unique ability to offer longevity insurance through payout annuities, if they are to maximize their asset retention. Payout annuities are annuity contracts that make regular, periodic income payouts to the annuitant at some predetermined point in time after the purchase of the contract.

This chapter focuses on the risks and opportunities for insurers when they convert qualified retirement or other saving into guaranteed payout streams. The consequent annuity payments can either be fixed in amount, or they can vary with the performance of underlying investments. Variable immediate annuities (VIA), which are payout annuities with funds usually invested in equities, have gained in popularity in recent years. Products such as these can transfer any of a variety of risks, from the individual to the insurer which, depending on the product, may include longevity, interest rate, credit, equity market fluctuations, and inflation risk. Benefiting from the "law of large numbers," in conjunction with creative product design, insurance companies can mitigate many of the risks they assume in offering these contracts.

For an insurer to make a profit on the product, however, the company almost certainly must retain some risk elements. Given the potential size of the retirement market and the increasing complexity of the related insurance product guarantees, an understanding of these products' potential risks to the offeror is essential to evaluating their financial position.

Our objective, therefore, is to explore the credit implications of assorted guarantees made by insurance companies offering payout annuity products in the retirement income market. As part of our analysis, we use a pricing model to quantify the risks to profitability (and solvency) from unexpected increases in longevity. Our modeling shows that future mortality improvements can have a material impact on companies with significant exposure to payout annuities. That said, we believe that the market offers substantial opportunity for the industry to attract new assets while meeting the financial needs of retirees.

Credit Risk in the Retirement Income Market

A brief look at recent insurance company failures in the United States helps illustrate the risks facing insurers and the role they play in the payout annuity market.

History of US Insurance Company Failures

The 1983 insolvency of Baldwin-United, a significant provider of single premium deferred annuities (SPDA), brought the issue of life insurance solvency to the attention of the general public. Though considered an annuity from a legal and regulatory perspective, the SPDA, acts economically more like a tax-deferred savings account or certificate of deposit. Though SPDA contracts almost always permit the contract holder to convert the contract's principal to a stream of income (the annuity) at the contract holder's option, this very rarely happens in actual practice (Sondergeld, 1997). Neither is this right given much attention in the product marketing process, since in most cases, the minimal contractually guaranteed annuity rates are based upon very low interest rates (e.g. 3 percent) and dynamically projected mortality tables. Thus if the contract were ever to be annuitized, the applicable annuity factors would most likely be higher; these more favorable factors would be used by the insurance company to set payouts. Some companies have significant amounts of older business outstanding with higher interest rate guarantees and mortality guarantees that were not based on dynamically projected tables, thereby increasing the value of the product's annuitization option to policyholders. Nevertheless, most of these options remain out-of-the-money, and policyholders would have to annuitize any in-the-money options to realize their value.

The issue of life insurer creditworthiness again grabbed headlines in 1991 with a rapid string of large insurer failures, including those of Executive Life Insurance Company, Mutual Benefit Life Insurance Company, and First Capital Life Insurance Company. The list was lengthened in 1994 and again in 1995 with the respective failures of Confederation Life Insurance Company and the holding company of Southwestern Life Corporation. Several other companies have also failed.

There are a number of themes common to these failures that provide valuable lessons. Many of these companies, for instance, had a product profile that was heavily weighted toward "spread-based" products such as SPDA and guaranteed investment contracts (GIC). They also often had short dated liabilities funded with insufficiently liquid and/or higher risk asset classes such as commercial mortgage loans, real estate, less-liquid private placements, or below-investment-grade bonds. Other problems included high leverage, regulatory issues, poor underwriting results, fraud, and problems in subsidiary or affiliate operations (Maloney, 1999).

The insurance industry has done much to improve the asset side of its balance sheet since the early 1990s. Yet exceptions remain and old risks continue to reappear in new products. In 1999, General American sought protection when it became unable to meet its near-term obligations because of inadequate available short-term liquidity. Illiquid assets and liability optionality continue to represent a potentially lethal combination that regulators and rating agencies must monitor closely.

Applying These Lessons to the Payout Annuity Market

While the life insurance failures of the past provide valuable lessons, it is also essential to anticipate future effects of changes in the industry's risk profile. For example, the importance of risks affiliated with the payout phase will rise as companies' liabilities become more concentrated in payout products, especially if more optionality is added to these products.

In our opinion, risks tied to the following two guarantees will become more prominent in the coming year.

Embedded Equity Guarantees

Many consumers planning for retirement seek equity market exposure with some form of downside protection. Insurance companies are responding to these demands with increasingly innovative product features such as guaranteed minimum income benefits (GMIB) and VIA with floors. Both of these product options are further discussed below.

Aggressive Payout Annuity Guarantees

Aggressive mortality, interest rate, or equity guarantees could expose insurers to material losses over the life of a payout annuity. These risks are heightened if a company guarantees payment streams to be made far in the future when there is increased uncertainty about the variables affecting the guarantee.

Mis-pricings of the above guarantees are unlikely to result in a dramatic "run on the bank" scenario culminating in a company failure, except in the most extreme cases. But a prolonged period of operating losses could severely weaken a company's capital position over time and reduce the overall financial strength.

Assessing Payout Annuity Market Opportunities for Insurers

On the positive side, there are a number of reasons to believe that the opportunity for insurers to meet retirees' income demands will grow significantly.

First, an aging population increases the demand for retirement products. By the year 2025, reasonably conservative estimates are that the proportion of the population aged over 65 in developed countries will increase to over 30 percent from just over 20 percent today. By 2050, this proportion will be over 40 percent. Consistent with economic lifecycle models of saving and consumption (Ando and Modigliani, 1963; Yaari, 1965), this will increase the demand for longevity insurance.

A second consideration is that the shift from defined benefit to defined contribution retirement plans has resulted in retirees assuming increased responsibility for meeting their retirement income needs. Instead of receiving a defined retirement income stream from the employer's defined benefit plan, more workers must personally manage their retirement funds during the accumulation phase as well as during the retirement base. Some might argue that employers offering defined contribution plans would recognize a responsibility to provide payout annuities, similar to the obligation to provide a diversified set of risk and return investment opportunities within a 401(k) plan. While this is not required, providing longevity protection would appear to offer substantial opportunity for growth in this market.

A third reason to expect market growth is that future retirees may not receive scheduled Social Security benefits, which should boost the demand for alternative retirement income resources. Deferred annuities, particularly variable annuities, have been a phenomenal growth area for the US insurance industry.

For all their success in selling variable annuities, however, insurers have thus far had little success in persuading individuals to convert their retirement funding accumulations into annuity streams, with the notable exception of TIAA-CREF, rated Aaa for insurance financial strength. Our best estimate is that the annuitization rate on variable annuities in the United States is less than 5 percent. Increasing annuitization rates will be crucial if insurance companies are going to retain the assets they have spent so much time and effort to acquire.

Extensive competition has already developed over control of assets during the accumulation phase. Section 1035 exchanges, allow an individual to transfer funds without tax consequences between two different insurance contracts, and noticeably these have negatively impacted the profitability of some large variable annuity writers. The Economic Growth and Tax Relief Reconciliation Act of 2001 (EGTRRA) also made it easier for participants to transfer funds out of 457 and 403(b) plans, further enticing insurance companies to find ways to retain assets through means such as annuitization.

In order for the payout annuity market to reach its full potential, however, the industry will have to convince distributors—including insurance agents, financial planners, and brokers—of the important role that payout annuities can fulfill in meeting client needs, and adequately reward them for their efforts to sell the product. When selling a payout annuity, a financial advisor gives up the valuable option to generate additional revenue from the account in the future, which can reduce the incentive to suggest such payout annuities. Companies have therefore been changing commission structures, by adding "trail commissions," to make immediate annuities more attractive to distributors.

The Size of the Market

The payout annuity market can be broadly divided into the annuitization and immediate annuity segments (Fenton and Hecht, 1999). As explained below, each of these segments can be further subdivided into fixed and variable payout annuity products. The "annuitization market" refers to the conversion of a lump sum of funds from an existing insurance contract into a defined payment stream. Note that we focus on the market in which individuals have some element of control over their retirement assets, as opposed to the traditional defined benefit pension plan. Annuitization is not a source of new funds to the industry but rather assures the industry continued retention of existing funds. Annuitizations in 2000 amounted to approximately $14 billion in the US Sales from the structured settlement and the terminal funding markets are not included in these numbers, as these products are not included in our analysis (LIMRA International, 2000).

Immediate annuities are new annuity contracts that initiate a periodic income payment at some predetermined point in time. Total sales of individual immediate annuities for 2000 came to $3.8 billion (LIMRA International, 2000). These figures exclude sales of TIAA-CREF, which had approximately $49 billion of payout annuity reserves as of year-end, 2001, including $17.7 billion of variable annuity reserves and $31.6 billion of fixed annuity reserves. Sales of VIAs are growing at a much faster rate than fixed annuity sales, although from a much lower base, as illustrated in Table 14-1.

Along with equity participation, annuitants also want security. Floor guarantees are therefore becoming increasingly popular as a component of VIAs, along with GMIB, in which the value of the option to annuitize at a guaranteed rate is dependent upon underlying account performance. Fliegelman and Robinson (2000) examined the credit implications of GMIBs along

TABLE 14-1 Annuity Sales Volume for US Market

	Fixed SPIA Sales (Billions $)	*Immediate Variable Sales (Billions $)*
1993	2.7	–
1994	2.6	–
1995	*	–
1996	3.0	0.2
1997	2.8	0.2
1998	2.4	0.3
1999	2.9	0.5
2000	3.0	0.8

Source: LIMRA International, 2000.

Note:
– No data available.
*Includes structured settlements.
This table lists the volume of annual sales for fixed SPIA and VIA during the 8-year-period ending in the year 2000. Note the increasing volume for VIA contracts during the last few years.

with other annuity secondary guarantees, but there are inadequate data with which to measure the current size of the VIA market. Further, there is a widespread lack of consumer appreciation for the longevity-insurance benefit of payout annuities.

The Role of an Immediate Annuity in Retirement

Financial advisors tend to envision a payout annuity as one element in the retirement portfolio. Savings, social security, employer pension plans and part-time work are additional financial resources for retirees. The combination of these resources should allow retirees to meet their financial goals, which include income required to maintain a desired standard of living; preservation or growth of at least a portion of those assets; funds available for emergency needs. While most consumers purchase life insurance because they are afraid of *dying too soon* and thus leaving family and loved ones in financial distress, older people buy immediate annuities because they are afraid of outlasting their financial resources should they *live too long*.

Immediate annuities (IA) provide valuable *longevity insurance* to the beneficiary that cannot be replicated by other investments through the use of a systematic withdrawal plan. Some payout annuities provide liquidity options and even protection against inflation. We discuss both of these features later in the chapter.

TABLE 14-2 Survival Probabilities to Alternative Ages (%) Conditional on Being Alive at 65

Survive To Age	*Survival Probabilities*		
	Single Female	*Single Male*	*At Least One from a Married Couple*
70	93.8	92.0	99.5
75	84.4	79.9	96.9
80	70.9	62.7	89.1
85	52.8	41.0%	72.2
90	31.6	19.6%	45.0
95	13.4	5.8	18.4

Note: This table lists the conditional probabilities of survival for a couple exactly 65 years of age. For example, the probability that at least one of the two survive for 20 more years, that is, to age 85, is 72.2 percent. Note that this number is far larger than the probability that either of them individually survives to age 85.

Source: Based on Society of Actuaries RP2000 data (www.soa.org/research).

To provide a sense of mortality patterns, Table 14-2 illustrates how long an individual can expect to live conditional on surviving to age 65. The first two columns show the probabilities of survival to a specified age for an individual female and an individual male, respectively. The last column shows the joint probability that at least one person from a married couple (both currently aged 65) will survive to the specified age. Interestingly enough age 85 is the typical "assumed" life expectancy, in most retirement planning calculations assuming that a lifetime annuity is not purchased. Table 14-2 shows that such an assumption exposes the retiree to considerable risk: at age 85 over 50 percent of individual females and over 40 percent of individual males alive at age 65, will still be alive. For married couples, the situation is even worse, with at least one spouse still alive at age 85 in over 70% of the cases. Consequently, if these individuals had used an age-85 life expectancy to plan their retirement income needs, it his highly likely they would exhaust their retirement resources (other than Social Security) while they were still alive. This *longevity risk*–the risk of outliving one's resources–is substantial and a main reason that we believe immediate annuities will grow in popularity. Clearly, retirees can protect themselves against this risk by purchasing protection from an insurance company.

The Role of the Law of Large Numbers In the Payout Annuity Market

Purchasing a fixed IA involves paying a nonrefundable lump sum to an insurance company in exchange for a series of periodic payments, usually monthly. With some products, the payments end after a pre-determined fixed period; these are called fixed-term (or period certain) annuities. With pure life-contingent annuity products, the income ends only upon death of the annuitant(s). Each of these annuities can also incorporate a refund of "unused" premiums upon death. Period certain and life contingency payment streams can also be combined in a single product, such as 20-year certain plus life.

Now, consider a group of five 95-year-old women each worried about outliving their retirement assets. US life tables show that there is a 20 percent chance that a random 95-year-old (white) female will die during the next year. Equivalently, in a large group of 95 year-old females, 20 percent of them will not survive for another year.

To protect against outliving their assets, these five 95-year-old women could enter into the following legally binding agreement. Each of the five would then contribute $100 to a communal fund that will invest in Treasury Bills yielding 5 percent. Then, according to the contract, at the end of the year, the *surviving* females will be entitled to split the proceeds of the fund.

The total contribution of 5*$100 = $500 will grow to $525 by the end of the year. If all five females are still alive—at 96 years of age—they will each receive $105. This is precisely their original $100 investment, plus interest. Nevertheless, what happens if one of them, which is what is expected, dies during the next year? The surviving four are entitled to split the $525, giving each a payment of $131.25. The remaining four survivors have effectively had a "return" of 31.25 percent on their investment. If two happen to die during the year, the remaining three each get $175, for a 75 percent "return" on investment. In other words, the survivors' returns consisted of their original principal, their interest, and a portion of the non-survivors principal and interest. By pooling mortality risk and ceding bequests, everyone gains. Technically, this agreement is called a tontine, also known as a participating pure endowment contract or, in this example, a participating one-period life annuity contract.

Of course, with only five women in the initial pool, the variation in what could happen might be wide, although only six things can happen. They might all die, and they all might survive or somewhere in between. However, with 10,000 such females entering a one-period annuity agreement, the *statistical law of large numbers* assures us that $1,050,000 will be split amongst very close to 8,000 survivors. In other words, the expected return from the contract—for the survivors—is (1,050,000/8,000) = 31.25 percent. The numerator is the total final value of the pool, and the denominator represents the survivors. The difference between the 5% return available in the market, and the 31.25% earned by the survivors are *mortality credits.* The higher the probability of death—that is the lower the expected number of survivors—the greater are the expected mortality credits. As one can

TABLE 14-3 Investment Returns Required to Exceed Annuity Implicit Return Assuming Survival

Age	*Death Probability*	*Required Return (%)*
55	2.26/1000	6.2
65	5.76/1000	6.6
75	16.34/1000	7.8
85	54.05/1000	12.1
90	95.84/1000	17.2

Note: This table displays the investment rate of return that is required to beat the implicit return from a fixed immediate annuity (FIA) at various ages, assuming a 6% interest rate pricing environment. Thus, for example, a 65-year-old (male) would only have to earn 6.6% during the next year, to end-up in a better position, compared to purchasing the fixed annuity. However, the same individual at age 95 would have to earn a (virtually impossible) 17.2% to beat the fixed annuity. Thus, the fixed annuity is relatively more attractive at higher ages. Assumptions: R = 6%, load = 0%, IAM1996 Table.

Source: Authors' calculations.

see from Table 14-3, at high ages it becomes virtually impossible to beat the implied mortality credits within a payout annuity through investment alone.

In theory, at younger ages it makes little sense for individuals to enter into an immediate annuity contract since the mortality credits are relatively low, and one can usually "beat" the implied returns through lower expense products or the using of alternative higher return asset classes. In practice, only insurance companies are typically allowed to create and manage such agreements to provide these mortality-contingent products. Most insurers go one step further and *guarantee* that annuitants receive a mortality credit enhancement, even if the mortality experience of the participants is worse (from the insurer's perspective) than expected, for example, if the participants live longer than expected. How can an insurer provide this guarantee? It does so by making careful and conservative assumptions about the rate of return earned on assets and the expected mortality experience. Furthermore, the greater the number of IAs an insurance company has on its books, the lower the risk of providing this mortality guarantee.

These are the ultimate economies of scale. In other words, the risk to the insurer might be significant if it sold only five such policies, but with half a million policies, the probability of significant statistical fluctuations becomes negligible. This, once again, is a direct result of the law of large numbers. It is important to stress, however, that there are two distinct categories of mortality risk that an insurance company faces when selling the payout annuity. The first type can best be described as a "small sample" risk. It reflects the chance that any particular annuitant will live longer than average. When faced with such a client, the insurance company is confronted with a payment stream that is longer than originally expected based on annuitant mortality rates. Actuarial theory has long established that this particular risk can be eliminated—and therefore should not be priced—by selling enough identical policies and taking advantage of the law of large numbers. Therefore, if enough policies are sold, the realization will converge to the expected.

The second type of risk is a subtler one. It is the risk that the insurance company overestimate the population's force of mortality, or, to put it in layman's language, that societal and medical changes will significantly lengthen average life expectations. The company can also misestimate the makeup of its customer base, selling to annuitants living longer than projected in pricing. This type of longevity risk cannot be easily hedged by appealing to the law of large numbers and selling more payout annuities.

Some insurance companies act as intermediaries but do not assume mortality or investment risk. Participating immediate annuities are structured so that individuals share with the insurer any unexpected favorable or unfavorable investment returns or mortality experience. Participating annuities shift a substantial part of the risk from the insurance company to the participant. The experience is not passed on immediately, but rather is borne by the annuitant pool and smoothed by the insurance company over a long time horizon. The provision is akin to the difference between a defined contribution and defined benefit pension plan. Both are meant to provide a pension, but the risk allocation mechanism is different. Indeed, the participating annuity structure greatly reduces the longevity risk to which the insurer is exposed.

An Engine for Future Growth? Variable Immediate Annuities

VIA are annuities with payments linked to the performance of a pool of underlying investments. By contrast, fixed annuity payments are set at issuance and are guaranteed by the insurance company, regardless of its investment or other experience. VIAs have increased in popularity and represent attractive potential since companies can earn a higher return on invested capital through a VIA than they can on a fixed annuity.

Though VIA payments may vary with any index or underlying investment, in this chapter we concentrate on VIAs backed by equity investments. Essentially, the principles of VIA are the same as those for a fixed annuity, except that the annuitants do not know in advance what the fund/pool will earn. Annuitants realize their investment returns only at the end of the year, and

TABLE 14-4 How A Variable Immediate Annuity Works: Monthly Payment Per $100,000 Premium + Unisex Age 55

AIR (%)	*Initial*	−20%	0%	+20%
4	$440	$334	$422	$510
5	$500	$374	$474	$574
6	$560	$415	$527	$639

Note: This table displays the initial and subsequent payments from a VIA under various market scenarios, and with a particular AIR selected in advance. For example, if a 6% AIR is chosen, the initial payment will be $560 per month at age 55. Subsequently, if the market declines by 20% during the next year, the payment at age 56 will be reduced to $415 per month.

Source: Authors' calculations.

then they split the gains among pool survivors. In the event that the investment earns a negative return (loses money), participants will also share in the losses, but the effect will be mitigated by the mortality credits.

All VIAs use an assumed investment return (AIR) to establish payout levels. Some VIAs allow the individual to select their own AIR, typically between 3 and 7 percent annually. Most commonly, contractholders elect a 5-percent return. To the extent that actual returns differ from the AIR, future payments are adjusted accordingly. Table 14-4 illustrates how this works.

For example, if an AIR of 4 percent is used, then a premium of $100,000 might produce an initial monthly payment of approximately $440. Subsequently, if the underlying market index dropped by 20 percent during the next year, the new payment would be $334, which–ignoring monthly compounding effects–is roughly $440 × (1 − 0.2)/(1 + 0.04). Note that the return, 20 percent in this case, is net of all expenses, including both fund level and contract expenses. On the other hand, if the market increased by 20 percent, the monthly payment would be $510, or roughly $440 × (1+0.2)/(1+0.04). Each year, the new payment becomes the benchmark, and the process begins anew. Technically, the 4-percent AIR functions as a "hurdle rate" above which payments are increased and below which payments are reduced. By contrast, if a higher AIR is selected, the initial payment is higher, but the hurdle rate is higher as well. Payments will only increase in subsequent years if the underlying index increases by more than the AIR.

The important point is that companies do not have basis risk on their investments, since investment guarantees are based on the actual return. But the insurer's profitability is still heavily influenced by market performance. To provide more payment stability to the recipient, some companies are now changing in the amount paid only once each year. In addition, market innovations have included creating floors to limit the downside and offsetting ceilings to restrict participation on the upside.

Risks in the Payout Annuity Market

Key risks to annuity providers include longevity and investment risk. Further, annuities may offer contract holders the right to receive surrender payments and obtain a commuted value, which creates even greater uncertainty for the insurance company concerning future cash flows.

Companies that do not properly price mortality and investment or equity market risk may not meet their profitability targets or worse. Our conversations with companies suggested that their post-tax returns on investment targets are typically 10–12 percent for fixed annuities, and over 15 percent for VIAs. The worst-case scenario for offerers of fixed annuities would be a prolonged declining interest rate environment combined with unexpected longevity improvements. For VIAs, a decline in the equity markets would also lower fees earned and could also trigger a minimum payout guarantee.

In what follows, we break down the various pricing elements and compare them to actual results. We also evaluate if a company offering a particular annuity product will be able to withstand unlikely scenarios that it may not have considered during pricing.

The Nature and Pricing of Mortality Risk

The sustainability of past mortality improvement has been a subject of substantial debate (Carnes and Olshansky, 1998). The value of annuity payouts may have been rising, of late because companies are not taking full mortality improvement into account (Poterba and Warshawky, 2001).

Appropriate mortality assumptions to use for pricing purposes depend on the universe of potential applicants. Companies offering annuities to the general public should expect a degree of adverse selection, as healthy applicants are naturally more likely to purchase longevity protection. Brown, Warshawsky, and Poterba (2001) measure the value of adverse selection at approximately 12 percent of premium for a 65-year-old man. Companies offering annuities to qualified pension plans must also consider the plans' expected male/female ratio, since by law they must price using unisex mortality rates. Women benefit from purchasing annuities based on a unisex table so a higher than expected ratio of women purchasers would reduce insurer profitability.

So, What Happens if Science Finds a Cure for Cancer and Heart Disease?

Clearly, the impact of major longevity improvements will depend on the exact timing and magnitude of scientific and medical breakthroughs.

TABLE 14-5 Impact of Alternative Assumptions on Single Premium Immediate Annuity Issue Age

Mortality	**Reduction (%)*	*Life Expectancy Spread*					
		Unisex 55		*Unisex 62*		*Unisex 70*	
Status Quo	0	82.9	+100 bp	83.8	+100 bp	85.6	+100 bp
Stroke and Pneumonia	−10	83.8	+85 bp	84.7	+77 bp	86.4	+60 bp
Cancer and Diabetes	−40	87.4	+39 bp	88.1	+4 bp	89.4	−67 bp
Heart Disease	−80	97.7	−36 bp	97.9	−111 bp	98.6	−257 bp

Note: This table displays the *ex post* spread that would be earned from single premium immediate annuity block of business, assuming an *ex ante* desired spread of 100 bps. Thus, for example, if life annuities were sold to a 62-year-old with the intention of earning a spread of 100 bps, then a 10% aggregate reduction in mortality (from the elimination of strokes and pneumonia) would reduce the spread to 77 bps.

Source: Authors' computations.

To quantify the effect of a substantial breakthrough on an insurance company's profitability, we have developed a simple pricing model (explained more fully in the Appendix).

Table 14-5 illustrates the impact of an unexpected improvement in life expectancy, driven by a constant proportional reduction in the force of mortality (hazard rate). These ratios roughly coincide with the average causes of death.[1]

To gauge the impact of major mortality improvements, imagine a situation in which a life annuity is issued and priced at age 62, with a 100 bp profit margin, assuming the SOA 1994 GAM (static, unisex) table captures the underlying population. The life expectancy at the issue age of 62 is 83.8, which is the life expectancy with no mortality improvement other than that already built into the actual table used to price the annuity, and the *ex ante* profit spread is 100 bp. If, however, there were suddenly an unexpected mortality improvement, the firm's *ex post* profit spread will clearly be reduced: the question is, "by how much?"

To answer this we must look a bit more closely at the precise causes of death. At advanced ages, approximately 10 percent of deaths can be attributed to strokes together with pneumonia, an additional 30 percent can be attributed to cancer and diabetes, 40 percent is due to heart disease, and the remaining 20 percent are accidents, suicide, and formally classified as "others" (Society of Actuaries, 1996). Likewise, the exact fraction will depend on the population in question, its sex composition, and ages at death. For now, we assume that the fractions are constant.

To evaluate the breakthrough scenario, we imagine that science found a cure to all strokes and pneumonia, reducing the force of mortality at each age by a factor of 10 percent. Curing cancer and diabetes lowers mortality by 40 percent, and eliminating heart disease, lowers mortality by 80 percent.[2] Thus, at each age, a *fixed fraction* of deaths is eliminated as a proxy for the reduction in various decrements.[3]

It is interesting that, the higher the issue age, the greater the impact on profitability of a given percentage improvement in mortality. For example, reducing cancer and diabetes ($f = -40$ percent), will still leave the insurer with a profit spread of +39 bp at issue age 55, but a −67 bp spread at issue age 70. One can do the same exercise with an individual annuity mortality table, such as the IAM or with some form of dynamic projection, and obtain results on the same order of magnitude. It is also interesting that an 80 percent reduction in the mortality rates, (by virtually eliminating cancer, stroke, pneumonia, and heart disease), adds only 10–15 years to human life. Alternatively, a 62 (unisex) year-old annuitant with a current life expectancy of age 83.8, would have to experience a 98 percent reduction in the force of mortality at all future ages, to expect to live to the biblical upper-bound of 120 years of age.[4]

Regardless of the actual methodology, the marginal impact is greater the older the issue-age of the business. In other words, at younger ages, the impact of a fixed percent reduction in mortality is lessened. More generally, it is essential to look closely at the process of determining mortality and the mortality improvement used in pricing insurance products, as well as the weighting of company and industry data.

Investment Risk

In developing an investment strategy for non-indexed fixed payout annuities, an investment manager is faced with the challenge of meeting fixed payments for an uncertain period. Insurers will take different degrees of investment risk to meet alternative pricing objectives. Credit defaults and assumed reinvestment interest rates are two key variables that insurers must consider.

Insurance companies typically invest primarily in bonds and other fixed income instruments. To attain high yields required to be competitive in issuing payout annuities, companies can purchase higher-yielding, lower credit-quality assets, or invest in markets such as private placements and commercial mortgages that offer incremental income. Clearly, defaults can have a material impact on profitability. A declining interest rate environment, combined with greater than anticipated mortality improvements, may also materially impact an insurer's profitability, particularly when the insurer is deploying shorter duration assets to back longer duration payout annuities. A dearth of attractive long-term assets can lead insurers to accept this kind of investment risk. Conversely, for firms invested in long, illiquid assets, a rise in interest rates could negatively impact profitability. Companies caught in this position may need to liquidate depreciated assets to meet payments.

Commutation Rights

In response to market demands, some insurers have offered annuitants the right to commute, or end, their contracts and receive at least a portion of their future annuity payments up front. In order to protect themselves against adverse selection from annuitants in ill health, insurers normally only permit commutation for a limited portion of the period's annuity payments. In these situations, insurers can control asset-liability mismatches by applying a market value adjustment (MVA) to the commutation. For a fixed annuity with an MVA, the discount rate used in determining the present value of future payments would be linked to a current market rate such as the 10-year Treasury rate. Unamortized expenses of the insurer would typically be protected by also applying a surrender charge that grades down over time.

Few companies offer the right to commute life contingent payments, mainly because of complications in determining the appropriate discount rate, the uncertainty of which is driven by mortality. The most common method to address the risk of adverse selection is to underwrite each annuitant seeking to commute life contingent payments. Companies offering such a feature must carefully consider all risks, including expense and legal ramifications.

The complicated nature of the product as compared to a straight annuity, implies that administration and sales training costs may be sizable. To protect against potential sales misconduct charges, firms must take steps to ensure that contractholders fully understand the commutation process. We believe that life contingent commutations will remain infrequent because of the complexities involved. Insurers may offer customers the ability to acquire offsetting life insurance, and to borrow against the "death benefit." This will allow annuitants to unlock the payment streams, albeit with a loan backed by an insurance policy. Another innovative proposal is to underwrite and sell long-term care insurance, together with life-contingent annuities, to offset these risks.

Risks in the Variable Immediate Annuity Market

Companies offering VIAs hedge against investment basis risk by linking promised payments to the actual performance of investments supporting the contract. An insurer's VIA product fees are also based on the account value, thereby linking the profitability of the product to the performance of the underlying assets. Notwithstanding the performance of the equity markets, companies will remain exposed to longevity risk. Consider a block of VIA experiencing higher-than-anticipated equity market appreciation, along with unexpected mortality improvements. Fees paid to the insurer will rise along with the associated assets, but the positive financial impact on the insurer of the increased fees must be compared with the negative impact of the increased longevity, which requires that the payments be made for a longer then expected period. The fact that a favorable equity market has increased the size of the periodic payment magnifies the longevity risk to the insurer. Conversely, lower-than-anticipated equity market performance diminishes the fees paid to the insurer. In this case, however, the longevity risk is not magnified by rising payments. In either case, an insurer can help offset its financial exposure to equity market performance by basing commissions paid to producers on the annuity payment stream.

Potential Liquidity Risks

Giving contract holders the ability to shift funds between the general account and variable account can also present risks to an insurer. Specifically, the possibility that policyholders might move between accounts *en masse* exposes the insurer to liquidity risk: there may be a need to sell a large block of bonds to fully fund the variable accounts.

Inflation-Indexed Payments

Companies offering inflation-indexed annuities must consider the basis risk of investing for the indexed payment. For the few companies offering annuity products indexed to the consumer price index, the scarcity of appropriate investments needs to be considered in the asset-liability management process.

Managing Payout Annuity Risk

To quantify the risk of payout annuities to an insurer, it is important to understand the incremental risk that these products add to a company's overall risk profile. For most insurers, payout annuities represent a very small portion of overall risk. The cost required to reduce the risk exposure from these products may not be justified. Nevertheless, prudence dictates that companies should have a longer-term plan for keeping their risk management process up-to-date with expanding sales. Companies also need to be sure that they are properly quantifying the risks in their products. This is particularly true for products with so-called cliff risks. Such products may meet pricing objectives in 99 percent of the scenarios, but they could still have very negative financial results in the remaining rare scenario. This can be the case with products such as a VIA or a product containing a GMIB.

Benefits of Diversification

One way that an insurer can mitigate the longevity risk of its payout annuity products is to take an offsetting position on mortality exposure though its life insurance products. Since the target populations for the different policies can be quite distinct, however, determining the diversification benefits can be somewhat difficult. On the other hand, there is some debate whether there are any substantial benefits from product diversification into IAs and life insurance. This is because IAs are sold primarily to the elderly, while life insurance is bought by the young and middle-aged. An increase in population longevity will adversely impact the liabilities of the former but only marginally influence the profitability of the latter. Furthermore, the duration and lapsation behavior of these differing liabilities are mismatched and hence cannot properly hedge each other. Although the mismatch argument might be true for (short) term life insurance policies, the argument is not as clear for non-participating whole-life policies. Both policies are sensitive, in opposing directions, to changes in the entire mortality table, albeit in different magnitudes. The issue becomes one of locating a proper hedge ratio in the face of uncertain mortality. In determining the ratio, one would need to look at the mortality table as well as product design, incorporating data on how susceptible a life insurance policy is to surrender. It is conceivable that much of the immediate annuity longevity risk can, in fact, be hedged using a properly calibrated portfolio of whole life insurance—even if the target group is much younger (see Milevsky and Promislow, 2002). For products with embedded equity guarantees, it may not be possible to diversify away the associated risks. Here the insurance company must look to other solutions, such as reinsurance.

Product Design as the First Line of Defense

Product design is the first and most important line of defense to protect an insurer's financial integrity and profitability. Often a simple product design change can significantly reduce the product's risk. For example, restricting the investment options of living benefit annuities such as GMIBs or VIAs with floors may reduce the volatility of returns and hence the value of the option granted to the contractholder. If a product feature cannot be quantified or hedged, it is simpler not to include it, irrespective of the demand. Doing otherwise is a potentially dangerous proposition, particularly for potentially expensive living benefit options.

Distributor and Customer Education

Increased education will be important to the success of the payout annuity market in the future. As product complexity increases, education will take on added importance, or else the potential for sales misconduct will rise. Contractholders must understand the consequences of being re-underwritten for a life contingent commutation, specifically that he or she will likely receive less money than if he or she were healthy.

Reinsurance Involvement to Map Out Risks

Reinsurance affords primary insurers access to the product design and mortality expertise of the reinsurers. Thus far, the US reinsurance market for fixed and variable payout annuities is poorly developed, mainly because of an absence of significant demand; some major reinsurers are also unwilling to accept longevity risk unless it is priced very conservatively. This is consistent with the reinsurance communities' expectation for steady mortality improvements, as evidenced by aggressive rates offered on life insurance contracts.

Looking ahead, the reinsurance market for payout annuities is likely to expand as primary company exposure increases. Long tailed payout annuity contracts may be attractive to offshore reinsurers that benefit from less restrictive regulation and lower taxes. Because of the long-tailed nature of payout annuity contracts, reinsurer strength will be an important risk consideration.

Conclusion

As the baby boomers reach retirement age, insurers will continue to look for ways to attract and retain retirement assets. Although payout annuity sales in the United States remain modest compared to sales of other insurance products, the benefits will be material for firms able to manage even a small portion of the growing pool of retirement assets. Insurance companies have prepared themselves for this growth by meeting consumer demands for liquidity, equity market participation, and minimum payment guarantees, with increasingly innovative products. As the market evolved, the next challenge will be for providers to protect the promises made.

Appendix

On a basic level, one can represent the price of, or the insurance liability created by, a \$1-for-life annuity in the following manner:

$$a_x = f(\mathbf{x}, \mathbf{q}, \mathbf{l}, \mathbf{r}, \mathbf{s})$$

In the above expression, **x** is the age at which the annuity is issued, **l** captures the expense loading, the vector **q** represents the mortality table, the vector **r** represents a term structure (yield curve) of interest rate, and the most critical variable **s**, is the profit spread. One can think of **s** as the difference between what the insurance company will earn on its assets, and what it "credits" the annuitant, net of expenses. Intuitively, the annuity factor is decreasing in **x**, and **r**, but increasing in **l** and **s**. In other words, older people pay less, and annuity factors are reduced in a higher interest rate environment. But, greater expenses and profit spreads will increase the price per dollar.

For example, in a flat $\mathbf{r} = 6$ percent yield-curve pricing model, one might see a profit spread on the order of $\mathbf{s} = 1$ percent, and a proportional expense loading of $\mathbf{l} = 10$ percent. In this simplified case—and with no fixed dollar loading—the annuity factor for the price of (or the insurance liability created by) a \$1-for-life annuity would be:

$$a_x = (1 + 0.1) \sum_{t=1}^{\infty} \frac{({}_t p_x)}{(1 + 0.06 - 0.01)^t},$$

where the numerator is the well-known conditional probability of survival. More precisely, if we use the Society of Actuaries 1994 Group Annuity Mortality Table (static, unisex), the actual annuity factors would be 15.69, 13.73, and 11.11, for ages 55, 62, and 70, respectively. Naturally, the younger the issue age of the annuitant, the more they must pay (and the greater the required reserves) for the same \$1-for-life guarantee.

In practice, the annuitant acquires a single premium immediate annuity (SPIA) with an initial sum of $\boldsymbol{W}$, thus guaranteeing a life-annuity of $\boldsymbol{W/a_x}$ for life. For example, a 55-year-old with \$100,000 would be entitled to an annual income of $\$100,000/15.69 = \$6,373$ for life. In the event of a period-certain guarantee, the annuity factors would be higher—since the survival probability in the numerator would be set to a value of one during the guarantee period—and thus the annual income would be reduced in proportion to the length of the guarantee.

This is, roughly speaking, how immediate annuity pricing is determined. In practice, of course, the valuation rate would be applied in the denominator to determine the required reserves, while the actual pricing would more closely resemble the above. For our purposes, however, we deliberately blur the distinction between pricing and valuation since we are interested in the broader impact of unanticipated longevity risk. For now, we imagine that every dollar of premium must be placed in reserves, but no more, thus ignoring capital issues and any possible surplus strain created by statutory valuation rates. The gap between the two will not change the main argument.

Now, imagine that science finds a cure to a specified decrement such as heart disease. In this case, the force of mortality would be reduced at each age by a given factor of x percent. On a technical level, the revised force of mortality would be related to the assumed pricing for mortality via the relationship:

$$\mu'_x = (1 + f)\mu_x,$$

where $f < 0$ represents the fractional reduction in mortality. We stress once again that we are approximating reality somewhat by assuming that a constant fraction f of deaths for any given age can be attributed to a specific illness, as opposed to an age-related fraction f_x. In practice, the number would vary. But, for our purposes we are interested in the effect of mortality improvements, as opposed to the reasons for these improvements, *per se.*

Furthermore, assuming the improvement occurs immediately after the annuity is issued, sold or priced, the true annuity factor should have been:

$$a'_x = f(\mathbf{x}, \mathbf{q}', \mathbf{l}, \mathbf{r}, \mathbf{s}),$$

where the prime symbol above the **q** denotes the true mortality vector. *Ceteris paribus*, for any given **x, l, r**, and **s**, the true annuity factor should have been *higher* for any given decline in the mortality rates.

The final step of our pricing analysis is to invert and solve for the profit spread that equates the original annuity factor that was originally used to price the annuity and the true (higher) annuity factor:

$$\begin{aligned} &\max \quad s' \\ &\text{s.t.} \quad f(\mathbf{x}, \mathbf{q}, \mathbf{l}, \mathbf{r}, \mathbf{s}) = f(\mathbf{x}, \mathbf{q}', \mathbf{l}, \mathbf{r}, \mathbf{s}') \end{aligned}$$

Mathematically, we are solving for the largest profit spread that equates the two annuity factors. Naturally, for any given level of mortality improvement, $\mathbf{s}' < \mathbf{s}$, and if the improvement is large enough (i.e. $f \ll 0$), the implied spread might be negative.

Notes

[1] Prices and reserves are based on the Gompertz approximation to 1994 GAM (static table), 10 percent expense loading, and a 6 percent (minus the profit spread) flat discounting. For example, if the annuity is issued at age 62, and mortality subsequently declined by 40 percent, the book of business will earn only four (bp), as opposed to the 100 bp used in pricing.

[2] From a technical viewpoint, the revised force of mortality would be related to the assumed pricing for mortality via the relationship:

$$\mu'_x = (1 + f)\mu_x,$$

where $f < 0$ represents the fractional reduction in mortality. When we reduce mortality, each and every q_x rate in the appropriate cohort table used to price the annuity is reduced by 10, 40, and 80 percent, respectively. For example, under an $f = -10$ percent shock immediately upon issuing the annuity, the modified cohort probability of a 55-year-old surviving to age 59, would be approximately:

$$(1 - (0.9)q_{55}) \times (1 - (0.9)q_{56}) \times (1 - (0.9)q_{57}) \times (1 - (0.9)q_{58}).$$

[3] In practice, of course, a properly detailed methodology would involve reducing each and every q_x by the fraction of deaths caused by any particular factor. We use

the word approximately above, because the actual mortality adjustment would have to take account of fractional age payment by perturbing the instantaneous hazard rate, as opposed to the q_x values themselves.

[4] An alternative way of interpreting the above table is to convert the so-called spreads, into a pre-tax internal rate of return (IRR) on investments; Appendix B illustrates this approach.

References

Ando, Albert Franco and F. Modigliani. 1963. "The Life Cycle Hypothesis of Saving." In *American Economic Review* 53(1): 55–74.

Brown, Jeffrey R. and Mark J. Warshawsky. 2001. "Longevity-Insured Retirement Distributions from Pension Plans: Market and Regulatory Issues." NBER Working Paper #8064.

—, Olivia Mitchell, and James Poterba. 2000. "Mortality Risk, Inflation Risk and Annuity Products." Pension Research Council Working Paper #2000–10.

—, Mark J. Warshawsky, and James Poterba. 2001. "New Evidence on the Money's Worth of Individual Annuities." In *The Role of Annuity Markets in Financing Retirement,* eds. Olivia Mitchell, Mark J. Warshawsky, James Poterba and Jeffrey R. Brown. Cambridge: MIT Press, pp. 71–105.

Carnes, Bruce A. and S. Jay Olshansky. 1998. *The Quest for Immortality.* Norton, W.W. & Company, Inc.

Corley Committee. 2001. "Report of the Corley Committee of Inquiry Regarding The Equitable Life Assurance Society." Faculty and Institute of Actuaries. September.

Fenton, John M. and Jonathan Hecht. 1999. "Making Payout Annuities Pay." Tillinghast-Towers Perrin.

Finkelstein, Amy and James Poterba. 1999. "Selection Effects in the Market for Individual Annuities: New Evidence from the United Kingdom." NBER Working Paper #7168.

Fliegelman, Arthur and Scott A. Robinson. 2000. "Bells and Whistles: Credit Implications of the New Variable Annuities." New York: Moody's Investors Service.

Holmes, Nicholas. 1999. "Not Yet Bleak House—The Implications of Guaranteed Annuity Options for the UK Life Insurance Industry." New York, NY. London: Moody's Investors Service.

Johansen, R. 1996. "Review of Adequacy of the 1983 Individual Annuity Mortality Table." *Transactions of the Society of Actuaries* 47: 101–123.

LIMRA International. 2000. Statistics provided to authors.

Maloney, Keven. 1999. "Life After Death—Moody's Examines Life Insurance Insolvency." Moody's Investors Service Special Comment, New York.

Milevsky, Moshe A. and David S. Promislow. 2002. "Can Insurance be Used to Hedge Annuities: An Introduction to Stochastic Mortality Models." Schulich School of Business Working Paper. Available at <www.yorku.ca/milevsky>.

Mitchell, Olivia S., James M. Poterba, Mark J. Warshawsky, and Jeffrey R. Brown. 1999. "New Evidence on the Money's Worth of Individual Annuities." *American Economic Review* 89(5): 1299–1318.

Poterba, James, and Mark J. Warshawsky. 2001. "The Costs of Annuitizing Retirement Payments from Individual Accounts." In *The Role of Annuity Markets in Financing*

Retirement, eds. Olivia Mitchell, Mark J. Warshawsky, James Poterba, and Jeffrey R. Brown. Cambridge: MIT Press, pp. 153–184.
Report of the Individual Life Insurance Experience Committee. 1996. "Mortality by Cause of Death Under Standard Ordinary Insurance Issues Between 1983 and 1988 Anniversaries." *Transactions of the Society of Actuaries* (1995–1996 Reports).
Society of Actuaries. 1996. *Transactions.* www.actuariallibrary.org.
Sondergeld, Eric. 1997. 'Annuity Persistency Study'. LIMRA International and the Society of Actuaries.
Yaari, Menahim E. 1965. 'Uncertain Lifetime, Life Insurance and the Theory of the Consumer'. *Review of Economic Studies* 32: 137–150.

Index